Bear Grylls was brought up on the Isle of Wight, where his late father taught him to climb and sail. A martial arts expert, Bear went on to spend three years as a soldier in the British Special Forces (21 SAS). He then had a free-fall parachuting accident in Africa, breaking his back in three places. Despite this, and after months of military rehabilitation, he went on to become one of the youngest ever climbers to reach the summit of Mount Everest.

Bear is the host of Discovery Channel's Emmy-nominated TV series *Man Vs Wild* (also known as *Born Survivor*) which is one of the most watched shows on the planet, reaching an estimated 1.2 billion viewers. Bear continues to lead record-breaking expeditions, from Antarctica to the Arctic, which in turn have raised over $2.5 million for children around the world.

Bear was appointed as the youngest ever Chief Scout on record, as figurehead to 28 million Scouts worldwide. He was made a Lieutenant-Commander in the Royal Navy, and is a best-selling author. He now lives with his wife, Shara, and their three sons, Jesse, Marmaduke and Huckleberry, on a Dutch barge in London and on a small remote Welsh island.

BEAR GRYLLS

TWO ALL-ACTION ADVENTURES

FACING UP

FACING THE FROZEN OCEAN

MACMILLAN

Facing Up First published 2000 by Macmillan
First published by Pan Books 2001

Facing the Frozen Ocean First published 2004 by Macmillan
First published by Pan Books 2005

This omnibus edition first published 2012 by Macmillan
an imprint of Pan Macmillan, a division of Macmillan Publishers Limited
Pan Macmillan, 20 New Wharf Road, London N1 9RR
Basingstoke and Oxford
Associated companies throughout the world
www.panmacmillan.com

ISBN 978-0-230-76152-0

579864

A CIP catalogue record for this book is available from
the British Library.

Typeset by SetSystems Ltd, Saffron Walden, Essex
Printed and bound by CPI Group (UK) Ltd, Croydon, CR0 4YY

Visit **www.panmacmillan.com** to read more about all our books
and to buy them. You will also find features, author interviews and
news of any author events, and you can sign up for e-newsletters
so that you're always first to hear about our new releases.

FACING UP

A REMARKABLE JOURNEY TO THE

SUMMIT OF MOUNT EVEREST

To Pasang and Nima
for saving my life that day in the Icefall.
I'll always be indebted to you.
&
To Shara, now my wife,
you were the reason for
coming home.

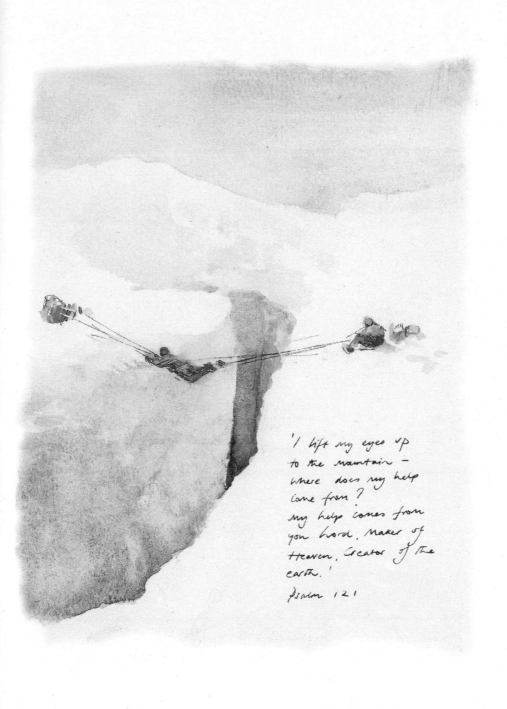

'I lift my eyes up
to the mountain –
where does my help
come from?
My help comes from
you Lord, Maker of
Heaven, Creator of the
earth.'
Psalm 121

Illustrations

▲

Foothills leading up to the Upper Himalaya

Summit	29,035 ft
Camp 4	26,000 ft
Camp 3	24,500 ft
Camp 2	21,200 ft
Camp 1	19,750 ft
Base Camp	17,450 ft

Foreword
Rev. Colonel David Cooper

▲

'How does it feel to have conquered Everest?'

I was at a lecture that Bear was giving to Eton College not very long after his return to the UK, after his ascent of Everest. He was with Mick Crosthwaite, who accompanied him on the expedition, and at the end of what was without doubt the best lecture on any subject that I had heard in my time at the school, he was asked this question by a member of the audience.

His answer was illuminating in more ways than one.

'I didn't conquer Everest – Everest allowed me to crawl up one side and stay on the peak for a few minutes.'

In that one sentence Bear showed an insight that he had gained on the mountain that all his years of schooling and time in the Army had not given him, though they may have prepared him for it.

In his book *Captain Smith and Company*, Robert Henriques uses climbing a mountain as a simile for the war he had recently fought. He was a member of a special unit during the Second World War and his simile has more truth to it than might be recognized by the casual reader who has no experience of war or mountains. It is no coincidence that so many soldiers have also spent a great deal of their time on mountains, and it is too facile to suggest that it is just for the training value.

Both war and mountains have the capacity to radically change one's perspective on the world and on one's place in it.

Without doubt it is the intimate involvement of life or death as an inevitable outcome that invests an event with such great value. When the chances are about even for each of these, it also invests it with a great capacity to change a person. Such an event is mountaineering.

For most of us our everyday life never presents us with this situation, and for those who it does, it is usually not sought for, but comes as a result of some disaster, man-made or natural.

This book is concerned with a person who has undergone a profound experience, at his own seeking, and we are privileged to be allowed an insight into the mind of the person who sought it. As a book it is difficult to parallel. Albeit one of the youngest Britons to ever climb Everest, his understanding and honesty, together with his self-awareness, is of a level that many never reach in a long life. What we his readers are privileged to share is a very personal account of his ascent, not just of the mountain, but of his humanity.

D.C.

Acknowledgements

▲

To those great men and women of the mountain: You are a credit to Nepal and I am lucky to call you friends. Sherpa Nima, Sherpa Pasang, Kami, Thengba, Ang, Pasang Dowa, Babu Chiri, Ang-Sering and Nima Lamu.

To the team: To Henry Todd and Neil Laughton for your trust and faith in me when it really mattered. Michael Crosthwaite, my friend and brother. I hold more respect for you than I could ever say. Captain Geoffrey Stanford, Grenadier Guards. Jokey Longworth. Edward Brandt. Andy Lapkas. Allen Silva. Michael Downs. Carla Wheelock. Graham Ratcliffe MBE. Ilgvar Pauls. Ali Nasu Mahruki. Scott Markey. I could not have been with better people.

To those we were alongside on the mountain: Tomas and Tina Sjogren for saving Mick's life. Bernardo Guarachi. Iñaki Ochoa. Bruce Niven. David Lim. The Singaporean Everest Expedition. Pascuale Scaturro. Captain Sundeep Dhillon RAMC. Tomi Heinrich. The Iranian 1998 Everest Team. You all epitomize the qualities that bring a mountain to life – strength, dignity and humour.

To those who loved and supported us: Mum and Dad and Lara for loving when it hurt. You're my best friends. Thank you.

ACKNOWLEDGEMENTS

Grandpa Neville for your love and smiles. You are the best example of a man I could ever have. James and Mungo. Shara, my angel, for your love, patience and kindness. You were with me all the way. Patrick and Sally Crosthwaite, Mrs Ronnie Laughton. This is your book as well.

To those who believed in us: To all at Davis, Langdon and Everest for putting your faith in me. Your willingness to reach out is why you have made DLE such a success. You are pioneers. Eve Theron. SSAFA Forces Help for all your support towards a messy-haired lout. You have made it all such fun and your work for the British Services is remarkable. Rev. Colonel D. Cooper, Richard and Sue Quibell for untold inspiration. Jay Martin and NSA, for your 'Juice Plus' support. Lewis McNaught. Stephen Day. Ginnie Bond and Becky Lindsay for your great patience and help.

For help in my research: Elizabeth Hawley. Paul Deegan. Royal Geographical Society.

To the best: Brunel Team – for always being there. Rev. Hugh Maddox, Ethel Bell and Nan for your prayers. Charlie Mack for your friendship. Sam Sykes for your time and energy in this entire project. Emma McK. Green Island. Tash. The Brigadier. Fozza. Ant . . . brrr. Annabel. Tom. Walter Scott, for all your editorial help. The late Colonel Anthony Witheridge. Judy Sutherland. Hugo M-S. Woggie. Brian and Vinnie. Dom S-B. Mike Town for showing me the hills when I was younger. The Big 'E' Squadron for your encouragement and humour. I'll always remember my time with you. Corporal Bob W. for your faith in me.

Bear
1999

CHAPTER ONE

DESERT PLUNGE

▲

The sky was beginning to fade, and the brilliance of the African sun was being replaced by the warm glow of dusk. We huddled together in the small plane and my feet began to get cramp; I tried to tense them and get the blood flowing again. The parachute made a comfortable backrest, but you always felt nervous leaning on it in case you damaged anything or accidentally deployed it. I shuffled again. As often is the case, there was no eye contact with the others in the little plane as we climbed up to now nearly 16,000 feet. People were engaged in their own little worlds – the air felt electric with silent tension.

As the plane banked to make another steep ascent, I glanced out of the little window down to the African basin far below; at that height you begin to see the curvature of the earth at the edges of the horizon. I felt a warm peace come over me.

Squatting there, cramped and nervous, I sensed a part of the magic that is found in edgy situations – a certain calm, a sharpening of one's senses.

The plane levelled out, people began to shuffle and become alert again, checking and rechecking equipment. We were all now crouching and someone reached for the door. As it slid back on its rails, the ferocious noise of the engine and 70 m.p.h. slipstream broke the silence.

'RED ON'. All seemed strangely still as we stared at the bulb flashing at us. 'GO'. It flicked to green. Andy reached out, looked far below, and then quickly fell away. Soon all the others had followed, and I was alone in the cargo area of the plane. I looked down, took that familiar deep breath then slid off the step. As the wind moulded my body into an arch, I could feel it respond to my movements. As I dropped a shoulder, the wind would begin to spin me and the horizon would move before my eyes. This feeling is known simply as 'the freedom of the sky'.

I could just make out the small dots of the others in freefall below me, then I lost them in the clouds. Seconds later I was falling through the clouds as well; they felt damp on my face.

I should come out of these soon, I thought, but instead I just kept falling through the whiteout. I looked to check my altimeter but it was hard to read.

'I've got to pull now and deploy; I'm too alone here.'

I reached to my right hip and gripped the ripcord. I pulled strongly and it responded as normal. The canopy opened with a crack that shattered the noise of the 120 m.p.h. freefall, as I slowed down to 15 m.p.h. As the buffeting ceased, I realized I should now be safely under canopy. I glanced up to check the symmetry of the chute as I'd often done before, to confirm that all its cells were open and working. They weren't.

I just stared for two or three seconds before realizing what had happened. Instead of the smooth regular symmetry of the nine or so cells above me, I had a chaotic jumble of silk. The force of the opening had torn part of the canopy in two. It flapped nervously and irregularly like two badly reined chariot horses tugging in different directions. I pulled hard on both my steering toggles to see if that would help. It didn't.

I tried to steer, but it responded slowly and noisily as if

straining to stay inflated. I watched the desert floor getting closer and objects becoming clearer and more distinct. My descent was fast, far too fast. Desperately trying to predict where the wind was, I realized I was too low to use my reserve chute – I'd have to land like this. I was getting close now and was coming in at speed; I flared the chute too high and too hard, out of panic. This jerked my body up horizontal, then I dropped away and crashed into the desert floor.

*

I woke and sat bolt upright in bed, sweating and breathing heavily. It was the third time I'd had this recurring dream of what happened those moments just before my accident. I tried each time to shake it from my mind; but the memories lingered. The fall itself had broken two, and seriously chipped a third, vertebrae. The Scottish doctor who had first assessed me said that I had come within a whisker of severing my spinal cord, and paralysing myself for life.

My back ached worse at night; the doctors had warned me of this, but still I winced each time the pain soared through my body. I held my head in my hands, then lay back down.

As I lay in bed for those initial months recovering, friends would come and visit me. I would struggle to get up to greet them. I'd put on my back brace, strap myself in and try so hard. It wasn't in my nature to be like this. I felt embarrassed. Part of me didn't even want them to see me in this way. I even remember trying to throw a rugby ball with a friend – until the pain stabbed again. My parents then encouraged me back to bed.

They had lived through hell after they initially heard of my accident.

During the week in the local hospital in Africa, I had managed to speak to my mother on the telephone. I took off the oxygen mask that I was breathing through, and tried to reassure her. Her voice sounded fragile, all those thousands of miles away. I hated myself for the grief I was causing. Since the moment I had returned, she had nursed and ferried me around all the doctors and hospitals like a saint. She knew that she had almost lost me.

For three months I lay in bed. My plans, my dreams of the future, hung in shreds. Nothing any longer was certain; I didn't know if I would be able to stay with the Army. I didn't even know if I would recover at all. It seemed as if in an instant my world had been turned inside out. I feared that this stinging pain in the middle of my back, of the nerves rubbing bone, would never leave me. I didn't want it to be like this.

Part of me feared that I would never recover well enough to be able to do all those things I loved. To be able to climb, to sail, even just sit in my favourite tree at home, high above the village and just think. It was this not knowing that worried me; nobody seemed to know – not even the doctors.

*

I was eight years old when my father gave me a mesmerising picture of Mount Everest. From that moment onwards I was captivated. I would sit there trying to work out the scale of the huge ice fields I saw in the foreground, and to judge how steep those summit slopes would really be. My mind would begin to wander, and soon I would actually be on those slopes – feeling the wind whip across my face. From these times, the dream was being born within me.

As a child, the tedium of the weeks at school was relieved by the thought of days ahead at home: climbing on the chalk cliffs in the Isle of Wight with my father. I was never back for more than a minute before I would be hassling him to come out with me.

I would clamber into my old hiking boots that were sizes too big for me; we would load up the car and the two of us would head for the hills. We would always take our two dogs with us, a Shetland sheepdog and a dachshund. The Shetland loved the scrambling on the slopes, but the little dachshund used to get thrown in a rucksack and carried along, viewing the world from out of the top buckles. And in such a manner were spent endless dreamy afternoons.

Winter was always my favourite time for these adventures, with the wind tearing across faces as we strode out together through the fields. We would scramble up the cliffs with me fighting to stay close to my father. From a distance the cliffs looked foreboding and treacherous and my mother would refuse to allow my father to take me up them. It made the climbs even more exciting – they were forbidden.

'You can never tell how steep something is until you rub noses with it,' dad would say. He was right. Up close the cliffs were only steep walks. Small sheep tracks laced their way in tiers up the face, giving us the chance to sit and rest every ten feet. My father would reach down with his hand and heave me the last few feet to each ledge. We would tuck in close to the cliff and gaze at the views across the island. They were beautiful.

Eventually we would come out over the top onto the grass and lie there, often to the bewilderment of some old couple on a cliff-top walk. They would gawp in bemused amazement – then totter off, shaking their heads with disapproval. It made the adventure even more real.

During these times my father would tell me stories of his climbing experiences in the Royal Marines; he would teach me all he knew.

'Always keep three points of contact on the face at any one time. Move slowly and always, always keep calm – however scared you are.'

When I see these cliffs now, the same feelings come flooding back. They make me smile. The cliffs look small and hardly very dangerous, but as an eight-year-old I always felt as if I was climbing the steepest face in the world. It made me feel different from the others when I got back to school. I had done something that I thought was really hard, and survived – and that made me feel special.

I remembered those days and managed a smile from my bed.

Lying, unable to move, inside all day and sweating with frustration, my way of escaping was in my mind. I felt I still had so much that I longed to do, and so many things left to see.

Suddenly all my dreams plagued me. I had taken my health so much for granted, but when faced with the reality of having it taken from me, those dreams, that before were neglected, came racing forward.

Lying in bed, strapped in my brace, gave me almost too much time to reflect on these things. I would rather not think about them. Forget them. Look at you, I thought, you've been in bed for months.

Time seemed to stand still.

I looked around my bedroom, and the old picture I had of Mount Everest seemed to peer down. I couldn't decide whether it was looking with pity or whether it was sneering. I struggled over to it and took it down. There was no longer any point in having it up.

My childhood desire to climb Everest felt further beyond the realms of possibility than ever. During those months lying there, I remembered my love of climbing with my father; my secret longing to one day see the world from the summit of the highest mountain. I remembered, but tried to disregard it as mere fantasy – as kid's stuff. It eased the pain.

CHAPTER TWO

REACHING OUT

▲

'That fine line between bravery and stupidity is endlessly debated
– the difference really doesn't matter.'

World War II British Air Force Pilot

After three months in bed at home, I was posted to an Army Rehabilitation Centre. I could move and walk around by now, but still the pain hounded me. Everything felt fragile and delicate. I winced if I turned a corner too fast. I felt pathetic.

For the next six weeks I spent all day every day being treated. Three-hour stints of stretching exercises under the close supervision of a medical 'physical training instructor' (PTI) would be followed by two hours of physiotherapy. Then we would start again. Slowly the movement returned, and I began to regain my strength. My confidence was coming back – I knew I was healing.

By the time I left the Centre, some eight months after the accident, I was recovering well. I had an almost full range of movement in my back and as long as I continued the exercises for the next four months, I would be – as the doctor said – 'better – and the luckiest man around'. Feeling slightly uneasy and with the cheeky grin of a three-year-old who's just been caught weeing in the paddling pool, I packed my bags and walked out of the main doors of the Centre. I had been very lucky.

This long road to recovery had taught me that life was precious. I had learnt this the hard way. I had come within an inch of losing all my movement and, by the grace of God, still lived to tell the tale. I had learnt so much, but above all I had gained an understanding of the cards that I had been playing with. This scared me.

*

It was a beautiful late summer's morning and by all accounts I had no reason under the sun to have such a dose of the blues; but I did, and I had them bad. I poured myself a glass of Ribena and thought of all that had happened.

After three extraordinary and unrivalled years with the British Army as a soldier with the Special Air Service (21 SAS), I made the difficult decision to leave. The nature of the job I had done was very demanding; if I wasn't lugging vast logs around some training area, I was tumbling out of the night-sky under a parachute. Whatever the field, the pace was always intense.

From the military point of view I had been given the 'all clear' to continue as before. For the present, I was declared 'fully fit' – the long term verdict though was a different story.

My parents insisted I sought the advice of various specialists, who in no uncertain terms told me that to continue such work would be 'madness'. They assured me that if I continued to military parachute with heavy loads and sustained a few nasty landings, then it would lead to severe arthritis in my back in ten years' time. There seemed to be a difference of opinion between the two camps of doctors. But it wasn't a risk I was going to take; I had been too lucky already to throw it away for the sake of a few more years with the Army. Still it was one of the hardest decisions I had ever taken; some of my best friends were still there. Disappointed, I felt compelled to 'hang up' my Army boots.

I felt that I had little choice; if I couldn't fulfil the fundamental requirement to military parachute, I was adamant that I didn't want to stay on as a 'non-active' member. My accident had cost me everything.

I loved my time with the army and feel a huge pride in having served with the regiment. Their professionalism and humour was unlike anything else I have ever known; they were to me a second family. When I first joined at the age of nineteen, to have been trusted and encouraged like a man is something that I will always be indebted to them for.

The majority of my Army-orientated school friends had joined the Guards or Cavalry, as Commissioned Officers. I felt strangely determined, though, to see military life from a different perspective – from the other end.

I had applied to join as a 'squaddie', the lowest rank available. From here, I was at ground level, the place where the real soldiers were. Nothing smart, nothing fancy, with no rank to separate us; just good, honest and, at times, wild people. It was the best decision I ever took. I made as good a comrade there as I could have ever imagined. We shared something truly lasting – friendships, born out of being cold and scared together. It was these soldiers I would miss.

*

Having now left the Army behind me, I began the daunting task of trying to find a career to follow. Choosing, or even seeing something that felt right, was getting harder and harder. As frustration upon frustration set in, the likelihood of having to perform a sensible staid job was beginning to raise its ubiquitous head – and it hurt. Everyone knows that tearing feeling between necessity's pull and your heart's pull. That balance between needing to pay the bills and having a dream. It is a difficult road. All I knew was that I was determined somehow to follow my heart, and was scratching around frantically for a route.

Rumour is a nameless child, and how exactly this one came to me I can't even remember; but it was one that was to have a profound effect upon me. I heard of an old friend planning to get a team together to try to climb Mount Everest. Neil Laughton was an ex-Royal Marines Commando: robust, determined, and as I came to learn later, one of the most driven men I had ever worked with.

Neil had been on Everest in 1996, the year that a storm hit high on the mountain, claiming eight climbers' lives in the course of twenty-four hours. This was the highest death toll ever claimed at one time in the history of Everest attempts. Out of the eight that died that night, some had actually frozen to death fifty metres from their tents. The others had found themselves caught out by the great 'goddess of the sky', having run out of oxygen, too late and too high on Everest's perilous slopes.

Climbing above 26,000 feet is unforgiving, and that night Neil had been pinned to his tent at Camp Four, cowering from the wind and fighting for his own survival – unaware of what was going on outside. Of the people to reach Camp Four, forty-eight hours earlier, Neil was among the few to return alive.

He was now getting a new team together to attempt once more to reach the summit of the world's highest mountain. What is it about a mountain with such fatal accolades that draws men and women to risk their lives on her icy slopes – all for the chance of that single, solitary moment on the top? Whatever it was, Neil seemed determined to go back, having got so close that tragic year. All I knew was that something deep inside me was stirring.

I thought of those days climbing on the hills at home as a kid. I had always climbed since then, and my love of the mountains had never changed; it was just the dream of Everest that I had suppressed. I had felt that I would never be strong enough after my accident, and I guess therefore, part of me had allowed the idea to die. Suddenly, and almost inexplicably, I was finding those long lost emotions were flooding back.

*

At the age of eighteen, an old friend and I were sitting around contemplating some sort of high jinks to get up to in the few months after having left school. The Indian Army became our target. Endless letters and pleas later, and the two of us found ourselves deep in the Himalayan foothills of North India, in the good company of a tall, elegant and turbaned General.

We spent a wonderful few months trekking through the valleys of Sikkim and Western Bengal, meeting eccentric expatriate gentlemen in the most unusual of places. At the end of the trek, after we had developed a hunger for civilization again, the General arranged for an evening of dancing girls to entertain us all – at his own 'humble dwelling'. The two of us rather tentatively sipped our glasses of whisky as these girls flung themselves around to ripples of delight from the inebriated General.

Soon afterwards he decided to 'retire' for an 'early night'. An hour later, exhausted by the visual stimulations, and apologizing for leaving the party a little early ourselves, we also 'retired'. We felt it only courteous to pop our heads round the General's door to thank him for his kind hospitality, before heading to bed.

As I peered round the door I was confronted by the extraordinary sight of the good General's buttocks, moving rapidly up and down above one of the servant girls. With his turban off and clothes scattered unceremoniously across the floor, he was so engrossed in his business that he never noticed me. I scurried back out of the room, deeply embarrassed. From then on we observed the General in a new light, and believed him emphatically when over breakfast he called himself a 'prancing stallion'. He, of course, was referring to his old cross-country days. We knew better.

During our last week with him, he escorted us to the Himalayan Mountaineering Institute in Darjeeling, a climbing school set up to teach advanced ice climbing techniques. I walked round the museum in awe, gazing at the endless Everest memorabilia on display. My excitement was uncontainable. Here was the culmination of all I'd ever known about climbing. Here were the memories of the élite; I was totally entranced.

Some of the General's final words to me out in India were an exhortation to 'one day try and climb the great mountain of Everest. If you train and try with all your might, and have just a little luck, then you'll succeed. And remember: take small steps; that is the key to climbing high.'

Sitting at home, remembering his encouragements, I slowly realized this was my chance. Here was an opportunity for embracing all I had ever dreamt of; I felt an irresistible urge to follow.

Maybe it had taken such a shave with death over the skies of Africa to allow this childhood fantasy to resurface; I didn't know exactly. But the Army had taught me a few things. The words from a speech by Roosevelt, that we had read so often, remained powerfully etched in my mind:

It is not the critic who counts, nor the man who points out how the strong man stumbles or when the doer of deeds could have done them better.

The credit belongs to the man who is actually in the arena, whose face is marred by dust and sweat and blood; who strives valiantly; who at the best knows in the end the triumph of high achievement, and who, at the worst, if he fails, at least fails whilst daring greatly – so that his place shall never be with those cold and timid souls who know neither victory nor defeat

. . . for those who have had to fight for it, life has truly a flavour
the protected shall never know.

Maybe now was the only chance I would ever get to follow this
dream. This dream of one day reaching the summit of Everest –
I felt it was now or never. I dug my old picture out from where I
had hidden it over a year earlier, when I was recovering – and
dared to allow myself the dream once again.

*

20 April 1997. After my second glass of home-brew cider at
10.00 a.m., designed to give me a little bit of extra courage, I
dialled Neil's number. The conversation was brief, to put it in
the most diplomatic of terms.

'If you're serious I need to know by tomorrow – ring me
then, I've got to go.'

Considering it had taken me most of the morning to decide
whether or not to call him, and then subsequently twenty minutes
to actually get round to saying I was interested in joining the
team, I thought his reply had been remarkably succinct. I wish I
hadn't stumbled and tripped over my words so much. I wondered
what he must have thought of me.

Like most of us, I have no shortage of weaknesses. One of my
faults, which is probably a reaction to bureaucratic and procras-
tinating senior Army officers, is a far too eager willingness to
accept things with absolutely no prior thought whatsoever. The
conclusion I draw is that it's far better to decide how good an
idea something is after the event; and on such a rock has been
founded a host of ridiculous mishaps and disasters. So, keen not
to break the habit of a lifetime, I rang him back the next day.

'Just give me the chance and I'll put my everything into this.
I'm deadly serious,' I said.

He agreed, on the basis of how I performed on an expedition
that October to the Himalaya. He wanted to have first-hand

reports on how I coped at high altitude, and insisted I join a team that was climbing the great peak of Ama Dablam – known commonly as 'the most beautiful mountain in the world'. Depending on how that went, I had now become the first member to join Neil in the British 1998 Everest Expedition. I decided not to tell him a word about my accident. I didn't think that he would ever understand.

As I replaced the receiver, I had a sinking feeling that I had just made a commitment that was going to drag me far out of my comfort-zone; and I felt more than a little uncertain about the wisdom of what I had done. But I had to look forward, I couldn't live in the memory of my accident; I wanted a fresh start. This was it and I felt alive.

My mother had always said, 'Commitment is doing the thing you said you'd do, long after the mood you said it in has left you.' She was absolutely right; the only problem was that I was now on the end of that commitment. For me, though, the decision had been made; the strength to stand by it was what I needed.

Subsequent moments of panic about the future were rapidly quashed by my fear of possible morning tube rides to an office job. I was going to throw my all into this. My toes began to tingle and I ran around the house making animal noises. I don't think anyone heard.

*

A few days later, I announced the news to my family. My prior decision to leave the Army had come as somewhat of a relief to them, and I guess they all assumed that I would now take a definite turn for the quieter life. They were right, that had been the intention; they had been through enough heartache with me already. But something was ablaze within me, and this dream to climb Everest just wouldn't leave.

I knew that only a tiny percentage amongst those who attempt this climb actually reach the top. Of those that do, I knew the numbers that achieve this on their first attempt is even smaller. Everest is no place to prove yourself. The likelihood of reaching the summit is so slim that you're inevitably setting yourself up to be disappointed. But I also knew that mountains are the place to express yourself. It was this expression that I now needed after my accident.

The fresh air of the mountains has always strengthencd me, and I longed for it again. Such a large proportion of my Army time had been amongst the hills, and I missed them. Here was a way back. The climb was a risk I wanted to take. There was more though. I still yearned to be able to look at my picture of Everest, and to know what those summit slopes were like, and to actually see the curvature of the earth from the top. It was a decision, I guess, I had already made long ago.

My parents and especially my sister, Lara, called me 'selfish and unkind', and then subsequently, 'stupid'. My sister and I have always been fiercely honest with each other, occasionally to our great irritation. But this on the whole, putting aside the occasional black eye, has always been the strength of our relationship. I am closer to my sister than anyone else, and I think it was this intimacy which provoked the hostility to the Everest idea in the months ahead.

Even when my parents came to accept, in the loosest sense of the word, the idea, Lara's loathing of that 'E' word remained. No amount of persuasion would win her round.

My parents weren't exactly a pushover either. Their acceptance of it came with the condition that if I died, then my mother would leave my father as he had been the first to endorse me. I felt awful. I had never meant to cause such chaos amongst the family, and part of me wished that I had said nothing, except that I was thinking about possibly taking a Thompson's coach trip for a few months around the British Isles.

Time, and my insistence that everything would be okay,

eventually won through and my parents, and even my sister as well, came to accept the idea. Their initial resistance then turned to this fierce determination to help me. Numerous times in the months ahead when I fell flat on my face, beaten by the exhausting road of finding sponsorship and having to train so hard, their support would pick me up, encourage me, and keep me going. Without their help I would have probably ended up on that coach trip around the British Isles. All I had to ensure was that I was right, when I promised I would be okay.

As it happened, four people tragically died on Everest whilst we were there. Four good, strong climbers. A Russian and his American wife; a Briton and a New Zealander. In truth, it wasn't within my capabilities to make these promises to my family. My father, I think, secretly knew that.

CHAPTER THREE

A WORLD APART

▲

'What is Everest without the eyes that see it? It is the hearts of men that make it big or small.'

Tensing Norgay

Legend has it that the Himalaya was formed in a violent struggle of the gods. While the Goddess Vishnu, known as the preserver of life, slept, the Demon Hiranyanksha leapt to earth and ravaged her with such severity that all her limbs were broken and contorted high up into the sky. From this struggle were formed the Himalaya, literally meaning 'abode of snow'.

Geology tells a different tale. About fifty million years ago the Himalaya and Nepal were a large sea called Tethys. As the vast continent of Gondwanaland slowly crossed the Tethys sea moving north, it eventually met with the shores of Asia. As they collided with mighty force, the impact drove the soft sedimentary rock of Asia dramatically upwards, as the harder granite of Gondwanaland bit into it. This wrenching and tearing resulted in the stunning creation of the highest, yet youngest of the mountain ranges on earth – the Great Himalaya.

The Himalaya stretches without interruption for 1,500 miles

all the way across the top of India. It's hard to visualize the vast scale of this giant land, but if we were to stretch it across Europe it would run the entire distance from London to Moscow. Full of the most gigantic mountains on our planet, the Himalaya houses ninety-one summits over 24,000 feet; all of them higher than any mountain on any other continent. Amongst these are thirteen of the earth's giants, standing over 26,000 feet, with Everest at the heart, the crowning glory of the physical world. Her summit lies, lonesome and wild, at just under nine vertical kilometres up – exactly 29,028 feet above sea level. A world apart.*

Numerous expeditions during the pre-war years took on the epic challenge of attempting to be the first to reach the summit of Everest. All failed, often with tragic results. These great men of adventure recognized the magnitude of the task in front of them. Mallory, who failed to return and was never seen again after his summit attempt in 1924, said beforehand: 'The issue of Everest will shortly be decided – the next time we walk up the Rongbuk Glacier will be the last, for better or for worse . . . we expect no mercy from Everest.' As time showed, he was tragically right; the mountain retained her secret.†

It was not until 1953, 101 years after the discovery that Everest was the highest mountain on earth, that she was eventually climbed. Just before noon on 9 May, Edmund Hillary and Sherpa Tensing 'stamped to the top with their teeth in the wind'.

Hillary wrote: 'My solar plexus was tight with fear . . . I

---

* A recent survey has established that the height of Everest has increased to 29,035 feet as a result of movement of the earth.
† The preserved body of George Leigh Mallory was finally discovered at 27,000 feet on Everest in May 1999. No camera, nor the body of his companion, Sandy Irvine, has been found. It is presumed that Mallory fell to his death leaving Irvine to die alone, sitting in the snow. A photograph of Mallory's wife, Ruth, that he promised to leave on the summit, was missing. The mountain's greatest mystery still remains.

wondered, rather dully, whether we would have enough strength left to get through. I cut around the back of another hump and saw that the ridge ahead dropped away and we could see far into Tibet. I looked up and there above us was a rounded snow cone. A few whacks of the ice axe, a few cautious steps, and Tensing and I were on the top.'

The news raced back down the valleys, reaching Queen Elizabeth on the eve of her coronation. *The Times* broke the story and the nation erupted at the British triumph. Morris, a young correspondent, wrote: 'The moment aroused a whole orchestra of rich emotions among the British – pride, patriotism, nostalgia for the lost past of the War and derring-do, hope for a rejuvenated future.'

The eventual success had come at last. The cost? Fifteen expeditions, the lives of twenty-four men, and the passing of over a century in time.

One of the reasons, I believe, that Everest was never climbed earlier was the fear of the effects that exposure to those sorts of heights would cause. Nobody knew whether the human body would be able to endure such stress. Similarly, before Roger Bannister successfully ran the four-minute mile, doctors declared that it was a physical impossibility; if you ran that fast, they said, your heart would literally 'burst out of your chest'. Likewise, the fear of what would happen to the human body so high on Everest was another unknown, waiting to be tested.

On the summit there is one third of the amount of oxygen that there is at sea-level. From about 18,000 feet the human body begins to deteriorate as it struggles for survival in the thin air. Above this height for weeks on end, you are on borrowed time. Your body, literally, is dying. Still today, forty-five years after the first successful ascent, the statistics of deaths on Everest remain constant. Out of every six climbers who reach the summit, one of those will die. Equipment improves, forecasts get more accurate, and technology changes, yet the mountain remains the same.

In all of Everest's history, still only thirty-six Britons have ever stood on her summit; a shockingly low proportion of those who have tried. She doesn't give her secret out easily, and she always has a price.

*

During the early 1990s, Nepal saw the emergence of commercial expeditions being launched to Everest. Climbers could now pay up to US$60,000 for the privilege of attempting the climb. This fee was intended to cover the logistical cost of the expedition, including all the oxygen, the permit to climb, as well as the cost of three months living on the mountain. The trouble was that advertising to get clients widened the market. Genuine climbers could rarely afford such fees. Instead the climb was opened to less fit and less capable clients, with little knowledge of the hills. The pressure upon expedition leaders to justify the cost often meant that these people found themselves too high on the mountain, dangerously tempting disaster.

It took until 1996, when the combination of a freak storm, and inexperience amongst certain climbers, resulted in that fateful pre-monsoon tragedy. On top of the eight lives lost that stormy night, the mountain took a further three lives the next week, bringing the toll then to eleven.

It wasn't only the inexperienced though who died up there. Among the dead was Rob Hall, the expedition leader of Adventure Consultants, and one of the most highly acclaimed climbers in the world. He endured a night at 28,700 feet, in temperatures of −50°C. Without any further supplementary oxygen and severely weakened by the cold, the mountain was about to show that no one, not even the best, were infallible.

At dawn, Rob spoke to his wife in New Zealand via a patch-through from his radio and a satellite phone at Base Camp. She was pregnant with their first child, and those on the mountain sat motionless as he spoke his last words to her, 'I love you. Sleep well, my sweetheart.' He didn't survive the day, unable to find the strength to move any more.

Shock ran through the climbing fraternity and the world at large. Fingers were pointed and blame was thrown around. The fact is that it took the lives of so many, and the desolation of so many families left behind, to show the climbing world that mountaineering cannot be purely commercial. People thought that they had found a formula that was fool-proof on Everest. But, as is the nature on high mountains, such systems have a funny way of breaking down.

People of course still make money by running commercial expeditions, but now the vetting of climbers involved is much stricter. The motives of these expeditions has now, for the most part, reverted back from being financially driven to what the essence of climbing is really about – namely a love of the hills. It's tragic that it took such a disaster to remind the world of such a simple lesson. Maybe it is a criticism of Western attitudes, and just showed a deep misunderstanding of the power of these mountains. Maybe it was just bad luck. In reality I think the truth lies somewhere in the middle. Whatever the answer, the fact is that mountains, like the sea, always demand a deep respect.

To the Nepalese and Tibetans who live under the shadow of the Great Himalaya, the nature of the mountains is well understood. Their force is a higher force, and their attraction is their beauty. Within Nepal, Everest is known simply as the 'goddess of the sky', or Sagarmatha. Even this name reflects their respect for nature. I guess that this reverence is the greatest lesson you can learn as a climber. You climb only because the mountain allows it. If it says wait, then you must wait, and when it allows you to go, then you must struggle and strain in the thin air with all your might. Listening to the mountain and having patience on it are the keys to survival.

Everest is so high that she actually creates her own weather-cycles round her. The huge mass causes such gravitational pull that a micro-climate exists around the mountain. The weather here can change in minutes, as wind and storm clouds flood through the valleys.

The summit itself stubbornly pokes into the band of wind that circles the earth at around 30,000 feet upwards. This band of wind blows continually at about 200 m.p.h. and is known simply as the 'jet stream'. The long plume of snow that pours off Everest's peak is caused by these winds, blowing frozen snow across the sky. It is hardly surprising that the temperatures high on the mountain can reach as low as $-100°$ wind chill factor.

Standing far above the clouds is this place, so wild, yet so beautiful, that I can so easily understand what Mallory meant when he described her as: 'rising from the bright mists, vast and forceful . . . where nothing could have been more set and permanent – more terrific – more unconquerable.'

At first sight, Everest is awe-inspiring beyond belief and holds a certain magic over the entire Himalaya.

For some reason, human nature through the decades is still irresistibly drawn to Everest, and I suppose always will be. The challenge, the beauty, the simplicity of nature, or maybe all three. I don't really know. All I know is that I am now sitting at my typewriter and looking at the picture of Everest in the glow of dusk beside me – the same picture that I used to look at as a wishful eight-year-old, and as a recovering patient. But now, having been so privileged to have crouched briefly on her summit, I view it in a new light; with an even greater awe. The mountain holds me entranced and still I burn with excitement when I see it. Sagarmatha is so much more than just the highest mountain in the world.

CHAPTER FOUR

MOVING MOUNTAINS

▲

Blake wrote in the eighteenth century that:

> 'Great things happen when men and mountains meet,
> That is not done by jostling in the street.'

For the time being, though, I was doing my fair share of jostling – madly charging around, trying desperately to find sponsorship for the expedition. The sum of US$25,000, when compared to the savings of a bottom ranked soldier, seemed as elusive as a pork pie in a rabbi's kitchen. Painting pictures to large corporations of the benefits of sponsorship and getting companies to catch the vision is the first and one of the hardest challenges of high-altitude climbers, and after 203 rejections it was beginning to take its toll.

Apparently it took Colonel Sanders of Kentucky Fried Chicken 1,009 'No's before anyone would support his idea of fast-food chicken. Most of us would have thought that maybe we needed to change our recipe. Like Colonel Sanders, though, this was my only card, so I kept plugging away.

Admin is most definitely my worst point, and I remember on one occasion dialling a number and speaking to someone who I thought was the marketing director of 'North Face' equipment. After twenty minutes of exuding down the telephone about the expedition, they informed me that I was through to a Sheffield industrial cleaning firm, and could I please hurry up with my booking.

I soon found that sitting at my desk with piles of proposals, numbers and names, was beginning to addle me in no uncertain terms.

I managed to escape from all this for two months during the build-up to Everest to join the team that was attempting to climb Ama Dablam. This was a commitment that I had promised Neil I would undertake; he would be eager to hear how I performed. For me, this trip was also a chance to clear my head a bit amongst the madness of the preparations for Everest, and to put in some valuable training.

Fitness was going to be fundamental on Everest, and I was now spending as much time as possible climbing and going berserk in the hills of Wales and Scotland. But I needed also to be training at greater heights. The other objective therefore of climbing Ama Dablam was to train at these higher altitudes and to see how my body would react.

Despite climbing with the Army and friends in European ranges, I had never been exposed to the extreme heights that Everest would present. If my body shut down, as can easily happen to people at those altitudes, there would be no point pursuing the dream any further. It was how I would react that Neil wanted to see.

In the 1960s Sir Edmund Hillary, on seeing the great peak of Ama Dablam in the Everest valley, described it as 'unclimbable'. Looking at her from the bottom, one can understand his sentiments; she stands impressively and majestically pointing straight up into the sky 22,400 feet above sea-level. Climbing it successfully would be an essential step on the road to Everest, both physically and mentally. This brought with it, though, a degree of pressure.

I spent five weeks living on this peak, pushing my body harder and higher. I was now testing my climbing skills to their limits, in situations where, rather uncomfortably, my life depended on them daily. A lifetime of concentration became crammed into the intense hours on her face each day – it left my body drained of energy and strength. I could hardly even think about Everest now. It was too large a step away. This climb itself was demanding my all. Unless I could perform here, what was I doing aspiring so much higher? Over and over I found I was telling myself, Just concentrate on the now. This is where it counts.

*

Finally, by the grace of God, I was huddled on the summit of Ama Dablam. As I squatted there, I glanced left through my goggles, and through the haze of the mist and howling wind I saw the peak of Everest slowly reveal herself. Strong, detached, and still two vertical kilometres above where I was now, Everest suddenly filled my mind all over again.

It had taken my all to be one of the few from our team to reach the summit of Ama Dablam, and now cowering there against the wind, feeling unable to take another step further, the sneer of Everest way above scared me. But something was drawing me. I couldn't explain it. It just somehow felt right. I knew that I would see the mountain again. For me, that time couldn't come fast enough.

Ten days later, back in Kathmandu, the capital of Nepal, the mass of Everest photos for sale in the market had me captivated again. More so now than ever before. To the commercial tourist, the pictures were just pretty postcards on the stalls. To me, though, each one seemed to jump out.

I know it's possible, I told myself. I've tested the formula, and it's worked. Put up with the discomfort and the pain, keep going and never give up, and understand that if you're moving up, then you're always getting closer.

Encouraged by how the climb had gone and this gut feeling that felt so strong inside, I returned home for the real phase to begin.

*

I was soon back in the 'jostle' of preparation. The team was gradually coming together now. Geoffrey Stanford, a Grenadier Guards Officer, aged twenty-seven, had joined Neil and me. He had climbed a lot in Europe and had done some high-altitude research in the Himalaya before – spending six weeks at 19,000 feet studying how the body copes and adapts to those sorts of heights. This, though, was to be his first attempt on Everest. His perfect manners and English exterior covered a grit determination; he was like a dog with a bone – a bone he wouldn't let go. A veritable British bulldog – but in black tie.

The final member of the team to join us was Michael Crosthwaite. I had grown up with Mick since I was a boy, and had climbed extensively with him over the years. Physically and mentally he was exceptionally strong, and because I remember him having chest hair at the age of eight (whilst I didn't) I had grown up with an inherent respect for him.

Straight out of Cambridge University, and fresh into the City Stockmarket, Mick felt he was rapidly going stale. In his own words he felt he had been 'swimming underwater for too long and needed to come up for fresh air'. Of 'fresh air', we assured him, there would be no shortage. Thus the pull of Everest had her enigmatic way with him; he made the brave decision to leave the City and join the team. The team was better off for it, and I was greatly relieved to have the company of a soul mate. With Neil and Geoffrey as such openly driven people, maybe the two of us could be a more 'relaxed' dilution for any tension in the future. Time would tell.

And so the team was finalized. It was small, strong, and despite consisting of very different characters, was bonded by a deep desire to climb this mountain. Neil had had the foresight to keep it small, the idea being that each member was to be capable of forming part of a summit team. We would need to work together, supporting each other constantly, and helping each other when required. I suppose, in some respects, this is similar to how a troop of gorillas operates in the jungle – picking nits out from each other's hair. In fact, thinking about it now, and remembering the state in which we cohabited a lot of the time on Everest, I don't think that this is too bad an analogy.

They say familiarity breeds contempt, but in the intensity of the relationships that we were to have, there was no room for this to be the case. We would be spending every day together for three months, living, eating, sleeping and crapping in some of the harshest conditions this world offers. Such experiences make or break friendships. As a team we were well aware of the need for trust and tolerance between us in the months ahead, and this needed to start now.

Three days after I had raised my first few hundred pounds for the expedition – a sum that felt like a drop in the ocean towards the total – I was loading some climbing equipment into Neil's car. My ice-axe accidentally scraped against the paintwork. Although my car is battered and covered in scratches which never really bother me, I knew Neil's TVR was first of all worth a lot more than mine and, secondly, was important to him. The next day, those precious few hundred pounds went towards paying for the repairs. This was somewhat depressing, but it was little things like this that I felt would make the difference later on. Neil appreciated it, and remembered.

Over the years the Army had sponsored a considerable number of Everest attempts. Out of all of these, only one had ever successfully reached the top. 'Brummy' Stokes and 'Bronco' Lane, in the 1970s, reached the summit in atrocious conditions. The bad weather then drove them back. In escaping, they suffered very severe frostbite and lost several toes to the cold; but they had heroically survived. Apart from this expedition, all the other military attempts had been turned away empty-handed; and much lower down.

One of the fundamental reasons, we believed, for this run of military sponsored teams not reaching the top was the size of their expeditions. They had always taken tens of people and mounted huge assaults, with the intention of eventually choosing just two or three to actually go for the top. Within a military framework, this inherently bred excessive competition rather than mutual support. In an environment such as Everest, this all too often spelt disaster.

Another mistake, I believe, was having too many chiefs and not enough Indians. Mountains are great levellers and care nothing for hierarchy – least of all 'chiefs'. From my time in the hills I have learnt a fundamental lesson: mountains are only ever climbed by 'Indians'.

So we didn't leave to any resplendent military fanfare. On the contrary, the Army understandably thought that we would go the same way as all the previous attempts. All we received from them was a promise of a party if we returned alive. I guess that is the way the world works.

With the team established, we started to train together as much as possible. My old motto of 'two steps at a time up the stairs' wasn't going to wash here. For months, day in, day out, we'd train, focusing hard on what lay ahead. Weekend after weekend was spent in the hills of Brecon, climbing for hours at a time with rucksacks loaded with rocks and thick dusty old books from home. I would then run for whole evenings during the week, along the miles of coastal hills in Dorset – cursing the British weather as I stomped across the steep fields.

Doing this endlessly, even when it was pissing with rain, cold and dark, and when all you really wanted to do was go out in London and be 'normal', was what would make the real difference later on. This is simply self-discipline. I had lived this sort of life before whilst training for the SAS selection, and swore I would never live it again. Yet three years later, here I was once more.

Mick and I worked a lot together, swimming countless lengths of the local pool – one underwater, then one on the surface, for hours at a time. This boosts one's ability to work without oxygen, making the body more efficient. Swimming in any rivers or seas was also fair game, but as it was winter, the excursions were rarely more than about three and a half seconds long, before we would be seen running frantically back to the relative warmth of the car's heater.

We would bicycle everywhere, run everyone's and anyone's dog round the woods in all weathers, until the ageing animals passed out with exhaustion. Even in dinner jackets, hills were rarely passed unclimbed as we scrambled to the top of them – often resulting in us being obscenely late for the party.

Despite sounding a little bananas, it was in fact the only way we stayed vaguely sane in the middle of the struggle of organizing all the equipment and sponsorship, prior to departure. My training was my secret escape, and, I guess, my chance to let go of all the tension that was accruing.

*

Time seemed to tick away with unusual speed. By now I had found one main sponsor, the Services charity, 'SSAFA Forces Help' (Soldier, Sailor and Airmen Families Association), who backed part of my costs for the expedition. They proved great fun to work with, as well as being outrageously efficient. Yet despite having got some of the way with SSAFA, I was still a whopping amount of money short.

Robert Louis Stevenson said that 'to be idle requires a strong sense of personal identity'. Obviously I was lacking this identity in the last month or so before we departed, as I roared around on my bicycle, trying desperately to raise the rest of the money.

All avenues were thoroughly explored, and on occasion Mick and I found ourselves in some quite bizarre situations, as we hungrily sought out the elusive 'financial remedies' that we hoped would satisfy our Everest fever.

This eventually led to us both standing on the pavement outside Richard Branson's house one cold and blustery evening, tucked behind a tree arguing over who was going to ring his bell.

'We'll do it together,' we finally agreed. It was 10.30 p.m. and we both felt like novice cat burglars as we grinned nervously in the street outside.

'On the count of three . . .'

We approached the door and rang his bell. The intercom crackled.

'Yup?'

'Ah, good evening, we've just popped round to leave a proposal for you, to see if Virgin might be interested in . . . click . . . Hello, hello?'

So before he had even heard what we had to say, Branson had rung off, assuming we were obviously there to sell him some toothbrushes or crimson dish clothes. But as he rang off, he made a fatal error: by mistake he must have leant against the 'door open' button. Mick and I looked at each other inquisitively as the door buzzed away in front of us. A quick glance around and without any further hesitation, we gave it a gentle nudge.

Seconds later, we found ourselves standing in Richard Branson's hallway, looking sheepishly around at each other, as if going to see the neighbour to announce that you've just run over their cat. We coughed loudly. And then a bit louder.

'Hello, hello . . . um, Mr Branson? Hello.'

Seconds later a furious house-assistant skidded round the corner of the landing and charged down the stairs, rather like the head mistress of St Trinian's. The two of us needed no further coaxing; we dropped the proposal in the hall and legged it out, as the front door was slammed ferociously behind us.

The next morning we sent the Branson household some very expensive Scilly Isle flowers, accompanied by profuse apologies with a PS saying that we hoped he had had a chance to read our proposal. We never got a reply.

But not all of our 'sponsor hunting' was so stimulating and generally the routine went something like this . . . 'Rummage for a clean shirt, and struggle into my grandfather's old suit. Venture halfway across London to endure a terrifying meeting with a frumpy PR woman with hair on her upper lip. Try desperately to maintain composure, but fail miserably and invariably manage to spill coffee down my front. Go home, peel off my suit and begin again.' God I hate suits.

This went on depressingly long, and I soon began to wonder if maybe there was something wrong. I bought some Clorets breath fresheners and kept trying.

Having dozed off, I was woken at my desk to the sound of Corporal Jones on the television, 'Don't panic, Captain Mainwaring, don't panic!' I yawned and turned it off. It was all too close. I picked up the telephone and carried on with the struggle.

A month later and still out of luck, I found myself in the unfortunate position of now being three weeks away from our departure date and still US$16,000 adrift. It was a cold February morning, and I was bicycling off to have a quick sandwich with a friend in the City. As I flew along the pavements, wearing only shorts and an old woolly jersey, covered with mud, I saw a firm called 'Davis, Langdon and (to my surprise ...) Everest.' They had to be worth a try.

I skidded to a stop, tried to flatten my hair and went in. A giant-sized photo of Everest adorned the wall of the reception. I gave one of my sponsorship brochures to the receptionist and asked if she would be kind enough to 'send it up to either um ... Mr Davis or Mr Langdon.'

The lady then leant forward and pushed her glasses back onto the bridge of her nose. As if annoyed to have been disturbed by this scruffy 'thing' in her reception, she told me that Messrs Davis and Langdon were the two people who had founded the firm in the early 1900s, and that therefore my request may be a 'little difficult'. I stood my ground and insisted, and eventually arranged for my brochure to go to the 'current' Senior Partner, then sauntered out and thought nothing more of it. I had done this a thousand times before, to no avail.

That weekend I spent at home with my parents in the country. Desperation was beginning to kick in. If something drastic didn't happen soon, then the expedition, for me, was off. I felt as if I was on this diddery old tight-rope and it was beginning to wobble.

'Why don't you pray?' my mother warbled from the kitchen. It had got way beyond that, I thought. But, in despair, I agreed. So my mother and I knelt in the field, with donkey droppings all around, and said a short prayer for some help. I was all too aware that if I couldn't find the remaining funds, I would have to withdraw from the team.

Forty-eight hours later a phone call came in for me. It was the Senior Partner of Davis, Langdon and Everest (DLE); they'd received my brochure and wondered if I would have a moment to come in for a meeting.

'Let me think ... this afternoon you say? Hmm, yep, I think

I'm free, but I better just check . . .' I calmly said, almost unable to even sit on the chair with excitement.

I raced up to London, squeezed into my suit once more, swallowed a breath freshener and hoped for my last shot to work.

The Senior Partner informed me that the founder of their firm had been a descendant of George Everest, the Surveyor General of India in the 1830s. George Everest had been the first man to properly study the height of this huge mountain in the Himalaya, and 160 years later and with the use of laser technology, scientists showed that he was accurate to within 0.09%. The mountain came to bear George Everest's name, and his descendant had founded the company whose coffee I was now drinking.

The team of people I was chatting with seemed a world apart from the slightly sour fat cats I had been dealing with elsewhere. They were interested, friendly and had a vision for how this expedition could work for them. Rather than purely wanting the PR from any media coverage, what they saw in it was entirely different.

They wanted a unifying focus for their company. They recognized that a successful company becomes successful from the inside out, rather than the other way round. What they wanted was a project to focus and excite all who worked for DLE, something that everyone would feel a part of. It seemed that I was fast going to become that 'something'. I swallowed nervously. I would have to start brushing my hair.

And so, with only fourteen days to go before we were due to leave, DLE came in as my main sponsor. The next day I went into the bank to pay in this huge cheque and the cashier's eyes lit up with delight as he asked me what I was going to do with the money.

'Get high,' I replied grinning, ' – literally!'

*

The countdown from then on was a blur of organising equipment; getting the correct sized high-altitude boots, sending them back and forth to modify them, and then getting the most suitable crampons accurately fitted. We had to make sure all the medical kit was in order with large enough quantities of the right pills and creams. Then it would be on to checking and re-checking the clothing. Outer-garments, thermal inners, windproofs, fleeces, silk inners, ice-axes, slings, harnesses; the list was endless. Sorting them neatly into the correct piles at home was a delight to our cat, who was convinced the latest in high-altitude goggles was a dead rat. But slowly, and with much help, it all began to take shape.

At the same time though, the fitness training ceaselessly continued. On one of my training sessions some weeks earlier, that actually took place on New Year's Day on the far north coast of Scotland, I was somewhat 'briefly' having my annual New Year's dip in the wild surf of the North Atlantic. As I emerged, clutching my wedding equipment that by now was looking as if it might never return to its former self, there stood a beautiful, well wrapped-up girl with hair blowing in the wind.

'Ah, sorry about this,' I muttered as I hopped around on one leg, trying to put my trousers back on, before falling over on the seaweed. 'I can explain everything.' I'm not quite sure what happened after that, but the girl on the beach, very bravely, became my girlfriend.

Our relationship wasn't exactly of the 'regular' variety, and Shara was thrown into the chaos of the final few months of preparation for an Everest expedition. They always say that if you want to terminate a relationship, then take up Himalayan climbing. Well I'd just started one, and it was good – I didn't in the least want it to end. I wanted to believe in 'if it's meant to be, then it will be', but when there's a lot to lose, such a motto is really hard to trust. My fears were beginning to show. Keeping everything crossed, I then disappeared for three months and found it a miracle that she was still there on my return. From now on I'll always swim on New Year's Day.

*

Our planned departure date was 27 February 1998, and that time was fast approaching. Because our team was relatively small, we had arranged to link up with a larger team who were also to be climbing on Everest. The aim was to benefit from the logistical ease of a larger group, whilst still enabling us to maintain the autonomy of a small, close-knit unit.

This larger expedition was being led by Henry Todd, a very well-known Scottish climber with huge experience and skill. It was with him that I had climbed on Ama Dablam, some months earlier. Rather like the Nepalese load-bearing yaks, Henry is huge, shaggy and matted, but in his case, somewhat better looking. We had been extremely lucky to have been able to join Henry's team, and without doubt were in the most capable hands around today.

The plan was that we would be climbing on the Nepalese side – the South-East Ridge. This was the original face that Hillary and Tensing climbed, and in the less than inspiring words of Kurt Diemberger, the famous high-altitude climber, 'this will always be one of the most dangerous routes.' Of the total 162 deaths on Everest, 101 of those have occurred here – on the Nepalese side.

The climb would lead us up from Base Camp into what is known as the Khumbu Icefall, a tumbling cascade of ice 2,500 feet high, that guards the way up to the first camp, Camp One. From here, the route follows along the crevasse ridden Western Cwm Glacier to Camp Two. The route then goes to the end of the Cwm, over the Bergschrund ice bulge, and then up the sheer ice walls of the Lhotse Face to Camp Three, 3,300 feet higher still. The climb then traverses the ice over the Geneva Spur, and then rises up to the South Col, Camp Four, our last camp.

From here the summit would be attempted in one final push. The route leads to the Balcony Ledge, and then up the South-East Ridge to the South Summit. Once over this and the famous Hillary Step ice-wall, the summit lies 200 metres ahead. We planned it would take about seven weeks of climbing to reach – if all went smoothly.

The first ascent by Hillary and Tensing had used nine camps during their climb. We were to use only four. The planning even at this stage, especially by Henry, was meticulous. Strategy and the effective allocation of resources is crucial in any attempt, and the four of us studied the maps and books like hungry students.

Henry was dealing with all the logistical side of the expedition, such as arranging the oxygen, the portage to Base Camp, the food, and more importantly, the Sherpas. The Sherpas, who are the local Nepalese climbers of the Everest region, would assist with the logistics on the mountain. Different expeditions would employ different Sherpas, but as with most factors on a mountain such as Everest, everyone would mingle and work together. This, in many ways, is the strength of the climbing fraternity.

For the Sherpas, climbing runs through their blood, and because of having been born at a high altitude, they climb with the strength of ten men. They became close friends by the end, and are truly some of the most wonderful people I have ever met.

Organizing these logistics though was a massive undertaking, but what would have taken all of us months of negotiations, Henry had a knack of being able to arrange in his sleep. He just quietly got things done.

*

The last weekend before leaving I went down once more to the Brecon Beacons with some friends. We walked all day, threw a rugby ball around in the evening, and slept in a sheep pen during the night. It was bliss.

A few days later we had a send-off party, for sponsors and

journalists to attend. Throughout the whole evening though I began to feel this anxiety. It was all happening very fast now, almost too fast. Part of me wasn't even sure that I really wanted to go at all. The champagne flowed, speeches were made, but as I sat through it all, looking at all my friends chatting away and laughing, I felt hollow. I'd never experienced this sort of loneliness. Even though here I was surrounded by all those I loved, part of me felt so alone. In forty-eight hours' time I would leave all of this far behind.

A radio station rang me the next day and asked for an interview. They said that they would like to do it on the morning show at 6.05 a.m. I gulped. I'm bad in the mornings at the best of times, but at 6.05 . . .

Early the next day, the phone rang; I sipped my morning cup of tea, and prepared myself for the questions. They ran thick and fast, and soon it was over. 'Easy.' In fact I even thought that I had done rather well. Ten minutes later though, the phone rang again. They said that I had sounded fast asleep and would I mind waking up and doing it again in twenty minutes. I apologized profusely, slurped two strong cups of coffee, and tried again – a bit more coherently. All was OK, and I consoled myself with the thought that first time round it must have been a crackly line.

The interviewer, though, had raised an issue amongst his many questions that I had been asked over and over again. He had commented that he always believed it wasn't possible for people in their twenties to be able to cope with the adverse effects of high altitudes; hence all well-known climbers tended to be in their thirties or forties, and never much younger.

I couldn't argue against this. It did always seem to be that the stereotyped climber was bearded and haggard. Well, I might have been haggard but I certainly wasn't bearded; in fact all I could really grow was a couple of grandma's whiskers on my chin. Maybe their assumptions were right. Maybe Everest was only for the hairy and older climbers. But there seemed nothing I could do about this, apart from believe Mallory when he said that 'climbing Everest is all about heart.' It seemed that this was the only card I had to play.

My last evening, I promised to go and have a drink with a friend. I bustled along on my old 1920s Dutch push-bike to a seedy bar in the depths of night-time London, and joined the queue to get in. It was heaving with people. The queue stretched right round the corner, and hardly seemed to be moving at all. I joined the end and waited in the chilly night. Eventually as I got closer to the door and was standing against the window of the bar, I spotted my mate inside. He was swaying from side to side, with beautiful girls draped all over him. I shivered in the cold.

He spotted me in the queue, and sidled over to the window. We tried to talk through the fogged up glass, but I couldn't hear. I then saw him gesturing something with his fingers. I squinted through the window. With a broad grin he held out his two fingers, and twisted them up the inside of the glass – symbolizing a man climbing up a mountain. He reached up as high as he could, then mimicked the man tumbling off. As he put his hand back in his pocket, he laughed out loud. I smiled at him from outside.

'I'll see you in three months, all being well; I'm not waiting in this queue any longer,' I shouted. Tim was then swept back from the window by the crowds inside, and was gone from view.

I turned and went home. I slept little that last night.

CHAPTER FIVE

AMONGST THE GIANTS

▲

'All men dream, but not equally, those that dream by night in the
dusty recesses of their minds, wake in the day to find that it was
vanity; but the dreamers of the day are dangerous men, for they
may act upon their dreams with open eyes, to make it possible.'

T. E. Lawrence, *Seven Pillars of Wisdom*

DIARY, 27 FEBRUARY:
Sitting in the plane finally on our way, at the end of a long,
very busy, emotional rollercoaster of activity – raising the
funds, organizing equipment, getting fit, staying healthy and
strong, and saying our goodbyes.

Peace at last. But also anticipation. It's time now to focus
on what's ahead – yet a nervous gulf hovers over us, as to what
the future holds.

Mick and I were travelling out about four weeks before Neil and
Geoffrey, the idea being to get a bit of extra time at high altitude
before the climb itself would start. We wanted to really begin to
focus on the job ahead; away from the 'busyness' of before.

One of the pieces of research I had done before leaving was
to contact a few of the British climbers who had successfully

reached the top of Everest. I hungered for any pieces of advice that they could offer. One of the recurring patterns that emerged amongst those who had achieved this and those who hadn't was that the former had often spent a few weeks beforehand training at an altitude of around 12,000 or 13,000 feet, in preparation. 'A time of focus before the battle' was how I heard it described.

And so the two of us found ourselves 30,000 feet up in the Qatar Airways first class section, heading for the Himalaya. Ironically, from a team of four 'tough' men, I now found myself alone with Mick, with whom I had shared rugby boots and maths books since the age of seven. Rather than feeling part of this hardened mountaineering team, off to wrestle with the extremes of cold and fatigue, I felt more as if we were going back to school at the start of term; as snotty, homesick kids.

But no one would have guessed it, as we reclined in our huge first class seats and ordered another drink.

Qatar Airways had very generously agreed, as sponsorship, to fly the team there and back. Having only ever flown crammed into cattle-class squashed between two sweaty squaddies, or with my parents, buried under piles of luggage, first class was a treat. I would love to be able to say how we drank the plane dry of complimentary whisky and champagne, and then needed to be wheeled off at the other end with Moët poisoning. But unfortunately that didn't happen, and the journey passed more or less in quiet anticipation.

Seeing this young couple in the row next to me, kissing their way across the skies, made me heinously jealous. I thought to myself how I would be able to do that soon; well relatively soon; like three months soon. Just a bit of discomfort along the way beforehand, then back to England and long kisses. I was annoyed with myself for feeling like this already.

The pilot brought us up to the cockpit and pointed out Mount Everest through the window, as we passed over Northern India. I pressed against the glass and there, as if piercing through a blanket of cloud on the horizon, stood that place of dreams. The frozen snow poured off the summit, streaming miles across the sky, as the jet stream pounded her upper slopes without remorse. I was transfixed as I stared at her – lonesome in the sky.

'Outside temperature's now reading $-55°C$,' the pilot commented. He looked at us and smirked. I tapped him on the shoulder, thanked him and went back to my seat.

I sat and thought of all that had happened in the last few days before leaving. Already it felt an age away. I wrote in my diary:

My best memory of all that I now leave behind is of that last weekend at home, when all the animals broke out. We put the Shetland pony in the field with the donkeys to see if they'd get on. They didn't. Olly, one of the donkeys, charged through the fence, through the trees, and vaulted a four-foot gate. The Shetland must have had something, as I'd never seen Olly so much as trot before – let alone jump. The pigs then got wind of the excitement and broke out of their sty. Hyacinth, the big female kune-pig, who can hardly walk as she's so large, did the 100 metres in about five seconds flat. The other donkey then tried to trample Hyacinth, and chased her eagerly along the river. By this stage Abraham, the cock, was flapping furiously, the ducks and chickens were fleeing in all directions from the chaos of the moment, and Mum and Dad were running round trying to make amends.

In many ways it was just another day 'at the ranch', but I guess it sums up all that I already miss about home.

Dad drove me to the airport, and looked ten times sadder than me, and I wondered if he knew something that I didn't. He lingered and lingered, until eventually we had to go through the departures gate. It was horrible. If something happens and

I don't come back, I just want you to know how much I love you both. Thank you for so much.

'Tough soldier?' – My foot!

And so we left England, praying that we would see her green grass again, three months later. All that now lay ahead was the mountain and how she was going to treat us.

*

The smog and diesel fumes of the ancient British-made buses engulfed us as we frantically loaded bags of equipment into the minibus. Kathmandu seemed exactly the same as it was four months earlier on my way through to climb Ama Dablam. The same hustle and bustle of Nepali officials claiming luggage tax duty, the same kids running around trying to assist in moving kit – all for a rupee or two.

The horns of the taxis hooted incessantly, as they fought their way through the mayhem of the rickshaw-infested traffic. We piled the last of our bags in and joined the flow, in search of a little backstreet hotel called the Gauri Shankar. Placed in the middle of the old part of the city, it is a small oasis of calm in the midst of raging chaos. The hotel is used almost exclusively by climbers, and they didn't bat an eyelid as we unloaded the mass of equipment. They were used to this sort of thing.

The rest of the day passed with a bit of shopping in the bazaar, a cold shower to wash off the grime of the city, and a huge Nepali-American supper. After a pretty restless night, our minds buzzing with all that was beginning to happen, we made our way at 5.00 a.m. to the domestic airport to pick up a small helicopter, bound for the foothills of the Himalaya. It was a relief to put in the earplugs, hear the rotors start, and lift off from the bustle of the city below.

I closed my eyes, leant against a sack of ginger, and breathed deeply. Forty minutes later, the rush of Kathmandu was far behind and we were flying across stunning valleys, rich with rhododendrons, with tiny mountain villages scattered intermittently along the hillsides. As we rounded the head of one of these valleys, we saw our destination: a small dirt landing strip perched on the side of a mountain at about 8,500 feet. The village of Lukla was nothing more than a tiny gathering of huts, clustered around a precarious runway.

The helicopter hovered above the ground, sending dust everywhere as the locals crouched from the blast. As we touched down, the Nepalese clambered round helping us drag the bags off the chopper. It then throttled hard and lifted off, disappearing from view as it dropped away down the steep hill, to return through the valleys to Kathmandu. We wouldn't see such technology again for a while.

Already deep into the foothills of the Himalaya at a height of around 8,500 feet, the village of Lukla is where we would start our trek in towards Base Camp. It would be a journey of some thirty-five miles. This distance would take us about twelve days to cover, partly because of the way one has to cross and recross infinite valleys and gorges that meander through the hills, but also because of the altitude difference that our bodies would experience. Base Camp is at 17,450 feet, and to reach this height safely requires giving the body enough time to adapt.

The strict acclimatization pattern that we'd have to follow would begin now. From this point upward, we would feel the strain of high altitudes. Acclimatization is all about allowing the body to adjust to having less oxygen to function with; and the key to this is being patient in how fast one ascends. The effects of altitude sickness can kill very quickly if this is ignored.

I had been told that the statistics of those who reach the summit of Everest successfully on their first attempt is something like one in twenty out of those climbers that try. We were both well aware therefore of the necessity to acclimatize well, as early as possible. This was to be essential if we were to have even a chance of the top. The struggle to stay healthy and to adapt to the thin air had begun.

DIARY, 1 MARCH:
It has taken all my energy and resourcefulness to raise the finance to organize this expedition for myself; I doubt if I could do that again. Because of this, I'm well aware that I've only got one chance up here.

Along the way will be harder work than I have ever known before, but I've got to throw my everything at this; and then it's home to fireplaces, the animals and hot chocolate. We're in the Good Lord's hands.

The little village of Toc-Toc was three hours' walk along the valley side, crossing wooden bridges over small streams and skirting round tiny batches of huts that lay along the route. The sounds of the yak bells ringing in the terraced fields and children fighting in the mud was all that broke the silence of the hills around us.

As we came round corners and glanced up through breaks in the trees, we would catch glimpses of the mountains far above us. Then they would be lost again from sight, and replaced by the immediacy of the flora all around. Glades of blue pine and juniper adorned the valleys, and their aroma reminded us of the refuge that these foothills provide from the cold and raw nature of the huge peaks far away and above.

Our first night in the valleys was spent at Toc-Toc, where we washed in the waterfall outside a little farm hut. A small family lived here, and fed us majestically on their homegrown vegetables and rice. We read by candlelight until 9.00 p.m., before settling down to sleep. The cushions were full of fleas and the wooden boards were hard on the body; but it felt good in its simplicity. Listening to the noises of the night, I dozed off to sleep.

I was woken abruptly in the depths of darkness to the heaving and retching sounds of Mick throwing up into a boot. Maybe the altitude was beginning to affect him, or maybe those vegetables had been just a little too fresh. Whatever it was, though, was sure making itself heard in Mick. The situation only got worse when, in the light of dawn a few hours later, I discovered that the boot Mick had grabbed had in fact been mine. Many apologies and a few cups of lemon tea later, Mick looked a better shade of green than he had at sunrise, and we slowly began to pack up our gear.

That day we were to reach the market village of Namche Bazaar, perched in the bowl of a hill at about 12,000 feet. This is the local trading place for the little villages scattered throughout the Khumbu Valley region. It is the last post of any vague civilization on the route through the hills, towards the Base Camp of Mount Everest.

Mick was weakened by his bout of food poisoning and was slightly concerned about making such an inauspicious start to the trek. He remembered hearing of some famous climber who had been intending to scale a peak out in this region, being forced to abandon the attempt after slipping a disc, chewing on a chapati – a local unleaven bread. I tried to reassure Mick that a bit of food poisoning wasn't quite the same and the two of us then set off, contouring along the valley edge before beginning the steep path up towards Namche Bazaar – avoiding at all costs eating any chapatis along the way.

After crossing a spectacular but precarious old rope bridge spanning a 300 feet deep gorge, we started up a long path through the trees towards Namche, two hours in the distance.

DIARY, 2 MARCH:
Steep terraced houses and plots of cultivated land form this little market town, high up in the forested foothills – it is the

most developed place I'll see for the next three months. It has a generator to supply the few houses with electric lights, and a primitive drainage system, covered by slabs of wood and stone, that runs through the streets. The place is full of small stalls selling endless amounts of old climbing equipment that expeditions have left behind on their return journeys.

Mick and I both bought a few final bits and bobs, or 'monkeys and parrots' as my old sergeant would say, that we might need as spares. We also took the opportunity to eat our last bit of vaguely decent food. We both know that from when we leave here tomorrow, the conditions will worsen, and the food we'll eat will be food that has been carried in – hence not quite 'Savoy-esque'.

A plump, middle-aged German lady, who is out here trekking, asked Mick if she could have his autograph, as she'd never met anyone who was attempting to climb Everest. I went and hid in the loo, chuckling away, as Mick floundered about trying desperately to escape this formidable woman's grasp.

The loos here are pretty primitive, and are generally just a hole in the floor inside a tiny wooden hut. Plenty of 'misfires' ensure that the wooden floor around the hole is well soiled, and that the pile of poo pokes through the hole like some sort of decaying pyramid. Because of being at 12,000 feet, it's pretty difficult to hold one's breath for very long, as you enter the little hut and desperately try to do what you need to do without inhaling. Inevitably you end up gasping for breath as you give up, and are left squatting there, puffing in the rancid smell. We hear a rumour of a loo further up, with a natural drainage system from a stream, making it beautifully clean. Maybe I'll try and hold on until we find it.

I told Mick that I was going to have an early night and was going to change and go down to pyjamas. Mick, slightly confused, asked me where 'Pyjamas' was, as if it was some Nepalese village he hadn't heard of. I chuckled – must be the altitude, I thought.

It is now snowing hard in Namche. This is the first snow we've seen. I wonder what it's like further up the Khumbu Valley.

It snowed all night, and at 7.00 a.m. we left Namche. We headed out into the mist, following the yak-trail towards the village of Deboche, five hours' walk away. As we started up the steep track, towards the Buddhist monastery at Thyangboche in the distance, the sun reflected off the muddy snow around us. Three hours later, approaching the monastic village, we could hear the monks' meditative chants. The sound seemed to waft over us like some soothing balm, as we climbed the last few hundred feet through the wooded slopes.

The monastery dominates the entire valley; and having been built laboriously by hand, chipping the rocks one by one, you could almost feel the solace of the place. The lama of the region, believed to be the living reincarnation of an ancient Buddhist deity, chanted from a parched scroll as we discreetly sat in the shadows at the back. After the ceremony we went outside the monastery and into an adjacent hut, where we sipped soup around a fire with some of the villagers. A couple of hours later, we headed out into the snow again, towards Deboche, half an hour further on.

Diary, 3 March:
Deboche turns out to be a cluster of only three houses and, as expected being higher up, is even more basic. The hut we are in is wooden, as are the beds; cushions now seem a luxury of the past. We all huddle round a fire as night brings with it the cold.

Two Buddhist monks are having a ceremony next to us, and are busy chanting and tossing rice around. They offered Mick and I some of their local alcoholic brew, called 'chang', which we sipped tentatively, having seen them coughing ferociously into it seconds earlier. Sharing drinks here is always a bit dodgy, as many of the locals suffer from tuberculosis, but being 'British', we felt it important not to appear rude.

We have found a lovely kitten here, which now follows us round the hut. The local name for cat is 'biralou', but this one seems alive with fleas, so Mick renamed it 'bira-fleas'. I wish that we could take it with us as our 'high-altitude' cat, but he says that it will make everyone scratch. I tried to tell him that I'd had fleas for years, but he wouldn't listen. The cat had to go.

The lady who runs the place here is apparently an old girlfriend of Edmund Hillary. She laughs beautifully, despite showing her only three black, rotten teeth. She seems to have chronic tooth decay though, and to be in real pain. She clutches her jaw and grimaces, smiles briefly, then carries on moaning. I feel pretty hopeless, as all I have to give her are some painkillers. So I have given her a large dose and told her to sleep. I'm suddenly a little worried that I've given her too much, especially considering the altitude that we're at. We haven't seen her again, I hope I haven't killed her!

That morning after a considerably colder night, the lady, who to my huge relief was still alive, woke us. It was dawn and she took us out through the trees to a clearing fifty yards away. There in the still of morning, some fifteen miles away, and five kilometres vertically above us, we saw the summit of Everest poking out from behind the huge mountain of Lhotse Shar. The early glow was catching the top, and she seemed so beautiful and remote as the wind drove the snow off her summit. Completely stuck for words, we both strained our necks and watched the sun rise behind her; then she was hidden again by the mist of day – gone.

I knew what Mallory meant when he said: 'Higher in the sky than imagination had ever ventured to dream, the top of Everest itself appeared.'

The sight of the mountain, so elusive, high, and impossible, filled my mind for the rest of the day. I had imagined that I would feel an excitement when I first saw her, but instead I just felt this dread.

*

Later on that morning, having each been given a cord necklace that had been blessed by the head Buddhist priest of the region, we left Deboche. The landlady, who had lived in the shadow of the mountains all her life, beseeched us to be safe; she assured us that the necklaces would bring protection. We thanked her and, deeply moved, headed on. We weaved our way through the snow-covered forest tracks, further into the heart of the mountains. From this height onwards, the flowers and trees would stop growing and the snows would really now begin.

DIARY, 5 MARCH:
This morning I had the treat of washing my hands in the freshly fallen snow. It's wonderful to see their real colour after the grime of the last few days. Everything gets much cleaner the higher up we go because it's colder, and bacteria and germs are less prevalent; it makes me feel much safer biting my nails!

Spent much of our rest-day today reading a book detailing the disaster on Everest in 1996; the disaster that Neil so narrowly escaped. I find it all too near. It's kind of hard to 'armchair' read a book that goes into graphic detail about how so many lives were lost in a storm high on Everest, when you're actually on the way out there yourself – and you're scared enough as it is. Still I guess the key is to learn from what happened. In many ways it boils down to being courageous when the chips are really down, and not just acting courageous when you're all safe and cosy. Courage should always be softly spoken. I must remember these things now.

A few hours later, we had arrived in the little village of Pangboche, the home of many Sherpas who live and climb in the Everest region. The houses were perched on the steep slopes of the valley, overlooking the gorge below. Many of these were full of climbing memorabilia, heralding past triumphs or disasters, and famous names lined the walls.

In this village, we were to meet Henry our expedition manager, who had been up here getting acclimatized, before having to head back to Kathmandu to arrange the collection of the oxygen cargo. Mick and I headed off to find him. He was staying with the head-Sherpa, or Sirdar, as they're known – called Kami. Kami's job was to organize the Sherpas who would help us carry supplies on the mountain.

The house Kami lived in was a beautiful, traditional Sherpa house. We entered through a tiny wooden door that led into a stable where the yaks lived. This was a small low room, with a packed mud floor, covered with straw. Through the darkness, a shaft of light revealed a wooden staircase going up into the main living area of the house. As the stairs creaked under us, we emerged into a large single room, where the whole family would live, cook, and sleep. A mud stove gently burnt in the corner, and the sun shone through the smoke that leaked from its side. Great yak furs lined the floor and beds, whilst yak droppings dried in the corner. These would eventually provide fuel for the stove. Tucked up in the corner of the room, grinning from ear to ear, twiddling his beard and sipping on a lemon tea, sat Henry.

We spent the afternoon with Kami and Henry, rummaging through barrels of equipment and checking all the supplies, so that Henry would know what had gone missing and be able to resupply it in Kathmandu. Everything came out; from tents to ice-probes for finding people under an avalanche, aspirins for thinning the blood and helping acclimatization higher up, to even mayonnaise. Hundreds of ice-screws, kilometres of rope, and a mountain of Mars bars. Once at Base Camp, resupply would be almost impossible, everything had to be checked and double-checked now.

Later on that day with Henry, whilst chatting to the Sherpas who had just come back down the valley, we heard our first piece of tragic news. A porter had been killed in the ice approaching Base Camp. Neither of us knew him, yet that evening there was a soberness amongst the three of us as we sat and heard what had happened.

The porter had been ferrying equipment up to Base Camp – a long trip that many of them do as an extra source of income. This time, though, he had been climbing over the glacier towards Base Camp too late in the afternoon, the time when the ice is least stable. Base Camp is perched at the head of the glacier, at the foot of the mountain, and the route is found by snaking one's way across the ice, amongst the huge glacial pinnacles that line the trail. As the climbing season approaches, this trail becomes better and better trodden – but in the early days, such as now, it was still pretty much virgin territory.

During the afternoon the ice is always weaker after a morning of sun on it. Apparently this porter had become disorientated, then lost, and they believe that an ice-bridge must have given way beneath him, sucking him away down the ice-smooth glacial streams that run beneath the surface.

Henry was returning the next day to Kathmandu, and warned us seriously against travelling to Base Camp at any other time than early morning – especially before any safe route was established. I prayed for the porter's soul and his family that night, and heeded Henry's advice carefully.

We spent much of that evening after Henry had left playing with some of the kids in the village. I lent a little girl of five the only pack of cards we had, hoping they wouldn't get too ruined. They were an important item for the times ahead. Secretly, though, I wasn't that hopeful, and pretty soon there were cards everywhere. Fifteen minutes later, it was wonderful to sit and watch this girl carefully tidy them all up, put them in their box, and place them back neatly alongside my diary. I smiled. I had learnt more about gentleness watching this than I would in months of charging around London. Funny really . . .

DIARY, 7 MARCH:
We walked for three hours today, up towards the last village before Base Camp – Dingboche, at 14,500 feet. We contoured along and up this huge wide valley that surrounds the beautiful and majestic peak of Ama Dablam.

I sat on a rock and studied the route I had climbed four months earlier. It felt good to see the peak, and to think that I'd stood on its summit. The mountain, though, still seems exactly the same as before – it's as if the climb has changed only me, and not it. As if only I'd been affected. I wonder whether, looking down, it even remembers me struggling, gasping for oxygen up those last few hundred feet to the top. Looking at it from this angle, part of me wonders how the hell I ever got up.

We passed the spot where Kami's sister was killed a few years ago in a landslide. It's strange seeing the torn scar in the hillside where the landslide happened; climbing over huge boulders of rubble that cover an entire village deep beneath them. Tentatively we made our way along the narrow path, with the ravine dropping away steeply to our right.

Two hours later we reached Dingboche. This village is situated at the foot of the huge mountains of Nuptse and Lhotse, with Everest behind them. Both Mick and I are tired today, and I think the altitude is now really beginning to have an effect. We'll rest here tomorrow, to try and recover a bit. It's this careful balance of rest, exercise and sleep, in preparing ourselves to be in the best possible state for the rigours ahead.

The tedium of such a strict routine is alleviated by the raw beauty of our surroundings. Vast mountains, the biggest in our world, rise straight up all around us, and when the wind blows through the valleys where we are, it feels as if the giants are stamping their heels.

A wonderful lady with a huge smile and only one eye, runs the lodge here. We piled up all the straw cushions and rested like the 'Princess and the pea' – a treat after the wooden boards of before.

I've just seen my face in an old cracked mirror, it was quite a shock – I hope it wasn't me who cracked it. Mick confirms that I look pretty rough, having not had a wash since … England. I can't say, though, that he looks like any Casanova!

At 6.00 a.m. we moved on from Dingboche, heading higher up still, towards Base Camp. We hadn't gone far, when we came across a great sight that I don't think I will ever forget.

Tucked into the side of the trail, stoically enduring the morning chill, sat two seventy-year-old English gentlemen enjoying some early morning breakfast. Seated at either end of a table that seemed to loll at a somewhat precarious angle on the rough ground. They both seemed lost in the ecstasy of spam and eggs at 14,500 feet.

We soon found out that these British eccentrics' ambition had been, for years, to walk through these valleys and to be able to see the 'Great Everest', as one of them said, 'in the flesh'. His eyes lit up with delight. We couldn't resist staying a while, and soon found ourselves, at their invitation, dining like 'kings' in the company of two fine 'queens'.

Whilst we sipped our tea at the end of the meal, the two of them became deep in conversation, arguing everything from the role of the Queen to the falling standards of British Rail sandwiches. Only when a punch-up over which was the quickest way from Salisbury to Bodmin seemed imminent, did we think it might be time to leave. Greatly inspired by seeing such extraordinary people in such an extraordinary place, we wished them luck and carried on – feeling much uplifted.

From there we followed a yak-trail, until we came up over

the lip of the valley. Ahead was a vast plain that stretched away into the distance, under the looming shadow of Mount Pokalde. We walked all morning through this plain, past the remains of old stables that had been used to house yaks. Soon we began to turn north, towards the foot of the glacier, upon which Base Camp is situated – still a day's walk away.

The path wound its way up through the mass of rocks that form the terminal moraine of the glacier. Buddhist shrines, called chortons, stand scattered along the route. Old prayer flags adorn these, and flutter away incessantly, beckoning you on your way as you pass them. The going had become progressively slower these last few days, and the thinner air was very noticeable now. Mick and I would stop every twenty minutes to rest, drink, and take the chance to savour the views of this barren land.

At mid-afternoon, we found a small hut with some Nepali porters inside, and joined them in drinking some tea. We then set out to try and reach Lobuche, before nightfall came. As we came over the moraine onto the glacier, we found ourselves in blazing late-afternoon sunshine. The main trail petered out into a small snow path, and the sun reflected strongly against our faces. A warm glow came over me; we were nearing the end of this long walk through the valleys to Base Camp. It wasn't far now. We'd be there tomorrow, God willing. We could just see in the distance, where the mountains met the end of the glacier – the place where it would be.

I wrote as we sat and rested:

We now can't see Everest at all, as it is hidden by the vast mountain of Nuptse, on our right. Even from Base Camp we won't be able to see her – not until we're 5,000 feet higher up, and well into the climb itself, will she reveal herself.

Two hours later we reached Lobuche, a clearing along the glacier with a few huts that accommodated those heading up to Base Camp. It was a foul-smelling place. Because of the nonchalance that the cold and altitude caused, people couldn't be bothered to keep the area clean, and they spent most of their time in the huts, drinking and complaining about the bleak conditions.

The loo here had degenerated into a seething mass of faeces, and nobody any longer even bothered to use it. Instead people crapped in any clear place they could find. The cold ensured that this place was never far from the hut. That night as I sneaked out to try and go myself, negotiating a route through the stinking minefield, I realized that hygiene was now a distant blur of the past.

That evening, as we sat wrapped up in our down jackets, round the tin stove that burnt the dried yak dung, we talked with the Nepalese who were there. Soon the chang was produced, followed not long after by an old guitar they had. None of them could play, and they were excited to hear that I did; that was until I actually did play, and then their enthusiasm somewhat waned. Well 'American Pie' isn't easy with six strings, let alone four. The next day, though, they agreed to let me borrow the guitar for the time I would be up at Base Camp.

As a lot of one's time is spent there mentally preparing for what lies ahead, I felt that to have a guitar was a real coup. Although I'm not sure the rest of the team quite saw it like that over the next few months. Heathens.

At 6.30 a.m. I strapped the guitar to my rucksack and we said farewell to the Nepalese. They grinned and bade us good luck in what the Tibetans call the 'poisonous gas': the thin air of high altitude. We lowered our faces to the morning chill, and headed off for the last five-hour stretch that would bring us eventually to Base Camp.

We hadn't got far, though, when the first effects of the food we had eaten began to kick in.

'Won't be a second, Mick,' I announced as I scurried off behind a large rock on the glacier to get rid of the better part of me that morning. But it wasn't all of me by any means. Frequent stops every ten minutes along the way followed, to the great amusement of Mick.

Getting the 'runs' though, is part of life when climbing in the hills of Nepal. The locals never wash much, and their food cannot be kept fresh for long – so their resistance to bacteria is therefore higher. I had been brought up on picking my pork chop up off the floor at home if I had dropped it, but, even for my stomach, some of the food we had at Lobuche was proving a bit much. The best and only way to cope with these 'part of life' occurrences was just to allow the body to work its course naturally. When it expels whatever is reacting against you, you feel instantly better. Bunging yourself up with Imodium or other diarrhoea tablets just delays the whole process.

By mid-morning I was much better, but a little dehydrated. We were slowly contouring our way along the side of the glacier, winding through the ice and debris of rocks that had been deposited along the route. These piles of rocks create a vast wasteland, and we followed an old yak-trail to avoid becoming disorientated. We were exhausted though by this clambering up and down huge boulders, and rests became more and more frequent.

Part of me felt maybe only now was I beginning to realize the 'enormity of the task ahead', to quote Mallory; the enormity of this challenge that maybe should have remained just a dream. I was struggling at even this height. How on earth was I going to be able to go up into the extreme altitudes that we knew lay ahead, kilometres vertically above where we were now, when I was currently worrying about the 100 feet or so of height change that day?

My goals at this time were so small, and I couldn't really focus on much more. But maybe that would be the key. I remembered hearing that to eat an elephant one has to start with a small bite. But at present I was having difficulty digesting even that.

As we continued along the route, we came to a cluster of stone memorials. These had been built in honour of some of the men who had died on Everest. Each one being about eight feet high, with a photograph wedged in the middle. These served as a chilling reminder of the authority of the mountain. Rob Hall's memorial stood quietly there, with a few prayer flags billowing on top of it. The tragedies keep happening, yet people still come back. I wondered if that showed bravery or recklessness; and couldn't decide. The numbers though tell the story simply – 162 lives lost on her slopes.

The final three hours towards Base Camp took us right into the glacier itself. From this point on, being so early in the climbing season, there was no established route, and we weaved our way along, heading in the direction of Base Camp. At certain points in the glacier, we would glimpse the Sherpas' tents in the distance. As we then descended back into the mass of rocks and ice, the tents would once more become hidden from view.

Dramatic drops that led down to frozen lakes below endlessly blocked the route. We would then be forced to try another route, winding through the maze of glacial rocks. Going up and down huge scree slopes and scrambling over these vast boulders the size of trucks soon left us both anxious and tired. We knew this was how that porter had got lost only a week earlier.

There was an entrancing quality to the surface of the glacier.

Much of it was covered in loose snow and rocks, but in parts we could see far down into the depths – beneath us were hundreds of feet of shimmering, glassy ice. On occasions the ground would groan as the glacier shifted below.

At this stage in the season we expected to find Base Camp empty, save for a small group of our Sherpas sent by Kami, who were starting to prepare the ropes and other equipment. It was them that we were hoping to meet. The majority of what we required for the climb, along with more clothing, would arrive by yak in ten days' time. So at the moment we had nothing more than just basic trekking equipment. I tucked my old chef's trousers into my socks to keep the draught out, and pulled my tweed cap down tight to avoid losing it to Tibet.

Everyone should permit themselves certain luxuries in life. Stan, for example, a very old friend, consistently made a point of stowing his pyjamas in his bergan on field exercises – to the bewilderment of his sergeants. But for me, my pair of tatty old chef's trousers and ultra-hairy Richard Hannay tweed cap filled my needs nicely. I think certain other climbers in due course showed a slight distress at the British attire around Base Camp, but as I'd once heard said: 'Beware: strength is often hidden in absurdity'; although in our case I'm not sure that was entirely true, but it was worth a try!

The wind began to get up over the glacier, and it got considerably colder. I wished now that I had some of my proper climbing clothes with me. I just wanted to reach the tents; it had been a long few weeks for the two of us out here, and we were both desperate to get there and start settling in. An hour later, though, we were still floundering around in the glacier, and not appearing to get much closer. We didn't talk, but rather just numbly dreamt of the sanctuary we hoped Base Camp would offer.

By the time we reached the tents it was blowing hard, and we were both cold and tired; but at last we had arrived. We went round to the flap of one of the tents, undid the zip, and peered in. The dirty faces of four Sherpas broke into welcoming grins. They were sitting round a tiny stove, clutching steaming mugs of hot tea.

'Why so late? We worried much. Come drink.'

We looked at each other and smiled.

We were now at 17,450 feet.

CHAPTER SIX

LAST CALL

▲

'Well here's another fine mess you've got me into.'
Oliver Hardy to Stan Laurel

DIARY, 12 MARCH:

Mick has a throbbing headache, and I can hear him throwing up outside his tent. He has hardly spoken a word in the last twenty-four hours since arriving here, and seems to be suffering quite a bit from the altitude at Base Camp. I'm putting on a semi-brave face, but feel pretty crap myself. It's all a bit worrying sitting here, and already feeling like this.

Early reactions of the body of not having enough oxygen in the blood are headaches and lethargy. The latter is never normally a problem; but when I've got to be helped in just getting a simple tent erected, it makes me feel pretty pathetic. Especially as I collapse in it afterwards and then look out of the flap, up to the vast mountain of Nuptse above, knowing that she hides the monster of Everest behind her.

I put down my diary, and thought that I would try to sleep a bit. Night had already come, and it was only 6.30 p.m. It felt bitterly cold – colder than I'd ever known. I saw on my temperature gauge that it was −20°C.

It was still winter time at the moment, and I knew that it would slowly begin to get warmer as the weeks went by, and spring arrived in the mountains.

I snuggled down into my sleeping bag, and closed my eyes. A bit of sleep should sort my headache out, I hoped.

Thoughts flooded my mind: I remembered the famous Everest climber Hornbein's description of Base Camp. He'd called it a 'world not meant for habitation'. I was beginning to understand. It made me question just how bright all of this really was. I wondered also how Mick was feeling and soon, bereft of any answers, I dozed off.

I woke up at 1.00 a.m. with a deep pounding in my skull. The literal 'bear with a sore head'. The stuffy air in the tiny, enclosed tent wasn't helping, and it was a toss-up between letting the harsh chill of the night frost come in, or enduring the headache from the less oxygen-rich, trapped air. I spent the rest of the hours until dawn with the zip closed, sipping at the lukewarm water in my thermos.

One of the factors of living at high altitudes is coping with condensation inside the tents. All one's exhaled breath freezes on the inner layer of the tent and around the top of your sleeping bag, and as the sun rises, this begins to drip. By 7.00 a.m. each morning your bag is damp, and you're invariably woken up by ice-cold water dripping on your face.

My first morning at Base Camp I spent half an hour trying to dodge these drips, and then reluctantly scrambled out of my bag, struggled into some warm clothes, and got out of my tent – squinting because of my headache.

Mick was still no better, and his tent was ominously still all zipped up. Little birds chirped round the front of his tent flap, and I sat there watching them, wondering jealously why they were only congregating outside his. It took a few minutes of observing this to realize that the birds were only there because they were feasting on Mick's sick that he had deposited there during the night. I grinned, and breathed in the cold crisp air as the morning sun began to shine on my face.

DIARY, 13 MARCH:
I'm trying to drink as much as possible to help the headache, but I certainly don't feel like eating anything. A small bit of rice was all I managed for breakfast with the Sherpas. Luckily the food will improve here dramatically when all the others arrive in a few weeks' time, but in the meantime we're strictly on 'Sherpa' rations.

I watched them all go off early this morning to begin work on the ropes, and to have a look at the first part of the climb. They seem so strong and at home at this height. I can only look on, 'sick' with envy – literally.

This morning I spent much of the time unpacking and sorting through my equipment. The guitar now seems a bit of a burden and I can't find any room for it in my tiny tent, now that it's full of kit. On top of that, it has broken a string during the night – it must have been too tight and have snapped in the cold.

Base Camp is already over 1,600 feet higher than the summit of Mont Blanc, the highest peak in Western Europe. Tucked away at the top end of a glacier, it sits in a barren landscape of rocks that are strewn like marbles across the ice. Often likened to the moon in its harsh and uninviting surroundings, pinnacles of glassy ice reach up, twisted and chiseled amongst the rocks. At this height nothing can grow.

When you first arrive, you struggle for hours to build a level platform for your tent, forging a base out of tiny stones amongst the ice. Glacial boulders balance precariously on pinnacles of ice, and as the glacier groans and moves beneath you, these shift and slide randomly about.

As the weeks go by, and the ice around moves, so does your tent. Soon you find yourself perched on a contorted bit of ground and you need to start again – repitching your eighteen square feet, of what becomes known simply as 'home'.

Mountains soar upwards on all sides, thousands of feet above. You can imagine the mountain gods peering down and viewing the tents as tiny orange specks amongst the miles of rock and ice far below. These mountains form a natural amphitheatre around Base Camp, and huge hanging glaciers are draped along the vast walls on all three sides. These collapse at all hours of the day and night, causing thunderous avalanches. Sitting here, you hope that your camp is situated far enough away, so as to avoid these terrors.

The noise of these avalanches shatters the silence of the place. As the weight of snow can no longer sustain itself, large sections break off and tumble like 'white thunder' down the sheer faces. The noise echoes around the mountains, shaking the foundations of the glacier as the avalanches plummet to earth.

These are extraordinary moments, as you hear the initial crack of the snow coming loose far above. We would scramble to the edge of our tents and stare out as the cloud of snow picked up momentum. We knew that we were far enough away from the danger; but still in the dead of night when we first heard those rumbles and saw the moonlight glistening on the tumbling mass of snow, our hearts stayed still.

These serve as a sober reminder of what lies ahead on the mountain, outside of Base Camp's 'safe' zone. In the mountains, avalanches kill more people than the cold and the altitude put together – here you're never allowed to forget this.

During those first few days Mick and I struggled to get used to this new environment. An environment that consisted of the cold, extreme altitude, and a wilderness of rock and ice. The occasional groan of the glacier moving beneath us at first frightened me. I was finding it hard not to be able to find refuge in anything familiar. No trees, no flowing water, no earth below us. The only comforts now seemed to be a second roll mat to pad out the sharpness of the stones beneath us and a battered old three-stringed guitar to strum.

I wrote in my diary:

> I think that the fear of what lies ahead accentuates the harshness of this place. I've never known an environment quite like it. I must learn though to think of this as 'home', as one thing is absolutely certain – Base Camp will be the tamest place on this mountain.

That afternoon, like many afternoons later on, I sought the solitude of my tent and whiled away the hours reading the letters that my family had given me before leaving. Tucked into one of the side pouches of my rucksack I found a note from my mother. It said simply, 'Angels are watching over you.' I folded it and carefully put it away.

*

I knew a couple of the Sherpas at Base Camp from the climb on Ama Dablam, namely Nima and Pasang; it was good to see them again. They are both great characters who live for the mountains, and take great pride in their climbing. They laugh ferociously at almost anything, and then can keep laughing at the same joke for hours. You couldn't help but like them. It was good to be spending time with them now, before the pressure started. Later on, we knew that we would be together in much less pleasant situations.

A couple of days later, Mick was feeling much better and was more his usual self. He is fiercely resilient, and recovering like this was typical of the way he overcame obstacles throughout the expedition.

Whether he was ill, or had taken a nasty fall whilst climbing, or was just feeling the frustration of endlessly waiting for suitable weather, he would always calmly ride through it. This would often involve him just quietly retreating to his tent, and sitting things out; coping with it in his own way. But he would never be beaten. Mick knew how to cope with hardship, and always seemed to emerge from it fighting. It was of no surprise therefore to see Mick, who had hardly been seen now for three days, climb out of his tent – smiling and fit again.

Because our families were very close, we had grown up as kids together. I will never forget his mother telling me before we left that she was confident Mick would be okay, as long as I was with him. But I felt the same reliance towards him. I sensed that I was stronger when I was with him, and he inspired me to work to my limits. Our partnership together, even at this stage, kept me going; and my respect for him grew daily. They say that if you see someone's vulnerability, then you realize their fallibility; but with Mick it was the opposite. In the weeks ahead I saw him almost daily at his physical limit, and this has left me with a deep admiration for the man.

Now that we had spent a few days at Base Camp, and Mick was feeling healthy again, we planned to pack a small rucksack of equipment and head back down the valley to about 14,000 feet, to train. We still had ten days before Neil, Geoffrey, and Henry's team would arrive at Base Camp, and we hoped to do a last week of climbing before they got here. We decided to leave the next day.

DIARY, 15 MARCH:
Another very cold night here, but I'm slowly learning the tricks of the trade. The most fundamental one being that to fill a waterbottle with boiling water before going to bed keeps the toes warm for hours, and evokes all sorts of good emotions.

The coldest hours are between 4.00 and 5.00 a.m. and by

that stage the water bottle is cold and lies uncomfortably in your bag. This morning I took mine out at 5.00 a.m. and it was frozen solid within forty-five minutes. During these early hours I just seem to curl up and hide away in my own little world – the world of my sleeping bag.

When the sun comes up, it burns so strongly because of the high altitude. Less particles to diffuse the rays makes the burning effects pretty obvious. Mick's already got panda eyes and we're both going this dark, dark brown. Rather than looking golden and sexy though, we just look this 'dirt' colour. Not that there's anyone to look sexy for, apart from three yaks. Talking of which . . . I wonder what the yaks like best, brown or golden . . . Hmm!

The sky also looks this wonderful deep blue colour, which seems to fade at the edges into a darker shade. I guess though that's to be expected – after all, we are 17,450 feet closer to space.

We headed back out of Base Camp the next morning – equipped with our rucksacks and fifty feet of rope. Once across the glacier, we were to head down to Dingboche, rest there and then climb the next day. But we found getting across the glacier from Base Camp harder than we had expected. The absence of any path meant that we wound our way through the ice in the rough direction we thought the edge of the glacier to be.

What should have taken two hours took us four, but eventually we found our way onto the ridge. The two of us sat exhausted and looked at the vast expanse of rock and ice that we had crossed. We didn't say anything as we stared, each of us lost in our thoughts – grateful to be on solid ground.

That afternoon, as we approached Dingboche, 3,500 feet lower down, we were relishing the prospect of sleeping in a hut with a warm fire, in the thicker oxygen. But when we arrived, the place was full of trekkers, now that the trekking season was fast approaching; and there wasn't room. We pulled out our little tent and put it up outside. It was a bit colder than being in the warmth of the hut and we didn't get our fire, but at least we could be in peace, and were able to hear the sounds of the night clearly.

The next day we walked for two hours, through strong wind and hail, down to the village of Pangboche. When we arrived we were starving and we tucked into a hearty lunch of rice, stewed vegetables, and yak cheese. We wanted to climb the ridge that led to the foot of Ama Dablam that afternoon, and to spend a night there acclimatizing; but now, curled up round the fire after a good lunch, we felt reluctant to head back into the weather and start climbing.

We both wanted to stay put, but we knew that we were due to meet a couple of friends in a few days' time, who had come out to see us. When they arrived it would be harder to train. We therefore felt it important to do some climbing these couple of days beforehand. So, reluctantly, we put on our thick clothing and rucksacks, and headed out into the snow, leaving the fire still burning.

*

We got rid of any superfluous stuff, and left it in the village. After crossing a small wooden bridge over a swollen stream, we began the ascent onto the ridge that would lead to Ama Dablam. It was hard work fighting against the wind and hail, and we tightened our fleeces around us to keep warm. I remembered the path we were on from when I had been here the year before; then it had been just rock and scree, but now it was covered in thigh-deep drift snow. After two hours we were beginning to tire. Even at these lower altitudes, the body becomes tired so quickly, as it tells you it needs more oxygen.

I led the way, kicking steps into the snow; but because of the thick mist that had now moved in, it was almost impossible to keep on the right line of path. The higher we got, the deeper the snow became, and at times, because of carrying forty-five pounds of rucksack, I found myself up to my waist in drift snow. Time and time again we would fall, as the crusty slabs gave way under our weight. The weather was worsening as the wind drove the snow ferociously across the slopes. My leather hiking boots had now frozen, and we were getting irritated by the slow going.

Eventually, three hours later, we reached Ama Dablam's Base Camp. We rested for a few moments. I was amazed by how different it appeared from when I was last there. The post-monsoon warmth of October had now been replaced by a stark icy cold, and the grass that I had lain on then, as I contemplated the climb ahead, was now snow-covered and desolate.

We had an hour and a half of daylight left, and decided to go a little further above the ridge before nightfall came, when we would be forced to pitch our tent. Minutes after setting off though, we found ourselves in even deeper drift snow. Mick was now leading, and soon found himself floundering in the loose powder. We kept going, but forty minutes later we had still only gone about 200 metres. We soon realized that we were getting into dangerous avalanche territory and decided to retreat the few hundred metres back to the mountain's Base Camp. We were tired; it had been a long day.

On our way back, part of a large slab of snow behind us groaned and cracked open. We hurried to the side, out of the danger. It stayed silent and still. We watched it carefully and then began to make our way tentatively back down, treading a fresh trail.

Back at the Base Camp, we found a site safe from avalanches, and tried to put up our tent in the howling wind. When we eventually got it up, we clambered hurriedly inside, cowering from the cruel weather. It was dark by now. My gloves and boots were frozen solid; I put them in my rucksack and stuffed the whole lot down my sleeping bag, in an attempt to thaw them out. We shuffled and tried to get comfortable.

The tent we had was known as a 'Himalayan Explorer', but it was so small that there wasn't exactly a lot of room for exploration; and the two of us, almost wedged on top of each other, tried to sleep.

At 8.00 p.m., we both woke up, gasping for breath. The tent was so well sealed that we had been breathing the same air over and over again. It felt as if we were at 114,000 feet instead of 14,000 feet. We cursed the tent and decided to rename the 'Himalayan Explorer', the 'Himalayan Suffocator'; we undid the flap a bit, lay back down and told each other stories late into the night. *The Lion, the Witch and the Wardrobe* was the crowning glory to us both falling deep asleep, exhausted by the day.

We woke at 6.30 a.m. It was now a beautiful clear day outside the tent, but still icy cold in the pre-dawn frost. We crawled out, grimacing as we put on our damp boots, and began to pack up our equipment. We found that the tent poles had frozen together, and refused to budge. Our hands were becoming freezing cold as we tried to free them.

Without the pressure of bad weather, though, everything seemed remarkably calm. We jumped up and down, trying to warm our feet up, and relished the fresh air. Soon I was busying myself trying to find some juniper under the snow, as Mick rummaged for his lighter. Five minutes later we had a lovely fire burning. We warmed our hands and our feet by the flames and thawed out the poles.

The warmth and smell of burning juniper made us feel glad to be alive. Alone in the hills on this stunning crisp morning, we waited for the sun to rise over the mountains.

As we left Ama Dablam's Base Camp and started down the ridge, the warmth of the new sun strengthened. For two hours we walked down in silence, lost in the joy of the moment, and revelling in the thought of the fresh omelette that awaited us back in Pangboche, only a few kilometres away.

That day we felt tired but happy. We just ate and wrote our diaries, and watched our kit steaming as it dried over the fire.

DIARY:
I'm feeling stronger now and I think our training is paying off. We have much to look forward to. Tomorrow we're meeting Emma and Alex, who have come out from England to trek in the valleys. Just the thought of them seems to lift our spirits. I hope they aren't shocked by my mountain smell.

We sat in the sun during the afternoon, and enjoyed the good hospitality of the Sherpa who ran the lodge. He was now elderly, but recounted stories to us of his days in the 'Great Mountains', as he fried rice over the mud stove. The day slipped by in such a manner, and we soon found that sleep swept over us.

*

The next day, with great excitement, we raced down the valley some four kilometres to the village of Thyangboche in order to meet the girls. We had arranged before we left England to meet them at 12 noon on that date, in the main lodge of the village. Nothing more had been said, and part of me wondered if they would be there. I hoped they would.

It had been a while since we had seen anyone we knew, and I was so excited by the thought of seeing friends. One of the joys of the hills for me is the way that life is so simple. One's focus is on living and expressing rather than keeping up or keeping on time. One of the downfalls of normal life is that you hardly have time to remember who you have seen in the past few days, let alone savour that time together. Out here, though, we knew these days together with our friends would be precious, before we began to wrestle with the mountain. I wanted to savour every moment that they were here.

We went into the lodge and looked around. There, curled round a fire, smothered in jerseys and rugs and grinning from ear to ear, sat Emma and Alex. It was as if a small part of England had arrived in these valleys to encourage us. It brought back feelings that I had never expected to feel. We sat up late that night and talked.

I fear that as the days went on, and we guided the two girls up towards Base Camp, I became more and more reclusive. I knew that soon they would be returning down the valleys. The higher we went, the harder work the girls both found it. I didn't want them to go. It spelt the point of no return for me, and I knew that the climb would start soon afterwards.

They had both struggled bravely up these vast hills and valleys in a determination to see Everest and to reach Base Camp. They had seen Everest now in the distance, but were still a few miles short of Base Camp and were beginning to struggle. They both felt dizzy and had bad headaches, and it was becoming obvious that they weren't enjoying this last bit. They would have to go back down the next day.

We had one last night all together. They both slept in a small wooden cubicle in the corrugated hut at Lobuche. Mick and I didn't even bother sleeping in the cubicled part. Instead we curled up as we were, still fully clothed, round the fire in the centre of the room. Early the next day, we helped them pack. They both felt awful. I was so impressed with their determination to have got this far, but for safety's sake they now needed to go down. Alex slipped me a note that said, simply, to be wise on the mountain.

If it's not right, then be brave and make those hard decisions. Come down.

The words sounded empty, but I tried desperately to acknowledge them. I knew she was right, and prayed that I would have the courage to do this, should the decision arise. And so, at 8.15 a.m. that clear morning, left two of my good friends.

Later that day I read her note. I reread it hundreds of times in the months ahead.

> It must be extremely tough knowing what's ahead, when there are so few people around. But keep your faith strong. It's times like this that it counts. I know the struggle that it's been for you to get this far, and I know you dream of the summit, but don't jeopardize everything else you've ever worked for. Nothing is worth losing your fingers or toes for, and remember, you're only twenty-three!
>
> Go with all my luck, and keep safe; I have this funny feeling that all will be okay.

I hoped she was right. I needed her to be right; but part of me doubted.

That afternoon we returned quietly to Base Camp, walking those last few hours along the glacier that had eluded the girls. The climb would now begin.

CHAPTER SEVEN

BREAKING THE ICE

▲

'We are the pilgrims, Master, we shall go
Always a little further it may be
Beyond that last blue mountain barred with snow
Beyond that angry or that glimmering sea.'

Special Air Service Regimental verse

From the peak of Everest, the land of Tibet lies sprawled out across the horizon to the north, as far as the eye can see. To the south, the summit looks over the vast range of the Himalaya, all the way down through the foothills to the Nepalese plain in the distance. No other bit of land stands above this point on the entire planet. Below the summit, though, lie days of treacherous descent, through a labyrinth of snow and ice that marks the way out of Everest's ruthless jaws.

The descent down the South-East Ridge is lined by faces of sheer rock and blue ice. These lead to a couloir of deep powder snow, and eventually on down to a col, some 3,000 feet below the summit. This col, the site of where our Camp Four would be, sits between the two huge peaks of Lhotse to the south, and Everest to the north.

From the South Col, the gradient drops sharply away, down a 5,000 feet ice wall, known as the Lhotse Face. Camp Three would be carved into the ice, a quarter of the way down this. At the foot of this ice wall starts the highest and most startling valley in the world. At one end of this would be our Camp Two, and at the other end, 2,000 feet lower, our Camp One. This extraordinary and vast ice glacier is known simply as the Western Cwm – or the valley of silence.

Pronounced 'koom', this huge hidden valley was named by George Mallory during the first Everest reconnaissance climb in 1921, doubtless from affection for his Welsh climbing haunts. The name has remained ever since. This glacier, hidden from view on all sides, slices its way through the centre of the surrounding giant mountains. Then, at the mouth of the valley, the ice begins to fall away.

As the glacier is funnelled through this mouth to the west, the glacier begins to rupture violently. Unable to sustain its own weight, the ice breaks up into a tumbling cascade of frozen water, with blocks of ice the size of houses, slowly shifting down the face. This is constantly moving at a rate of about one metre a day, breaking and collapsing its way down; thus making the mountain dangerously unpredictable. Similar to when a flowing river narrows through a ravine, turning the water into frothing rapids; likewise here, as the ice is squeezed and forced down, it begins to 'froth'. It is this gushing frozen river that is called the Khumbu Icefall; one of the most dangerous parts of the ascent.

At its feet lies Base Camp, a safe distance away. The noise of thousands of tonnes of ice, constantly shifting and wrenching, breaks the silence of every night there. The Icefall never rests.

The late Lord Hunt, in his account of the first ascent of Everest in 1953, describes this moving mass of ice like this:

A sheer precipice, overhung with thick slices of blue ice more than 100 feet in depth, which peel off in massive slabs at intervals during each day. As you look at it, you might expect to hear the roar of that immense volume of foaming water which, after flowing peacefully to the brink of the cliff above, is now plunging down with terrifying power. But it has been gripped by the intense cold, frozen into immobility, a silent thing, its force restrained. But not quite. For this labyrinth of broken ice is moving, its surface changing, making it the most perilous of problems to surmount.

Sitting at Base Camp, some forty-five years after Hunt wrote that, the Icefall didn't seem to have changed a bit. Holding my mug of sweet tea that had been made by Nima Lamu, the young Sherpa girl, I shielded my eyes from the early sun. Only 400 metres in front of us, shimmering and detached, lay the Icefall. At that moment, all was quiet.

The responsibility this season for building and maintaining a route through the Icefall was borne by Henry and our team of Sherpas. These Sherpas had now been up here for two weeks, preparing the ladders and ropes that would be used extensively in the ice. Already they had created a route through about three-quarters of the Icefall, roping ladders together in order to cross its yawning crevasses. They had been working fast. This morning was no different, and at 5.00 a.m. they were at the foot of the Icefall, putting on their crampons, and preparing for the risky work ahead. The smell of burning juniper wafted over my tent, as the last bit of branch crackled into flames.

Each morning the Sherpas would burn this as an offering to the 'goddess of the sky', to pray for their safety that day. In the future you could tell the days when climbers were in the Icefall, by the amount of juniper that was smouldering around Base Camp.

I wrote that morning, in the cold of dawn:

29 March, 6.15 a.m.:

Base Camp is now a lot more busy. The Singapore expedition arrived yesterday, plus about three-quarters of the entire Nepalese yak population, needed to carry all their equipment. I've never seen so much stuff, and we've even heard rumour that they have the facilities to carry out advanced dentistry. This makes Mick and I look like true amateurs as we argue over who's got the tin of plasters. I hope all our equipment arrives soon, so that I don't have to feel quite so pathetic as I sit here freezing in these ruddy old chef's trousers that flap like flags in the wind. Even I'm looking forward now to a pair of long johns.

The Sherpas, during our absence down the valley, have constructed a stone building out of the rocks around Base Camp. It is covered with a tarpaulin and has a table of carefully balanced stones in the middle. It's very impressive, and reflects their quiet but strong character. It has all been built with no fuss in just a week. Back in sunny Dorset we'd still be arguing about who was going to be the 'foreman'.

Most of our time at Base Camp will be spent in this 'mess tent', as the Sherpas call it. It is a key part of Base Camp, and all our little tents surround it.

Mick and I started flattening some more tent sites yesterday for the rest of the team when they arrive, and we hope to finish these today. It's good to take some exercise and throw some rocks around, in an attempt to level out some ground. I'm feeling much stronger now.

Supper last night was blooming 'dal-bat' again. The standard Sherpa food – rice and lentil soup. Delicious once; okay twice; but desperate the twentieth time on the trot. We can't wait for the arrival of the others, plus the better grub.

Mick sat in the mess tent last night in his 'Base Camp' shoes – namely his trainers. At night though, it is still bitingly cold, and is made even parkier by wearing trainers on an ice floor. He looked in envy at my snug moon-boots. Halfway through supper he announced that he was in grave danger of losing his toes from frostbite before he'd set foot on the hill.

Mick ended up eating supper whilst suspending his feet six inches off the ice; it kept me amused all evening.

By now, though, Mick and I were beginning to get itchy feet. The girls had left two days ago, and the others were due to arrive sometime soon. We wanted to keep up our strength, and asked the two climbing Sherpas over supper if we could follow them up into the Icefall the next time they went. We wanted to get a feel of the place, and to help our acclimatization. It would only be a climb of some six hours but we knew that time spent above the height of Base Camp could only give us an advantage when the others arrived, as our bodies would be more adapted to the higher air. Nima and Pasang agreed to it, and carried on eating. Tomorrow would be a rest day. We would start with them the morning after that; an hour before dawn.

> DIARY, 30 MARCH:
> This morning was spent with the two of us sitting in the sun on our roll-mats, chatting and preparing our equipment. We measured harness lengths, adjusted slings, taped up ice-axe handles with foam to prevent the frozen metal sticking to your gloves, and then endlessly rechecked everything we had done. I've never felt on the one hand so prepared, and on the other so unprepared. However fit and experienced you are, the moment you enter the Icefall you're plain 'gambling'. And in my experience, I've never come out of a casino yet in credit.

As well as the Singapore team, a couple of other climbers had also now arrived at Base Camp. The first of these was a pleasant but slightly brash climber from Denmark, called Michael. This season was to be his second attempt on Everest. He was determined to climb the mountain solo, and without any supplementary oxygen. So far it had eluded him. On his previous attempt, the months of climbing lower down, carrying huge amounts of kit, had drained his body too much of those vital energy reserves needed to enable him to climb higher up. At the crucial time, he had been too exhausted to carry on.

This year he was trying again. He had Sherpa support at Base Camp, plus a radio communications officer with whom to keep in contact higher up. Their camp, like the Singaporeans', was also a hive of the latest modern advances. This time though, instead of being medical advances, they were nutritional.

Michael would begin each day by stirring up these colourful and glutinous concoctions of high-energy, high-protein, high-everything drinks. He guaranteed us that these would propel him, as he said, 'like a rocket with bad wind, up the mountain'. We felt somewhat disadvantaged eating normal food, rather than any exotic blend of pills and shakes. His friendship with us started off badly when he sauntered into our tent to announce what was on his food menu that night. It consisted of lasagne and pizza. The two of us hadn't heard those words for a while and instantly hardened to him, as we continued nibbling on our rice and dal-bat.

In due course, though, as we shared experiences together, he became a friend and confidant; but it took some time. Such a driven character was often hard to stomach at Base Camp, when you just wanted some space and a bit of quiet time alone.

The other new person that had arrived at Base Camp was a kind-faced Bolivian climber called Bernardo. Standing only five foot something, with a grin that was as broad as he was tall, Bernardo was gentle and full of laughter. Over the next eight weeks he became a close friend. Born and bred in the Bolivian hills outside La Paz, he was a true mountain man, with a wealth of experience. In 1994 Bernardo had been attempting to climb Everest from the north side. After two months of climbing, and only hours from the summit, Bernardo heard of a German climber in trouble. He turned back to assist in the rescue of this climber, and managed to save his life; but it had cost Bernardo the summit. He had made the right decision, but in the blur and haze of high altitude, such decisions can become hard to take. It was a credit to his strength and will-power that he had so bravely turned around.

After four years of trying to raise the sponsorship to climb again, Bernardo was once again at the foot of the great mountain. He was hoping to be the first South American Indian to reach the top of our world's highest peak. Bernardo spoke very limited English, and once he discovered that I spoke Spanish, the floodgates opened. I was drowned in a barrage of conversation. I think Bernardo had missed the banter, having walked in silence through the valleys for over two weeks. I just sat and listened, enjoying his clear South American accent, as we discussed the climb ahead.

Bernardo, having just reached Base Camp, needed to rest for a few days – but wished us both luck for our preliminary climb in the Icefall. He said he would be watching us through his binoculars, and finished his mug of tea by saying, '*Vaya con Díos*' or 'God's speed.'

DIARY, 30 MARCH, DUSK:
We had fried spam tonight for supper. A treat the Sherpas had been reserving for this last meal, before starting the climb. Despite the fact that we suspect spam has now been banned in England, as it's so unhealthy, it was a great luxury to us both here. It tasted as delicious as anything I can remember.

All my kit is immaculately laid out ready for dawn, when we'll start into the Icefall. I feel a real 'spod' with everything so neat and tidy. If Shara could see this, she'd be amazed.

I just seem to lie here, endlessly mulling over all the possibilities of what I'm about to do. The build-up and fear is so exhausting mentally, and those death statistics are so unhelpful. Ruddy statisticians; nothing better to do than worry those who are actually doing things.

Earlier this evening as I was getting into my tent, I heard this huge, shattering crack reverberate round the valley. A vast wall of snow from the side of a mountain behind us, known as the Lho-La Pass, collapsed. A thick cloud of snow, fifty feet high, came pouring down the sheer slopes. As it picked up speed, the roar grew with it, as the snow rolled down towards Base Camp. I was scared it might reach us in the middle of the glacier, but instead, as it plummeted to the floor at the valley's edge, it billowed up like an explosion, hundreds of feet high. From here it took five minutes to settle slowly, and eventually left an eery silence hanging over the place. It was the most awe-inspiring sight I've ever seen, and a sober reminder of tomorrow.

I seem so full of fears about everything. The cold, the risk of death in the falling ice, the pain of the climb itself. There seems so much ahead. Nobody minds pain occasionally, but the prospect of being at my physical wit's end for the next two months terrifies me, as I stand here at the starting gate. What happens if Mick dies tomorrow, on day one? Or if I do? I pray for the Good Lord's protection over us. Taking gambles like this just isn't healthy. I feel knotted up inside. All I seem to have to hold on to are my stuttering faith and my memories of those I love at home.

Sleep didn't come at all that night, as I lay thinking about what was now only a few hours away. The cracks and rumbles of the Icefall seemed especially loud to me; or maybe it was just my ears being over-sensitive to their groans. I tossed and turned, looking every half an hour at my watch to count the time remaining until my alarm would sound. I just wished for deep sleep, so that I would be strong the next morning. But it never came.

*

Leaving the warmth and security of a sleeping bag for the cold chill of night is one of the worst parts of climbing. The cold that the night provides, ensures greater stability in the Icefall. It is during these night hours that much of one's climbing has to be done. By day, not only is the ice weaker, but the temperatures soar dramatically. Trapped in the ice, with the heat of the sun blazing down, has been known to literally sap the strength from a man. Skin becomes burnt in a matter of minutes if not protected, and temperatures that have an hour beforehand been in the minus 20s°C, can now rise to over 80°F.

Early starts, like this morning, would become matter of fact by the end; but in that pre-dawn chill, leaving my warm sleeping bag was, mentally, the greatest struggle. It was times like this, when I was still sleepy, that I felt the most vulnerable and alone.

As I sat up, the condensation that had frozen within my tent shook all over me, covering me with icy flakes. Struggling to get into my knee height, high-altitude boots shook the tent even more, and engulfed me again in icicles. These boots alone weigh more than most people's entire shoe collection put together, and fastening them took almost ten minutes. Reluctant to actually unzip the flap of the tiny tent and allow the wind in, I dressed as much as I could in the confined space of the tent. I rolled over to put my harness on, and pulled it tight around my waist.

'Morning Miguel,' I stammered, in the direction of Mick's tent.

'*Hola Oso* ("Morning Bear"),' the reply came. Mick was learning Spanish very quickly, now that Bernardo and I had been speaking it continually.

My sister had named me 'bear' as a baby, and I have no idea why. I certainly wasn't hairy and rarely growled, but for some strange reason the name had stuck. I had hoped that by the mature age of seven and a half, I would have grown out of it; yet here on this frosty morning at the foot of Mount Everest, at the age of twenty-three, the nickname still remained. I shook my head and smiled.

And so went our standard early-morning greeting. Whether

it was at Base Camp with our tents only inches apart, or higher up the hill, with our bodies only inches apart, the greeting each time that we had to get up was the same. Said with cheerful irony, it invariably made one feel better. It made you feel that you weren't alone in being cold and miserable.

We both emerged from our tents; it was 5.30 a.m. As Mick sorted out his rucksack, I went to try and crap behind a rock. Dawn was always the best time for this, as all the faeces were frozen and didn't smell. As the sun warmed Base Camp each day, the stench of the makeshift stone hole, smeared with misfires, was pretty rancid.

The challenge I found that early morning was undoing an all-in-one windsuit, whilst trying to keep it off the ground, then squatting, wiping and trying to keep my hands warm, all at the same time. That first time of doing it all dressed up was a shambles. But practice would make perfect; and of practice, I knew, there would be plenty.

We tried to force down some Sherpa porridge, but only really managed a few mouthfuls. I was nervous, and felt sick swallowing the stodgy mess. In hushed voices, as if not wanting to awake the Icefall, we said goodbye to the Sherpa cook, Thengba. We then gently lay a small branch of juniper on the fire and watched it crackle into life. We put our rucksacks on and followed Nima and Pasang through Base Camp, to the foot of the Icefall.

For twenty minutes we snaked our way through the rock and scree, heading for the entrance to the ice. The trail of bootprints left in the slush of yesterday afternoon had now frozen solid, and showed us the route. The entry-point was marked with a bamboo cane that the Sherpas had left. I looked back at Base Camp, and could see the smoke of the juniper still smouldering away. I hoped the prayers would work.

We were the first Western climbers to be entering the Icefall this year. So far only the Sherpas had been into her depths. We sat on the ice at the bottom, with jagged pinnacles rising up above us on all sides. As the Icefall flattens at its end, it fluctuates along, rolling in these crests of contorted ice. Hidden amongst the pinnacles, away from the view of Base Camp, we sat and began for the first time in months to put our crampons on. A mixed feeling of excitement and trepidation flooded my body. At last we were beginning the task that had been a dream for so long. I yearned just to get started, to get my teeth into it. I felt that once the bit was between my teeth, then it would be easier to hold on to. But with it came that nervous, sick feeling. Ahead was the unknown.

We began to weave deeper into the maze. Our crampons bit firmly into the glassy ice, with their fresh, razor-sharp teeth. It felt good. As the ice steepened, and we began to climb further into the frozen labyrinth, the ropes started. The days of hard work by the Sherpas showed us the route, as the ropes snaked away into the distance. We clipped our karabiners that were attached to our harnesses on to the fixed line. The rope twisted up and over the walls of ice in front of us. A few strong pushes and we would clamber over their lip, lying there breathing heavily in the ever higher air.

There ahead would then be the next contorted ice face that beforehand had been hidden. As we went higher we began to see Base Camp below us, getting smaller in the distance.

I was getting used to wearing crampons again and stepped carefully to avoid tearing my windsuit on the sharp teeth. I was rusty, and twice the blades sliced a gash in the material as I tried to kick a crampon into the ice.

The dawn brought with it some haze and soon Base Camp was obscured from sight. We checked our equipment again, and kept moving on. The pace behind the Sherpas was steady and manageable; I was feeling good. Despite now going higher than I had been since we had arrived in Nepal, I was coping okay in the thinner air.

Soon we came to the first of the aluminium ladders that spanned the yawning chasms that appeared amongst the broken ice. Elaborate systems of ropes secured these ladder bridges, but still occasionally we would reach a point where the crevasse had shifted. Here the existing ladders would be suspended, twisted in the air, ropes torn apart as the weight of the moving ice wrenched the structures asunder. We would wait and watch as Nima and Pasang, who were also known as the Icefall 'doctors', would get to work repairing and fixing the route across.

All work in the Icefall was undertaken in silence. It was safest like this. During the regular breaks that we would take, the Icefall doctors would quietly smoke, leaning against the ice walls all around. Smiles would be exchanged. As sections were repaired, we would continue on up. We would change onto the new rope, clip in, and start across the precarious ladders, with the crevasses stretching away into the blackness of the abyss below us. The Sherpas believe that some of the crevasses are so deep that they come out in America. Looking deep into them, I could understand their reasons. There was something sinister about the nature of these silent tears in the ice.

We would focus carefully on each step across. Our spiked crampons would slide on the metal ladders until they gripped in a groove and held fast. Only then would you step again, your eyes keenly focused on the ladder and not the drop below. That was the key to crossing these safely.

We didn't want to have to test the strength of the ropes that we were clipped into. They were a precaution rather than a lifesaver. Because of the amount of rope required in the Icefall, the standard of the rope was low. They were designed really just to support you as you climbed, rather than be able to cope with the strain of a long fall. It was thin multi-purpose rope, and you would not want to rely on it in an emergency. Instead, we would just have to be cautious with each step.

Once across, we would be panting heavily; we would unclip and clip into the next rope ahead, and move away from the danger of the crevasse edge. Then we would rest and recover our energy.

Four and a half hours of this slow progress, and we were getting right into the heart of the Icefall. Tucked under the shadow of an overhang, we drank and rested. It wasn't the safest of places, but then again nowhere was on this frozen waterfall. The sun was now getting stronger. As we rested, we covered our heads and faces with our hoods to protect ourselves from the glare and reflection all around us. We knew the danger of the sun in this place, and carefully reapplied the thick sunblock.

We started moving again, following the 'doctors' up through the broken mass of ice. We would shuffle over giant ice cubes and frozen bridges that lay at 50° angles, right under the face of a dark overhang. I knew that what we were standing on had, a day ago, been part of the overhang now above us. We could see where they had peeled off.

Soon we reached a flat area of plateau, about halfway through the Icefall. We thought we could see the top of the Icefall, far above and in the distance; but we weren't sure. It was noon.

The Sherpas then announced that they were going to remain on this plateau, to finish repairing a section we had just crossed. The two of us agreed to carry on for a couple of hours, to try and reach the three-quarter point before returning to meet them, and all descending together. They told us to turn around before 2.00 p.m. at the latest. We had now been in the Icefall for six hours.

We set off alone. I led the way, feeling still relatively strong. It was wonderful and freeing to be alone here with Mick, climbing together, communicating silently, and working our way up the Icefall, where only the Sherpas had been before.

It was good to have that focus of concentration where your mind is uncluttered and thinks only of the job in hand. Our minds felt sharp as we kicked into the ice and secured ourselves to the next rope. The air felt fresh as it filled our lungs. Your body needed all the oxygen it could get from each breath and it seemed to savour the moment as the air rushed in. It felt good.

The route now steepened and a series of ladders strapped together leant against huge forty-feet vertical ice blocks. The overhangs became bigger and more sinister. We were careful to be precise in what we did, and became acutely aware of our surroundings. We didn't talk. At 1.45 p.m. we could go no further. The route ahead had collapsed the night before, and a jumble of vast ice blocks lay strewn across the face. The rope shot vertically down below us, drawn as tight as a cable, as it stretched under the weight of the ice around it. I looked at Mick behind and he pointed at his watch. We were at our time limit and needed to turn around.

I was just ahead, and noticed that I was standing in a particularly vulnerable part of the Icefall. I felt suddenly very unsafe and started down towards Mick. Suddenly, 200 metres to my right, I heard a large section of ice break off. The block tumbled, like a dice across a board, down the Icefall. I crouched, just staring. As the snow settled behind it, I got to my feet, then hurried my pace down towards Mick. I wanted to get out of here now, I felt too exposed.

The colour of the ice where we were was dark blue, and pinnacles reached over us, 100 feet high. It seemed unstable and flaky, and was beginning to drip from the heat of the sun. It is at this time, in the mid-afternoon, that the Icefall is most dangerous, as it melts, and parts begin to collapse.

Racing all in one go under these overhangs that cast menacing shadows was impossible; the body wouldn't allow it. Repeatedly we would be halfway through, then would be forced to stop and recover our breath, still deep within the jaws of the overhang. But there was nothing we could do; the body had to stop and get more oxygen.

Once safely out the other side we would sit and recover and encourage the other to follow quickly. We were new to the Icefall and were trying to learn its tricks.

Soon we were out of the nasty section and back among more familiar territory; ahead we could see the plateau where we had left the Sherpas. We passed through the part that they had been repairing. We could be no more than 100 metres from the Icefall doctors now. I was looking forward to seeing them, and then getting down. We had been in the ice for almost nine hours now and were tired. Little did I know that the day was far from over.

As I came round the corner of a cornice, I could hear the whispered voices of Nima and Pasang nearby. Energy flooded back and I leapt from ice block to ice block down towards them. Ten yards later I needed to stop and rest; they were close now. I smiled at the sound of their hushed and tentative tones.

I unclipped, and clipped into the next rope down, and leant against the ice, recovering. Suddenly the ground just opened up beneath me.

The ice cracked for that transient second, then just collapsed. My legs buckled beneath me, and I was falling. I tumbled down, bouncing against the grey walls of the crevasse that before had been hidden beneath a thin veneer of ice.

The tips of my crampons caught the edge of the crevasse walls and the force threw me across to the other side, smashing my shoulder and arm against the ice. I carried on falling, then suddenly was jerked to a violent halt, as the rope held me firm. The falling ice crashed into my skull, jerking my neck backwards. I lost consciousness for a precious few seconds. I came to, to see the ice falling away below me into the darkness, as my body gently swung round on the end of the rope. It was eerily silent.

Adrenalin soared round my body, and I shook in waves of convulsions. I screamed, but can't remember what. My voice echoed round the walls. I looked up to the ray of light above, then down to abyss below. Panic overwhelmed me and I clutched frantically for the walls. They were glassy smooth. I swung my ice axe at it madly, but it wouldn't hold, and my crampons just scraped along the ice. I had nothing to lean against, no momentum to be able to kick them in. Instead the flimsy stabs with my feet hardly even brushed the surface of the ice. I clutched in desperation to the rope above me, and looked up. 'Hold, damn you. Hold.'

I grabbed a spare jumar device from my harness. (This is a climbing tool that allows you to ascend a rope but won't allow you to slip down.) I slapped it on to the rope as added security. Suddenly I felt strong pulls tugging on the rope above. They wouldn't be able to pull me out without my help. I knew I had to get out of here fast. The rope wasn't designed for an impact fall like this. It was a miracle that it had held at all, and I knew it could break at any point. The pulls on the rope above gave me the momentum I needed to kick into the walls with my crampons. This time they bit into the ice firmly.

Up I pulled, kicking into the walls, a few feet higher every time. I scrambled up, helped by the momentum from the rope. Near the lip, I managed to smack my axe into the ice and pull myself over. Strong arms grabbed my windsuit and hauled me with great power from the clutches of the crevasse. They dragged me to the side, out of danger, and we all collapsed in a heaving mess. I lay with my face pressed into the snow, eyes closed, and shook with fear.

Nima and Pasang sat with their heads in their hands, breathing heavily; then glanced furtively around. Known to be two of the bravest, most hardened men of Everest, the Icefall doctors now looked visibly shocked. They knew that it had been close. Mick was still trapped on the other side of the crevasse that had collapsed. Nima laid a ladder down and Mick shuffled tentatively across. He put his arm round my shoulder and said nothing. I was still shaking.

My confidence plummeted. Mick had to escort me the two hours back down the Icefall. I clutched to every rope, clipping in twice. I crossed the ladders a different man; one who had experienced that thin line between life and death. Gone was the brash certainty of before, when I had confidently shuffled over them. Instead each one now took me what felt like an eternity to cross. My breathing became harder, and all my strength seemed to leave me.

My elbow was stiff and swollen, having been smashed against the hard ice walls of the crevasse. I tried to use my good arm to descend with, but I knew it didn't bode well.

Lying in my tent alone that night back at Base Camp, I found I was shaking as it began to dawn on me just how lucky I had been. Undoubtedly I owed Nima and Pasang my life.

I wrote:

31 MARCH, MIDNIGHT:
My whole body feels drained. The emotions of today just overwhelm me. I feel dehydrated and worn out by nine hours' hard climbing in the intense heat of the Icefall. It's also beginning to dawn on me just how lucky I was. It could have so easily gone the other way. I can't quite fathom how the rope held my fall. I have this vision of the crevasse below me that fills my mind – it scares me.

Over supper this evening, the Icefall doctors spoke in rapid voices, using vivid gestures, as they recounted the episode to the other Sherpas. I received treble rations from Thengba, but found I couldn't eat anything. I needed company but at the same time felt this thirst to be alone.

My tent that before was so organized and tidy, with everything in pristine condition, is now a jumble of ripped windsuit, gaiters and boots, from where my crampons tore them as I fell. I'll start repairing them tomorrow. Thengba has said that he'll help me with this. His smile as he said this warmed me like nothing else. Never has a mouth full of black teeth been so attractive. He's a kind man.

It's now midnight and all is strangely quiet outside. I long for rest, but my mind is too busy thinking the same thing over and over. I dread going back into the ice.

I really miss Shara, and my family. I long for the company now of friends; of Charlie, Trucker, and Ed. I wonder what they are doing right now. Maybe if I pray for them then they'll pray for me; I really need it now.

I dozed for an hour earlier, but the crevasse dominated my dreams. Falling is this helpless feeling, where you are powerless against it. It strikes those same emotions of my parachuting accident. I pray for protection against these nightmares, please.

Through all my experiences with the Army, and breaking my back like I did, I have never felt so close to dying. It leaves me with this deep gratitude for all the good and beautiful things in my life. I don't often think about it, but the bottom line is that I don't want to die. I've got so much I want to live for. It makes me question why I'm even taking these risks at all.

Despite the immediacy of the fear, it still somehow feels right to be trying. My expectations are maybe becoming lower, but I'm going to stay. I just pray with my whole heart never to go through such an experience again. Tonight, here alone, I put in words, 'Thank you for helping me, my Lord and my friend.'

CHAPTER EIGHT

WARNING SHOTS

▲

'He who has a "why" to live, can bear almost any "how".'
Nietzsche

The morning of 1 April was glorious. Sitting on the ice in the warmth of the morning sun, I started to stitch my ripped kit. My elbow was still swollen and ached annoyingly whenever I bent it. Mick sat beside me and we talked of the mountain and everything that lay ahead. It was all that was on our minds.

'At least I don't have to explain to Neil and Henry that you're no longer with us,' Mick said jokingly. 'Although it would have meant I could have your roll-mat, I suppose.'

'Thanks for that, Miguel,' I replied. 'Anyway if I had copped it, then you'd have nothing to do today – talking of which, can you give us a hand stitching this gaiter?'

We felt happy as we peacefully sat and worked. The others were now only two days away.

That afternoon, as we reclined in our separate tents, sprawled out like two Pompeiian philosophers contemplating the wonders of the great outdoors, we suddenly heard the voices of two females; we came alive at once. Only minutes earlier we had felt so lazy that we had argued over whose turn it was to go and refill the waterbottles ten yards away; now, inspired by the sound of two girls, we both leapt out of our tents like primed gladiators.

'Hi, are you an expedition climbing here?' one of them asked.

'Ah yes, um, that's right,' I replied. 'You look tired, can I get you . . .'

'Yeah, come on in and grab a cuppa,' Mick replied, bustling past me, and beating me to the mark.

The afternoon was spent in happy abandon as we whiled away the time, chatting in the mess tent. It turned out that the girls were out in Nepal for three weeks, with a party of trekkers. They were the only ones from the team to reach the goal of Base Camp. The rest of the team had given up, too exhausted.

'All the boys were so gung-ho, and called us "slow coaches" the entire way, but we're the only ones to have made it in the end,' they said.

It was a familiar tale. Altitude is a great leveller, and time invariably proves that the tortoise up high always beats the hare. These two tortoises were the prettiest we had seen in a while. The yaks didn't get so much as a passing glance for the rest of the day.

The afternoon, though, was soon coming to a close.

'Look, you guys better get going before it's dark. You'll need three hours at least to get back to Lobuche down the valley,' I said with great pains. Mick looked like a homesick boy, saying goodbye to his parents for the first time; but only I could tell.

They filled their flasks with hot tea, and began to wrap up warm. As they did so I scribbled a note to Shara, and wrapped it in a home-made envelope, addressed to her home, back in England. It read: 'Don't forget me while I'm away. You have my word I'll come back. I love you. Happy belated birthday. Bear.'

They carried it back with them, promising to post it on their return to civilization. I said I would have to owe them the postage, and longed more than ever to see Shara. I had told her nothing about my fall, I thought it better that way. I just hoped my note would reach her. Three weeks later, Shara picked up a tatty envelope that had just flopped through the letter-box to the floor; she picked it up, opened it and smiled.

*

That night, the two of us were alone again. The wind blew gently across the glacier; I lay curled inside my sleeping bag, listening to its rhythm, until eventually sleep swept over me. My body needed this rest, and I slept until just before dawn.

Lying in those early hours between four and six in the morning, I allowed my mind to drift. I was getting used to this place now. I felt safe in the seclusion of my tent; and was coping better with the low temperatures at night. My confidence was slowly coming back.

By the time we emerged that morning, the two Icefall doctors had already left to work in the Icefall. They had had their rest day and were eager to try and push the route through to the lip of the glacier; all the way to Camp One. They had started early. Our day carried on in the blissfully slow pace that characterizes so much the reality of mountaineering – the 'rest' times.

The human body has to rest in between bouts of extreme physical exertion. The altitude means that the body is already under pressure as it tries to cope with the lack of oxygen in the air, and thus these periods of recovery up high need to be longer than at sea-level. The body is fighting two battles: the thin air, and then the recovery. It takes time and patience, but because you are away from the hassles of 'normal' life, you feel free to soak up the energy that the hills around you provide. There is time to just be.

Late afternoon, an increase in noise from the mess tent meant that something was wrong. We went to find out what was happening – more from curiosity than anything else. We weren't prepared for what had happened.

'It getting late. Where Icefall doctors?' Thengba mumbled. 'Normally back two hour now. Dark not so far way.'

He was right. At 6.30 p.m. most nights now, it would get dark and the stars would begin to appear in the night sky. It was already 5.30 p.m. and the sky looked somehow different and menacing; something felt not quite right. 'Why were the doctors so late?' I could find no answers.

Mick and I scanned the Icefall through the binoculars; we could see nothing that resembled tiny figures on the ice above us. The wind had been slowly picking up all day, and as dusk fell, the Icefall became hidden in a swirling mist. The other Sherpas and Thengba were frantic. The doctors were still not back.

Thengba, five foot and a tiny bit tall, with knotted, dirty black hair, cut untidily round his ears, fiddled nervously with the stove. It wouldn't light. He shuffled on his worn Reebok trainers with no laces in them, and tried to fix the pump of the petrol burner. He licked the end of the plunger and squeezed it back in, and then started vigorously pumping pressure into the tank. Eventually the petrol ring crackled, then burst into flame.

All the Sherpas huddled around the stove, chatting nervously in low fast whispers. For the third time in ten minutes, everyone hurried out of the tent into the darkness to scan the Icefall, hoping to see a light or some indication of the Icefall doctors. Still there was nothing, and the wind was getting up by the minute. The Sherpas looked to Mick and I for help. We had been the only other people at Base Camp to have gone into the Icefall; but we could offer no answers. As the minutes dragged on, the options available to us dwindled.

Mick and I talked together, desperately trying to assess what we could do.

'Okay, let's look at this logically,' Mick said. 'They have either become trapped by the ice or alternatively one of them could be injured and is trying to make it back down slowly. If it's not one of these, then . . .'

We were both well aware of the dangers up there and knew that there was a strong possibility that they might have been killed. Why else were two of the most experienced Sherpas out so much later than ever before, with no sign of any light up on the mountain to indicate they were alive and moving? They were up there now in treacherous conditions. The Icefall was being blown by ferocious winds that were whipping snow across the ice. The wind cracked against the canvas of our tents and the noise carried across the glacier. The situation was worsening.

As we tried to reassure the Sherpa cooks, we knew secretly that the two Icefall doctors could either be dead or fighting for their survival. They were not equipped to last a night in these conditions. They always climbed with the minimum of personal equipment, so as to allow them to carry more rope and ice screws. Dressed only in thin clothes, designed for six hours' work in the heat of the day, the cold could claim their lives all too quickly.

We seemed helpless. What can we do? I thought. Come on. In these conditions we would be unlikely even to find our way though the maze of ice, in order to find the start of the ropes. The frozen footprints that showed the way before, would now be covered in six inches of snow. The ropes would also be buried, and climbing in such conditions in the depths of the Icefall would be virtual suicide. Unable to see crevasses that lay hidden by thin layers of freshly fallen snow would be like walking into a death trap. The chances of surviving it would be slim, and the likelihood of finding two dead men would be high. The frustration this brought was untold, as we sat and waited. It was now 10.00 p.m. We knew time was running out for them up there.

Bernardo sat with us in the tent, the strain of the last few hours written across his dark brow. We had lit a strobe light at Base Camp for the Icefall doctors to see if they were alive; to give them hope. I doubted, though, that they would be able to see it, as the beam seemed to get swallowed by the mist and swirling snow. All we could do was make hot flasks of tea in case we heard anything, and then just wait and pray. The minutes dragged on like hours.

*

By midnight there was no change. We agreed that all we could possibly do was try to sleep for a few hours then get up before dawn, and set off in hopefully better weather into the Icefall. Heading up, even in those conditions would be extremely unwise, but it was our only chance of finding them – alive or dead. It was a hopeless situation, and the prospect of the Icefall in those snow-covered conditions terrified me. I went to my tent, and knew that we had no other choice – we would leave at 4.00 a.m. I dreaded finding the two men, who had hauled me to safety only days earlier, dead. It confused me; it was all happening too fast.

As I lay in my tent, I could hear Mick shuffling inside his. He was getting his boots and harness ready, and sorting out any other kit he would need. It was cold and pitch black outside, and his flash-light flicked busily round his tent.

We were together in the thick of it, a million miles from the safety of home. Everyone at Base Camp looked to us both. Even the Sherpas from the Singaporean team had refused to join us, when we had asked for their help. They had not had their Buddhist ceremony yet, where they pray for protection on the mountain. To venture into the Icefall beforehand would be tempting the goddess's anger to the extreme. They would not do it. The responsibility fell on us two alone. We were the only people who had been in there before and knew the route.

We lay and tried to mentally prepare. I wondered what the doctors were thinking at this moment, if they were still alive. They knew we would come as soon as the weather allowed us a chance; until then I prayed that they would have strength in whatever they were facing. I drifted in and out of sleep.

*

At 1.30 a.m. I heard the clanking of metal on metal. I knew the sound so well; your harness makes that noise as the karabiners and descenders hit each other. Someone was moving slowly, very slowly. I hurried into my boots and down jacket, grabbed my headtorch and scurried out into the night. Mick emerged from his tent as well, and there, moving towards us through the wind and snow was Pasang, shuffling at crawling pace. He was covered in snow from top to bottom, his cuffs had frozen solid, and icicles hung from his goggles and hood. He waved wearily in the direction of the Icefall.

'Nima come long way behind. Very slow, tired. Need help, very tired,' he stammered.

Thengba was up, spouting with excitement in very fast Nepalese. He was ushering Pasang to the tent. We sat him down, and filled a mug with tea. There would be footprints to guide us now – we had to get going to try and find Nima. We left Pasang with the other Sherpa cooks, and hurried out. Thengba refused to let us go without him and raced off into the darkness following the prints, muttering to himself under his breath. I knew that Nima was his best friend.

Thengba was completely under-dressed; he wore his same old holey trainers and had no gloves. He was too scared to think, and had rushed off. He wanted to find Nima. We caught up with him and tried to persuade him to turn back, otherwise he would get frostbite. He refused and insisted on following us into the Icefall. The footprints were becoming covered again but we could still make out the vague impressions through the fresh snow. We shouted and waved our lights into the distance as we went. We had to find Nima soon.

Thirty minutes later and only 500 metres further on, we were in the middle of the flowing ice, at the foot of the Icefall. The wind was atrocious and it was bitterly cold at this time of night. Thengba shuffled along behind.

Suddenly round an ice pinnacle emerged this figure, stumbling drunkenly through the snow. He moved like a man of a hundred years old. Hunched and weak. He collapsed to rest in the snow. We hurried to him.

'You're okay, Nima. You're safe. We'll be home soon,' we reassured him. Mick gave Nima his headtorch so that he could see where he was going more easily. It brought some life to his steps. He wanted to show us that he was strong; he didn't want to let us down. He soldiered on with great effort a few more stubborn yards, until we forced him to rest and drink from the flask. Then he collapsed.

We tried to help him undo his crampons, now we were out of the steep ice. It would help him move freer. He wouldn't let us initially; he was too proud. Even though his fingers were stiff with cold, he tried to free the buckles on his crampons. But his fingers wouldn't work and he reluctantly allowed us to help. When we got them off we noticed that Thengba was silent.

A quick glance revealed that he was shaking with cold having rushed out into the storm so ill-equipped. It was Thengba who now needed the help. Even Nima in his depleted state recognized this. They were the oldest of friends. Nima was the mountain man, Thengba the cheerful cook; Nima knew that his friend was not used to coping in these conditions. We struggled to get Thengba wrapped up and Nima to his feet, and then all slowly began to get moving. We must have looked a sorry sight as the four of us staggered into Base Camp; but by grace, these two extraordinary men, who epitomized man's ability to resist the forces of nature, were still alive.

As we drank tea and ate noodles round the petrol stove in the tent, the smiles began to appear. Thengba had his dearest friends back again; he felt safe now. As we warmed ourselves and sat huddled around, the story of what happened slowly emerged.

They had got so close to completing the route to Camp One, that they decided to work a little longer, to save having to return through the Icefall again the next day. They wanted to complete the job that had taken three hard weeks of work to put in.

As they reached the last part, they saw ahead a sheer thirty-feet wall of ice that would lead up to the lip of the Icefall. Working together, Nima climbing and Pasang supporting the end of the rope, they started up the face. It took time to ascend and secure the route, as they screwed pitons into the ice, through which to feed the rope. Neither had watches and at dusk they were forced to turn around and return back towards Base Camp. Once it was dark it became a different battle.

They had been so busy that they had worked too late; neither had noticed the menacing weather coming over them. The clouds brought darkness with it earlier than normal, and with only one headtorch their progress became slower and slower as the battery gradually died. By 8.00 p.m. the battery was dead and they were still dangerously high. By now the storm was in full force; they could see no further than five yards. Crawling on their hands, they slowly descended through the Icefall.

Three times Pasang came within inches of being swallowed by the ice, as the snow-covered ground in front gave way to reveal perilous crevasses. Each time Nima behind had held the rope fast, and stopped him falling. It took five hours to descend the route in this manner. But they knew that they could not afford to wait until morning. The cold would not allow it. If they stopped moving in those temperatures, the mountain would cruelly claim another two victims.

At 1.30 a.m. Pasang had staggered past my tent – his karabiners clinking.

*

Lessons had been learnt: you have to watch the time in the Icefall, you must have sufficient equipment to cope with emergencies, and always a headtorch each. These are fundamental; but the doctors were masters, and all masters get lazy. It is their great determination and quiet strength that brought them back in those conditions. Conditions that would have devoured lesser men. Despite this, they knew they had been lucky. Smiling and much warmer, two slightly subdued Icefall doctors went to their tents to rest. It was 3.15 a.m.

The whole of Base Camp had been waiting with baited breath. Relieved, we sat with Bernardo and a couple from the Singapore team, sipping tea along with a bit of chang for 'medicinal' purposes! We were grateful for the strobe light they had placed at Base Camp – it had helped guide the doctors down. There had been nothing more they could have done; none of them had yet been in the Icefall.

Bruce, the Singapore team's Base-Camp manager, who was as un-oriental as a Yorkshire pudding with his broad Scottish accent and mannerisms, cursed the taste of the chang.

'It's a Jack Daniels I need at a time like this,' he joked, as he took one last swig before returning to his camp.

Soon we were back in our own tents – the wind was steady. The sound was soothing and I fell fast asleep.

*

At 4.30 a.m. I woke abruptly. I could hardly hear myself think there was so much noise. It was still dark, and the fierce howling of the wind shook my tent until I feared it would collapse. I felt instantly wide awake, and spreadeagled myself across the inside of my tent to hold it down. The wind came in gusts. A small lull of still, then ... wham! The tent would be almost lifted underneath me and the sides whipped so ferociously I feared they would rip. Snow poured in through the vent at the back of the inner-lining, as it blew in waves under the outer canvas. It then swirled around my tent. I tried to jam some equipment against the vent to stop it, but it was in vain. It still poured in.

Mick was fighting the same battle. He had managed to build up some equipment against the lining of the tent, but still he was soon lying in about four inches of snow.

We both resorted to the only option available. We climbed deep inside our bags and sealed ourselves from the snow and cold air. For two hours the mountain goddess seemed to blow mercilessly, creating this fearsome howl of an 80 m.p.h. wind, screeching across the ice. Base Camp was being pounded.

'Bloody hell, Bear, this is crazy, budge up,' Mick shrieked, as he unzipped my tent and squeezed in. 'No point us both losing our tents, we might as well make sure one survives. Mine's even worse than this, I was in deep snow.'

We had to shout at each other to be heard above the wind.

'Thank God the doctors got back. If they were still out in this they'd have survived about ten minutes – no more,' I yelled.

'Tell me about it. I almost got blown off my feet coming three yards to your tent,' Mick replied.

I felt safer with Mick. We sat huddled together, wondering how long this outcry from the mountain would last. These were jet-stream strength winds. What the hell are they doing at Base Camp? I thought.

By 7.00 a.m. the wind seemed to be dying gradually. Still though, snow licked across the glacier at a frightening speed. All the Singapore team came and gathered in our mess tent. Mick and I, by now, had also abandoned my tent for the bigger communal mess one. About fifteen of us in total, including the exhausted Icefall doctors, whose hopes of a long-deserved rest had been shattered, gathered round the stone table.

The tent looked like some scene out of a holocaust movie, with pots of ketchup and sacks of rice covered in a layer of snow, resembling the fall-out dust from a nuclear explosion. Snow had blown in through every hole and tear in the structure, and the driving wind had whipped in loud claps against the tarpaulin.

As dawn came we assessed the damage. In the few days beforehand, Mick and I had ensured that our tents were tightly secured; we had done this almost out of boredom, rather than anything else. There had not been much else to do, except secure tents and prepare equipment. We were lucky, it had paid off.

The Singaporean camp had been hit on higher ground; tents had literally been torn apart. Out of a total of twelve tents, only two now stood. The others were scattered in shreds – poles and canvas having been blown across the glacier at the mercy of Mother Nature. Bernardo's supply tent lay limp and in tatters. The magnificent blue structure of the day before was now a sorry combination of bent poles and ripped canvas.

The Sherpas seemed frightened, and nervously declared that this was the worst storm that any of them could remember at Base Camp for at least fifteen years. We looked on in silence at the carnage that the wind had left.

Like battle-weary troops, the Singapore team were now forced to leave Base Camp. Their tents were ruined; they needed a re-supply, and that would take time. They would wait for this in Lobuche, and train in the meantime in the surrounding valleys.

All of us, in some way, I guess, had arrived with swollen ambitions; we expected to control the way everything would go; we all assumed our equipment or our own strength would be enough; we thought we had a fool-proof system. Disaster is never far away when man assumes to have control over anything –

never more so than with nature. As is the way with mountains, our puny systems have this funny habit of breaking down.

These thoughts dominated my mind as Mick and I found ourselves virtually alone again at Base Camp. I was viewing the mountain in a new light now. I felt as if we were trespassing by even being here. It was as if we were being given warnings. Maybe we weren't meant to ever 'climb the Great Mountain', as the Indian General had said.

We were still here though, and were still alive. I almost didn't dare look up in the direction of the summit. It seemed too far, too ambitious. But as is the nature of the human spirit, the flame somewhere still dimly glowed. I allowed myself a sneaking look up and quietly dreamt.

CHAPTER NINE

BROTHERS IN ARMS

▲

'Think where man's glory most begins and ends,
my glory was I had such friends.'

Yeats

The solemn chanting of the Buddhist priest echoed round the glacier. The Lama, as he is referred to, scattered sacred flour and rice into the air at sporadic intervals, then watched as it pattered down like rain across the ice.

The Lama was buried in his fervent prayers, oblivious to his surroundings. He sat cross-legged on a tattered old mat laid across the rocks. He was dressed in an old crimson monastery cloak that wrapped round him several times over, and his old leather shoes seemed to have been repaired with twine more times than one would deem possible. His physique was small and wiry, and his face, withered and wind-beaten by a lifetime in the hills. He smiled eagerly at us as a large branch of juniper crackled into flame.

The only indication of which century we were in was his woollen hat. Bright yellow with a huge bobble on the end; it dwarfed his face. The look of pride in his eyes suggested that he loved this hat. It had a certain 'something' that other priests we had seen were lacking. Perhaps this eccentricity was the reason why he had been sent up to us by the monastery. He had travelled twenty miles into the snows to administer what appeared to us at Base Camp to be our 'last rites'.

Neil and Geoffrey had arrived with Henry the day before. Henry had completely failed to recognize Mick because of the thick beard he had sprouted in only three weeks, and because of my grime he only recognized me by my chef's trousers. Base Camp had come alive and the Lama's ceremony marked the formal start of the climb. This was the Sherpas' big day.

In preparation, they had built a stone altar upon which the Lama would raise the Buddhist prayer flag at the end of the ceremony. But at the moment it looked naked, standing alone, towering above the rocks. The wind gently blew across the ice and the sun was already getting hot. The Lama continued his chanting, and we all sat serenely round about, watching the bobble hat move as his head shook in prayer.

The ceremony is called the 'Puja', and the Lama spends an entire day chanting and offering food and alcoholic sacrifices to the mountain goddess. It is the most important part of the climb for the Sherpas: without the mountain's blessing, none of them would venture any further. Such is the strength of their conviction. On the other hand, once the Puja is over, the Sherpas gain this great courage. They are now clear to climb; whatever happens afterwards is their destiny. Much of their courage comes as a result of a successful Puja.

Even Nima and Pasang had undertaken their own, slightly less elaborate Puja ten days earlier, for just the two of them. It was essential. Their work had started earlier than the other Sherpas, and like all work in the Icefall – they needed their share of luck.

It was now 11.00 a.m. and the ceremony at Base Camp was

in full flow. The Lama invited us to bring our ice-axes and crampons to him for a blessing. Everyone scrambled to their tents, rummaging equipment together for the Lama. We all placed it at his feet, and as the metal of the axes and crampons clinked together, the Lama tossed more juniper onto the fire, chanting ever louder.

Suddenly the chanting stopped, the noise of the fire was all that remained. The Lama raised his arms aloft, and signalled for the Puja pole to be brought forward. With great solemnity – faces displaying intense concentration, the Sherpas slowly raised the prayer pole into position. From the top of the pole, four lengths of prayer flags, each thirty yards long, were stretched across the glacier and secured under large stones. The protection of Sagarmatha had begun.

The tone then changed abruptly. We were each given sacred flour and rice to throw in 'prayer', and food and drink to consume. An old gasoline container, brimming with clear liquid, was produced from under wraps. It was the dreaded chang.

I grimmaced at the first sip. The smell brought back memories of drinking cheap vodka in the bushes at school, where I had ended up unconscious after drinking what felt like straight turps. I had vowed that I would never touch it neat and in such vast measures again. The Sherpas were insistent, though, that I drank more to appease their mountain goddess. Too much more and I would not need any protection, as I would be flat out on my back for the rest of the expedition, unable to climb. Still, keen to keep them happy I took another swig and winced. I swore that this was worse than the cheap vodka. Surely they wouldn't mind, I thought to myself, if I put a bit of orange juice in it and pretended I was drinking a cool vodka and orange in the garden at home.

A combination of altitude, and not having drunk more than a couple of sips of alcohol since the flight over, ensured that the ceremony rapidly deteriorated into chaos. The Sherpas' tolerance to alcohol seemed even less than mine, and soon the chanting of the Lama was drowned in the drunken banter of the Sherpas, as they threw sacred flour wildly around like confetti.

The scene was soon like the final throes of a children's tea party, with all of us covered in food and drink – food and drink that even the Lama was unable to avoid getting covered in. I am sure the monastery would have disapproved but – oh well – the Lama seemed to be loving it. If Sagarmatha's protection relied on the joviality and chaos of the Puja, then by all accounts we had nothing to fear on her slopes.

The day slipped by and the tension of the weeks fell away. The Lama still sat cross-legged, grinning and chanting away songs and prayers that I am sure were slowly becoming gobbledegook. He reached over, and swigged at the petrol container of booze. Sitting there, his face covered in sacred flour, he was the picture of religious delight. The only thing that now looked sober was his bobble hat – and even that was tilting at an extraordinary angle.

Evening came, the Lama staggered to his feet and left, and a stillness swept over the camp. I sat on a rock and surveyed the carnage of where the Puja had taken place. It was a mess of rice and biscuits strewn across the ground, and the last bits of juniper were still smouldering in the ashes. The prayer pole towered above Base Camp like a vigilant sentry and the prayer flags fluttered in the gentle breeze. They are designed simply to carry the prayers up to the mountain as the wind caresses over them. As they swayed in the breeze, I hoped they would work.

Two days from now we would return to the Icefall, this time as a complete team – the aim being to reach Camp One. The departure of the Lama and the stillness of dusk beckoned in the next stage of this adventure. The festivities were over and from now on things would become much more serious. Everything we had worked so hard for over the last year, everything the Puja had been about – all the prayers for protection – now lay menacingly in front of us. My head was beginning to hurt from the chang, and as I sat on a rock with Mick, Neil and Geoffrey zipped inside their tents either side of me, I found myself looking out at the Icefall. The ice shimmered in the glow of dusk and my mind wandered in a semi-drunken haze.

DIARY, 2 APRIL:

The peaceful ease of the last few days, when Mick and I were alone, has now gone. All was very quiet then as we sat and talked and waited for the others to arrive. Now that they are here, the energy that a group of ambitious, highly driven climbers creates is very evident. There is a purpose to everything, the camp is a hustle of bodies busily organizing equipment and discussing plans.

It's good to see Neil out here; we've spent so much time together in England, planning and discussing, that it is a relief to see him in the flesh and to be getting ready together. He's as confident as ever, a bundle of energy and humour – and part of me feels a little slow around him. Mick and I have been alone with the Sherpas so long that to be thrown into the deep end of banter and conversation feels a bit strange. Part of me misses the solitude that we have enjoyed. But we are here, God willing, to climb this mountain, however impossible it now seems. That is our aim. I hope I'll live up to the promises I've made. The promises to be strong and dependable when it counts.

The tension and excitement is already here, hidden under the surface of people; you can just sense it. It's like the rollercoaster has left the dock. Tonight there's a funny feeling in my stomach.

The other teams were also beginning to arrive at Everest Base Camp. The Singapore team had returned, newly equipped, along with three American teams and an Iranian team who were hoping to put the first Iranian on top of the world. Base Camp was now more like a small village, with huddles of tents scattered randomly across the glacier.

The other climbers, under the logistical umbrella of Henry Todd, had also arrived. Inclusive of our four-man team, the total number in Henry's group was twelve. We would all climb together for the majority of the route, then at Camp Three we would separate in different directions. The eight Everest climbers would traverse north to the South Col, while the other four would make their attempt for the summit of Lhotse – the fourth highest mountain in the world.

Outside our immediate team of Neil, Mick and Geoffrey, I had never met most of these other climbers. Apart from Henry, the only other person I knew was a very experienced climber from Colorado called Andy Lapkas. We had climbed Ama Dablam together six months earlier, where I had gained a huge respect for this man. Tall, lean, and quietly spoken, but with a cheeky smile and sense of humour, Andy was a thoroughbred climber. He had climbed Everest in the early 1990s. After two months' preparation he had reached the summit in a staggering final climb – without the use of supplementary oxygen.

The two of us had laughed together on Ama Dablam about the appalling state of our cars back home, and how they both had broken down before leaving. Silence would then fall, as we both wondered how on earth our girlfriends put up with driving around in our clapped-out old bangers – then we would laugh again. I was pleased to have Andy climbing with us now, even though higher up he would head for Lhotse.

Also climbing Lhotse were Nasu, a Turk who had previously climbed Everest from the north side, and Ilgvar, a Latvian who had climbed it from the south. Sitting in the mess tent I felt dwarfed by the strength and achievements of these great men; we were in honoured company amongst such experience. I tried not to be daunted, but secretly felt a little small.

Scott was a doctor from Canada, who had been hoping to be part of the Lhotse team. Tall and friendly, he had managed to twist his ankle severely whilst being chased by a yak on the way up to Base Camp. Although he saw the funny side of this and went along with the inevitable jokes, it was a great disappointment to him. He had spent a lot of time and energy training for this climb, not to mention the financial cost, and it now looked over before it had begun. Such is the nature of climbing. Luck holds a big hand in any ascent and for Scott, luck had dealt him a bad card. He would try to rest his ankle and climb later on in the expedition, though realistically he held out little hope. For now, he was to stay at Base Camp as our doctor. We would need him.

Also on the Everest team was Carla, a Mexican lady trying to be the first Mexican female to the summit. She had given her all for the chance to climb here, having taken three years to raise the funds. Quiet and friendly, she hid a fierce determination to make it to the top at almost any expense.

Allen Silva was an Australian climber who was part of the Everest team. Blond and wiry, he had climbed all his life in the Himalaya. Allen didn't say much, and seemed cold towards us. Perhaps seeing me in chef's trousers and tweed cap, with a wispy beard that only grew under my chin, he maybe thought that I was out of place and unserious. I may not have looked as sensible as possible, but my heart burned with desire to climb high on this mountain. The more he doubted, the greater my determination was to prove him wrong in my strength and reliability.

Allen's coldness upset me. We needed trust up here between us, trust in who we were, and in what we had done; but he wasn't giving it. If he wanted to see us work before he gave his, then we would show him we were trustworthy. Henry sensed Allen's coldness and reassured me.

'I know your background and we've climbed together before – take no notice of Allen and just do what you did on Ama Dablam, okay?'

The faith Henry and Neil had in me was what counted, and in this they never wavered. I was the young one. But they trusted me and I wasn't going to let them down. They gave me something to live up to.

Another climber on the team was an Englishman called Graham, who had climbed Everest a few years beforehand, on his second attempt from the north. He was hoping to be the first Englishman to climb Everest from both sides. Easy-going and competent, he was an asset to any team. A true Newcastle man, he professed to doing his training 'in the pub with a glass of ale and a cigarette'. His strong eyes and prior achievement, though, told a deeper story. Here was a man who could climb with the strength of ten men. We had heard it from others, and could see it behind his Geordie grin.

Michael was from Canada, and a friend of Scott. One of the most celebrated rock climbers in Canada, Michael had spent his life in the mountains of his native land. Sponsored to the hilt by North Face equipment, Michael was trying to reach the summit of the 'Big One', as he would say. Cheerful and kind, with a vulnerable streak that lay hidden under his 'outdoor image', Michael already looked apprehensive. Seven weeks later, I was to spend one of the most nerve-wracking nights of my life, squashed alongside him at Camp Two. All our experience suddenly seemed to count for nothing; we were both just scared. Michael was a good man, and I sensed it within hours of meeting him.

As part of the team we also had a communications officer, who was to be running the radios for us from Base Camp. Her job was to keep us in touch and informed on the mountain. Jokey was already a friend and when I offered her the job in London she leapt at it. Jokey was due to finish her contract as a producer with Carlton TV, and when Neil agreed to it, she joined us.

She was used to working with loads of technical equipment, and on arriving at Base Camp with Neil, she took to her job like a duck to water. People had had their doubts that she could even reach Base Camp, and feared that she had too little mountain experience to run the radios. But like so much in life, and especially in the mountains, determination wins through. Jokey showed all those doubters up as she threw herself courageously into the job; she did it well and for us to have a lovely smiling face to come back down the mountain to was a joy. No one could have done the job of communications officer better.

She would have to leave us at the start of May, and was due to be replaced by Ed Brandt.

Now that everyone had arrived, Base Camp was busy. People went quietly about their things – whether it was rummaging through hold-alls of kit or shaving in a bowl of warm water. We were getting ready. Ahead would lie two months of living and working in very close quarters – and for the time being, we were slowly getting to know each other.

The process of the climb meant that we would have to ascend then descend the mountain continually. This would allow our bodies to acclimatize to a high point, before coming back to Base Camp to recover. It is how you climb a high mountain. You reach the threshold of altitude that your body can cope with, then come back down to rest. Then up a bit higher to acclimatize to a greater height and then down again. The whole time you are fighting the danger of illness, altitude sickness, avalanche and bad weather. Luck has to come into it. We all knew that to be successful here so many factors would have to come right, and that inevitably included luck. Every day I prayed for it – for the Good Lord's luck.

They say that to climb Everest successfully, you actually climb the mountain five times over – in the process of going up and down. It is a giant game of snakes and ladders, and like in the game, the higher you go, the further you have to fall.

The highest that our bodies would be able to acclimatize to would be Camp Three – at about 24,500 feet. Beyond that we would be into what is called the Death Zone where the human body cannot survive for long. You cannot digest food and you weaken rapidly, due to the body's starvation of its vital fuel – oxygen. From then on, we knew we would be on borrowed time – even if our bodies allowed us to reach that height. Our aim had to be to try to acclimatize to Camp Three as soon as possible. We hoped this would be some time around the last few days of April.

Our fight would then be against the weather. The fierce jet stream winds that pound the upper slopes of Everest make the mountain completely unclimbable – their strength would literally blow a man off the face. But twice a year, for a matter of only a few days, the winds abate.

The warm, moist air of the monsoon, after crossing the Bay of Bengal, then carries on further north. As it meets with the mountains of the Himalaya, it is forced upwards. This wave of warmer air creates a small bulge in the jet stream, raising the height of the winds by a few thousand feet – leaving Everest strangely silent. At Base Camp, lying in your tent, you can hear the deep rumble of the jet stream far above you, as it licks across Everest's summit. It is a constant roar that serves to set the boundary that man can reach. When the winds lift for those precious few days as the monsoon passes over, the mountain is climbable. When, and for how long this period lasts, is the gamble you take.

This break may only be a matter of days, maybe two, maybe three. If you are not in position high up at the right time you miss it, and all has been in vain. After the period of calm, when the winds have been lifted, come the storms. The mountain is then smothered in these monsoon snows.

The whole art of high-altitude climbing is as scientific as it is artistic and passionate. All going to plan, we reckoned on the chance of a summit bid in early May. All that was ahead was unknown. If we could be sure of one thing, though, as we prepared ourselves those last few days before starting, it was that the mountain would never act as we hoped or expected. We never assumed it would.

*

Various journalists and sponsors had come out with Neil to cover the start of the expedition. Most of them made it all the way to Base Camp, but a few were hampered from making the last few miles because of illness or altitude sickness. Those that made it arrived laden with rucksacks, blue in the face and grinning ferociously. They were trying hard not to look too tired; after all this was only Base Camp! I tried to reassure them that there was no disgrace in being tired, and that when we had first arrived we looked like ageing cart-horses on our final delivery round. I'm not sure quite how much this helped them but still . . . it was good to see them.

Patrick was a journalist from a London financial magazine who was out here scribbling profiles on the team, but I couldn't help feeling he was in the wrong place for a big financial story. He had kindly remembered that when we were having our sponsors' send-off party in London, I had expressed a certain regret at not being able to have the odd smoke for three months whilst away. I smiled when, over a cup of tea, he tossed me a packet of cigarettes, saying that he thought they could be handy – post-climb. He was right and I hurriedly put them on the stone ledge of the mess tent, along with various other 'sacred' items we had, that provided us with some light at the end of this Everest tunnel.

At the end of these long months, we would have sat for countless hours in the tent drooling over the contents of this 'shelf': a bottle of Moët et Chandon large enough to sink the *Bismarck*, a box of Belgian chocs, and the now infamous pack of Benson and Hedges. Hope keeps spirits alive higher up, and every little bit, I reckoned, would help.

One of the other journalists' questions to me was again on the issue of my age, and the disadvantages of being so young and hoping to climb so high. Again I had no real answer. It annoyed me that he had raised the issue; it was okay in London, but not out here, not now. It was all too close. The answer to his question was something that time alone would tell.

Those few days with the 'journos' and sponsors at Base Camp were a relief. Many of these guys had become good friends, and seeing them was a welcome break from the tension that was already beginning to emerge. Their departure, though, came all too soon. The Camp, which had been brimming with people for two days, was suddenly reduced to just the team; it was still busy but was now noticeably quieter. The focus returned to the mountain.

The 'journos' had looked in horror at the Icefall in front of us, and we had laughed at the time. Now they had left, we looked differently at the ice 200 metres away looming up into the mist. It had that dangerous beckoning look that it is infamous for. I ignored it and busied myself in our final preparations.

I wandered round to have a chat with Bernardo, the Bolivian, and carefully stepped over the ice and rocks in my moon boots towards his tent. He was sitting on a large stone chatting with someone else – both facing out towards the Icefall.

'*Hola Oso!*' Bernardo grinned. 'Come and have tea, and meet my friend Iñaki.'

Iñaki was a Spanish Basque climber, who was hoping to climb Lhotse this season. He smiled from behind his sun glasses. His

Spanish was harder to understand than Bernardo's clear South American accent, but we got by – more or less.

'*Qué?* Once more, Iñaki. Sorry?' I said, apologizing my way through the conversation.

Iñaki was a friendly and experienced climber who had just got married to a beautiful Spanish girl. He missed her already. It was hard not to like Iñaki. He told Mick and I later that day of what happened when he had tried several years earlier to climb Everest. We listened eagerly.

'I was strong lower down on the mountain, and was excited. After six weeks of carrying equipment up to Camp One and Two, and then twice up to the penultimate Camp, Camp Three, I was acclimatized. All I needed then was the weather. Ten days later we got the forecast we needed, and I reached Camp Four three days later.

'In the Death Zone at that height, it was cold, bitterly cold. As I set off into the darkness, starting the sixteen hour climb to the summit, three thousand feet higher, I was finding it hard to see through my goggles. It was so dark as there was no moon and my torch was getting dimmer and dimmer. The wind had dropped, and I made the decision to take my goggles off. When your mind is numbed by the asphyxiation of the thin air, you act irrationally. I should never have removed my goggles in those temperatures.

'By the time I reached the South Summit, only two hours from the top, I could no longer see. My eyes had frozen to my eyelids; I was effectively blind. My partner helped me down the route to safety, but it took four days to see properly again.

'It's a risk up there guys. Don't ever take your goggles off, promise? Heh – you'll be okay. More tea?'

I knew that golden rule, but I reminded myself of it once again. Mick looked uneasily at me and smiled. I didn't want to be sitting around endlessly discussing any longer – I wanted to be doing it.

Charles, one of the American climbers who had tried to climb Everest four times, also came and joined us. He was English but now lived in the States. He seemed polished and smooth, and seemed to have got Base-Camp living down to a fine art. I felt jealous of all his gadgetry; he even had a mini dustpan and brush to clean out all the rock sand that got blown into his tent during the day. I could use one of those, I thought. My tent is like lying on the beach in Bournemouth it's so dusty and sandy.

Charles was friendly enough, despite reminding us of all the risks, and the likelihood of failure – none of which exactly helped my waning confidence.

'Don't even bother coming to this mountain unless you're prepared to come back, again, and again. It's almost unheard of to achieve it first time. I mean, I've been here on this hill four times now; Edmund Hillary took, I think, three attempts to climb it before he reached the top in 1953.'

I didn't have the resources, though, to try it three or four times. For me it was now or never. If the mountain didn't allow it, if it was out of condition and the weather never broke, then so be it, but if it gave me the chance I swore that I would be there. It made me boil inside. Neil felt the same. When I told him of Charles' views, he had a twinkle in his eyes.

'Don't listen to it, Bear, okay? It's just talk,' he insisted.

After his experiences on the mountain in 1996, Neil had now shown the courage to come back and try again – but openly he said that it was now or never; he never wanted to be scared by this mountain again. His face showed his determination to do it; it is what made him Neil. Although we were so different in temperament on the surface, we both shared a hidden something underneath. I understood him.

Tomorrow at 5.00 a.m. we would be together as a team at the

foot of the Icefall. We needed a good sleep, so the four of us left the mess tent early.

DIARY, 6 APRIL:
We will be climbing tomorrow for the first time as a team. The four of us will go with Andy, Ilgvar and Nasu – all of whom have climbed Everest before. I feel under pressure to climb well and live up to their standards; it frightens me. All these guys are the top climbers in their countries, and in the top group in the world. I feel rather like a seven-year-old who has been substituted, due to a flu epidemic, to play in the under 13's rugby team.

I suppose that I've got to forget about what they've done, and concentrate on what I'm doing. This is also the first time back in the Icefall since my fall. I find it really hard to talk to anyone and say that I'm frightened of it. Luckily Jokey has been sweet and we sat and talked about it in my tent. I can say things to her without feeling I'm being weak.

She's just gone back to her tent and left me a note to say everything will be fine. I hope she's right. She also left me Byron's *Don Juan*, a tiny miniature book to read, which is kind of her – if I can't get to sleep I can read myself into a slumber.

I want to talk some more but she'll probably be snoozing by now, and anyway I must get some good rest; tomorrow I need all my strength.

Henry has managed to wangle the use of a satellite phone for us, as ours was fused on the way out. Someone plugged it in at Namche Bazaar and the place almost exploded like a firework. The phone was a jumble of burnt out fuses. Emotionally, it was one of the more expensive firework displays.

Everyone else has called home today. Part of me held back though – I don't know how helpful it would be to speak to my family. My feelings for them are going berserk and I just want to get up to Camp One and down safely before I call. I hope I don't regret that decision.

As ever I pray for your protection Jesus. Night, night.

*

Adrenalin surged round our bodies those hours that we climbed together before dawn. It was our first time as a team in the Icefall and the synergy of this made me feel strong. I was loving the dawn chill and focus of energy that I was experiencing, as we cautiously made our way through the jumble of ice above us. The moon reflected off the ice in strange silhouettes. Our lungs heaved continuously in the thinner air; our earlier acclimatization trip didn't seem to have made it any easier.

Clip off one rope and on to the next, check the lock of the karabiner, then move on. It was routine now. We passed the spot where Mick and I had been forced to turn back last time. Nima and Pasang had found another route through that area of collapsed ice. It was 7.30 a.m., the sun would be getting strong soon. I thought that I could see the lip of the Icefall that would eventually bring us to Camp One, but I wasn't sure; it was probably another false horizon.

The long, slow, worrying hours in the Icefall were relieved somewhat by the hope of Camp One – somewhere above us. On the lip of the Icefall, where the first slabs of the glacier begin to peel off into the tumbling frozen river below, we would be safe. From there we would have our first sight of the vast Western Cwm Glacier that leads to the approach walls of Everest in the distance. I longed to see this hidden valley, and to be safely out of the Icefall. It can't be far now, I thought.

Only 100 feet below Camp One, the route through the ice had crumbled. The ground had opened up during the night and swallowed the ropes; the remains of these hung like threads above the gaping chasms that seemed to disappear into the darkness below. There was no way we could cross these crevasses. We would have to find a new route through, but that would take time; precious time that at this height in the Icefall we didn't have. If we could not reach the relative security of Camp One soon, we would have to retreat. The Icefall was no place to be trapped in the full strength of the sun. We had experienced that before.

A decision had to be made quickly. We all squatted and considered the options. To construct a lengthy three-ladder bridge over the chasms was the only one available. Finding another route round the crevasses always tended just to reveal more obstacles and lengthen the time spent in the Icefall; the bridge was agreed, but it could not be done today in the heat. Depressingly, we were being forced again to return to Base Camp.

The journey back was tiring; we were drained by the climb. We had channelled all our strength into reaching the lip, in the hope of staying at Camp One a night to acclimatize. Now, though, we had been forced to retreat, doubling the time spent amongst the ice; we hungered for relief from the heaving of our lungs and the burning heat of the sun.

Mick was slowing down as the descent dragged on, and was wobbling between sections of rope. He didn't look at us or speak.

'Come on, Mick, the Icefall gets more and more dangerous from now on, we've got to keep going. Remember let "fear be your guide",' Andy hollered. These words would become a catchphrase for us throughout the rest of the expedition: 'Just let fear be your guide.'

Mick pushed on down, treading carelessly now over the ladders. Tiredness at altitude does this; you become dangerously nonchalant about your actions. Things that would terrify you when you were thinking normally are treated with wistful disregard as exhaustion sweeps through your body. The temptation to ignore a rope and not clip into it was strong. It was easier just to loop it through your gloves and shift lazily across the ladders. I tried to resist this temptation; after all, last time it had saved my life. Still, our minds got tired, and haste often took precedence over safety. This is why accidents happen up high, we all knew the routine yet often still ignored it – such is the desire for relief from the fatigue. The prospect of Base Camp took on a meaning that is almost impossible to explain.

*

During the next few days that we spent at Base Camp resting and recovering, Geoffrey began to look ill. The colour faded from his cheeks, and his guardsman banter waned. As he sipped tentatively at his noodle soup, we knew that something was wrong. He hardly emerged from his tent, and would only appear for one meal each day. He was getting weaker, yet stubbornly tried to hide it. By the third day it was obvious that this wasn't just a passing bout of food poisoning; he was weak and ill.

Scott, our team doctor, soon diagnosed it. Giardia. Immune to all but the strongest dosage of antibiotics, this Asian illness is carried by the spreading of germs found in faeces. Resulting in severe vomiting, diarrhoea, fever and dehydration, a bout of giardia is curable but is deeply debilitating; and what is more – it was spreading.

Maintaining peak health is crucial for exerting this sort of energy. The height we were at, even at Base Camp, meant that the body was already significantly weaker and less resilient. Getting giardia weakened the body drastically. Geoffrey took the medication and began the frustrating road to recovery at 17,450 feet.

Those early weeks of April, the conditions were perfect for climbing. We had to try and reach the height of Camp Three as soon as possible – if we were to have even a chance of the summit later. We couldn't wait for Geoffrey to get better, and had to carry on. We all knew the situation, yet when it happens to you it is hard to stomach. Geoffrey never baulked, and like the gentleman he is, he encouraged us to continue without him. We had no choice.

The next trip through the Icefall we were a depleted team. An early start ensured we had time to spare if we encountered another major collapse in the ice; but this time the route was okay. The bridge-ladder at the lip of the Icefall was now in place, as a few of the other teams had passed through. As the three of us started across the last ladders that we knew led to Camp One, our excitement grew. It had taken so long just to reach here; we longed to be out of the Icefall like never before.

The ladders creaked and groaned as Neil shuffled across in front of me. They swayed with each step he took. I followed on, and in the middle, as the ladders sagged, I noticed the knots that leashed the ladders together beneath me. I hoped that not too many crampons had stood on these, and tried not to look down.

Soon the three of us were squatting, tucked into an ice ledge under a twenty-foot overhang that led to Camp One, now only a stone's throw away. We were panting heavily, and spent two minutes getting our breath back. We looked at each other excitedly, we knew that once over this lip, a whole new world would open up. We would be able, for the first time, to see the great Western Cwm, hidden from Base Camp, and only visible to those who have survived the Icefall. I yearned to see, in the flesh, the sight that I had only seen in photographs. It was only feet away. Neil cleared the lip swiftly, leaving a lingering silence behind him. He stared at a land that held tragic memories for him; two years on, he was again at the foot of the mountain.

Tucked into the ledge below, I found myself panting frantically; I hadn't even started. I was nervous that I wouldn't be able to clear the lip. I dug the tips of my crampons into the ice, and leant in close to the ice wall, still breathing heavily. The ice felt cold against my face, and I looked down between my feet into the crevasse below.

Look up, come on, never look down, I thought to myself.

I swung my ice-axe into the wall above, stepped twice up the face and rested, hanging on my jumar. It seemed to hold my weight securely as the teeth gripped into the rope. I moved on slowly up the wall. Another swing of the axe and several more steps up, and I was lying on the snow at the top. As I squatted on the lip, undoing my jumar from the rope and recovering my breath, I looked out behind at the Icefall. It tumbled away beneath me in this jumble of giant ice blocks; I could no longer see Mick below. I flicked the rope to tell him that I was off the line. He clipped in and the rope went taut under his weight.

I turned round slowly and stared in amazement at the sight ahead. The scale of this giant land in front mesmerized me. Walls of rock and ice, thousands of feet high, swept up from the glacier sides and the valley meandered away to the east in a haze of silver and white. Behind us and far below, the tiny speckles of orange tents showed where we had come from, five hours earlier; Base Camp now seemed an age away from this vast land we were seeing before us. Neil smiled at me.

'Not bad, eh?' he said.

'It's why we climb, Neil. This is why,' I slowly replied.

The sun was rising as Mick scrambled safely over the ledge to join us. He grabbed our hands, and we gave him a haul to his feet. He shook the snow from his windsuit, tied off to the top rope and knelt, leaning on his ice-axe as he looked in awe at the valley ahead.

Hidden from the telescopes that would be peering up from Base Camp, we walked tentatively around on the flat ice, feeling, as Hillary had once said, 'like ants in a world made for giants'. The plateau we were on was eerily silent, apart from the wind blowing softly down towards us through the Cwm. In the stillness of early morning we stood breathing deeply in the thin air and surveying the destruction of the Icefall below us. My imagination had never assumed this new land to be so beautiful. Camp One had now been reached. It was 8.30 a.m. on 10 April.

CHAPTER TEN

EASTER ON THE ICE

▲

'No gentleman ever takes exercise.'
Oscar Wilde

'Himalayan Hotel' was the name given to the tents we were now using – yet it was misleading. The name to me had always conjured up images of some sort of luxurious, spacious affair with a comfy en-suite bathroom and soft, fluffy towels. But I had been mistaken in these assumptions. The so-called 'Himalayan Hotel' was about five feet by four feet, hardly high enough to kneel up in, and full of four hairy, tired and irritated men. Camp One was . . . different.

Neil, Mick, Andy and I shuffled all our equipment around trying to dig out enough room for our bodies to recline in some vague resemblance of comfort. It wasn't easy. Using our rucksacks to lean on, and our weighty high-altitude boots as foot rests, we tried to get settled.

'Bear and Mick, stop humming ruddy Cat Stevens and go and fill this sack with ice; we've got to get drinking soon, we're all dehydrated,' Neil said sternly.

He was right, the headaches confirmed this. These are a

discomfort that you have to endure when climbing up high; they are the first symptoms of a lack of oxygen in your body and are almost impossible to avoid at these heights. Four men squashed together in a tiny tent, recycling the same stale air, with all the flaps sealed to keep the never-abating wind out, hardly helped to relieve these headaches.

It would be a relief to clamber out and get some fresh air. The stench inside the tent was rotten. In the day you can get out every now and then – but not for long without protection from the debilitating heat of the sun. But when night falls, bringing with it the cold, this is a luxury you cannot enjoy – you just have to grin and bear the cramped discomfort.

Mick and I struggled into our boots. They were now steaming as the condensation and sweat was beginning to dry. We shuffled onto our knees, unzipped the flaps and crawled out. The strength of the sun suddenly hit me and I quickly put my sunglasses on. The glare of the sun reflected on the ice can leave you snowblind in a matter of minutes if you are careless. The two of us grabbed an ice-axe each and started hacking at a corner of blue ice at the edge of the plateau.

When the sack was full, we dragged it slowly back to the tent, stopping to rest only once on the ten yard journey. Even at this height a small amount of exercise leaves you exhausted. Back at the tent, thirsty hands reached out and hauled the sack inside – it is this ice that we would melt in the small stove to make our water.

'God knows where the hell they're going to put that,' Mick chuckled, 'there's not even room to swing a cat in there.'

We enjoyed a few more deep breaths of the fresh air, then squeezed back into the tent. An elaborate system of string had been tied across the tent with socks hanging off it, drying. I clambered past and collapsed back in my slot between Andy and Neil.

In the heat of the sun the tent was always burningly hot. Mick measured the temperature on his smart, new-fandangled watch. At regular intervals he would then announce in horror that it had gone up – again.

'This is bloody ridiculous!' Mick cursed. 'I thought Everest was meant to be cold. If I'd wanted to be sweltering I would have gone to Mallorca. Open the flaps a bit, Neil, and sod the wind.'

We were all stripped down to our underwear or at times even less, to try and keep cool. It didn't really work, and the sight of us all together in this neolithic state would have qualified for some horror show, as we lay sprawled across the tent. We used our windsuits and down jackets to lean on, but they just tended to stick sweatily and annoyingly to our backs.

Neil almost invariably chose the worst spot in the tent. Not only did he always find himself in charge of the tiny gas stove – trying to balance the huge pan of ice on it – but he also always seemed to pick the wettest patch. A puddle of condensation and spilt water was already forming under Neil's roll-mat – causing much amusement as he madly fumbled, trying to rearrange his few square feet of sleeping bag.

Having consumed a mugful of oxtail soup that had taken two hours of pain-staking work to prepare, a moment of relative calm would generally ensue. This would then be shattered by the gentle hissing sound of Mick, leaning to one side and urinating into his pee-bottle. If it was clear, then a satisfied sigh was heard, signalling that he was rehydrating well; if it was still dark brown, he would swear, and throw some more ice in the pan. The length of time it took to melt ice at this height was almost twice as long as at sea-level, as the gas burnt at a lower temperature – making rehydration a lengthy process.

I started to laugh and shook my head for no apparent reason at all, apart from the absurdity of this life we were living up here.

Soon everyone was smiling. It seemed so surreal. In this most extraordinary place; a place that I could never have envisaged, I somehow felt happy. Despite being crammed between Neil's sweaty armpits and Mick's honking feet, for some reason I loved these guys. The four of us were perched in a tiny tent, two metres from the edge of the most treacherous Icefall I had ever seen – yet all seemed strangely okay.

That night at Camp One was colder than any before. The heat of the sun was replaced in minutes by a bitter coldness, as darkness swept along the Cwm. We fastened the zips and slid deep down into our bags. Mick's temperature gauge had gone from 31°C to now almost −25°C. I was worried it would explode – through confusion.

All four of us curled in close to each other for warmth, and tried to sleep. I knew that I was still dehydrated, as my pee was brown and I still had a pounding headache, but there was nothing I could do. I had drunk almost continually during the day, but it obviously hadn't been enough. That night I couldn't sleep at all. I couldn't even turn as I was wedged between rucksacks and bodies. I cursed my aching head and hid myself into the depths of my sleeping bag.

*

At 9.00 a.m. the next day, we unclipped off the last rope at the bottom of the Icefall. We sat and breathed deeply in the thicker oxygen of Base Camp, trying to recover some energy before staggering the tiresome fifteen minutes over the glacial rocks back to our tents. We had left Camp One early at 5.30 a.m. and had come through the Icefall as swiftly as we could. Charles, from the American team, had reminded us some days before that the 'more times you climbed in the Icefall, the greater the likelihood was of being in the wrong place at the wrong time.' This off-hand comment of his had annoyingly lingered in my mind for the entire journey back down, and I vowed not to listen to the 'scare-talk' again that seemed to fly around Base Camp – I felt it was unnecessary.

Funnily enough the one person apart from me who got most worried by the unpredictability and danger of the Icefall was Bernardo. He would stomp around counting on his fingers, as if working out detailed probabilities of having a block of ice the size of the Taj Mahal fall on him. Whoever was nearest would always rapidly reassure him, and soon his smile would spread eagerly across his face again. Everyone loved Bernardo.

That morning, as we wandered back across the glacier, the happy face of Jokey standing in her fleece hat outside the comms tent beckoned us home. We dropped our packs – which were now much lighter as we had stashed some of our equipment at Camp One – and had mugs of hot lemon thrust into our hands by the smiling Sherpa-cooks.

Base Camp no longer seemed the hostile place that I remembered it to be only weeks earlier, but instead now had the full appeal of 'home', as I dried my kit in the sun and lay safe in my tent listening to my tape of the Gypsy Kings. All was much better, and what was more, I noted that tomorrow would be my favourite day – Easter Sunday, 12 April.

'Jokey, listen, tomorrow's Easter Sunday, and I thought we could hold a service. We could have a reading in Spanish from my Spanish New Testament for Bernardo and Iñaki, then maybe you could sing a solo, how about "Amazing Grace"?'

'No way, Bear, I . . .' Jokey retorted.

'Wonderful – thanks, Jokey, I'll write out the words for you later. In E major okay? Great.'

Jokey laughed; she knew she wasn't going to get out of it. Besides, far more people would come if they knew a stunning girl was singing – and we needed all the support we could muster;

already Graham was grumbling in his Geordie way about having a 'sodding religious service'.

Neil and Mick rallied round, announcing the news to the other teams. Most thought we were stark raving bonkers and some thought it was a piss-take, but the four of us felt determined to pull it off – come hell or high avalanche.

*

A surprising number of people turned up that crisp Easter Sunday morning, squashed in the stone mess tent. I felt as happy as I had ever been. I decided to call home later to wish them a Happy Easter, as well. It had been a while now since I had spoken to home, and I wondered how my family and all the animals were – all those thousands of miles away, and thousands of feet lower down. Easter always does that to me; evokes all those homely thoughts.

Neil brought everyone to silence with a firm clap. The room fell silent.

'Over to Friar Bear,' he said grinning away.

We prayed for protection on the mountain, and I read in faltering Spanish from St John. Jokey sang 'Amazing Grace' beautifully, even if all the words did get a little muddled. Bernardo chuckled like never before.

The highlight though was saved for the end. As I produced the bottle of Glenfiddich whisky, I saw Henry's eyes light up with delight, as if saying, 'about bloody time.' We had stuck firmly as a team to our rule of only ever drinking for medicinal or religious purposes, and this was a religious one, so we would enjoy it.

Communion that morning on the ice at 17,450 feet was magical. Easter eggs and the bottle of Glenfiddich circled the congregation not once, not twice but three times before it came back to me. Bernardo thought it must have been Christmas as well as Easter as he swigged eagerly from the bottle. The service then ended and the tent turned into cheery laughter for the rest of the morning. It hadn't quite been High Church but it would do.

As I sat on the rock outside my tent with my feet brushing the ice of the glacier beneath me, I reread the words of 'Amazing Grace' that Jokey had sung. They rang so true.

> Through many dangers, toils and snares I have already come,
> 'tis grace that brought me safe thus far and grace will bring me
> home.

I never got to make that Easter day phone call home as the Danish climber Michael refused to let us use his set any more. Tension was building amongst the climbers at Base Camp, and Michael had lost his temper with us over how we had rigged the satellite-phone up to the batteries. It all seemed a bit absurd to us, as Michael shouted at everyone about misusing his property. We seemed to be the brunt of his frustration for no logical reason. He was feeling the pressures of the climb and looked tired. No one held it against him – we all needed to let off steam occasionally, and no one really took it personally.

We were to head back up the next day again to Camp One and, from there, on to Camp Two. We spent most of these rest days sleeping – or rather just lying there, dozing in our tents with very little on. I would reread letters that Shara and my family had given me before leaving. I never got bored with them.

*

That loathful time in the pre-dawn chill before leaving Base Camp was as bad as ever. The alarm sounded but I didn't need it, I was awake anyway. With frost from inside my tent falling all over me, I struggled for the umpteenth time into my boots. They were looking worn now, and carried the scars of the Icefall –

being covered in stitching and masking tape. These very expensive and tough-wearing, high-altitude boots were made theoretically to go on and on, but all the climbers out here had said that they never really lasted more than a season. I was beginning to understand why.

All through the night I had heard Neil coughing. The dry air of the high altitude causes this – the Sherpas call it simply the 'Khumbu cough', after the valley that we were in. Neil was suffering worst of all, and it bugged him; he knew all too well that it was weakening him. He shrugged it off if we mentioned it. I knew he was secretly taking eurythromycin, a chest antibiotic, but he refused to admit this. It was something he could do without, and our suggestions were unwelcome. He felt it was his problem. We knew Neil's mentality and just left him alone, but his deep hacking preyed on him, and wouldn't leave him alone. That early morning it was worse than usual.

Together in the mess tent I tried to stuff some porridge down, but it wouldn't go. I nibbled on a Mars bar instead. It was 5.30 a.m.

At the foot of the Icefall we met the Iranian team, and shared some boiled sweets amongst each other, as we put on our crampons. The Iranians seemed in good spirits. They started into the ice before us, and soon we were close behind them, moving a little faster. As we progressed through the Icefall, higher and further into its depths, the overhanging, fragile ice walls seemed to loom all around. The route had changed quite a lot, as large sections had collapsed. Vast blocks of ice hung as if on threads above us. As we reached the shadow of one of these, the Iranian team suddenly broke into loud chanting.

The golden and unspoken rule of never speaking whilst amongst these pinnacles was being breached. The four of us had only ever communicated in whispers or hand-signals, and we stood there shocked as their fervent prayers grew in volume.

The noise was lethal in these surroundings. We didn't know whether to shout at them to be quiet or whether to keep silent and not add to the noise. Part of me felt this anger and part of me wanted to laugh. It was so surreal to be in this position with these Iranians singing away as the walls of ice cast huge shadows over us. They had surely picked the worst part of the Icefall to start this.

We were suddenly driven by this urge to get past. Without saying a word, we skirted quickly round the Iranians, unclipping and then clipping on the other side of them. We weren't going to hang around here – even if it was prayer time. When we reached what we thought was a safe ledge, we sat and rested after the sudden burst of energy. We chuckled to ourselves at the situation as they began to catch up. At least this ledge was relatively safe.

As the Iranians caught up they suddenly sped up and raced past us. We had hoped to keep in front but they gave us no chance.

'Dangerous here,' they said as they went by.

'Yes, I know,' we replied, 'the Icefall's lethal.'

'Not the Icefall in general,' they replied, 'I mean, the part you are sitting in now is dangerous. Look, big crack in ice below.'

We looked around and suddenly noticed the crack. What we had taken for a safe ledge, out of danger, was actually a cornice. Through the centre of this ran a thin crack. We leapt up and shuffled off it towards the now laughing Iranians. Looking back at where we had perched, we couldn't even understand how the ice hadn't collapsed, it was so delicate. It looked ready to go at any moment. We had been lucky and had been helped by them. As the saying goes, 'he who laughs last, laughs loudest', and they had won this one. We sat all together for a few minutes resting.

From then on we were happy to follow, but at our insistence, their chanting stopped until we were out of the Icefall.

Neil's cough had been a persistent noise alongside me through the ice. Every five seconds he would hack this deep, dry cough. He now swore openly at it. It was slowing him down considerably and we were happy to go at the Iranians' slower pace, to help Neil. The cough was obviously debilitating him.

One of the strengths of a small team lies in its ability to help each other and to know everyone well enough to be able to do this. Many times ahead Neil would help me, but for now it was he who needed it. We encouraged him and took more rests than we would have normally done. Secretly though, we longed to get out of here. Time spent playing this Russian roulette with the Icefall was time too long. As Andy would say, 'just get through it as quick as you can, as each step in it is a gamble.' It was 9.00 a.m. when we all eventually stood aloft the tumbling ice below.

By Neil's own admission, there had been a time during the last two hours when he doubted he could even continue, as he felt so weak. It just went to show that even the strongest are not immune from the mountain's strain. Climbing Everest is about heart more than everything, and Neil was showing this again. That vital ingredient inside had brought him those precious few steps closer to his dream. A dream he was giving so much for.

We were slowly learning the tricks of living on the mountain, or maybe we were just becoming numb to the discomfort; whatever it was, that second time at Camp One was better than before, and I even slept a few hours during the day. My acclimatization must have been working. As the day wore on we found various ways to relieve the boredom of watching ice melt. I took the time to get some pictures of Mick and I dressed in nothing but boots, rucksack and ice-axe, standing above the Icefall. This wasted countless minutes and kept the team amused for hours afterwards.

During the photo session, as we were both posing naked, feet astride, with expressions of bizarre origin, two Singapore climbers emerged exhausted over the lip of the Icefall by our tents. As they looked up in anticipation of beholding the wonder of the Western Cwm, they were met instead by myself, stark naked, hopping across the ice telling Neil to get a blooming move on as my tackle would soon get frostbite in this wind. I think I slightly ruined the moment for them.

The Everest team within Henry's group had now been split into two parties, us three being with Graham, whilst Geoffrey was to join the others – Allen, Carla and Michael. His giardia was now better, and to his credit as soon as he felt on the mend he was determined to reach Camp One for a night. Whilst we had been resting at Base Camp, Geoffrey had completed his acclimatization night above the Icefall. As he was coming down to rest, we had passed him on our way up to Camp One. He looked happier and fitter, and was back on track. It was a shame not to have him in our group, but that was the way it had gone. We knew the weather wouldn't wait for us and we had to push on to Camp Two, regardless.

*

The next morning at Camp One, the frost in the tent was infinitely worse than at Base Camp, and at 5.00 a.m. I sat up to pee in my bottle, shaking the tent. The others cursed as icicles fell down on their bags. Dressed in inner-boots and windsuit I then went outside to have a crap. We had dug a hole right on the lip of the Icefall and it seemed dangerously precarious, dropping my trousers and squatting quite so close to the edge. I hurried and finished as quickly as I could. It wasn't quite like at home with a newspaper, sitting there for hours on end, enjoying the leading articles in the local rag.

The best way to get out of the tent in the early mornings was to get dressed and packed up, one at a time, until everyone was sitting inside the tent ready. Then one at a time, we would shuffle to the entrance of the tent, put our crampons on with our feet outside the door, then clamber out. We were getting used to this now and soon the three of us and Andy were heaving on our rucksacks on the plateau outside the tent. It was still bitingly cold at this time, and we pulled our hoods around us tight.

Our sacks were heavier than before, laden down with the various items that we had stashed previously at Camp One, as well as all the new equipment we had brought up from Base Camp. We were each carrying full down salopettes, down jacket, sleeping bag, two roll-mats, headtorches and batteries, inner fleeces, a large quantity of freeze-dried food packs, cameras, and two litres of water. We helped each other heave them onto our backs and set off into the vast whiteness of the Western Cwm. Despite being heavy, they weren't a scratch on what they would be when they contained two large oxygen cylinders, higher up. We knew these carries lower down would strengthen us for the times higher up.

The great Cwm lay before us, as we made our way slowly along the valley. Fifty yards, then a rest – pacing our steps. The Cwm sloped up in giant steps of ice every few hundred yards or so. Sometimes we would contour along these on tiny snow trails, and sometimes ladders roped together would span the thirty-foot high walls. We would clamber up the metal rungs and peer over the top to see the next level of glacier ahead. At other times we would just simply clip our jumars on and dig our crampon points into the ice and battle up and over these small vertical lips.

The route zigzagged its way across the valley floor, slowly gaining altitude. The crevasses were becoming more frequent, and were now wider and deeper than in the Icefall. Several climbers had had very narrow escapes in the last few seasons, when the ground beneath them collapsed to reveal one of these monsters. Their ropes alone had saved them.

The Sherpas by now had found a route through to Camp Two and we followed the trail religiously. Even if we needed to go to the loo, it had to be done on the trail. It wasn't worth stepping off it, even a yard. We remained clipped to the ropes even when it seemed flat and stable. The floor had hidden secrets below it and we didn't want to risk anything.

The crevasses, that were now every hundred yards or so, needed at least one or two ladders to cross them. The drops below seemed sinister as they disappeared into black. We would clip in twice and shuffle across. The famous Scottish climber Mal Duff, who had died suddenly of a heart attack at Base Camp a few years earlier, had once commented that 'only on Everest would these crevasses be considered safe'. He was right. We were gaining confidence and found ourselves skipping over the ladders with dangerous disregard. But there were too many to worry about all of them. You would never get anywhere stopping and debating each one, you would be too exhausted from mental fatigue.

The pace got slower and slower as we wound our way along the deep snow of the valley floor. We were desperately trying to reach Camp Two at the top end of the glacier, before the sun got too strong in the sky. The Western Cwm in the heat of the day can rise to well above 80°F, as the sun reflects on the ice and the heat becomes trapped by the walls of rock and ice, thousands of feet high on either side. We needed to reach Camp Two within five hours to avoid this heat trap. It was 7.30 a.m. and already the shadows of the ice were being replaced by the glare of the sun.

As we came over one particularly high lip in the glacier, we saw for the first time the face of Everest in the distance. Hidden from view before, by the Nuptse corner, the mighty summit now loomed before us, still some 8,000 feet higher. It took my breath away. So far the only glimpses we had had of the summit were from the trek up to Base Camp. Even then the huge wall of Lhotse and Nuptse had hidden the majority of Everest, and all we could see was the summit ridge with the wind howling the snow off the top; and always so far away. Now here she was up close. She was no longer hidden by these other mountains but instead looked vulnerable and exposed. It was as if we had walked unsuspectingly into the goddess's home – I felt as if we were looking upon royalty indeed.

There was no longer any ambiguity as to where the summit was. We had come round the corner and the vastness of her black rock and ice face soared up into the clouds. As the sun rose over the top of Everest, its rays filtering between the wind and snow from the summit, we sat on our packs, silent and alone. The feeling of that sight is still strong now. All I could think was that whoever created this was a genius.

There we sat like specks in a white sea of ice, with Camp Two still far away on the horizon. Those last few kilometres across the glacier to the moraine, where Camp Two was to be put, were longer than I could have ever imagined. Mick, Neil and I plodded in each other's footsteps – slow, laborious, considered steps. Twenty at a time was all we could manage, before we needed to rest. We would take it in turns to count silently, before announcing quietly – 'twenty'.

We were drained by the altitude and heat, and Camp Two never seemed to get any closer. The climber David Breashears once remarked on this heat, 'you literally pray for a puff of wind or a cloud to cover the sun, so you can keep moving on up the Cwm.'

After four hours of battling against this, Camp Two was clearly visible – it was now so close. Those last hundred yards dissolved into a haze of discomfort and eventually we dropped our heavy packs on the rocks and drank. Camp Two wasn't much considering the effort we had given to reach it; in fact it was grey and dull. Tucked into the shadow of the vast wall of Everest above, it seemed forboding and unwelcoming. Shingly rock covered dark blue ice that ran into water in the heat of midday. Nothing was solid but instead everything was sliding and slushy. I tripped trying to scramble over a small ledge of ice. I was pissed off and tired and couldn't be bothered with all this.

We slowly set about the task of erecting our tents. At Camp Two, around 21,200 feet, we were to have an advanced Base Camp, with separate mess tent and now one tent between two people – it would be luxury – but setting those tents up was irritatingly slow. Our tent sponsors had promised that they could be erected in minutes; we proved them wrong. Half an hour later of slipping on the ice, and still it looked limp and incomplete. We measured the base, secured the canvas, and started digging a platform into the moraine, upon which to site it.

My head was pounding, and I was dehydrated. Bent double, scraping shingle off the ice for an hour and a half, just exacerbated the headache.

Everyone was suffering from the effects of the altitude here, but eventually, two hours later, Mick and I had our site flattened. It wouldn't have passed any tests with a spirit-level but it was the best we could do at that height. It would have to do. We sprinkled a few more handfuls of shingle in a last vain attempt to level it, then moved the tent into place; it fitted more or less. We knew that in two days the sun would melt the ice around the tent and that our once almost flat site would soon resemble a model of the Pyrenees – still, there was nothing we could do. We snapped the poles into position, weighed the flaps down with rocks and crawled in, exhausted. Tomorrow would be a rest day, giving us a chance to get used to the height.

That night as the sun disappeared from the Cwm, we experienced a new sort of cold. It was deeper and seemed to penetrate through even the warmest sleeping bag. My nose was running and I felt the snot freeze as it dangled from my nostril. I shook Mick to show him; he groaned. Mick and I both felt awful. It is a lingering dullness in the body, coupled with a pounding headache and slight nausea. Neither of us had eaten much that evening, despite being drastically in need of sustenance. At this height, even without the levels of exercise we were taking, the body needs to receive almost three times the amount of calories that it needs at sea-level. At the moment we just weren't getting it.

In our tent Mick was dozing. It is the best solution for this discomfort – to numb the mind and lie in a haze. I shuffled to my knees to urinate before settling into my bag. As I knelt and peed into the bottle, the plastic warmed my hands as it filled up. It felt good. The tent was at a slight angle and full of sharp lumps, and I shuffled on my knees to ease the discomfort. Suddenly the pee-bottle slipped through my cold fingers. Urine spilled everywhere. I clutched frantically for the bottle, but by the time I snatched it up the majority of a litre of dark brown stinking piss was already chilling inside the sleeping bag – my sleeping bag.

On the mountain there is nothing more personal than this item. You cherish it, watch over it, and relish in it, as you spread it out each day. It is your chance to escape for those hours inside it; away from the reality of the situation that you are in, as you try to forget. Mine was now a soggy, stinking mess. It would soon freeze on the ice. I wiped as much as I could away with my fleece, I had nothing else to use. I had to keep my thermals dry at all costs. Soon my fleece was damp and I stuffed it down my bag. I would try to dry it overnight. All damp kit, such as socks and inner boots, always went down the bag. Here they were warm and would slowly dry – that was unless you had poured urine all down the bag earlier.

Mick had suddenly come to life. He thought it the funniest thing since we had set foot in Camp Two. He had hardly uttered a word since arriving, and now bounced back. At least it had made him feel better – bastard.

'Well that's a relief, Mick, I was worried I might be too comfortable,' I added. We had a rule – the more dire the situation the more relieved we would appear. It had a funny way of defusing the most stressful of situations.

'You lucky thing, I wish I could have a sleeping bag full of piss!' Mick retorted.

He soon turned over, lying there quietly chuckling every five minutes until he eventually went silent. I had climbed into my bag wearing the minimum of clothes. I didn't want everything to get wet. I didn't sleep at all that night, and lay there, longing for the warmth that I knew dawn would bring; but dawn came all too slowly.

*

I was up early, even though today was a rest day. It was 5.30 a.m. and I could now see in the pre-dawn glow. I dressed in all my down gear and clambered out of the tent. The mess tent was next door, and I poked my head in. The Sherpas were still asleep and I quietly sneaked out. I looked down the valley – the mist seemed to linger at the end, above the Icefall far below. People at Base Camp would be staring up into this thick cloud, yet for us up here above it all, the mountains were crisp and as clear. Nothing stirred.

Soon the Sherpas were up and we all huddled in the tent, sitting on bundles of rope that were to be used higher up on the mountain. We held warm mugs of tea close to us and sipped noisily. Steam poured from our mouths as we breathed out. The tent was full of equipment for the route up to Camp Three, some 3,300 feet further up. This next part, from Camp Two to Camp Three, was to prove one of the hardest sections of the climb.

At the top of the Western Cwm stands the seemingly unscaleable 5,000-feet wall of ice, known as the Lhotse Face. Ranging in angle from 50° to 80° in steepness, it stretches away into the sky. The great peak of Lhotse stands at the tip of this face. Menacing dark blue ice as hard as rock lines the face in a shimmering glaze. It appears a haunting sight as you strain your neck to study it. What appear to be small lumps on the face, some three-quarters of the way up, prove under the binoculars to be vast ice seracs, under one of which we would place our Camp Three.

The angle and exposure of this face meant that our Camp would have to be hacked into the ice, to create a platform. Once under the lee of one of these seracs, the tent should be safe from any avalanches that came down the face. The idea was that the snow should clear over the top of the serac, sparing the tent below. It seemed a little hopeful, but was better than nothing.

Sitting on the equipment that the high-altitude Sherpas would be using up to Camp Three, we quietly talked.

'Listen, I think we should try and recce the top of the Cwm today. If we can try to find a good route round the Bergschrund crevasse at the foot of the Lhotse Face, it will be good for our acclimatization and will make the job of the Sherpas much simpler when they start,' Andy suggested.

I saw our rest day floating rapidly out of the tent before my eyes.

We looked at each other. We knew it made sense, but our bodies wanted to hear otherwise. They lost the battle, and would have to endure another day of punishment. This would now be our third day of exercise in a row, and I knew we needed rest soon. I switched my focus to the rest we would have at Base Camp a few days from now. Nobody was going to rob me of that one.

We all tried to shovel some muesli down with some hot water, then feeling full after about two mouthfuls, we went to get ready.

The sun was still low in the sky when we roped together on the ice. If you have too little rope between you and the person in front goes through the ice, then they would take the next man with them; too much rope and it was clumsy and almost impossible to pull someone out if they fell. We measured the distances between us carefully.

As the morning progressed and we snaked our way tentatively across the upper slopes of the glacier, our excitement increased. Neil was in front, meticulously prodding the ice with each step. Despite the slow pace, the altitude meant that we were soon tired. We leant on our axes as we rested between steps, all of us doubled over in a line.

Every now and then Neil would find a thin snow covering ahead. His axe would penetrate through to reveal a dark abyss below. We would shuffle along until we found a narrow part then take it in turns to leap across. The others would take the strain, give the nod, then you would run three yards and leap across the unknown. As the dark crevasse soared by below, you hoped the ground on the other side would hold. When the ground gave a resounding thud, you sighed. You would then move on a bit and adopt a firm position for the next man. In my case this was Mick. His hatred of this crevasse-jumping was apparent, yet without question he would throw himself across like a fearless three-year-old on skis. I couldn't help smiling. He's mad, was all I thought.

*

C4

C3

C2

C1

Mount Everest

Summit 29,035 ft
Camp 4 26,000 ft
Camp 3 24,500 ft
Camp 2 21,200 ft
Camp 1 19,750 ft
Base Camp 17,450 ft

BC

Clockwise

Bear and Mick during the Puja ceremony at Base Camp.

Bottom's up! Geoffrey breathing oxygen and trying to rehydrate at Camp 4 (26,000 ft) before the second summit attempt.

Pasang, the Icefall doctor. One of the bravest men on the mountain.

The complete team at Base Camp. *Back row*: Graham, Mick, Michael, Bernardo, Iñaki, Javien, Andy, Bear, Henry, Carla, Ilgvar, Ed, Geoffrey, Kipa, Lakpa. *Front row*: Allen, Nasu, Neil, Lo, Kami, Dowa, Pemba, Pas, Ang

Main photograph: Yaks ferrying equipment up through the snows towards Base Camp.

The imposing Lhotse Face
Icewall at 24,000 ft. The
blue ice shimmering in
the moonlight.

Crevasse-crossing in the Icefall at 18,500 ft.

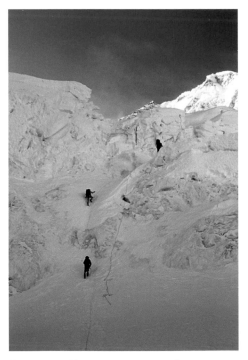

Slowly working our way through
the icefall.

The Western Cwm at dusk.

Right: One of the corpses on the mountain that serves as a sober reminder of Everest's authority.

Main photograph: Dusk at Camp 4. The highest camp in the world at 26,000 ft. The clouds are pouring over the lip of the South Col.

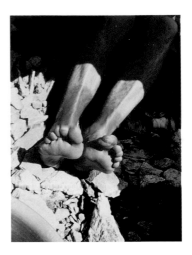

Clockwise

Bear on top of the world. 7:22 a.m., 26 May 1998.
Summit of Mount Everest at 29,035 ft

Neil's frostbitten feet. The result of our long wait
beneath the South Summit.

Bear back at Base Camp for the last time. Still
sweaty and drinking Moët in the midday sun.

The four of us post-climb. The tension falls away.

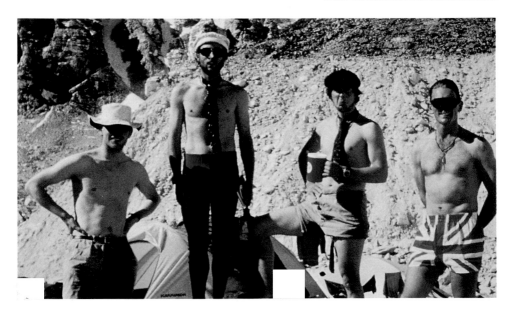

No Western climber or even any Sherpas had been this high, so far this year. We were treading on virgin territory on the ever-changing surface of the glacier. The excitement welled up, and I felt strong. Here I was with those I knew so well, alone and isolated in the rawness and wonder of nature; and it made me feel good.

Soon we found ourselves climbing methodically and slowly up near the foot of the vast Lhotse Face. Up close, the scale and angle of it seemed more severe, and I felt my frailty like never before. This land of the giants dwarfed me, as walls of rock and ice thousands of feet high soared away from me on all sides and in front. I could only stare in disbelief. My life didn't even seem to register on a scale here. I was nothing amongst these.

I remembered how God says He values us even more than these mountains, and it confused me, as I stood feeling so intimidated by them. Yet the more I just looked at these hills, the more I felt part of them. Here we were, nature, God and man, and strangely all three were beginning to feel in harmony, as if He was right there with us.

From the foot of the Lhotse Face we could look directly up the 5,000-foot ice wall. Around us lay hundreds of small fist-size rocks that had fallen down the face, and embedded themselves into the glacier ice. One of these travelling at the pace it would, down sheer blue ice, would kill a man at once. We couldn't stay here long.

We stood tentatively at the lip of the Bergschrund crevasse, peering in. This huge crack in the ice, where the Lhotse Face starts and the Cwm ends, was thirty feet wide and seemingly bottomless in depth. It seemed surreally quiet. We looked around for a few moments then headed quickly away from the danger-zone of falling stones. We had done well and had laid out a good route for us all in the weeks ahead.

The excitement of climbing so freely, without fixed ropes or ladders to cross the crevasses, had kept fatigue away – but the descent brought it flooding in. We were tired now and moved as swiftly as we could back down towards Camp Two, following our footsteps precisely.

*

We all slept better that night at Camp Two, as our bodies welcomed the release from the exhausting concoction of exercise and altitude. It was almost impossible to replenish the body with enough fluid at this height. However much we drank we always seemed to remain dehydrated. That night as I peed in my bottle, I clutched it firmly like a baby does a doll. Nothing was going to let it slip through my fingers this time. Once bitten twice shy; and the first bite had been miserable. The urine was still dark brown; a depressing colour. The only consolation was that Mick's was even darker. We compared colours in the fading light and Mick was forced to admit defeat. It came as no surprise that we both had headaches.

At 8.30 a.m. the next day we were back down at the top of the Icefall. We had covered the distance between Camp Two and One in only two and a half hours, as our bodies enjoyed the richer air as we descended through the valley. By 10.45 a.m. we were back at Base Camp. Whilst we had sampled the beauty of the land of the giants somewhere up there in the clouds above, back at Base Camp nothing seemed to have changed. I liked this. It was about the only constant factor in our existence up here; that Base Camp was welcoming, mostly sunny, and full of food.

Jokey, though, seemed worried. I don't think it had hit her what we were doing until now. All of us were gaunt. Our skin was burnt a dirty, black colour from the fierce sun, and our faces looked drained. Having no idea of what was up there causing all this made her imagination run wild. All she saw was us disappear in the early mornings into the cloud and reappear days later looking battle-weary and weak. It distressed her.

In our haste to reach the sanctuary of Base Camp and the prospect of one of Thengba's fresh omelettes, we had hurried down too fast. The weariness of the last few days engulfed me that last hour through the bottom of the Icefall. I didn't linger long with the others, and was soon asleep in my tent. I woke at noon and wrote in my diary:

Life here, with all the fears we carry, coupled with the remoteness, the cold and discomfort up high, makes me appreciate the good things at Base Camp like never before. The simplest of things become the focus of hope: the thought of speaking to home, or the prospect of mayonnaise.

I'm weak after the last few days and this dehydration seems unconquerable. I've got a bit of sunstroke after the descent today. I was careless and couldn't be bothered to wear my hat, and am paying the price now. My hands are annoyingly blistered from the ropes running through them on the descent, and my shins are bleeding from the boots rubbing the front of my legs. They say pros don't get injured as they look after themselves so well. I must be showing my real colours – colours of 'not-so-glorious amateurism'.

The pain in my elbow from my fall in the crevasse lingers on. Whenever I lean on it, the bones grate and I yelp like a puppy. All in all I feel about as tough as a limp flannel. Still, I guess as long as I'm giving my all, that is what matters; it's just that I feel a bit beaten up at the moment.

I count the days until I can run in the fields at home with the animals, climb trees, sit in front of big fires, lounge in bubble baths, and sleep on soft pillows.

The more time I spend here the more I believe the only way to survive is to stay close to Jesus. At Camp Two I read Mick and Neil some good passages from C. S. Lewis's *Screwtape*

Letters that I had torn out and stuffed in my pack. It talks about true freedom. They fell asleep!

After one of the finest night's sleep that I had had in Nepal I woke to Mick bellowing, 'Morning, Oso.'

I replied, as per custom, with a resounding, 'Morning, Miguel.'

Mick had obviously shared in that good night's sleep. All our bodies were relishing in the rest and thick air. Today I really would call home. Michael was up the hill and his communications officer let us use it again on the quiet. It still cost us $7 a minute.

'Mum, it's me.'

'Bear ... it's ... BEAR!' she shouted, summoning everyone around.

It was wonderful to hear all their news. All the animals were well, and Mungo my nephew was now walking. Lara promised that he had even said 'Mamma', although Dad swore that it was the poor baby just being sick. I smiled.

I told them that we were going to try to reach Camp Three soon, and then it would be the waiting game for the jet-stream winds to lift, before we could attempt a summit bid. I told them about my narrow escape in the crevasse in the Icefall.

'You fell in a what ... a crevice?' Mum warbled.

'No, in a crevasse,' I replied.

'Speak up, I can hardly hear you.' She tried to quieten everyone around her, then resumed, 'Now, about that crevice ...'

'It doesn't matter,' I chuckled.

I promised I would call again when we got back from Camp Three in a week or so's time, then hung up.

When I came out of the tent everyone was laughing, having listened to our conversation. Allen confirmed his belief that poms were mad, and Neil sat there grinning away.

Geoffrey had gone back up the hill with the others on their acclimatization climb to Camp Two – so we missed again. He seemed to be going well, which was encouraging. Scott, our doctor, was recovering from his sprained ankle and was hoping to climb soon, even if only to glimpse the Western Cwm. I admired this courage.

Having spent so much time alone at Base Camp whilst everyone else was climbing, he was beginning to miss his fiancée desperately. It showed. In many ways, one of the hardest factors of climbing such mountains is the time away from loved ones. These are feelings, though, that everybody knew, and everyone coped with in their different ways.

Henry had also had a bout of some illness that irritated his Scottish temperament; it wasn't in his nature to be ill. Three days later he was better and had now gone up with Geoffrey to Camp Two. Base Camp was left relatively quiet. We chatted to Charles again, who mentioned that, according to the statistics, only one in four of us would summit. Sitting alone reflecting on this, I thought of who it would be in our team. They were all so powerful: Graham, Neil, Allen – they were amongst the top climbers of their countries. I felt that it could not logically be me. I knew my only hope was to ignore the statistics; it was just that they seemed quite heavy. Neil, as ever, said not to listen to him.

'We're a team, okay. Just keep doing what you're doing. The difference between those who make it and those who don't is that the latter stop believing they can – their spirit goes. We've both got that spirit, you know that deep down, Bear, all right?'

We only had one more rest day at Base Camp before our last acclimatization climb up to Camp Three at 24,500 feet. Henry had reminded us over and over again that it was this stage that was make or break.

'If you can reach Camp Three in reasonable time, in under

seven hours, and cope more or less with a night at that height, then you're qualified in my book for a summit bid. If you're too slow then I can't risk you any higher. You'll come back to Base Camp and stay here.'

Henry had laid down the parameters. As leader of the overall expedition and in charge of the logistical support, what Henry said went. He had been climbing here for years, and his specialist knowledge of Everest was immense. He nearly always climbed up to Camp Three or Four – but no higher. He was there to ensure safety for the summit teams. His altruism in this brought him his satisfaction.

'The joy for me is the climbing in these mountains and helping summit teams be successful. Over the years I've developed a pretty good feel for those who will and those who won't make the summit on Everest. When somebody gives their all and achieves it, it changes their life. You can see it in their eyes. In helping them achieve that is my satisfaction,' he would say.

We all knew the pressure upon us to perform well on this final preparatory leg. We could not afford to make a mistake now. If we were to be on the summit team, we had to show our capacity to work to the pressure, and climb with strength and, above all, kindness. Up high, there is no one more unpopular than the selfish man.

We were all getting ready and focusing on Camp Three. We discussed the most effective way of climbing the blue ice, debating different crampon techniques. We all knew that at that height, with that sort of gradient, there would not be room for error. But we were hungry to do it. I didn't want to wait any longer.

That evening, talking with Scott, he told of the years of preparation he had done for this climb. Being out here, seeing the mountain but with a weak ankle, his ambition now was just to see the Western Cwm. That was all he wanted. I felt humbled. What was I doing aiming for the summit? Scott was training for this climb while I was still at school, yet he is only hoping to reach the Western Cwm. Maybe I was reaching too high. This troubled me that evening as I sat alone in my tent.

But I knew that I had to stretch myself further, and reach beyond my grasp. I felt this burning urge to go higher and I longed to witness the summit. The beauty of the places on the way there was unquestioned – what I had seen so far had stunned me in its sheer scale and beauty, but I felt there was more. My eyes and heart were for the summit, and my dream was to reach it with the Person who had created it. I wanted this to be my journey.

CHAPTER ELEVEN

MAKE OR BREAK

▲

'Unless you try to do something beyond what you have already mastered, you will never grow.'

Ronald Osborn

It was 5.00 a.m. and eerily still at Camp Two. Mick had been tossing and turning all night, cursing his inability to sleep.

Today was make or break for us. We had reached Camp Two by mid-afternoon the day before, after a seven-hour climb from Base Camp. It had been the first time that we had done the route all in one go without a night at Camp One en route, and it had taken its toll. We had hoped our acclimatization would have lessened the pain, but the strain of climbing all the way from Base Camp showed. Our pace had been reduced, again, to twenty small steps at a time.

One of the irritations of such slow moving and so many breaks was that it gave you too much time to reflect on the discomfort. I had hardly even looked at the Lhotse Face in the distance; it was too big a leap. It had taken all my reserves just to get along the Western Cwm.

Fourteen hours later I was squatting in the chilly air of dawn, checking my pack was secure and adjusting my crampons for the last time, before setting off in the hope of reaching Camp Three, some 3,300 feet higher. I felt mildly sick.

Camp Three is on the threshold of where the human body can survive. Any higher and the body begins to feed off itself and slowly shuts down; you are then on borrowed time. How the human body reacts to this strain varies amongst people; but as I had been repeatedly told, 'altitude adaptation grows with age', and age was something that was working against me. I prayed that my body would cope. It had to. This was the real tester. If I failed to cope up at Camp Three, I would return to Base Camp and never go back up again. My body would be one of the many that cannot cope with the lack of oxygen. Looking at the vast Face before me, I tried to imagine being up there. I couldn't.

'Okay, let's get going, we need to be well onto the Face by the time the sun comes up. That only leaves two hours to reach the foot of it,' Neil announced.

We had hardly spoken that morning. We were all nervous, and lost in our own thoughts. Much rested on the next seven or so hours.

Thirty yards after setting out from Camp Two we were still on the scree and ice moraine, trying to reach the firmer glacier ice that would lead up from there. Neil was in front, and suddenly slipped on the ice. We stopped as he got to his feet and started again. A yard later he slipped again, and fell awkwardly on the sharp stone and ice surface. He swore at the top of his voice, and slammed his ice-axe into the glacier bed. He was pissed off.

We all felt the pressure on us now, and floundering thirty yards from Camp was bugging for Neil. It was an unnecessary irritation. I understood. We all just sat there for a bit. We didn't need to speak. We just needed time as a team alone, out of Camp Two. We sat there for five minutes just being together. Neil had just expressed what we all felt. We were feeding off each other now, and gaining strength from it.

We started up again and followed our route to the Bergschrund slowly and deliberately, trying to save our energy for what was above. All was silent apart from the crunch of ice beneath our feet as the teeth of our crampons gripped in the ice. The same methodic, high-pitched crunch that rang in my ears with every step. It felt hot already and it was only 6.30 a.m.

As we approached the start of the Face we sat for ten minutes and rested. I handed round some glucose tablets. I used to suck these continually; it was something to do as you leant on your axe with your eyes closed breathing heavily, trying to summon up the energy to move forward. It acted as a distraction from the discomfort.

The wind was blowing gently across the ice; it was a small relief from the heat as we started up the ice. As we kicked the points of our crampons in, we would lean on them, test their grip, then push another small step higher. A couple of these, then we would need to rest. The leap we were making in altitude of 3,300 feet was huge – considering the altitude we were at. Even on our trek into Base Camp we had only been climbing around 900 feet a day, and that was some 10,000 feet lower down.

We knew the risks in pushing through this boundary, but because of the severity of the gradient we were forced to take it. Logistically it would be almost impossible to site two camps on the Lhotse Face – it was too risky avalanche-wise, and would result in the human body spending too much time too high. Everything considered, it was reckoned that to reach Camp Three and then get down quickly, was still the best way of acclimatizing to the body's threshold. As soon as we had completed our trip to Camp Three we would then return back to Base Camp for one last time; from then on it's all weather driven.

For five hours we continued slowly up the blue ice, each step deliberately placed. Mistakes on here could not be rectified. We would slide our jumars along the rope, then check the teeth had gripped, before leaning back to rest, letting the harness take the strain. The jumar is attached to your harness via a short rope known as a sling; you had to trust all these links to hold you – you had no choice.

At the end of each rope, we would clip in with a second sling and karabiner to the next rope – make sure it was secure, then unclip the jumar and move that as well. It was routine but you couldn't afford to be careless. The Lhotse Face has claimed so many of the deaths on Everest that mistakes went unforgiven. The concentration drained us as much as the climb itself.

When resting, our crampons would grip the ice and we would lean back on our harness. Looking beneath us, the ice shimmered away into the distance. I could see the small chips of ice that my crampons had dislodged, tumbling down the sheer face below. The sling holding me was as tight as a bow string under the weight of my body and heavy rucksack. We had tried to keep the weight of these to a minimum but still it was uncomfortably heavy as it bit into our shoulders.

I shuffled my feet to relieve the pressure of the heavy boots on them. Bent at an angle, the hard plastic dug into your shins, and the blisters I had from before were still sore. Jokey had helped bandage them, but the plasters were rubbing off now. I tried to shuffle them again.

Neil described it later as 'like being tortured', which made me feel a little better, to think that someone else loathed it with the same deep vengeance. There was nothing remotely pleasant or romantic up here now – it just hurt.

The wind picked up the higher we went. We stopped to tighten our windsuits around us. I clapped my hands together and snow shook from my fleece gloves. I didn't even have the energy to look down any more. I couldn't be bothered.

As we climbed higher we lost ourselves in our own worlds. Each of us was fighting our own battle here. The danger of slipping hung in our minds continually.

After six long hours, we could just make out the seracs above us. I saw Bernardo abseiling down towards us. He had reached Camp Three the day before. He looked confident.

'Not far now, Bear, over two more lips then see Camp Three,' he said as he reached me. The Sherpas had reached it yesterday as well, and had spent the afternoon putting the tent in. They were fitter than us up here, their bodies coped better. Up higher everything would level out: Western climbers and Sherpas would climb at the same frighteningly slow pace. The altitude would ensure this; but still up to Camp Three the Sherpas were faster. They had done their job well; Camp Three was in and they were now returning with Bernardo. They smiled broadly at us as they passed us on the ropes. They understood our pain.

As we emerged over the final lip I could see the tent wedged under the serac, 100 feet above us. It looked precariously perched, but to us it symbolized everything cosy, as we edged our way towards it. The tent flapping in the now stronger wind looked the most alluring yet elusive sight I can remember. The cold had set in and it was now snowing hard. The wind swept the snow across the dark ice and up into our bodies. My hands felt icily numb and I tried to shake warmth into them. The fleece gloves acted to stop the metal jumar and karabiners sticking to our hands.

Camp Three didn't seem much closer and I had been moving now for a further twenty minutes.

Mick was a little behind Neil and I, and, as we both rolled over the ledge of Camp Three, we looked over and down at him. He was stationary. Another weary step, then a rest. He must have looked at us with envy, so close yet so far away. Come on, Mick. He never gave in, and eventually, freezing cold, he staggered to the ledge. A cold smile swept slowly across his half obscured face. The three of us were at Camp Three.

*

Andy was already in the tent, having left Camp Two a couple of hours before us. He was tired and irritated, but so were we all. The tent was tiny and four of us crammed inside, wet, with all our equipment, and boots, was a feat that a champion 'Twister' player might have struggled with. We fought to find space to squat.

Sachets of dried food were scattered across the floor messily, and we crammed our sleeping bags against the tent wall that was wedged against the ice face behind us. This side of the tent seemed a dull colour in comparison to the lighter, outer facing edge. I leant against the ice with my sleeping bag behind me, and tried to get comfortable in the limited space.

The headache that I thought I had left behind at Camp Two was with me again, stronger now. I swallowed four more aspirins.

In such close quarters, when you are tired, thirsty, with a headache, trying to melt ice continually on a tiny worn stove, and crammed into a corner against a cold wall of ice, requires a certain degree of tolerance from everyone. If ever friendships were to be tested it was now.

We knew each other so well, and knew how we each reacted to things, that things got done relatively smoothly and quietly. We must have appeared like 'old hands' as I helped Neil jam a roll-mat on the ground, as he passed me my headtorch from my pack, and as we grinned at Mick peeing in his bottle two inches from my ear. Nobody ever told us it would be a holiday; and we never expected it to be easy. It was just good, in a bizarre sort of way, to be here all together.

Once your boots were off you didn't leave the tent. Several lives had been lost by people putting their inner boots on, going out for a second, then because of being careless and dozy from the altitude, slipping on the blue ice. It was their last conscious act, before finding themselves hurtling at breakneck speed down the 5,000 feet glassy face, with only a yawning crevasse at the bottom to meet them. Being careless up here can all too easily have fatal consequences.

The Singapore team had left Camp Two at the same time as us, but hadn't made it to Camp Three. We heard on our radio call that evening that they had turned round after four hours. The weather had looked nasty. They would try again tomorrow. A warmth came over me; the three of us and Andy had made it. God knows how, but we were here, on the side of the Lhotse Face at some 24,500 feet above sea-level . . . and Mum and Dad. The thought made me smile.

The daylight was dying fast and we used our headtorches to keep watch over the stove that hissed away incessantly in the corner. I leant against my pack, wedged between Mick and Neil, and closed my eyes.

The sporadic snorts of Mick clearing his dry throat, and the deep hacking of Neil's cough, were the only sounds as darkness swept across the mountain. I tried to doze.

'The tent . . . it is just ahead, no, it's gone. What's happening? There it is again, so close . . . now it's moving away. Stop, please.' I was locked in this never-ending cycle of pain, desperately trying to grab the tent, but never being allowed to. I just kept plodding on, I begged my mind to let me give up, but it refused. There seemed no escape. 'Stop . . .'

I opened my eyes and realized I was inside the tent. I tried to shake the nightmare from my head. I never wanted to see another rope or karabiner again.

At midnight I heard Andy mutter angrily to himself, 'Oh, for fuck sake, come on!' He wasn't finding rest either. I took another aspirin. Maybe it would help me sleep, as well as ease the headache. It didn't work.

*

I opened my eyes when I heard the sound of someone peeing in a bottle. It was Mick again. I hadn't even gone once yet.

'Mick, can't you ruddy do that lying down,' I whispered.

'It's too big,' Mick replied.

I knew that I would need counselling on my return, to get rid of that image of Mick always kneeling, grinning and pissing this brown, stinking urine into his see-through bottle. For a long time afterwards if you said 'Mick' to me, then that was the image that leapt to mind. Everyone else had perfected the art of peeing whilst lying down; everyone, that is, except for Mick. He, as they say, liked to do it kneeling.

As dawn arrived we began the irksome task of trying to disentangle ourselves from the mass of limbs and equipment in the cramped tent. We tried to get the stove to light but it had frozen solid. I unscrewed the parts, removed the small gas filter to allow the gas easier access, and stuffed the various different bits down my bag. Ten minutes later it had thawed out and lit on the third attempt.

An hour later we had each drunk a warm mug of water and were dressed, fumbling around inside for last-minute things. My gloves were still damp, but at least were warm when I squeezed them on. As I manoeuvred myself from the tent, the fresh crisp air filled my nostrils. Waiting for the others to emerge, I sat and looked around. The heavy snow and driving wind of yesterday had been replaced by beautiful stillness. I was transfixed.

We were now two vertical kilometres above Base Camp, and still one and a half vertical kilometres off the summit. Mountains that before towered far above us, at Base Camp, were now level with us or below. I felt like a predator creeping slowly but surely

171

up on the sleeping giant of Everest. But today we would undo all that slog. We would now have to descend again to Camp Two, then Base Camp. The thought of retracing all those sweat-earned steps depressed me; but it was our only option. The human body cannot acclimatize any higher, and in the process of slowly catching this monkey, we were being forced to retreat.

Sitting there, I glanced across to where Camp Four, the South Col, would be. The traverse above that led to the Yellow Band and then on to the Geneva Spur looked terrifying as it glistened in the early sun. Above these features, somewhere to the north, lay Camp Four. I let my eyes scan the horizon above, wondering if the weather would come right and allow me any higher. I prayed it would.

As I looked back down the valley I realized the severity of the Face we had climbed up in the wind and snow, only fifteen hours earlier. I checked my harness as I sat there.

Those few minutes that I sat, while Mick, Neil and Andy got ready, I experienced a stillness that I thought did not exist. Time seemed to stand still. I didn't want the moment to end.

*

It had snowed heavily in the night and the ropes were now buried under several inches of snow that lay delicately on top of the glassy ice. It would make the descent much harder.

Soon we were ready and carefully checked each other's harnesses. It was worth the few seconds it took, and could save a life. Then slowly we started down. The rope ran through our figure-of-eight abseiling devices, and buzzed as we picked up speed. I found it thrilling bouncing over the ice, leaning out, trusting the few pieces of cord that held us firmly in place. The ropes, under friction, were warm to touch as they raced away above us. I tried not to think about the thousands of feet of sweat and toil that now flew through my hands. I didn't want to remind myself that I would have to do it again on the way to Camp Four and the summit; the prospect hurt too much.

On the way down we saw the specks of a few other climbers coming up. It was the Singapore team and an American climber. They must have left early. We passed the Singapore team and wished them luck. The American was fifty yards below. I was feeling tired by now. The strain of a night so high up was making me dozy as I came down, and the thrill of the descent was beginning to wear off. I just wanted to get down.

As I unclipped past the American, I groaned hello then clipped on past him. I was getting clumsy. Suddenly I lost traction in my crampons and skidded down the ice. The rope knocked the American sideways. I tripped onto my back and the sheet ice whisked me away. Just as I began to accelerate, the rope jerked me to a halt. A second later the American smacked into me. We both lay motionless for a few seconds, facing in to the slope – then clutched frantically for the rope.

'Are you okay? Man, that was close. Keep your points dug in,' he said almost casually.

'Yep, I'm all right, I'm sorry, I lost grip suddenly. Are you okay?' I replied frantically.

'Yeah, yeah, but lucky this rope held, eh?'

We worked our way up carefully to the anchor point of the rope, and breathed deeply.

I buried my head in my jacket as my chest heaved. I had been lucky – again.

You can't afford mistakes like that – you know that, Bear, I told myself.

The two of us grinned at each other. Only in such a precarious place can an accident like that bond people. In any other situation it would result in arguments and a punch-up, but up here you are both struggling to do your best in a dangerous game. The mountaineer's temperament is very laid back, and at times of stress like this it showed. He shrugged it off.

'Hey, forget it,' he said.

I carried on slowly down, carefully watching each step I placed. It had been my first mistake on the mountain and it could have been my last. I felt ashamed, as if I had somehow let the others down. They were more forgiving, though, than I was to myself.

'Getting some downhill practice in up there, were you, Bear?' Mick joked. I grinned back at him sheepishly.

I hated having close shaves like that – I vowed it would be my last.

*

Back at Camp Two the tension fell away – we were ecstatic. Our final acclimatization climb was over. Michael and Scott were both there as well and shook our hands. I think they envied the fact that we had the prospect of a good rest awaiting us back at Base Camp. They were still hoping to climb some of the way to Camp Three in the next few days, depending on how Scott's ankle held up. I think, though, Scott knew he was near his limit. We sipped the warm mugs of lemon tea and talked. Scott and Michael looked at us a little differently now.

We had proved we could cope at our altitude threshold and survive. We all knew that this boded well for a chance of the top. No one said this as there were too many other factors that could stop us, but deep down we knew we had done all that had been asked of us. I couldn't help feel a tinge of pride. We had done okay.

The next day, we left Camp Two carrying the minimum of gear. Most of what we had ferried up would be needed for a summit bid. It would wait for us there. The route down through the Cwm – for the first time – felt pleasant. Our bodies revelled in the rich air. We crossed the crevasses with confidence, not due to altitude-induced nonchalance but because of pride. We were almost back.

I breathed deeply at the top of the Icefall, as we gazed down into the depths below. The more I saw it, the more I dreaded going back in. I guess that as we were getting closer, the stakes increased; suddenly there is more to lose. I clipped into the rope and dropped into the ice, leaving the Cwm behind me. All went smoothly until half an hour later.

Neil had just reached me, and Mick was waiting two yards further on. Suddenly we heard a piercing crack as a slab of snow tumbled, bouncing across the ice boulders. The snow engulfed the north side of the Icefall, creating this deep rumble. We crouched and watched as the cloud of snow settled only a few hundred feet away.

As we squatted, we could see Base Camp clearly below. Binoculars would be watching us from there. We moved efficiently down the ropes with fresh vigour. We're too close to screw it up now, we're too close, I thought.

By 12 noon we were gazing back up at the now-silent Icefall. Jokey's voice broke that silence. I think she summed it up, as she candidly muttered under her breath, 'Bloody men, I don't know.' A smile spread warmly across her face and she hugged us excitedly. It was good to be back.

CHAPTER TWELVE

SUMMIT FEVER

▲

'Now that I'm here, where am I?'
Janis Joplin

I woke from a deep slumber to the sound of excited voices outside my tent. Sherpas were scurrying around frantically. All of us shuffled from our tents to see what was happening. A Nepalese porter, who was not from the Khumbu valley area, was moving quickly towards our camp. He looked tired. Strapped from his head, an old canvas band supported the weight of a wicker basket laden with various things. He shuffled into camp, grinned, and eased the weight from his back.

Sherpas grouped round him and questioned him eagerly. Soon all went quiet, the Sherpas moved aside and the porter turned to us.

'British expedition? British?' He mumbled in pidgin English, 'Telephone from Lukla, long journey. English man two days behind.' He produced from his basket a small box, covered in polythene. He smiled as if he knew how much this cargo meant to us.

Since our own satellite telephone had exploded dramatically

at the hands of the rickety generator in Namche Bazaar all those weeks ago, our communication back home had been minimal. Using Michael's telephone had caused endless friction, and would have required a mortgage to have used it at all regularly – thus hampering our desire to ring home. At last the replacement phone from British Telecom had arrived. Jokey shone with pride. She had organized it via e-mail, and could hardly believe her eyes that it was now with us.

It had travelled out with her replacement communication officer, Ed Brandt, who had sent it ahead by runner from Lukla after flying into the foothills. He knew it would reach us sooner that way. The porter had carried it at high speed up to Base Camp in only four days. The pace showed. He sat sipping milk tea, wrapped in blankets, and mumbling with the Sherpas in between swigs. Ed would be still somewhere in the valleys beneath us, but he had done well. Our communications home were now up and running.

*

Most of the team were now back at Base Camp and we only awaited the return of Nasu and Ilgvar after their ascent to Camp Three. They were the only two from our party still not back.

Geoffrey had also reached Camp Three successfully, along with the rest of the Everest group, Carla, Graham, Allen and Michael. Scott, though, was now returning to Base Camp for the last time. He had decided his injury would prevent him going any higher. He had witnessed the extremes of the mountain and her beauty, but would not risk going further. From Camp Three onwards you enter another world. A world where only the fittest and lucky survive. He had decided not to continue. He had done extraordinarily well already.

Henry had been to Camp Two and was acclimatized to that altitude. He also made the decision not to go higher. He would supervise the summit teams from either there, or back at Base

Camp. Time would decide. Base Camp, for now, was busy feeding exhausted, hungry men and women.

We were now receiving, almost daily, very accurate weather forecasts from Bracknell in the UK. These, for the price of $500 a go, gave us the most advanced precision forecasts available anywhere in the world. The latest climatic information was gathered there. It was coined from satellite and weather centres round the world, as well as from commercial jets flying at altitudes of up to 45,000 feet. All these sources were sending regular weather updates back to the Bracknell base – and for a price we could access it.

Our lives would be dependent upon the accuracy of these forecasts up the mountain. Being caught out unawares up high was fatal. Bracknell could help prevent this and were able to determine wind strengths to within four or five knots accuracy, at every thousand feet of altitude. Such information was invaluable, but as with all forecasts, they were only predictions. Three weeks later Neil and I would find ourselves fighting our way through deep snow towards the summit in winds of up to 50 knots. Wind that was not meant to be there. If we had known this, events might have turned out very differently. But for the moment, the forecasts came pouring in. The entire team would then crowd round eagerly to see what the skies above us were bringing. It still didn't look good.

When the summit is being clipped by the jet-stream winds that pound her day and night at over 200 m.p.h., any summit attempt is impossible. At Base Camp on a still night we could lie in our tents and listen to those winds some ten thousand feet above us. The sound seemed to shake the mountain.

For now we were waiting for those early signs of the monsoon to arrive in the Himalaya: the time when the winds over Everest's summit begin to rise. The snow then ceases to pour off her like a smoking volcano. At that time, a stillness descends and the mountain beckons those who have waited.

For the time being, the summit was still being blown ferociously. We didn't have to be able to see; we could hear it. We tried to busy ourselves at Base Camp as we began the waiting game. There was much to do.

We tested the oxygen canisters again and again. We learnt the correct flow rates for the Russian-imported oxygen regulators. Formulas had to be learnt by heart. Up high there would be no time for complex mathematics – the brain would be working too slowly. Simple sums become impossible. I was bad enough at these at sea-level, let alone in the Death Zone.

A flow of 2.5 litres a minute on a 1,500 litre canister would last just over ten hours. Call it ten to be safe. The orange 'poisk' canisters were smaller and would last five or six hours. Different regulators attach in different ways to different canisters; we had to be able to operate these with mitts on and in the dark. It could save our lives. We endlessly practised together in the mess tent. Watching me fumble and drop things as I tried to do it blindfolded was a source of great amusement to Mick, Geoffrey and Neil – but then it would be their turn. The mistakes had to be made now, when it was warm and safe. We all knew this.

Initially the days passed quickly as we prepared ourselves. We watched, one morning, two Nepalese porters loading up barrels of human faeces on their backs to carry down the valley for a fistful of rupees. They smiled away as they made the loads comfortable on their backs. It was good manure for the crops lower down in the valleys – they were over the moon.

Before leaving they laughed and joked with the Sherpas, hugged, held hands in the Sherpa fashion, and drank tea. Not once did they wash their hands. Still – easy come, easy go. This was good old Sherpa-style. The poo-bearers, as we called them, then disappeared amongst the rocks across the glacier, heading down the valley carrying their precious cargo. I doubted somehow they would have any problem with the Nepalese National Parks Police, rummaging through their bags for smuggled goods.

We spent that afternoon playing Neil's 'Great stone throwing' competition. As the day progressed, so did the silly games. In the middle of an absurd bout of one-legged volleyball, played with a makeshift bundle of cardboard and masking tape, Allen walked past us and glared. He could not understand us, and certainly could not correlate the risks we were about to take with us larking about now. He dismissed it as unprofessional. For us, though, we were letting off steam from the fear of all that lay ahead. We wanted to laugh and relax – just a bit.

That evening the radios crackled with news that was serious, deadly serious. Our joviality of the day switched in an instant. Someone was in grave trouble up the mountain.

'I repeat, I am seeing a figure three-quarters of the way up the Lhotse Face stationary, I repeat, stationary.' The voice of the Singaporean at Camp Two sounded worried.

'It's beginning to get dark up here and we don't know who the hell it is. He's running out of time if he doesn't start moving.'

The radio crackled frantically for the next two hours as people tried to find out what had happened. As darkness swept through the valley, those watching from Camp Two lost sight of the figure. It was getting cold and the wind was picking up. Nobody could survive at 24,000 feet in those conditions if they were not moving. At Base Camp as we listened, we prayed silently. There was nothing else we could do. We had all been on the Face and knew its dangers. What the hell, though, was this climber doing up there now?

The American team, along with Nasu and Ilgvar, were the only people at Camp Three. It had to be one of them.

Nasu and Ilgvar responded to our radio call – they were safe.

The Americans, though, weren't responding. At 10.00 p.m. they at last replied.

'We are missing Jim Manley up here. Has anyone any news?' they asked wearily from their precariously perched tent on the Lhotse Face.

Angry voices followed. Why had they been so slow to reply? Why had they left it so late to notify anyone that one of their party was missing? The Americans had no real answer. The drug of thin air had a hold of them. They were almost too tired to even speak.

'Where the fuck is Manley?' Graham asked bluntly. He had grabbed the radio in rage and now fired questions at the Americans some 7,000 feet higher up.

'You've got to go and find him, and now,' he continued.

But the Americans couldn't. They were too tired and knew that there was nothing they could do in this weather.

'We reckon Jim's turned back down the Face. To start looking in these conditions would be just too risky,' they argued. 'None of us are in any shape to survive out there. We're too exhausted. Can you see anything from Camp Two?'

The mist and darkness obscured any chance of seeing the figure – the figure of Jim Manley. The attention turned to Nasu and Ilgvar. They were less tired, having been at Camp Three a night already. They would have to start a search – themselves.

'Nasu and Ilgvar, listen – Jim could still be out there. If he's turned back then it's okay, but we don't know. There is a risk he could have severe oedema or be unconscious on the ropes. We need you to descend and try and find him. Are you in a state to try this?' Graham asked firmly. A long pause followed.

'Roger that. We'll try.'

They emerged twenty minutes later from their tents. Fighting blizzard conditions, they made their way laboriously down the frozen ropes. An hour later Nasu's voice crackled on the radio.

We all huddled round hoping that they would have found Jim alive. Nobody spoke a word.

'No sign, Base Camp, of Jim, I repeat, no sign,' Nasu shouted into the radio over the noise of the wind. The radio cut dead.

As they both continued their descent towards Camp Two in the gale, the reality of what must have happened slowly began to dawn on us all listening. Jim must have fallen some time ago, as the mist hid him from view.

By the time Nasu and Ilgvar reached Camp Two there was a soberness over the whole mountain. They had done all that had been asked of them. Their exhaustion from the descent left them weak and drained as they sat in their tent. It was well past midnight. Nobody wanted to sleep; yet there seemed nothing to wait up for any longer.

*

'Base Camp, do you copy?' a panicked, weak voice mumbled through the radio. Click. Everyone swung round towards the sound.

'Hello, Base Camp,' the voice echoed again. 'This is Jim. Do you copy?'

The radio-net burst into conversation.

Jim had been too tired on the ropes to move. He had drifted in and out of a deep exhaustion and had just clung to the rope as night came – too tired to move or care.

Eventually he carried on past one more serac and spotted a tent to his right. It was empty, as it was one of the other teams' tents, left now at Camp Three ready for the summit bid. He clambered wearily in, left the radio off and lay there fully clothed and closed his eyes. At 12.30 a.m. he came to and turned on the radio to call Base Camp. People were furious; it was a call too late.

As he had slept Nasu and Ilgvar had risked their lives on the Face to find him. They must have passed within metres of him as he lay in the lone tent. Exhausted and distraught, they had to report the news that they had reached the bottom of the Face and Manley had not been there. We all knew what that had meant.

The next morning saw frantic apologies from the Americans who had been too tired to help, and countless apologies from Jim. Nasu and Ilgvar returned to Base Camp. The apologies were irritating to hear. Nobody cared about apologies – it was too late. The incident was shrugged off, nobody blamed Jim – it was the nature of climbing, that things can so easily go wrong. Yet it had sparked a fire of emotions. Emotions that had been brewing for a while. The tension of what lay ahead up there blew these feelings wide open, and Base Camp slowly turned into a huddle of nervous, anxious people. We had been out here now for over two months, and the volatility and frustration amongst the climbers was beginning to show.

*

Jokey would be leaving Base Camp in two days; her time with us would soon be over. As arranged beforehand, she had to return for her sister's wedding in mid-May. Scott would also accompany her; the mountain, unfortunately, no longer held anything for him. It would be sad to lose him and his medical expertise. Ed Brandt, a friend of Neil's, would be taking over from Jokey. He was due any day now. Jokey's last few days passed slowly. The strain on the climbers at Base Camp made it a less pleasant place to be, but Jokey had lived through it all with us. Part of her didn't want to leave. She had been with us from the start, and now at the key time she was having to leave. Her face said it all.

'I so hoped to be with you when you went for it. It's horrible packing up and seeing you still waiting for these jet-stream winds to lift. I know your frustration,' she told us, as we sat all together in the tent, her last evening. I knew that in under a week she would be at home in Norfolk drinking tea with her family, and

Everest would be only a memory. Part of me longed to leave as well, but our ambition seemed to hold us prisoner here – awaiting a final showdown with the mountain. I felt a little stranded.

'You will be okay. I just know it,' she said. But she didn't know. She had never seen above Base Camp – that desolate land of ice far above the clouds that now hovered over Base Camp. She didn't know what went on up there. But I longed to believe her. She had been a friend to all of us at Base Camp, and we would miss her.

When she left, I didn't even wave her off. I sat in my tent and tried to focus on what lay ahead up there. A new phase was now beginning.

*

The fact that Ed Brandt's face wasn't as good-looking as Jokey's was all we thought, as he staggered into Base Camp that first week in May. As communications officer, his job of keeping us informed and in touch on this final stage would be crucial. The comms tent at Base Camp was a bit ropey and torn, but it would be a place where he would spend many restless nights in the coming days and weeks, as he waited for our radio calls. A few of these, and Ed's face definitely wouldn't be as pretty as Jokey's – no one's would be by the time the mountain had dealt her last set of cards to us. A hand that, as of yet, was still our most feared unknown.

Ed had brought with him what Mick called our 'ESLs': our 'Emotional Support Letters'. As he dished them out to the four of us, we grabbed them and ran off to our respective tents. For the next two hours Base Camp was unusually quiet as we lay and reread our letters from home. Each one became thumbed a hundred times. I couldn't help but squirm with excitement as I read them. From my sister, Lara, my parents, my grandfather, and from Shara. A wad of sweet-smelling, ink-stained, carefully sealed reminders of all I missed so dearly.

To my precious son,
We do miss you so much, and think and pray for you continually. You are in God's safe hands – I can't wait to hear some news from you.

The pigs, Hyacinth and Violet, are growing fast and now even come for walks with us very obediently. We have built a duck pond for the ducks, Sam and Isabella, in the corner of the farmyard, and they love swimming up and down. Isabella was trodden on by Hyacinth and has broken her leg – at vast expense the vet has made her a little cast for it. Dad suggested it would have been cheaper to shoot her and have her for supper. But she has just laid five eggs and I am hoping that she will go broody.

All my love, Mum

My father talked of more practical matters:

Do just bear in mind that you must only go as far as you can. There is no loss of face if you turn around, for whatever reason. Already you have gone so far and seen sights that most of us can never imagine. We are both so proud of you, our bestest, but remember, only, son.

God's speed, Dad

Common practice on Everest is a period of rest before a summit attempt, down the valley below Base Camp. The thicker, more oxygen-rich air allows the body to sleep better and recover faster than at the debilitating altitude of Base Camp. The body's metabolism begins to work more effectively and you strengthen quickly. On returning to Base Camp the body is as strong as it will ever be. It will need to be.

All of our team were now off the mountain. The wait was now for the weather. In the meantime people debated the merits of going down the valleys to rest. On one hand the body recovers well, but on the other hand you risk picking up diseases that the trekkers have brought in. On top of this, you also risk being away when the crucial time comes – the time when the jet stream is beginning to lift. Andy had been robbed of a chance of reaching the summit of Everest almost ten years earlier, when the weather came right and he was too far down the valley to be in position to use it. He never forgot this and warned of the danger. The four of us had to make personal decisions about what to do.

Neil and Geoffrey announced that they would go down to the village of Dingboche some six hours below Base Camp. Mick and I decided to stay. We dreaded leaving and opening up the possibility of missing our chance. If only we had known the length of time that we would have to wait, we would have gone down as well. We were to be waiting in total for over three weeks. A far cry from the hope that Jokey and all of us had held, of an ascent by 1 May.

So we stayed. The eighteen square feet of our tents was now home to us. We had all our letters, and little reminders of our families. We felt reluctant to leave them; they comforted us. I had my small sea-shell I had taken from the beach on the Isle of Wight that now hung from the roof of my tent; Shara had written in it my favourite quote that I had used so often in the Army: 'Be sure of this, that I am with you always, even unto the end of the world.' St Matthew 28.20. I read it every time I went to sleep. I liked my 'home' at Base Camp.

DIARY, 7 MAY:
Alone again with Mick – waiting. It gives us time to think, but also time to be scared. It's almost too much time.

Any self-expression is so stilted up here. At home you can do handstands and run and swim, but here the waiting and worry of injuring yourself before the big push makes life so bland. Self-expression is really now reduced to just trying to be kind and gentle with people around us. There's not much else that we can do.

We are all so ready; we have done as much preparation as

we can. I never believed this possible, but it's now true. All our kit is neat and sits ready for the green light. Our harnesses are checked and carefully arranged; we know our way round them blindfolded. Knots can be tied in seconds with mitts on and crampons attached in any conditions. All we can do is wait and hope a break comes, to allow all this work to lead somewhere.

There comes a time when preparation no longer counts. I know that ultimately it is not how quickly I can tie knots that will make the difference, but rather how strong my heart is – how much I really want this, how much I will be able to endure up there. It is this spirit that counts for everything. I pray that mine will be strong.

Iñaki left yesterday for the summit of Lhotse, for what the Spanish call a 'posicuela' – an early bid. He will be at Camp Two now, preparing to leave for his summit attempt. I wish him all my luck. He knows it is a risk as the mountain isn't really ready for him, but he misses home. If anyone can do it, though, he can. Tomorrow evening we will know if he has made it or not.

Tomorrow evening came and the radio buzzed into life. 'Iñaki to Base Camp. I'm turning round. It is just too windy and I've hit deep snow, no way can I go on. I'm turning home,' came his muffled and tired voice from somewhere just above Camp Three. He had bravely tried to climb Lhotse alone, but the way was barred. He would be exhausted. It had been a long day for him, having started his bid at 11.00 p.m. the night before.

Three days later he tried again. Once more the mountain stopped him. The fierce winds and strong sun had now left him blinded. It was the same as had happened on Everest all those years earlier. Confused and disorientated from his effort, he staggered drunkenly down the Lhotse Face. He had to reach Camp Two and rest. He could hardly see out from his goggles. His eyes were puffy and swollen. His visibility was reduced to a vague squint; he knew he had to get down fast.

Back at Camp Two he knew it was all over for him. He would leave Base Camp after two heroic solo attempts, to return to the warmth of Spain and the comfort of his new bride. We all admired his efforts.

Patience on the mountain, especially on Everest, is the key to climbing successfully. It is one of the reasons that Everest climbers tend to be older. They have more of it. Ultimately it is the mountain who says whether you can climb or not. We are but pawns in this game – the decisions all lie with the mountain. The Sherpas say that the mountain goddess reviles pride and arrogance on her slopes. They are both killers up there. We knew that we had no option but to wait quietly for our chance, and pray it would come.

I remembered how in *Pooh Bear*, Eeyore worried, Owl contemplated, while Pooh just was. We also needed to learn this. We had to be content with just being. But sitting there was hard – so hard.

Climbing Everest involves so much more than I ever dreamt. People on our return would only be interested in whether we reached the top. To the media and those who don't know, that is their only question; but there is so much more. As I waited, I thought back to all those endless days training at home, day after day; I remembered those weeks of climbing out here before the others had arrived, pounding up and down the huge hills that surrounded the valleys lower down. I remembered the pain and jubilation of coming through the Icefall that first time unscathed, and of reaching the heights of Camp Three. Yet no one would even mention these afterwards. Their only question would be: 'Did you reach the top?' It was as if the weeks of fear, discomfort and endurance counted for nothing; when in reality, they count for as much as the summit.

Neil and Geoffrey soon returned after three days' rest. For us nothing had changed; we still sat in our tents, me in my chef's trousers and tweed cap, Mick in his long-johns, and both of us lost in our own world of resting, eating and thinking. I envied the break Neil and Geoffrey had had. They were rested and healthy and had missed nothing. We should have gone as well, I thought.

I phoned home regularly now. It was the only relief for us here. I had nothing much to say except that I missed them and that I longed to be home. Neil and Mick teased me mercilessly about my conversations.

'Bear, look, you don't have to ask every time you speak to your family, how each of the animals are in turn, okay? I'm sure they would tell you if they weren't okay. I mean, you must use up hundreds of pounds on asking how ruddy Olly the donkey is, and how Sam and Isabella the ducks are. It's ridiculous,' Neil joked.

But I liked to hear. It was my link back.

I also spoke to SSAFA, one of my sponsors, who mentioned that I had received an invitation to Buckingham Palace for the Young Achievers Award. I felt honoured, but also a fraud. I hadn't blooming climbed it yet. Couldn't anyone understand that a gulf the size of the Atlantic still stood between me and the top? No one seemed to realize this.

I rang some great friends who live near my family in Dorset. The father, a wonderful eccentric Colonel, loved by everyone, answered the phone.

'Hello, Colonel, good morning, it's Bear here,' I mumbled.

'Hey everyone, it's Bear calling from the summit of Mount Everest. Quick.'

'Uh, no, Colonel, I'm at Base Camp. We're still waiting for these winds to lift, I'm not at the . . .' I tried to tell him.

'Marvellous, Bear, congratulations. The summit eh . . . boy,' he interrupted.

He refused to believe I was at Base Camp. After all, I had

been away for over two months now – I couldn't possibly still be at Base Camp. But I was and no, I hadn't reached the summit. I despaired.

Six months later, after I had been back in England a while, the Colonel left me a message on my answerphone. I had given him a rock from the summit of Everest inscribed with a verse saying, 'Be still for the Glory of the Lord is shining in this place.' Some weeks earlier, he had been diagnosed suddenly as having terminal cancer. His voice was weak and shaky on the machine, and he simply said, 'Thank you, Bear, for my rock, thank you from the bottom of my heart.' By the time I heard the message he had died. I wept at home. A true gentleman now lived in heaven.

*

Mick and I decided to get out of Base Camp for a day. We wanted some exercise, having been lying around for now almost ten days. We packed up and left in search of a 'supposed' Italian research station in the valleys below, somewhere off the beaten track. There was rumour of pizza and pasta. We left in high spirits.

Ten hours later, nine of which had been spent walking, we returned. The Italian research station turned out to be a hut that served spaghetti and spam. We should have suspected as much. Spam. We just couldn't seem to avoid it. It seemed to follow us round everywhere. We were fed up with eating it for almost every meal at Base Camp, couldn't people realize it was 'banned' in England. Sure as eggs are eggs, we should have known that the research station would produce the infamous tinned meat. We had two mouthfuls then left, and arrived back at Base Camp as night fell – chuckling and well-exercised. 'Flipping Italians,' we announced.

The forecasts were still bad and were now accompanied by a

warning that they would get worse. We shook our heads. It was ridiculous. We began to suspect that this season could be like the last one – in the autumn of 1997, when not one single climber reached the summit of Everest. The weather hadn't allowed it. This was fast becoming a possibility now as well. Mick and I agreed to see what the next day would bring and then decide whether we also should go down for a proper rest. But the next day brought tragic news. Things weren't going right.

*

The Sherpa bustled into Camp. He looked scared and nervous. He spoke quickly.

'Man dead. Altitude sickness. He dead,' the Sherpa muttered. We listened to what had happened.

The trekker was Japanese. He was one of a party getting close to the crescendo of their trip – approaching Base Camp. They had all failed to recognize the symptoms of altitude sickness in this man. He had carried on up, when he should have gone down. It was his last and worst mistake. By late afternoon he was in the late stages of pulmonary oedema. His lungs began to fill up with fluid, and his breathing became more and more laboured as he choked in his own blood-filled lungs. By evening he had died of a heart attack, induced by pulmonary suffocation. At 17,000 feet the altitude had claimed its latest victim.

Rigor mortis soon set in. They needed to get the body into a basket, in order to carry it back down the valleys to where a helicopter could collect it. The body, though, was now rigid and those around him were unable to bend it. Left with only one option they twisted the body and leant on the back until it gave way and broke. With a shrill crack the spine split in two and the body could be squeezed into a basket and carried down.

It came as a deep shock to us all at Base Camp. We hadn't

known the man but he would have a family somewhere. It was such a tragic waste of life. A waste that could have been avoided if the symptoms had been recognized earlier.

At the small village of Dingboche, halfway along the trek to Base Camp, is a small hut called the 'Himalayan Rescue Association'. Resident Western doctors work here, researching the effects of high altitude on the body. They are all volunteers and do three-month stints in the mountains as part of their research. They lecture daily to trekkers on the effects of mountain sickness, predominantly pulmonary and cerebral oedema. These Japanese had obviously opted not to hear the lecture. It was a fatal decision.

We had visited the doctors en route up to Base Camp and had chatted endlessly about the climb ahead. They offered fresh and new advice to us. We listened carefully. They measured the oxygen saturation levels in our blood and monitored pulse and blood pressures.

The danger they warn trekkers about is going too high too fast. The body reacts differently with different people, but the symptoms are pretty universal. Severe dizziness, headache, vomiting, and laboured breathing; these all mean one thing – go down. It's as simple as that. A descent of some 1,000 feet can make the difference between life and death. We all had to have an expert knowledge about all this.

Pulmonary oedema affects the lungs; the capillaries dilate under the lack of oxygen and the lung-cavities begin to fill up with blood. Eventually the climber suffocates in a frothy mixture of mucus and blood. Cerebral oedema affects the brain. The lack of oxygen to the head makes the person severely drowsy, with searing migraines. This causes the brain to seek oxygen by absorbing more blood. If this continues the brain eventually swells and then dies.

Both these conditions can kill in hours, if not recognized.

Even more so with the heights we were to be going to. We took this deadly seriously, as we had witnessed it at first hand.

DIARY, 10 MAY:
Thinking of what happened to this poor man terrifies me. He died of altitude sickness some 400 feet vertically beneath the height of Base Camp, and we are sitting here preparing to go some 12,000 feet above Base Camp. It seems crazy.

I'm going to get out of Base Camp tomorrow, my head's going berserk. I need space. The storms that were predicted are soon moving in, so we can't climb yet. I'm going to go down to Dingboche to rest, get some food that isn't spam, and then sleep. I need to get away from everything for a while. I pray for the Japanese man's soul.

CHAPTER THIRTEEN

TORN APART

▲

'Luck and strength go together. When you get lucky you have the strength to follow through; you also have to have the strength to wait for the luck.'

Mario Puzo

As we snaked our way back down the valley leading away from Base Camp, I felt a deep pain in my shins. Each step I took, sent this pain shooting through my leg. I winced. I didn't mention it to any of the others – I didn't want them to know.

Mick, Neil, Geoffrey and Ed were with me. We had all decided to go down to Dingboche at 14,000 feet to spend our precious few rest days – it was our recovery time before the summit bid. For Neil and Geoffrey it was their second time down below Base Camp. Dingboche was low enough to ensure that the thicker air would replenish our bodies, and the prospect of cheese omelettes provided an added incentive to get there.

I couldn't shake the pain from my shins. Each time I stood on the hard rocks of the glacier, they stung viciously. I knew what it was, I had seen enough people in the Army suffer from it. Invariably it had hindered them continuing any exercise. I almost refused to acknowledge it was what I thought.

Shin splints is the severe bruising of the muscles at the front of the lower leg. It comes from excessive pounding on hard ground. It makes walking agony. I turned up the volume of my Walkman and tried to ignore the pain and just enjoy the richer air. It didn't work.

As we tumbled into the lodge at Dingboche and threw our packs into two double cubicles, I sat and rubbed them hard. I had to rest them or I would never be able to climb up high. This was an added burden that I could do without.

I told Mick about it that evening as we sat alone on our tiny wooden beds in the lodge. There wasn't much he could do.

'Brufen, Bear. That's what you need, and masses of it,' he suggested, in between writing his diary.

The old Army favourite for numbing pain. Technically designed as an anti-inflammatory, it takes the swelling away. I swallowed three of Mick's small supply.

'Thanks, Miguel.'

For three days we sat in the lodge, eating and relaxing in the fresh air. It was the break I had wanted. I tried not to think about the mountain. Every night, after taking several Brufen, I would sleep soundly. I hadn't slept like this in seven weeks. It was wonderful. As I rubbed my shins every night for half an hour, Mick and I chatted in our room. Our minds invariably drew us back to the mountain.

Our second day there, the weather turned. The winds far above us were now blowing fiercely. We could see the clouds licking across the wall of Lhotse above us. It meant that Everest would be taking a severe punishing behind. These were the storms we had expected. Dingboche was cold and blowy; Everest, though, 15,000 feet above, would be atrocious as the cold front pounded into her. At least everyone was now safely off the mountain, I thought. I wondered what damage the storm would cause to our camps up there.

A day later we returned to Base Camp. The shins felt better going uphill, but any little descents still stung madly. Thank God it's all uphill to the summit, I thought. I didn't even think about the descent, I knew it would hurt. I tried instead to forget about my shins and focus on the climb ahead.

As we crossed the last part of the glacier back to Base Camp we became stuck behind a trail of yaks heading across the glacier. They would be bringing supplies in. I offered to help the Nepalese ladies herd them. I grabbed a stick and started shouting and prodding the big, lazy animals to move. It took my mind off the tedium of the walk.

'Hooii, come on, move, you oafs,' I hollered from behind. Mick chuckled.

I was sure that they were becoming more attractive, then I reminded myself how long we had been in the hills. What the hell, I thought, and gave them all names. Dolly was the best-looking by far.

Base Camp was the same as ever. People wandered languidly between tents, clutching large mugs of hot lemon, and chatting with each other. It was relatively peaceful. The majority of people were still away, resting down the valley.

We heard from Henry that our Camp Two had taken a severe beating in the storm and that possibly our Camp Three was destroyed. We didn't know. We would take spare tents up with us on our ascent just in case. Great, more stuff to carry, I thought.

That night I went to sleep early. I had looked forward to being in my tent again. I had quite missed it; my little home. I noticed, though, as I lay down that I had a bit of a cough and sore throat, but I didn't think it was anything major. It had started whilst we were walking back from Dingboche. It was a minor irritant, that was all. It should be gone by morning, I hoped. I didn't give it a second thought.

*

I fumbled frantically in the dark for the zip of my tent. I undid it quickly, pulled myself out and threw up violently on the ice. I lay there in the freezing air, panting for breath, with my head hung low. It was 1.00 a.m.

I stayed in that same position, hunched in the porch of my tent, for what seemed like an eternity. I had a throbbing head-ache. My throat felt like sand-paper, and my ribs shook with each deep spluttering cough.

I must have picked it up in Dingboche. 'Damn. I was stupid to go down.' Descending to the more disease-prevalent valleys is the risk one takes in order to get a good rest. In my case it was a serious mistake. I lay awake until dawn, trying to squeeze the migraine from my head by shutting my eyes tight. It didn't work.

I sort of knew that the next forecast we would get would be different. I just had a feeling inside. We had had bad forecasts now for so long that the tension, even after a rest, was growing. People had risked a lot for a chance of the top, and waiting for the right weather is draining. Everyone felt this. For some the wait had been too much. Iñaki had taken his chances with his two early attempts. But they had failed and time still marched on. Much longer and the monsoon would be here with the snows, and then it would be all over.

It looked as if that transitional period between the two seasons, where the winds lift for those crucial few days, might not happen. We waited for the news.

The fever sent shivers up and down my body, I felt drained and weak – and looked it too. Andy, who worked as a physician's assistant back in Colorado, had taken over from Scott as our doctor. He took one look and quietly came and talked to me. He was the only person I felt like speaking to. He soon diagnosed it as a chronic chest infection, which my body was struggling to recognize. That was why I had been sick as well.

One of the greatest dangers of being ill at altitude is dehydration. Your body works so much slower that fighting disease is a long process. As the days go on, dehydration sets in – slowing the body's recovery even longer. Andy gave me a course of eurythromycin to start. These antibiotics would fight the infection; but it would take time. Time that I suspected I wouldn't have.

My greatest fear came true later on that morning, when Henry entered the tent with the forecast. People sat around looking determined and eager. They shifted in their seats. They longed for the news that the winds were beginning to rise; I dreaded it.

'Okay, good news at last. It looks as if we're going to get the break around the 19th. That gives us five days to get up there and in position. We need to start working towards this, okay?'

Henry, for the first time in weeks, appeared deadly serious. He knew this game all too well. You have got to wait and not fight, but when it suddenly shows signs of clearing, then you've got to go. We had done the waiting and now it had come. The moment I had longed for and the moment I now most feared.

I lay in my tent, struggling to move. My body shivered even in the sun, and my joints ached with the fever. I was too weak to eat properly and the journey to the mess tent to fill my water-bottle left me shaking uncontrollably. I was in no state to go anywhere. My mind tried to fight the fever, refusing to acknowledge it – but it was obvious. There was no way that I was going to climb now. I slowly felt it all slipping away like sand through my fingers. Then came the anger.

DIARY, 14 MAY:
Neil has just come to see me. I knew he was coming and knew what he would say. He had to say it.

They have got to leave Base Camp tomorrow morning for their attempt. There isn't the time to wait for me to recover, it could take over a week at this height. I knew he was right. I told him that I may be okay tomorrow morning, in which case I would come as well. He looked doubtful. He knows I won't be better by then.

We have done everything together and suddenly now the team is being torn apart. Why? I just can't understand why.

I've given my everything just for a chance to climb this last part and now I see it slipping away. We've worked our guts out on this mountain for seven weeks. Given so much.

I find it hard to write. My mind swirls with this sodding fever, and the feeling of anger and upset. Please, not now. Just please make me better, God. Please.

That afternoon the improvement I had told my mind would come never came. I lay sweating in my tent as the others scurried around in preparation. I rang my sister. I didn't have anything I wanted to say to her. I just wanted to hear her voice. I missed her.

'Promise me you won't go up while you're like this. Promise, Bear. Don't be stupid. You know what would happen, okay?' Lara said in a panicky voice. She was right. Classically it is how people die. They are ill, the time comes, the pressure is on and they go. As they ascend their body begins to shut down. It happened to Scott Fischer, one of the climbers who had died in 1996. He went up on antibiotics, still weak. The body can only put up with so much, and in the extreme heights above Camp Three it is at its limit. A sick body cannot survive. Scott died. Lara made me promise again. I was promising away my dream.

I began to turn my anger against God. I had felt it was all so right, but was now being kicked in the teeth. Maybe He had never even been with me. I felt let down. I hadn't been ill like this for ten years. I couldn't understand why. I pushed God aside in my mind. 'I'll get better tonight without Him.'

Lying there alone in my eighteen square feet of tent, something came into my head that I hadn't heard for five years. Not since my great-uncle Arthur had died. He had been a naval padre in the Second World War. Arthur was one of seven children. There were now only five left. One had died at sixteen from Weil's disease at school and one of the twins had been shot in the War. Those that now remained were all over seventy-five. As Arthur lay on his bed dying, he turned to my grandfather and whispered something to him. My grandfather had then subsequently told me, and I had never forgotten it.

His words had been simple: 'Remember this if you remember nothing else. When God goes, everything goes. Never let your faith leave you. Promise me.'

The words rang in my head. I said out loud, 'I won't, I promise.'

I slept peacefully for an hour after that. There must be a purpose to it all, I thought, there must be.

That night was probably the longest of the expedition. I was dry, I was safe, and I was near my friends – but I felt for the first time a real sense of loneliness. In a matter of hours Neil and Mick, along with Allen and Carla, would leave Base Camp for the first summit attempt on Everest's south side for over six months. I had not been included. I would be a liability, I was far too weak. I would not survive. It wasn't a decision that I had to make; the decision had been made for me by Neil and Henry. I lay, feeling so alone as the night dragged on. I didn't want to sleep.

Henry had insisted Geoffrey stayed behind as well. Graham and Michael, the remainder of the Everest party, were also ill with the same fever. The three of us and Geoffrey would form the reserve summit party. It had to be like this. Us three were ill and to have Geoffrey on the first attempt would unbalance the numbers. Logistically there were enough supplies to cope with a summit team of four. Five would be too large and leave the reserve team too small. Geoffrey was kept back to join us – if there even was a chance for the second summit team. I doubted there ever would be.

The Lhotse team were also leaving this morning for their attempt. The three of them, Andy, Nasu, Ilgvar had looked focused the previous night. They had eaten well and retired to their tents early. Today was important for them as well.

I felt, though, that I was no longer in the élite. I had held my ground but had fallen at the last fence. I dreaded watching Mick and Neil leave in a few hours' time, without me. For the first time, I was no longer terrified of leaving; instead I was scared of staying.

At 5.00 a.m. I heard the first rustles from Mick's tent. This morning there was no 'Morning, Miguel' to be heard. We both knew things were different. I remembered Mick's mother assuring me that she knew everything would be okay, as long as we were together. The words rang in my mind. I retched from the fever, but kept it down. The illness was still rampant. I had no choice, I had to stay.

Ten minutes later Neil and Mick whispered to each other in hushed tones, as they put on their harnesses in the cold air of dawn. I thought of them looking at the sky above as we always did before leaving. At dawn it seems so fresh and new. I could hear them clapping their hands through their mitts to keep warm. I knew those feelings. I had done it with them so many times. They would want to get moving soon. Now was the coldest time of the night.

As I levered myself to the flap of my tent, my head spun. I cursed the fever. Mick and Neil were both crouching outside to say goodbye. I didn't know what to say.

'Just be careful, guys, eh? Just be careful,' I said, looking them each in the eye. 'Wise decisions, okay? If it turns nasty up there just get down. The mountain will always be there.' The words sounded hollow as I spoke. They knew all this. How I envied them.

Mick knelt, shook my hand and held it.

'You should be here, you know that? We'll all be up there together, okay?' he said quietly.

Yeah, I know – together, I thought.

At 5.35 a.m. the four of them left Base Camp. I could hear from my tent their boots crunching slowly and purposefully across the rocks towards the foot of the Icefall. The sound soon faded. All I could hear then was the wind beginning to pick up across the glacier as the dawn beckoned in a new day. I lay back down. My tent had never been so bleak.

*

The radio crackled to life. Ed rushed to the comms tent and arrived at the same time as Henry. They grabbed the handset.

'Say again, over,' Henry ordered sternly.

'Henry, it's Andy. Neil has passed out.'

I could hear them from my tent, five yards to the left.

'I'm with him and he's come round now – but I'm worried,' Andy added.

Only two hours into the Icefall, Neil had begun to feel dizzy. Ten minutes later, his body was suddenly overwhelmed with heaviness. He collapsed on the rope and fainted. He had come round but fainted twice more in five minutes. He didn't know why. They radioed in as they sat amongst the ice. They rested and made Neil drink; ten minutes later they started slowly on their way again.

By 8.30 a.m. they were all safely in Camp One. They put Neil in the tent and began brewing whilst they discussed what should happen. Andy and Henry talked quickly between themselves on the radio. Neil should come down. Something was wrong. He shouldn't be fainting.

Neil took the radio.

'Look, all is fine, I was a bit dehydrated and nervous and was probably pushing myself too hard in the Icefall. That's all. I feel fine now and okay to go on. What's more, there is a fine Baxter's soup on the go. I couldn't possibly leave it,' Neil said unconvincingly.

Secretly he knew he should descend. Going on when something is wrong is lethal. But Neil was not coming back. It was a risk to go on, but it was a risk he decided to take. We hoped his desire for the summit wouldn't cloud good judgement. I couldn't decide if he was being brave or stupid, or whether the two met somewhere in the middle – I wasn't sure. But I knew Neil would make the right decision. We trusted his judgement. He decided to go on and review everything from Camp Two. We knew what that meant. He was going up.

DIARY, 16 MAY, 1.30 P.M.
Base Camp has a silence about it that I have never known. I've never been the one staying behind before. It seems strangely empty. Tents are sealed and stay sealed. No humming or laughter can be heard from inside them. It's like a ghost town. Only the hacking coughs of Graham, Michael and I disturb the peace.

We all sat at lunch in silence. They both look weak from the illness. I think I am stronger than them and am slowly getting better, but I'm not sure. We're certainly no advert for 'healthy living in the mountains'. We are thin, weak and look a putrid shade of green. We shuffle around slowly to refill our bottles before retiring to our tents to lie down. I hate being like this. I can hear Michael groaning in his tent. It's frustration as much as anything. I can understand it. I groan as well, but only in my head.

This morning I whiled away the hours by trying to work

out how many meals Mick and I had eaten together in a row. It took my mind off thinking of them climbing higher and higher with every minute that passes. I worked it out to be 264 meals together in a row. It's no wonder that breakfast felt so strange. He wasn't there to be rude to me. I miss him. I told the others of my mathematical calculations; it raised a smile.

I just pray nothing happens to them up there. They are already showing signs of strain and nerves. Neil should not have fainted like that. They seem vulnerable. But I guess we all are. I realize this more and more the longer I stay on this mountain. The pretences of strength have gone.

I wrote on about our third day of being in Nepal that I feared for Mick's safety. I haven't felt it again until today. I pray he is safe.

It turned out to be a strangely prophetic feeling.

*

Later that day I felt stronger. That night I slept soundly all the way through. The antibiotics were working. My throat still felt painfully swollen, and my cough was heavy – but the phlegm was now looking clearer. Any exercise, though, even walking to the mess tent, left me hacking ferociously. My ribs ached. But somehow, deep inside, I knew that I was slowly getting better.

The next day the forecast came as a shock. We had received a severe warning of a cyclone approaching Everest; the news was that it would be forming into a typhoon. It was scheduled for the 21st or 22nd. It didn't give them much time up there. If it came on the 21st that would be the day they would hopefully be returning to Base Camp – in four days' time. If things went wrong and it came earlier, it left them no room to manoeuvre.

The typhoon was predicted to drop five feet of snow on the mountain. Such an amount would instantly make the place a death trap. Anyone still up there would, in the words of Henry, 'be unreachable. The snows would cut them off for good.' Mick and Neil's schedule looked tight. At Camp Two later that day they sat and tried to work things out. If it came on the 21st they would just be okay. It was another risk, but it was calculated. They would take it. Their planned rest day at Camp Two before heading up would have to be foregone. There wasn't time. The cyclone was moving ever closer.

That afternoon I made a difficult decision. I told Henry that I was fully fit and wanted to go.

'What's the point, Bear? When this cyclone comes, that's it. I know it's disappointing, but that's the nature of the game,' Henry said firmly.

'No, Henry, that's not it,' I replied.

'Drop it, Bear, okay? Just drop it.' He was tired as well. We had all been here a long time. He felt the frustration as well.

He came and talked to me later. He hadn't meant to snap at me. It was difficult for us all. We discussed the options available.

'If you were sensible you'd bite the bullet and realize there is nothing you can do but stay here. I don't believe you're fully fit, and if this ruddy storm comes we need to get everyone and as much kit as we can off the hill, as quickly as possible. Going up in the hope of a summit bid is a waste of time, Bear,' he said quietly.

'Don't worry about it being a waste of time,' I replied. 'If there's the smallest chance that the typhoon moves away I want to be in place. If it is still on course it will only take me five or six hours to get back from Camp Two if I have to. It will give me plenty of time,' I exaggerated.

'What's more,' I continued eagerly, 'I'll be in a position to help the guys on their way down, and if the typhoon comes I'll be able to carry one of the tents down. I'll be an extra hand.' It was the best argument I could offer. I needed to cough, but held it in. I wasn't going to win this battle, then lose the war by coughing and showing I was possibly not fit to go. My throat felt dry and the cough tickled irritatingly.

'Yeah, okay, if that's what you really want, there's no harm.' Henry chuckled, he liked a bit of fight. 'Go with Geoffrey, take two radios, and help me liaise with these guys on their bid. You're too impulsive, you know, and that can be dangerous. Joking apart, just don't expect too much. I'd be surprised if the typhoon doesn't come, you've seen the satellite photos. It's heading straight here.'

I slapped him on the shoulders, and hurried to see Geoffrey. He would be pleased. His patience had won through the first battle. I looked forward to climbing with him. For the first time in a long time I was looking forward to being in the ice.

*

I couldn't bring myself to call my parents that afternoon. I was breaking too many promises. But I longed to speak to someone. I rang one of my dearest friends, Judy Sutherland, a lady who lives in London with her two daughters. I imagined them in their cosy house with their phone ringing.

'Hello?' Judy replied softly.

'Judes, it's Bear ... yes, I'm at Base Camp. Judes ... can we pray? Would you mind?' I had rung her regularly over the years, often in times of difficulty; each time we had prayed. But this time it felt different; more serious. My spirit soared as we spoke together from the two extremes of our world. I felt, strangely, right next door.

By morning we would be gone. One last time up the Icefall. Up above into those clouds I had spent so many hours staring at from Base Camp; up into the unknown. As Mallory had said before he left for his last vain attempt over seventy years ago, 'from Everest we expect no mercy.'

I tried not to think of my parents or Shara. I didn't call them.

It would be too hard. I had promised Shara that we would go sailing when I got back, somewhere hot, really hot. I had to make it back for that. I felt driven again.

I still coughed like a nineteenth-century chimney sweep and was still swallowing antibiotics like they were smarties at my fourth birthday party, but I felt alive. I could see a glimmer of hope shining very faintly. It was all I had to hold on to. That storm had to change directions. East or west I didn't care. It just had to move.

7.25 P.M., 17 MAY (My last diary entry)
We are leaving in under ten hours now. The weeks of resting and waiting at Base Camp, at last, are over. But we are going up with nothing guaranteed. I still only feel about 60% fit, but it is now or never, I know this. The weather seems certain not to change; the typhoon is still on course, but yet despite all this I feel excited. I feel hopeful.

I just hope for the Good Lord's strength in everything ahead. I pray for His protection on the mountain, and I long for His health to fill my body. Thank you . . . oh, and a good night's sleep would be superb.

CHAPTER FOURTEEN

STONE'S THROW

▲

'Be not afraid of moving slowly, only of standing still.'
Chinese proverb

The two of us approached the lip at the top of the Icefall. I clipped my karabiner into the last rope that lay between us and Camp One. It was 7.20 a.m. We had made steady time. We were in no rush, we had all day to reach Camp Two in the distance. I coughed hard and phlegm filled my mouth. It was dark against the ice as I spat it out. Still infected, I thought.

I kicked my crampon into the ice wall and squeezed my body upwards. The points of my crampons held me firmly in place. The rope tightened above me; I rested for several seconds. As I neared the lip, I suddenly felt the strength go from my legs. I had never felt this before. My mind raced, I felt panic sweep over me. I struggled even to stay steady, pressed in against the wall. My legs could hardly hold me; they felt like jelly. I just leant in against the ice. 'I have to breathe, take it slow, relax.'

I slowly felt the panic subside, and the strength return. I shuffled up the last four feet of the ice wall and collapsed on the plateau at the top. I flicked the rope to tell Geoffrey behind me that the rope was now free. He clipped on and it sprang taut.

I never worked out why that had happened. Why I had suddenly felt so weak. My legs had just given up. It didn't bother me, apart from one thing. 'What about if it happened again on the final ice wall of the whole climb?'

This ice wall, some forty feet high, is simply called the Hillary Step – after Sir Edmund Hillary, the first man to have ever climbed it. At an altitude of some 28,700 feet, a terrifying ridge leads along from the South Summit. The Hillary Step is all that then blocks the way up to the true summit. If this 'Step' is climbed successfully then only a gentle 200-metre crest remains. This leads to the top of the world. I thought of that loss of strength. I could get so close, but then not have the energy to get up. The thought scared me. I tried to forget it.

We made our way slowly through the Cwm towards Camp Two. I noticed how much weaker I was. The cough was hampering me. My ribs hurt as I breathed in the thin air. Over and over I told myself, 'you're getting stronger, you're getting stronger.' I believed it, but still hurt.

At 3.30 p.m. we reached Camp Two. I felt drained and dizzy. We sat and drank with our rucksacks at our feet – our windsuits open to the waist to let the cool breeze in. The two Sherpas here, Ang and Thengba, plied us with hot lemon. I had missed their big smiles since I had last seen them. It was good to be here.

I knew that Mick and Neil would be somewhere between Camp Three and Camp Four. They would be breaking into new territories, going higher than at any point so far on the expedition. I wondered if we would be able to see them.

We had studied the route in detail. It was a treacherous traverse across the Lhotse Face and a long haul up what is known as the Geneva Spur. This spur leads to the hidden wasteland of the South Col, Camp Four. The Sherpas pointed out the climbers to us through the binoculars. They were dots on a vast canvas of white, far above us. Squatting exhausted in Camp Two, looking up through the glasses, I no longer envied them. I was too tired. I dozed in a haze against the canvas of the tent as the sun shone in the afternoon heat. I forgot everything for a brief time.

*

It was 11.00 p.m. that evening. I had tried to sleep but my mind raced. Mick and Neil would leave Camp Four any minute. They would be getting dressed. Not an easy task with four people in a tiny tent at 26,000 feet in the dark.

They didn't radio to say that they were leaving; I guessed that they were too busy. I wondered what the weather would be like up there. At Camp Two the wind blew steadily along the Cwm.

Up at Camp Four life was less pleasant; much less pleasant. Almost every climber who was hoping to attempt a summit bid was up at the South Col that evening. The longer than expected wait at Base Camp had made people anxious. When the break had come, they had all hurried up towards Camp Four. They reached it after a three-day climb. The disasters of 1996 had started with too many climbers attempting a summit bid at once. This seemed dangerously similar. Almost twenty-five climbers now waited that evening anxiously at Camp Four.

The danger would come in having hold-ups on the ropes at the Hillary Step. This had to be avoided. Bodies cannot survive the cold and the waiting at those heights. What's more, people didn't carry the oxygen to be able to wait for hours. Once you left Camp Four you were alone and on borrowed time. There would not be time to wait for others on the ropes ahead. Neil and Mick knew this. Neil had witnessed it before at first hand. With this in mind, they left ten minutes before the others.

Whilst at Camp Three the day before, Mick had found that

our ice-axes we had left there to secure the tent with were now frozen deep beneath the Face, covered by the storm. Mick spent two hours digging frantically around the tent, trying to get them out. He desperately needed his axe higher up. Exhausted, he eventually had to give up looking. It was impossible to break the ice. Nothing would budge in those temperatures. We had lost the axes but because of them the tent had miraculously survived the blizzards. Our axes deep under the ice had held it firm.

The storm had pounded Camp Three severely. It had taken its toll, especially with the other more exposed tents. The winds had literally ripped some of them from their holdings. The remains could be seen by us from Camp Two through the binoculars. Scattered and torn canvas flapped out from the Face. Those teams had been forced to carry more tents up to replace them. It was heavy and burdensome work and used up precious energy. Energy that everyone would need desperately above that height, as they entered the Death Zone.

At Camp Four Neil had tried to help Mick find something to substitute as an ice-axe. The most exposed col in the world is no place to hunt for anything. The danger of coming across one of the many bodies lying nearby is high. You never want to look too closely at anything. The place has seen too much. Besides, the wind blows so severely that time out of the tent has to be kept to a minimum. Still, though, they hunted around under old ripped tents for something that could act as an axe for Mick. They found an old snow stake and a piece of wood. It was all there was and the weather was getting worse. It would have to do. In the tent they bound the two pieces together. It was far from ideal.

Mick was at the end of the tent and thus found himself in charge of the boiling water. Four people with a mass of equipment squashed in a tiny tent made the job impossibly hard. People shuffled to make some room.

Suddenly the container of boiling water exploded. It had somehow formed a seal that had locked tight as the pressure built up. Scalding water now sprayed out of control over Mick. He ripped his clothes off in seconds. He was annoyed more than he was hurt; he felt it was a bad omen. His clothes were soaked. He cursed being up there. Later he said, 'I wondered at this point if I should be there at all.'

*

They dozed and continued melting ice until 10.00 p.m. They would leave some time in the next two hours. It would take that long at that height to get ready. They nervously began to sort their equipment out.

At 11.10 p.m. they left Camp Four. The full moon had been on 11 May; the ideal summit time. By now, though, over a week later, the moon was fading. They would need all the light their headtorches could provide. But batteries don't last long in those conditions.

The jet-stream winds were silent, the night was still, and they left earlier than intended. They wanted to be ahead of all the other teams up there. It was a good decision.

Leaving Camp Four, Mick felt unsure about his oxygen supply. His mind wandered vaguely as to a reason why. He reached behind him and checked the flow-rate gauge again. It read 2.5 litres/ min. That was right. He let it fall back down to his side. He tightened his mitts again and carried on. He knew he was going slowly. Something wasn't right. But there was nothing he could do in the dark and in those temperatures. It was well below −30°C.

Five hours later, the trail of climbers was snaking its way slowly up the unroped ice, towards the Balcony Ledge at 27,500 feet. At 1,500 feet below the summit, this is the first objective to reach after leaving the Col. They were moving slower than expected. Mick's headtorch, despite having had a fresh battery in it, had now failed. It had got dimmer and dimmer, until he was eventually left to grope his way up the ice in the darkness. The lights of those ahead were all that showed him the route.

At 6.15 a.m. dawn arrived. Sitting on the Balcony Ledge, they changed oxygen canisters. They removed their goggles, exposing their faces to the elements for a few seconds. Neil snapped the ice that hung from his mask; it was frozen condensation. Then their faces were hidden again, as the breathing apparatus was refitted and the tanks heaved onto their backs. Nobody spoke.

The weather that had looked so promising at midnight seemed now to be turning. Few even noticed. Michael the Danish climber, who had been hoping to climb solo and without oxygen, was no longer there. He had turned around at 5.00 a.m. Oxygen is what keeps the body warm up high. Without it Michael was slowly freezing. He knew he would die if he carried on. He bravely turned back; his attempt was over.

The climb above Camp Four is where it all counts. It is the great leveller and the great divider. So many climbers manage to fight the Icefall, the Cwm, even the severity of the Lhotse Face, yet it is this part, the final part, that makes the difference. It is here that people fall away. It is here that all the real work happens. Michael had tried, and no doubt he would try again in future years. For now, though, he was exhausted. His body could take no more. He was experienced enough to recognize this. Turning back for Camp Four is a frighteningly difficult decision. Michael had the courage to take it.

Other climbers were also forced back. Some were struggling with their oxygen, some knew deep down what was, and what wasn't, possible. These also turned back. They say that it is at the actual gates of a new world that most turn back. It was true; many were now turning back before it got too late. One can argue that they were the sensible ones.

Another climber slipped after half an hour of the ascent; he tumbled down the hard ice to the Col 100 feet below. He had broken two ribs and struggled back to the tents. He was lucky to have been still so close. Had that happened higher up it might have been very different. He sat the time out anxiously at the Col, waiting for news from those still climbing. It was to be a long night.

Mick and Neil still pushed on. Carla was slow behind them but continuing at all costs. Her courage was showing itself. She hung on. Allen was also quietly climbing. He didn't say a word but stayed firmly with them. By 7.00 a.m., back at Camp Two, we had still heard nothing.

Various Sherpas were putting in some stretches of rope below the South Summit. It was hard work on the steep ice face, which was now covered in loose powder snow. None of the route so far had been roped. Rope was heavy and had to be carried, and was therefore used very sparingly and only on the most exposed sections.

Everyone knew the dangers up there, but the altitude seemed to numb people's minds. Nobody cared. Climbers tottered dangerously on the Face beneath the South Summit, their crampons scraping loosely across the ice under the snow. Any small section of rope was clutched at frantically. In those conditions it is almost impossible to make ropes 100% safe. They are all dodgy, but people didn't care. If they saw a rope, it spelt safety to them. Their minds weren't capable of interpreting them as anything else.

At 10.05 a.m. Neil reached the South Summit. The true summit was within his grasp and he knew it. He sat and looked in amazement at the view ahead. He could see the final ridge that led to the Hillary Step, and above this the gentle slope that would lead the final 200 metres to the summit. His heart raced. He knew that this was his chance. In 1996 the disasters had robbed him of the chance to go above Camp Four. Two years on he was here again, only this time the summit was within reach. Nothing was going to take it from him. He felt strong, and glanced hungrily along the ridge ahead. He waited anxiously as the lead Sherpas and several American climbers arrived. Mick should be here soon, he thought.

Something told Neil that things were not going right. In the blur of high altitude, the realization of what was happening slowly began to dawn on him. Over the next ten minutes the dream that had eluded Neil once was going to elude him again. Anger welled up inside him as he heard various American climbers arguing. Their voices were slow and laboured, but the message was clear. Somewhere along the way there had been a misunderstanding over who had what rope. Suddenly, here at 28,700 feet, some 335 feet below the summit of Everest, after so much work and risk – the reality dawned. There was no more rope.

Whose fault it was, and why, will always remain a mystery. These things happen in the world above 26,000 feet. It is a scary and surreal place. No one had intended the error, but it had happened. These professional men were suddenly reduced to floundering, exhausted wrecks. There was nothing they could do. It would be impossible to continue along the corniced ridge without any rope. It would be suicide. Continuing was not even an option. The head Sherpa there, the great Babu, confirmed this. Even Hillary had used rope here. Without any, it was too dangerous.

The snow was now pouring off the summit again. The winds were returning. The sound alone told them that; that deep, penetrating roar. They cowered in the snow on the South Summit. They had one choice and they had to act quickly. They had been motionless for too long. They had to retreat. Neil stared through his goggles at the summit only a few hundred feet above.

He slowly let his head fall forward. All he felt was an emptiness. He turned and never looked back. He started down a different man.

The radio call came ten minutes later from Neil, from just under the South Summit.

'We've had to turn back. There's been a screw-up with the rope,' he muttered slowly. He sounded drained. 'We've just left the South Summit. We're all okay. I'll call in from the Col. Neil out.'

Henry at Base Camp could only hear the crackle of the radio. The full message couldn't reach him. I relayed it to him from my tent at Camp Two. At random times on the mountain, the weather prevents the radio signal travelling very far. It was one of these times. At Camp Two, even I could only just hear. I sat in my tent and wondered what the hell was happening up there.

Things then began to go very wrong and, as is the nature on high mountains, when this starts, it can all begin to happen very quickly. This was no exception.

*

I was woken from my doze at 10.50 a.m. as the radio flared into life with the sound of a voice. It was Mick's. He sounded weak and distant. He was calling me.

'Bear at Camp Two, this is Mick, do you copy?' he mumbled.

'Roger, Miguel, go ahead,' I replied. I sat up and held the radio close to me.

It crackled furiously and all I heard was something about oxygen.

'Mick, say again. What about your oxygen? Over.'

There was a short pause as he fumbled with the controls through his mitts.

'I've run out. I haven't got any.' The words echoed round the tent.

His tank must have been leaking since he had first used it, I thought. He would have been suffocating as he climbed. I couldn't understand what had gone wrong with his tank. They had been checked and double-checked. I tried to find an answer. No one, though, would ever know, it didn't matter. All that mattered was my friend, my best friend was now dying some 6,000 feet above me and there was nothing I could do.

'Keep talking to me, Mick. Don't stop. Who is with you? Mick, tell me,' I said firmly. I had to keep him talking. If he stopped talking and lost consciousness I knew he would never come down. If he couldn't move up there, then I had to get a picture of who else was there. It might be his only chance.

'Allen's here. He's got no oxygen either. We're sitting here . . . It's not good, Bear.'

I knew that. I felt hopeless. We had to find Neil. Their survival depended on someone being above them.

'Mick, come in, Mick?' No reply came. 'Mick, do you read?'

A minute later his voice came back on the radio.

'Getting ready to assume the "dying in Asia" position, Bear,' he slowly said. We had joked for years about the 'dying in Asia' position, whenever we felt things were becoming dire. It had only ever been a joke. In our wildest dreams, though, we had never imagined a conversation like this. 'Mick, for God's sake. Mick?' I weakly replied.

'Bear, I reckon Allen has ten minutes to live. I don't know what to do.' Mick cut off. I tried to get him back on the radio but no reply came. Nothing came from him for twenty minutes. They were the longest minutes of my life.

I sat alone in my tent. Geoffrey didn't have a radio. I felt lost and feeble. Mick, come on, move, please, I pleaded with him in my mind. I prayed he could hear.

*

Mick describes what happened up there:

As I approached the South Summit, I sensed that something was wrong. People were turning back. I couldn't understand what was happening. As a climber passed me coming down, he told me the news. We would have to turn back. The words, I remember, shook me. My mind swirled. 'Turn around now?' I reeled in disbelief. The climber carried on down, and I was left with no choice but to face the reality. For some reason it was over. I turned slowly around.

I decided to check my oxygen levels before descending. It was a precaution only. I reached for my gauge. I stared at it. I tapped it. It must be wrong. It read – 'empty'.

This was ridiculous. I should still have ten hours left. I stood against the ice, stunned. I checked again. At 28,500 feet, though, you do not argue with your gauge. You can't afford to. I had to head down fast. Within minutes, though, I was without oxygen. I sucked frantically on the mask. Nothing came out.

The effect of having no oxygen is not dramatic, you do not collapse to the floor as if suffocating. Instead, slowly, your thinking, movement and coordination become more difficult. I just sat and clung to the few ropes in place below the South Summit.

Slowly and uncertainly I started down them. A yard at a time, sitting on my arse. I didn't have the energy to stand. It was a slow process and people started overtaking me on their descent. You would expect this to lead to complete panic, given the situation. But no panic came. This is one of the most dangerous things about being at altitude, the lack of oxygen causes a sort of drunken acceptance that is almost impossible to snap out of. People asked if I was okay. Strangely I found myself saying that I was fine.

On reaching the end of the roped section, I found Allen slumped in the foetal position in the snow. He also had no oxygen. He seemed in an even worse state than me. It was then that I radioed for help and spoke to Bear at Camp Two.

Only a few climbers were still above us. Neil, one of our Sherpas called Pasang, another Sherpa named Babu and two Swedish climbers, Tomas and Tina. Tomas and his wife Tina were on their third attempt to reach the summit of Everest. In all, they had spent almost nine months over three years in the pursuit of their dream. Once more it had eluded them. They were among the last to be turning back. It was them and their Sherpa Babu who found the slumped figures of Allen and myself.

When they came across us, huddled in the cold snow, they knew they had to act fast. Time was running out. By pure chance Babu was carrying a spare canister of oxygen. Something that is very rarely ever done. Extra weight is not something that one wants up there. But we were lucky; the great Babu was carrying some extra – for an emergency. Here it was.

We had lent them some oxygen before at Camp Three, so they owed us a favour. I now needed it with my life. Babu offered it, before I could ask. They saw what was happening and needed no prompting. They saved my life.

Neil and Pasang then located an emergency cache of oxygen nearby. They gave one to Allen and forced us both to our feet. They made us move. I staggered on like a drunk. I was too tired to care.

Having been without oxygen now for over an hour my body had a serious oxygen deficit. I swayed in and out of consciousness as my body tried to absorb this fresh tank. I was fighting for my survival. I was only able to manage two or three steps before my legs would buckle beneath me with exhaustion. I could never have imagined being in this situation. The exhaustion ensured that I was not aware of what was going on. All I remember was desperately trying to stand and move. Yet my legs were like jelly, and no amount of will-power seemed to override this. I was amazed at my own weakness.

At the Balcony a fresh oxygen cache awaited us. I sat and gasped into the mask. I turned the regulator up to four litres a minute. It was an extravagance I could now afford, Camp Four was in sight through the wispy clouds far below. Only 1,400 feet of descent stood between us and the relative sanctuary of our tents. It wasn't far now.

Tomas, Tina and Babu, by lending oxygen to Mick, undoubtedly saved his life up there; and without Neil and Pasang's help, Allen's story might have been very different. They had all showed the sort of courage that the mountains demand. Without their help, history might have claimed another two victims to Everest's toll.

From the Balcony they staggered down together slowly. It would soon be over; Camp Four appeared again briefly in the mist. The tents looked like specks below.

Slow and tired, his mind wandering in and out of a haze of consciousness, Mick maintains that he remembers little about this part. He descended deliriously, his feet shuffling like those of an old man, down the icy slopes. Mistakes were too expensive up here, but he no longer cared. He stumbled on. He had to get back to Camp Four.

They were so close, yet were still in such dangerous terrain. Descending sheet blue ice without any ropes is hazardous at sea-level, up there it was lethal. To the east of the Col lies the treacherous Kanshung Face; to the west, the Lhotse Face. Each at least 5,000 feet in height. A careless slip would kill. Mick staggered down, the drug of thin air overwhelming him.

Neil could do nothing as it all happened so suddenly; he could only watch on in horror. It was all so quick.

Mick describes the next few minutes:

Neil had insisted that I descend with Pasang, both of us roped together. Pasang was the fittest up here and most able to help. He leashed a rope between us; I hardly even noticed. Some time later, maybe twenty minutes into the descent, I just suddenly felt the ground surge beneath me.

There was a sudden rush of acceleration as the loose top snow, warmed by the sun of day, slid away under me. There was nothing I could do. I hurtled down the sheer Face on my back, skidding along the ice below. Then I made the fatal error of trying to dig my crampons in to slow the fall. The force with which we travelled catapulted us through the air in a violent somersault, as the points of my crampons caught in the ice. The two of us, still roped together, accelerated even faster, the horizon nothing but a vague swirl around me. I felt that this would be my end. I knew what was below on either side.

I thumped back onto the ice, still on my front hurtling downwards. I lost all sense of anything at that point. I shut my eyes. I felt the undulations of the ice rippling across my chest. Then suddenly in a moment of relief I felt myself slowing in some deeper snow. But only a second later I was accelerating away again. I resigned myself to the fact that I would die somewhere down the Kanshung or Lhotse Face. I didn't know which; it didn't matter.

For a second, and the final time, I felt my body slow down. I bounced and twisted over a few rocks then slid to a halt on a ledge. I just lay there motionless trying to take in what had happened. I would not open my eyes. I lay there shaking for what seemed an eternity.

Suddenly I heard voices around me. They were muffled and strange. They were ... Iranian. I couldn't believe my ears. I tried to scream to them but nothing came out. They surrounded me, clipped me in and held me. I started to cry and cry.

They escorted Mick, shaking and in tears, back to the camp only 200 metres away. Others found Pasang also shaken. Somehow they had become disconnected in the fall. No one could understand how. No one cared. They were safe. That was all that mattered. Neither, miraculously, were seriously injured. Luck or fate, who knows? An hour later they both sat cramped and shaken in the tent. Mick passed his mug to Pasang, his hands still shaking. He managed a small smile.

When they reached us at Camp Two, forty-eight hours later, they were shattered and shaken. They looked like different men. Mick moved in a daze, slowly across the glacier. He didn't even seem to have the energy to look up, to look at us. He was lost in his world of fatigue; deep fatigue. They collapsed by the tents. Neil smiled; he had done all that had been required of him, and they were safe. Mick just sat and held his head in his hands. It said it all. It had been a long three days.

The Lhotse team were also now back at Camp Two; they also were weak and drained. They had fought for some twenty-two hours from Camp Three, up towards the gulley that would lead to the summit of Lhotse. Deep snow had forced these giants of men back with the summit only a few hundred feet above. They also had been plagued by problems with their oxygen sets. It is the nature of the conditions. However robust and well tested everything is, nothing is guaranteed up there.

They talked little back at Camp Two. They had given their all, but still had been turned away empty handed. I felt shocked at how resilient these vast mountains were, and I felt humbled at how little all these efforts had come to. I don't think that I had ever realized just how truly hostile these mountains can be.

*

That night Mick and I talked together, quietly and slowly. I admired Mick more than ever. I longed to have seen all he had seen up there, even with the price he had paid. He was still shaken and wore the scars of a man who has survived a different place all together. Even his clothes told the story. His windsuit was ripped in eight places, huge gashes appeared where the material lay open. His down trousers oozed feathers from rips all along them, and he had lost every bit of spare kit he had – gloves, waterbottles, photographic equipment, fleece hoodover and head-torch – all gone. He had returned from his attempt, robbed of everything. The mountain had claimed it. But he is a survivor and late that evening as we prepared to sleep he prodded me. I sat up and saw a small smile spread across his face.

'Bear, next time let me choose where to go on holiday, okay? Your choice was lousy.' As he spoke, I began to laugh with all my being. I needed to, so much had been kept inside. We hugged. Thank God he's alive, I thought.

*

The next morning they slowly left for Base Camp. They desperately needed rest. Their attempt was over. Mick just wanted to be safe. That was all he wanted. I watched them head out into the glacier, and hoped that I had made the right decision to stay at Camp Two.

We had received a forecast at dawn. Henry had announced that the typhoon was slowing and that it wouldn't be here for two days. By tomorrow if it was still moving towards us I assured him I would come down. But while there was a hope that in the next few days it might move away, I insisted on staying up here – ready. It was a difficult decision, but somehow it felt right. I sat and watched as they slowly became blurs on the ice.

Geoffrey disagreed with my decision and had left to go down with the others. I was the only one of the team to stay. It was risky being up here with the likelihood of a typhoon at any moment. I knew that I wouldn't be able to go up until we knew exactly what was happening with it, and that wouldn't be for a few days. On top of this, the longer you stay at Camp Two, the weaker your body becomes. It is a fine balance between acclimatizing and deteriorating. Too long up here and I might find myself without the strength to go higher. For a place of convalescence, Camp Two, at 21,200 feet, was a miserable choice. But I stayed and I was never quite sure why.

I sat and watched until they were all gone from sight. It was now just Thengba and Ang in one tent, and me in another. We had one radio, one pack of cards, a few torn pages from my Spanish New Testament, and a sack of dehydrated food. It was already my fourth day at Camp Two. I had no idea how long my body would keep what little strength it still had.

CHAPTER FIFTEEN

ALONE

▲

'Man's loneliness is but his fear of life.'

I threw the playing cards across the floor of my tent in frustration. It was a stupid game anyway; I hated Patience. Two days ago I decided that if I got all my cards 'out', then the weather would give me a chance – if I didn't then the typhoon would move in. I had lost, so made the contest the best of three. Two days later it was 37–38 to me in the lead, but victory still just eluded me. I lay back down and just stared at the roof of the tent. My socks swayed gently as they dried on the string, slung across the poles. I flicked them impatiently.

These past few days had been the longest days I had known. My watch seemed to have slowed down, and the monsoon drew ever closer to the mountain, beckoning in the time when Everest would be buried again under five feet of snow.

My days revolved around the midday radio call from Base Camp, when they would give me the forecast. The call was scheduled daily for 12 noon. Keeping it to certain times saved battery power, and batteries were crucial. I always slept with them down my sleeping bag. It was the warmest place for them and where they would last the longest. I waited anxiously for the forecast today. It was only 9.15 a.m. and already I was fiddling with the radio; checking the squelch just in case.

I desperately longed for news that the typhoon would move away. Yesterday it was reported to be stationary. Today would be vital. I waited anxiously. I knew that we were running out of that precious commodity: time. I checked my watch again.

At 12.02 p.m. the radio came to life.

'Bear at Camp Two, it's Neil. All okay?' I heard the voice loud and clear; the reception was good today.

'Yeah, in the loosest sense of the word,' I replied, smiling.

'I'm worried you may be going slowly insane up there, am I right?' Neil joked.

'Insane? Me? What do you mean?' I replied. Neil chuckled into the radio.

'Daft,' he replied. 'Now listen, I've got a forecast and an e-mail that has come through for you – from your family. Do you want to hear the good or the bad news first?'

'Go on, let's get the bad news over with,' I replied.

'Right, the bad news. Well, the weather's still shit. The typhoon is on the move and heading this way. If it is still on course tomorrow you've got to get down. I'm sorry. We all hate it.'

He had said it straight. I paused before replying. I knew he would say something like that. I had prayed so hard, yet it hadn't worked. I shook my head.

'. . . and the good news?' I asked dismissively.

'Your Mum has sent a message. Says all the animals are well.' Click.

'Well, go on, that can't be it. What else?'

'Well, they think you're still at Base Camp. Probably best that way, you know. Otherwise your mother may just suddenly turn up,' Neil chuckled.

'I'll speak to you tomorrow,' I replied. 'Pray for some change. It will be our last chance, eh?'

'Roger that, Bear . . . oh, and don't start talking to yourself. Out.'

'How's Miguel getting along . . . Hello, Neil.' He hadn't heard me.

I dismantled the radio and put the batteries down my bag again. I had another twenty-four hours to wait. It was these moments just after the radio call which felt the longest. I lay back down and shuffled the cards once more.

*

That afternoon I walked for twenty minutes up the glacier to the Singaporean Camp Two. I wanted to see if I could borrow some cough medicine. I had finished all mine but still I was being kept up most of the night heaving and spluttering. I wondered who would be in their camp.

Only a few Singaporeans remained now at Camp Two. The rest had returned to Base Camp some days ago, after their summit bid had failed that fateful night that Mick had fallen. The two who were still here undid their tent flap. One of them was the leader of the team. We sat and chatted for a while. It was good to have company.

'No, Bear, I'm not going any higher, it's my ribs. They're screwed,' the leader said. 'It's all this coughing. I've managed to actually crack two ribs, I've been coughing so hard. It hurts to breathe. It won't let me go any higher.'

I sympathized with him as I coughed hard into my jacket sleeve. My own ribs were taking their own pounding up here. I asked if they had any extra cough medicine.

They produced a vat, the size of about four waterbottles. Across the front in felt-tip was written 'cough medicine'. My eyes lit up. I had been swilling my cough medicine from a tiny pot, the size of a shot-glass. It had made no difference. I filled a big mug full, chatted a bit more then shuffled carefully back down to my own tent. This should cure me, I thought, I mean, just look at the colour of it. It reminded me of diesel oil, but it should do. I took a giant swig and smiled as it soothed the inflamed back of my throat.

*

As I wrestled with life and solitude at 21,200 feet up the mountain, back in England at Mick's parents' home all was very different.

Mick's father had been following the team's progress closely on the internet, from his office. Various other teams were keeping their web-sites updated daily, and by the time of the summit attempt a few days earlier they were updating almost hourly. Such was the advance of the Americans' communication that during the confusion everyone had encountered at the South Summit (at 10.00 a.m. on 19 May), Mick's father, Patrick, was receiving live reports on their progress. He knew his son was up there at the same time and shared in the disappointment when he heard they were being forced back, having got so close. Nothing, though, prepared him for what he heard next.

An American report came through saying that a 'British climber had fallen', nothing else was known. The words flashed up on Patrick's screen. He stared in horror. It was 8.45 a.m. in the City, the heart of London.

For the next three days he heard nothing more on the incident. Why? What had happened? Couldn't they say? Had someone died? Was it Mick? His mind raced with the possibility, the strong possibility, that the 'British climber' reported to have fallen might have been Mick. Our satellite phone was switched off at Base Camp. Everyone there was too busy trying to get Neil and Mick off the mountain safely. Patrick could get no more news.

He dared not tell his wife, Sally. He couldn't. He describes those days and nights as the most 'agonizing experience imaginable'. He is a man of great strength but even he was shaken. He recounts: 'What was so hard was not being able to share it with Sally. I couldn't, as I didn't know for certain. I couldn't work, sitting there, looking at the screen in front of me, the screen that had given me the news originally – it made me feel sick. I dreaded facing the reality. The possibility that our only son was dead.'

It was not until Mick eventually returned to Base Camp that he was able to ring his father and tell him he was safe. Mick had had no idea that Patrick knew anything about it. Relief swept across his father's face. A relief that only a father, I guess, can know. Mick assured him all was okay, and announced that he would not return again up the mountain. Ever. He knew only too well how lucky he had been. He took off his Everest crampons for the very last time. He thought of me still up at Camp Two, and looked knowingly up the mountain.

Meanwhile, some 3,700 feet above Base Camp, I waited for that next and final forecast, longing with all my heart for a chance. That chance was now in the hands of the weather.

That night in my tent I could hear the deep rumble of the jet-stream winds above me. The sun had disappeared down beyond the bottom end of the Western Cwm. It left me all alone. I curled tight inside my bag and closed my eyes. I really missed the others.

*

I crept out of my tent long before dawn. The glacier looked cold and hostile as it swept away to the west. I zipped my down jacket up and stumbled across the ice to have a crap. It was 4.30 a.m. I waited for the sun to rise whilst sitting in the porch of my tent and wondered what it would bring today.

Thengba and Ang were still asleep in their tent. I wished that I was also.

I couldn't believe that all the work we had done so far, boiled down to today. I prayed for the umpteenth time, for that answer to my prayers. The typhoon had to move or peter out. It had to. My mind wandered to being up there; up there climbing in that deathly land above Camp Three. That land where, as I had read, only the 'strong and lucky survive'. Please. I dozed off dreaming about it.

By ten o'clock I was ready on the radio. I rechecked the strength of the batteries. They were nice and warm. I looked at my watch again. Come on.

This time they called early. It was 11.58 a.m. I jumped for the set.

'Yep, Base Camp, I've got you,' I said anxiously.

'Bear, you dog. It's come.' The voice was excited. It was Henry speaking.

'The forecast has said that at 11.00 p.m. last night the cyclone began revolving, and has spun off to the east. They think it will clip the Eastern Himalaya tomorrow, but nowhere near here. We've got a break. They say that the jet-stream winds are lifting again in two days. How do you think you feel?'

'We're rocking, yep, good, I mean fine ... I can't believe it. Alrighty.' I punched the air and yelped. Thengba came scurrying across to my tent and peered in inquisitively. I howled again. Thengba grinned and climbed in. I couldn't stop patting him violently on the back. He laughed out loud, showing all his two black teeth. He kind of understood. It had been a long five days.

Neil was already preparing at Base Camp to come back up. Another chance had suddenly opened and he had to take it. It might be his last attempt ever. He had openly said that if he was turned back this year as well, he would never return. Already he had climbed to 28,700 feet and now only a few days later he was preparing to go up again. It was unheard of. People said that his body would not be able to cope. They didn't know, though, what was going on inside him. Just one last attempt. My last one, he thought. And this time something excited him more than ever before.

Mick was staying firmly at Base Camp. He was still in shock. He needed rest. He helped Geoffrey and Neil pack up one final time. If this failed we all knew our attempt was over. The monsoon hovered down in the Nepalese plains, awaiting its grand entrance. In one week's time, we knew it would all be over.

During the course of the day, both the depleted Singapore team and Bernardo had left Camp Two towards Camp Three. It meant that they would be a day ahead of us in the attempt. This was good. They would have valuable information on the conditions above the South Col. I prayed that they would be safe. Those of us still on the mountain were a small group now.

*

By 7.00 p.m. that evening, Camp Two was again full of friends. Neil and Geoffrey were there along with Michael and Graham, both now recovered from their illness. Carla and Allen had also come back up for a second attempt. The weariness of trying again showed dreadfully in Carla. Her body was crying out for relief. She looked understandably gaunt and frail. Allen took two hours longer than everyone else to arrive. The fatigue was showing in him as well.

The Lhotse team were also back. Andy and Ilgvar would try once more. Nasu, alternatively, had decided to leave Base Camp the day before to return to Kathmandu. I wouldn't see him again now. He believed he had actually reached the summit of Lhotse on the first ascent, as he was ahead of the other two. Andy didn't really believe this. He knew that the summit had been still too far away. An air of doubt hung around it all; but no one would ever really know.

I was so relieved to see Neil arrive at Camp Two. He smiled and we hugged. We both knew the chance that was ahead of us – words weren't needed. I had missed him especially.

Darkness came quickly or maybe time just seemed to race by, now that others were here. It was funny how the minutes had crept by so slowly for almost nine weeks in total. Nine weeks I had waited for this chance. And now that it was here, the minutes didn't seem to be able to go slowly enough. Despite the excitement, part of me dreaded what lay before us. In less than ten hours, the struggle would begin. I knew the next four days, God willing, to the summit and back to Camp Two, would be undoubtedly the hardest of my life. But there was a purpose to it. At its end was my dream that I had held on to for so long. The summit of Everest, I felt, was waiting for us.

I shared my tent that had been all mine for so long with Michael, the Canadian. As I had got to know him over the past two months I had come to like him a lot. He had a tenderness under his outdoor rugged image that I couldn't help but warm to. He was as scared as I was. I could tell.

He busied himself nervously in the tent; sorting out his kit, rechecking each item meticulously. Counting glucose tablets, checking the length of straps for waterbottles that would hang round our necks (the best place to stop them freezing), checking the simple things which are always the first to go wrong: spare gloves, spare goggles, tape, blister kit, ready-tied prussik knots for emergency rope work, you name it, it all came out and was checked. It took our minds off things.

We shifted around tentatively, trying to give each other some room. I knew Michael needed space to be alone before it all started, we all needed it, but we had to try and cope with what we had. I understood. I tried to quietly rest as he sorted his things out. I lay back on my rucksack and closed my eyes. I felt that mixture of fierce excitement and deep trepidation. I couldn't quite believe what now lay before us.

The words that my grandfather had written to me in one of the letters that Ed had brought when he arrived, rang in my head.

They were powerful words to me. At ninety-two years old, he had a wisdom that cut right to my core.

'Keep on in there, your struggles are a triumph for guts and Godliness.'

The words guts and Godliness struck me hard. It was all that I aspired to. I knew somehow my grandfather understood me.

That night we tried desperately to sleep. From 5.00 a.m. the next day, the biggest battle of my life would begin. I found it hard to even pray.

Michael and I shuffled nervously all night. I peed at least four times. Michael chuckled as I rolled over with my pee-bottle and filled it again.

At 4.45 a.m. I started to get ready. It was invariably always the worst time; the time when you felt warm and cosy and were trying to shake the heaviness from your eyes. By 5.15 a.m. I crawled out of our tent and breathed deeply in the morning chill. It would allow Michael some space to get ready.

We tried to eat some porridge oats with hot water. I added masses of sugar to try and make it taste a bit better, but still I could only manage a few gulps. My mind was elsewhere. I was worried that so long up here would have made me weak, that my body would be drained from living at Camp Two, and would have used up my vital reserves. But I had to be strong enough now; I knew that I would soon find out.

At 5.45 a.m. we all met on the ice and sat in silence as we put our crampons on. I had done this so many times in the last two months, yet this morning it felt like my first time. As we started off, leaving Ang and Thengba watching from their tent, I hoped with all my heart to see them safely again four days later. Much would have happened for better or for worse by then. The glacier ahead of us leading up to the Bergschrund and the Lhotse Face seemed eerily still. I felt a mild sickness inside. It was nerves.

My cough was still there but irritated me less now, or maybe

I was just used to it; resigned to the discomfort. The angle steepened as we neared the ropes of the ice above us. The Lhotse Face loomed away far above.

In silence we started up towards Camp Three. I hoped it wouldn't take as long as last time. I hoped to be able to reach it in around five hours.

By 10.00 a.m. we were well into the climb. We moved methodically and carefully up the blue ice. It crunched, then splintered beneath our crampons as they gripped firmly with each step we took. I leant back on my harness and reached into my windsuit. I pulled out several glucose tablets. They tasted sweet in my dry mouth. I swigged at the waterbottle that hung around my neck and looked around.

Five and a half hours of climbing, and the tents were only 100 feet away. It still took twenty-five minutes to reach them. I climbed with Graham. We were both slow and tired. It showed with him especially. He swore under his breath. It was all taking so long. I tried to keep patient and just keep moving slowly. The principle was that if you were moving up, however slowly, you would eventually reach your destination. It is just that the process hurt so much.

We collapsed into two tents. Neil, Graham, Michael and I in one, Geoffrey, Carla and Allen in the other. We settled down to the odious task of trying to melt ice. The gas stove had blocked again; frozen solid. I undid it, rubbed it, and put it back together. The flame flickered and then lit.

I thought of my ice-axe buried under the ice outside the tent. I had known that it would be impossible to retrieve; Mick had told me so. I had borrowed an axe instead from Pascuale,* an American climber on the mountain. I had picked up his spare

* Pascuale Scaturro successfully reached the summit of Mount Everest late in May 1998.

axe the day before from Camp Two, assuring him jokingly over the radio that I would stay alive to return it. He made me promise. He was a friend and knew the risks up there. 'Be careful' had been his last words to me.

Up in the tents at Camp Three we tried to get on with things quietly. Living in these close quarters, under pressure, when you are scared, tired and thirsty, is a sensitive business. My time in the Army had helped me in learning how to live with people in confined spaces like this. I had spent enough cold nights in a patrol huddled together waiting for dawn. This was much the same – only a little higher! I needed this training now as we settled down for the night, squeezed in the tent, tucked into the ledge in the ice here at 24,500 feet. The other thing the Army had taught me was about going that extra mile. About pushing yourself that little bit more, and how the finish is always just after the point at which you most want to give up. I reminded myself of this as I lay cramped between all the kit and stinking bodies. I would need that discipline more than ever before now. That extra mile; that little bit further.

Carla, despite our advice to the contrary, had insisted on coming up with us to Camp Three. Henry at Base Camp had refused to allow her up. He knew that she was too tired. She had given her word that she would only go up with us from Camp Three if the winds died down. Henry knew that in anything but perfect conditions she would not survive. Her body was completely drained after her first attempt. The forecast would be given to us at 6.00 p.m. at Camp Three; it would decide Carla's fate. If the winds higher up were above 40 knots, she would have to turn back.

The radio crackled with the voice of Henry from Base Camp.

'The winds are going to be rising, guys. You've still got a window, but the conditions are far, far from ideal. I'm sorry, Carla, but you are going to have to come down. I can't risk you up there. It's too dangerous,' Henry announced. There was a long pause.

'No way, no way. I'm going up. I don't care. I'm going up,' Carla retorted angrily. 'You can't make me come down. Not after I've come so far.'

Henry erupted down the radio. 'Carla, listen, we had a deal. If the winds were strong you would come down. I didn't even want you up there but you insisted, but now the ride ends. We had a deal and you come down. That's the end of it.' He was worried having her loose up there.

She burst into tears, shouting in Spanish at him. I felt for her like never before. She had given so much for this chance. And now, this close, she was being forced back. I knew what she must be feeling. I would be the same. But Henry was right, she wouldn't make it in the winds up there. It wasn't her fault; she had used her strength on the first attempt. She didn't have that same strength now. It had taken her three hours more than us to reach Camp Three. If she was slow like that higher up, she would die. We all knew this and tried to comfort her in the tent.

It slowly dawned on her that she would go no further. Her dream was ending here and it hurt. She was one of the most determined women I had ever met, and the grief now showed all over her face. She sobbed quietly to herself in front of us. She knew secretly that it was the right decision.

We sat for the best part of an hour in silence. I noticed that my headache had now returned for the first time in ten days. I cursed it and tried to drink some more of the disgusting, luke-warm water in my bottle. I longed for something cool to drink; I swallowed an aspirin.

*

Geoffrey and I were the first to leave Camp Three. We wanted to leave at different intervals to avoid any delays on the ropes. At 5.45 a.m. the two of us climbed out of the tent and began fixing our oxygen masks. It would be our first time on the mountain breathing supplementary oxygen. We had experimented in breathing the oxygen at Base Camp, but never under extreme exertion and never so high up; I wondered what difference it would make.

We squeezed a large tank into our rucksacks, fitted the regulator and made sure the lead was free and the gauge not caught up in any straps. I hoisted the rucksack onto my back and tried to make it comfortable. It weighed me down and sat awkwardly on my shoulders. It felt four times as heavy as it had when we were testing it at Base Camp; and even then it had been an effort to lift. I shuffled again. It felt a little better.

The balance between the effort needed to carry the heavy tanks and the benefit the oxygen gives, is a constant debate. The conclusion generally is that the benefit of the oxygen outweighs the weight, but not by much. The air above this height now becomes so thin that it is almost impossible to live. Only a very few exceptional and physiologically different people can climb free of supplementary oxygen above here. Even the majority of Sherpas use oxygen high on Everest.

The tanks form what is known as an 'open system', where the regulator allows a small trickle of oxygen to flow through the mask. This amount can be adjusted to give between 1 and 4 litres of oxygen a minute. This combines with the normal air you are breathing to marginally boost the level of oxygen inhaled. But not by much. The body needs to breathe about thirty litres of air a minute during extreme exertion; if you used a closed system, of breathing compressed air, the tank would last minutes. It would be impossible to do, as you can only realistically carry one or two tanks at the most. The 'open system' therefore is the only real method of using supplementary oxygen up high. A trickle of oxygen mixed with normal air is all this provides.

Generally we would climb on 2.5 litres a minute. This was

deemed the most efficient rate. But even this, at these extreme heights, was hardly enough to stay alive, let alone moving at any pace. But as they say, 'it is just enough to do the stuff.' But there was no scope for mistakes in this. The majority of the bodies we would encounter up above Camp Four had died because of one thing: not enough oxygen. Their bodies had slowly suffocated to death, and the lack of oxygen in their brains made them hardly even aware of what was happening.

I double-checked that the tubes were free and not snagged up. I checked the tubes were soft and that no condensation had frozen inside them. I checked my mask was tight around my face, then carried out the same procedure with Geoffrey. Our eyes caught each other through our goggles and we knew it was time to start across to the first rope that would lead on and up the Lhotse Face, towards Camp Four, somewhere far above us.

Within ten yards though I felt as if I was choking on my mask. I didn't seem to be getting any air from it. It was suffocating me. I ripped it from my face gasping frantically. I hung on my harness from the Face, tubes and connections wrapped round me in a chaotic jumble. This is crazy, I thought. I tried to untangle myself. My mask swung freely beneath me. I found that I had to remove my entire pack to free everything before trying again. I checked the air-bubble gauge that told me that oxygen was flowing. It read positive. I refitted the mask and carried on.

Five minutes later, nothing seemed to have changed. 'For fuck's sake,' I swore in a muffled cry, as I tried to gulp air through my mask once more. I could hardly breathe with it on. I found myself throwing my head back to get a deeper breath, but still I felt stifled by the mask. I tried to keep going but couldn't. I stopped again and tore it from my face, gulping in the outside air.

It was working; everything said that it was working. I couldn't understand it. It felt as if I was trying to run a marathon uphill, with a pair of rugby socks stuck in my mouth. I was gasping without getting relief. Geoffrey stooped behind me, leaning over his axe. He was also struggling. He didn't even look up. We were both lost in our own worlds; trying desperately to breathe.

I replaced my mask, determined to get used to it. I knew I had to trust it. I had been told over and over to trust it. The only place that I would get life from up here was the Russian fighter pilot's mask that covered my face. I had no choice but to keep it on.

I continued on up, slowly but methodically, I was not going to take my mask off again. I tried to ignore the pain. The rope stretched away above me, straight up the Face.

An hour later Geoffrey was some way behind, but I kept plodding on, three steps at a time. The ice crunched away beneath me.

Eventually the route started to traverse across the Face. Away to my right it soared upwards to the summit of Lhotse far above. To my left the ice fell at an alarming angle straight down to the Western Cwm, 4,000 feet below. It shimmered menacingly as the sun that was now rising glistened on its blue veneer. I couldn't afford a mistake up here now. I tried to stop my eyes looking down, and focused on the ice in front of my feet. Slowly I began to cross the Face towards the rock band that divided the Face in two.

The Yellow Band, as it is known, is a 150-feet high stretch of sedimentary sandstone rock that was once the sea-bed of the ancient Tethys sea. As Gondwanaland and Asia had collided, the rock was driven up into the sky. Millions of years later here I was traversing towards it, now only some 4,000 feet beneath the highest point on our planet. It seemed somehow surreal, as the Band loomed closer to my left.

At its foot, I clipped on securely to the rope that the Sherpas had fixed only two weeks earlier. I hoped it was secure; it was all the protection that I had up here now.

I glanced up and could see the sandy, yellow rock rising into the wispy clouds that were now hovering over the Face. I knew that once over this, Camp Four was only a few hours away.

My crampons grated eerily as they met rock for the first time on the climb. They made a screeching noise as they scraped across it. They found it hard to grip, and would only hold when they snagged on a lip in the rock. Leaning back and out from the rock, I rested on my harness. The rock and ice seemed to sweep away below as the Face above steepened.

I turned outwards and tried to sit against the rock, with my crampons jammed into a small crevice beneath me. I leant back, desperately trying to get oxygen into my body, sucking violently into the mask. As my breathing calmed down I looked at where I had crossed. Camp Two was now but a tiny speck in the hazy distance below. I remembered how I had sat there and watched Mick and Neil climbing up where I was now. I checked my karabiner once again on the rope.

As I cleared the steep Yellow Band, the route levelled out into a gentle traverse for 500 metres. At the end of that was the Geneva Spur that would lead up to Camp Four. My body began to feel the excitement again.

The Geneva Spur was named by the Swiss expedition in 1952, the year preceding Hillary and Tensing's epic first ascent. It is an anvil-shaped black rib of rock that lunges out from the ice. It rises steeply up to the edge of the South Col, the small saddle that sits between the two great peaks of Lhotse and Everest. The Geneva Spur forms the last major hurdle before the Col, the place of our final camp.

There was a raw simplicity in what I was doing. My mind was entirely focused on every move I made; nothing else clogged my thoughts. It is this straight simplicity that I knew drew men and women to climb. Man is living to his utmost, straining everything towards one single purpose. It made me feel alive.

I would aim to reach a point in the ice just in front of me with each few steps I took, but invariably I would be forced to stop short; my body needed to rest and get oxygen. I would lean on my axe and stare at the point a few yards in front that had eluded me, then start moving again, determined to reach it in the next bound. In this manner I slowly approached the Geneva Spur.

I passed the point where the Lhotse route led. Up above I could see the tent where Andy and Ilgvar had rested yesterday afternoon, before their summit attempt. Far above that, I could see the tiny specks which were them struggling up for the summit. They still had a long climb ahead of them. I prayed that they would make it, and kept shuffling along.

As I started up the Geneva Spur I could see Geoffrey below and far behind me. He seemed to be moving better now. I wanted to keep in front and pushed on. Behind him I could see the figures of the others below, Neil, Allen and Michael, moving slowly across to the Yellow Band. Carla would be on her descent now. I didn't know whether I envied her or felt sorry for her. I pushed the thought from my mind.

I climbed steadily up the Spur and an hour later found myself resting just beneath the lip. The Col awaited me over the top. I knew this, and longed to see the place I had heard and read so much about. The highest camp in the world at 26,000 feet, deep in the Death Zone.

I hated the term 'Death Zone', it conjured up images that I knew were all too real up here. Mountaineers are renowned for playing things down, yet it had been mountaineers who had coined the phrase. I didn't like that.

It would be my first time in the infamous Death Zone. I wouldn't have time now to worry about how my body would cope. For me, this was my chance.

As I pulled the last few steps over the top of the Spur, the gradient fell away to reveal a dark shingly rock plateau. As I swivelled slowly on my crampons, they grated against the slate under them. I swore I could see all of Nepal below. I sat, stunned and alone. Slowly, blanket cloud began moving in beneath me, obscuring the lower faces of the mountain. Above these, a horizon of dark blue sky lay panned out before me. I knew I had entered another world.

CHAPTER SIXTEEN

ABOVE THE CLOUDS

▲

'If I go up to the heavens you are there, if I go down to the place
of the dead, you are there also. If I ride the morning wind to the
ends of the ocean even there your hand will guide me, your
strength will support me . . . I can never be lost to your Spirit.'

Psalm 139, vv.5–10.

Adrenalin filled my tired limbs, I just longed now to see the Col.
Two hundred metres of clambering over the shingly, black rocks
and the saddle appeared. I knew at once that this was it.

The South Col is a vast rocky area, the size of four rugby
pitches, strewn with the remnants of old expeditions that had
been here. Empty oxygen canisters lay scattered about randomly;
they told a hundred tales. It was here that in 1996, in the fury of
the storm, men and women had struggled to find their tents. Few
had managed. Their bodies lay within metres of the flat area,
many of them now partially buried beneath ice and rock. It was
a sombre place; a place where many now rested eternally. A grave
that many of their families could never visit.

People talk of rubbish dumped at the Col; it is a false image.
The vastness and desolation of this wild, windswept place dwarfs

the few items left here. The fragments of old tents and canisters were never left intentionally, they were left in desperation. They were the only marks of men and women who had struggled frantically to save their own lives. There was an eeriness to it all.

My impression of the Col was one of isolation. It was a place unvisited by all but those strong enough to reach it. No helicopters can reach above Camp One at the highest, let alone up here. No amount of money or technology can put a man here; only a man's spirit could do that. I stood motionless as I surveyed the place. The wind blew in gusts over the lip of the Col and ruffled the torn canvas of the wrecked tents. A sense of excitement swept over me. I gazed in disbelief.

Two tents, one from the Singapore expedition and the other belonging to Bernardo, stood alone in the middle of the Col. Both groups had come up the day before. The tents were now empty. The two Singapore climbers and Bernardo were somewhere above us. I wondered what they were going through right now. I thought of the Singaporean leader still at Camp Two. He would be willing his team-mates on. The whole of Singapore awaited news of this attempt. I hoped they had succeeded.

We had agreed beforehand to share Bernardo's tent. I found it and climbed in slowly. At this height everything happens in a strange form of slow motion. The effect of the thin air makes people move like spacemen. Slowly and deliberately I shifted inside and removed my pack and oxygen tank. I'll lie down for a second, I thought. I fell back in a heap.

I was woken suddenly by the sound of Bernardo returning. I still had my pack on. I sat up wearily as he peered into his tent. He smiled, his face looked tired but radiant. I didn't have to ask if he had reached the summit, his eyes said it all.

'Beautiful, Oso. Beautiful.' Bernardo repeated the words again and again, in a dreamy voice. I admired his strength. He had done it. We huddled together in the tent. He seemed so alive. Much more so than me. I smiled at the thought.

The two Singapore climbers also returned. They too had been successful. I tried to imagine the jubilation of the rest of their team back at Base Camp. Soon Singapore would be celebrating the country's first ascent and rightly so; these two climbers had risked and given their all. They collapsed in their tents. Unlike Bernardo, their exhaustion was written all over them as they literally staggered the last few yards to their tent and disappeared. They would leave the South Col tomorrow; a triumphant, drained pair.

Bernardo stayed twenty minutes with me and then left. Adrenalin was carrying him. He wanted to return to Camp Two that afternoon. Only a man like Bernardo, born and bred in the Andes, a climber and guide all his life, with two previous attempts on Everest behind him, could do this. He left the tent with a big smile.

'It's all yours, Oso. *Vaya con Díos.*' The same words he had said almost six weeks earlier.

*

Two hours later Neil and Allen arrived. They had overtaken Geoffrey and Michael. The stronger seemed to be shining now. Neil shook my arm excitedly. We were here at the Col together. That togetherness gave me strength.

Geoffrey and Michael also soon arrived with four Sherpas. Three of them would climb with us to the summit, and one would come with us as far as the Balcony Ledge. They would help us take a spare oxygen canister up to this point. There, we would need to replace our canisters with a fresh tank for the final part of the summit bid. The plan was that this fresh tank would last all the way to the summit and back to the Balcony. As we then came down, with our tanks getting low after ten hours' use, we would be able to collect our half-empty ones previously cached at the Balcony, and carry on down the last leg to Camp Four. It didn't leave much margin for error.

As they arrived they informed me that Graham, an Everest summiteer in his own right, had turned round 300 feet above Camp Three. He had felt too weakened by the illness that we had both had, and knew from experience that he would never have the energy to reach the summit. He had headed down after Carla, dejected. He had given so much. But it wasn't his time.

We both had the same illness, but somehow I was still here. What did he know about the next stage, that I didn't? I pushed the thought aside and helped to put up another tent.

*

The Col is a deathly place, where humans are not meant to survive. The thin air that I felt, as I removed my mask in a bid to conserve oxygen, seemed to burn my lungs like frozen fire. At this height the human body begins to deteriorate fast. It cannot recover, but instead begins to eat into its own muscle and bone in a struggle to survive. You cannot digest food and the clock continually ticks away.

We struggled frantically to erect two more tents. The weather was worsening and we needed shelter fast.

We pulled a tent from its stuff-sack and tried to pin it down. The wind ripped it from our groping hands and the material flapped wildly as we tried to contain it. In the confusion of wind and high altitude, what should have taken us minutes to put up, actually took us an hour and ten minutes. We got colder and more irritated as we tried to force wrong poles into the wrong slots. We had done it a thousand times, we could do it blind-folded, yet here we were floundering like drunks trying to get a tent up. My hands were getting bitterly cold.

As we finally secured the last corner with a pile of black slab rock, the wind was roaring ferociously. A 70 m.p.h. gale was driving the clouds over the lip of the Col towards us. We huddled in the tents and waited. Waited for night to come.

Michael, Allen and Geoffrey were in one of the larger tents, and the Sherpas were in the other. Neil and I made do with the one-man tent that Bernardo had left. We had struggled to squeeze into it, and all our kit was piled up at the windward end. The tent was missing its outer skin, and the inner had several gaping holes through which the wind raced. I tried to block them with my rucksack. The wind just whistled instead. I wriggled in an attempt to stretch my legs. We would have about nine hours to wait like this before we would leave.

We slowly began to settle down to the odious, but essential, task of melting ice. At this height the gas burns at a much lower temperature. What took a long time before, now seemed to take for ever. Physiologically it is almost impossible to drink fast enough to stay hydrated in the Death Zone; but when it takes two hours to boil a small pot between two, the task of replenishing ever diminishing fluid levels becomes a losing battle. We thirstily sipped at the mug of hot water. What had taken so long to produce seemed to vanish in a minute. Restlessly, we began again.

We had to be hydrated to stand a chance of surviving a period of seventeen hours of extreme climbing in the Death Zone. During that time, eating or even drinking would not be possible. Two pairs of inners and then a huge pair of outer mitts ensured that fumbling for a nibble of anything was impossible.

As for drinking, I knew that our waterbottles, however hot when we started, and wherever they are kept, would be frozen in half an hour in these temperatures. Putting them down your front was now pointless as they would be far too inaccessible. Windsuit, down suit, then fleece, made certain of this. Up here, every bit of warm kit we carried would be worn. Fully clothed, one looks like something between an astronaut and a fighter pilot as you stagger clumsily about. Nothing up here is easy. But despite the inability to drink, still people carried one or even two waterbottles. It was force of habit. They would both quickly freeze but they are a security that no climber can comfortably leave behind.

Sitting in the tents awaiting nightfall, I felt this deep sense of impending doom. I was already exhausted and dozy from the altitude. The thought of seventeen hours, the longest marathon of my life, weighed down by heavy oxygen tanks, terrified me. I didn't feel strong enough. I lay there waiting, more scared of the night ahead than I had ever been.

I knew that all our hard work was for this next twenty-four hours, but still I just wished it would pass away. I tried to convince myself of all that lay the other side of it. Home, families . . . Shara; but even all my memories seemed strangely distant up here. Maybe they felt the same about me. I wondered who really cared right now. I reached for my mask and breathed slowly. I would allow myself five minutes breathing on it. It would be no use reaching nightfall and having no energy to move. I gave myself this treat every half-hour or so.

The lethargy one feels at this height is extraordinary. The lack of oxygen slows the body down to a crawl. Laziness just fills your limbs. You just can't be bothered. Just don't care. That's the danger of this place, it creates a blind nonchalance. It took me ten minutes to turn over and reach to my left to get my pee-bottle and urinate. Everything was in slow motion. My urine came out a deep dark brown. Neil chuckled. It meant that I was losing our competition over who could rehydrate the fastest. I was still severely dehydrated and we hadn't even begun. I grinned weakly back at him.

'Let's wait until we see yours,' I mumbled and turned over.

The zip of our porch was broken. It fluttered only half closed. From where I lay I could see the route ahead. It looked menacing as the wind licked across the sheer ice, picking up loose fragments of powder snow and chasing them away. I thought of all that had happened.

I could see the place where Mick had fallen. It seemed strangely still in that ice gully. He had been so lucky; or had he been protected? My mind swirled. I thought of all those brave and famous mountaineers who had sacrificed their lives in the pursuit of their dreams up here. I thought of those who hadn't wanted to sacrifice anything, those whose lives had been cruelly robbed from them. The numbers were too many. These people were determined fighters, yet the mountain had beaten them. It confused me.

I wondered if we would reach the top. It felt so distant; maybe we would get so close like the others, turned away empty-handed; or maybe fate would make another turn, where we would join the bitter ranks of those who never came home. I had never felt a fear of the unknown like this before. I fiddled with the pot and lay some more ice gently inside.

On the first successful expedition here in 1953 with Hillary, they had used an extra camp above the Col, which they had placed near the Balcony. We, though, had no more camps. Experience up here had concurred that it was more effective to try to climb it all in one go from the Col. It made this last day and night horrifically long.

In 1996, when those tragedies had struck, the entire route from the Col upwards had been roped. This year we had none, until just under the South Summit. It made the majority of this climb dangerously exposed. Ropes could not compensate for mistakes this time. Mick's fall had shown this. It had to be perfect from here on. Errors were out of the question. It increased the pressure for us.

It was 7.00 p.m. exactly. Half an hour to go. At 7.30 p.m. we would start the laborious task of getting dressed and ready. It would take at least an hour and a half. By the end, no parts of our body or face would be visible. We would be transformed into these bizarre cocooned figures, huddled, awaiting our fate.

I reached into the top pouch of my rucksack and pulled out a few scrumpled pages wrapped in plastic. I had brought them just for this very moment. I unfolded them carefully and read.

> Even the youths shall faint and be weary, and the young men shall utterly fall: but those who wait upon the Lord shall renew their strength: they shall mount up with wings as eagles; they shall run and not be weary; and they shall walk and not grow faint. Isaiah 40, vv. 27–31.

I felt that this was all I had up here. My God was the only person I felt who understood me now. I knew that back home my family would be strangely unaware of what I was going through. These words were my only comfort. They would ring round my head for the next night and day as I climbed.

*

Darkness seemed to cover the mountain in minutes. The moon was now almost entirely hidden; we had missed the ideal full moon by over two weeks now. It made the visibility very low.

As night came, the wind seemed eerily to die away. The tent no longer shook with the force of the gusts. The jet stream no longer roared. It seemed as if the mountain was beckoning us towards it. And like willing victims, we began the lengthy task of getting prepared.

Halfway through the ordeal of dressing, Neil took his last piss. He was looking forward to winning the 'clear pee competition': the ideal way to be, before starting. He should win, he had drunk continually all afternoon. He knelt and pissed. It came out a deeper and richer brown than mine. He looked down in anger. I smiled.

'I think that concludes the event, Neil. Winner's prize is the last swig of the mug,' I mumbled with relish. Neil laughed. I swigged.

Twenty minutes later we sat squashed together in the tent, hidden under a mass of down and fur. I had put a fresh battery in my headtorch; I would need it. In the cold, batteries last a tenth of their normal time. I fitted it round my fleece hat and switched it on. The beam flashed brightly as it darted around. We crawled slowly out. It was time.

*

We had decided to leave at 9.00 p.m. intentionally. It was much earlier than people normally left. Our forecast, though, had promised strong winds higher up. These were reckoned to increase during the next day. We wanted, therefore, to do as much of our climbing at night, before the winds got any worse. On top of this, was a desire just to get going. The wait disturbed me. I wanted it all to start or end, but not to linger. I fidgeted nervously with the mask over my face.

Geoffrey, Allen and Michael emerged from their tents. They heaved the tanks onto their backs and moved slowly towards us. It was almost impossible to recognize who was who. The only sound was of their crampons scraping across the rock under them.

The Sherpa tent was still all closed up. Neil hurried them. They mumbled at him. They were tired. They said that they would leave in a few minutes. They told us to go on; they would follow behind. We didn't argue.

We turned towards the Face some 300 metres in front, and started moving. Someone's crampon pierced an old gas bottle. It hissed violently. No one even looked at it. There was something mystical about the five of us moving slowly across the Col. We must have seemed like shadows being drawn towards the darkness. Soon the tents were invisible behind us in the night.

As we reached the ice, the gradient steepened dramatically.

We bent lower into the slope and moved steadily up, our headtorches swaying slowly as they lit up the ground in front of our feet. Our world became that light. It showed us where to kick our crampons and showed us where to place our ice-axe. The light was all we knew.

As the time passed the group spread out. It was natural. You can't afford to wait for everyone. Not up here. Each of you is fighting your own private war for survival. Your own private war in your mind as to why you keep going.

The group naturally divided into two. Allen, Neil and I led the way, and Michael and Geoffrey followed behind. They both soon fell way back. After two hours, as the three of us perched on a small lip of ice, we looked down below. The two lights of Geoffrey and Michael seemed distant and small. The Face here seemed steeper than anywhere else on the mountain. We were still dangerously without rope. I dug my crampons in, hoped they would hold, and leant back against the ice.

'Are you scared?' Allen asked me quietly. They were the only words any of us had spoken so far. The words seemed faint through his mask.

'Yes, a little,' I replied, 'but not as scared as I would be if I could see the angle of this Face,' I added, peering out into the black. It was true. It was too dark to see the danger; all you could see was the intensity of the snow and ice, lit brightly by your torch in front of you. We stood and turned into the Face again and carried on up.

As we climbed I seemed to lose myself in this surreal world of torchlight. Two steps then a rest. Was my grip secure? I shuffled. Neil and Allen were only yards from me, but somehow we were each alone. It was the most lonely work I had ever done. I clung to their heels even when my body said rest. I didn't want to lose them. They were all I had up here.

At midnight we came across this deep powder, drift snow.

We hadn't expected this. It drained our reserves as we floundered about in it. Each step we took forward, our feet would slide back in the loose snow. It took three steps just to make the ground of one. Snow filled my mask and gloves, and my goggles began to steam up.

I swore to myself. Where the fuck is the Balcony? It must be soon. I looked up and the ice and rock ledges disappeared above into darkness. I shook my head. I knew I was tiring.

For the next two hours, I resigned myself to the fatigue. I didn't care. I wouldn't swear when snow filled my goggles, or as I slid backwards; I wouldn't swear when the lip ahead was another false horizon. I just kept following and forgot everything.

*

At 1.00 a.m. we came over one more ledge and collapsed in the snow of the Balcony. A sense of excitement refilled my body. We sat now, as high as Lhotse. We were now at 27,700 feet above sea-level. I turned down my oxygen to 1 litre a minute as we weren't moving, and waited. I lay back against the snow and closed my eyes. It was to be a long wait.

We had to wait for the Sherpas to arrive. They were bringing spare oxygen canisters. We would swap our half-empty ones for fresh tanks. Those should then last to the summit and back to the Balcony. It would give us about ten hours to complete the round trip. The time factor up here was your oxygen. If you weren't going to make the summit and back in that time, you had to have the self-discipline to turn around. But discipline can get blurred when the summit is in sight; it is why people die.

The three of us sat huddled in the snow and waited for the Sherpas, Geoffrey and Michael to arrive. It was bitterly cold, a deep, chilling cold. It was − 45°C.

I curled into a ball and tried to keep warm. My toes began to feel numb even when I moved them.

At 2.00 a.m. there was still no sign. None of us talked. We

buried ourselves in our own worlds, trying to fight the cold and the likelihood of frostbite. On such a small flow of oxygen, frostbite comes easily. I wiggled my toes again and held my hands close to my chest. 'Come on.'

Suddenly the entire sky lit up before us, the mountains flashed as if in daylight, then disappeared again. I looked up sharply, then looked at Neil. The lightning flashed across the horizon once more and the thunder then rippled through the valleys below.

This shouldn't be here, I thought, what's going on?

Seconds later the sky flashed again. It was an electric storm. It was moving up through the valleys. We sat some 5,000 feet above it. I had never seen anything like it in my entire life. I stared, open-eyed in disbelief. We looked at each other nervously and knew what it meant.

If that came up towards us it would be fatal. It would turn the mountain into a raging mass of snow and wind. 'It can't come over us. It mustn't,' I mumbled.

Unbeknown to us three, huddled into the snow at the Balcony, Geoffrey and Michael were also fighting a battle on the slopes way below us.

Geoffrey was having problems with his oxygen set. The flow wasn't running properly. It choked him and his pace slowed drastically. Alone, and separated from Michael, he moved tentatively. He turned to see what the flashes were. The storm below shocked him. He struggled on but soon realized it was futile. He would never make it at this pace. He faced the frightening possibility that he might have to retreat from the mountain. He sat and tried to think, his mind swirling in indecision.

He, though, had the courage and discipline to do what others before had refused to do and ended up paying for with their lives. He got to his feet and slowly turned round. He had to retreat to the relative safety of Camp Four. His attempt was over. He had no choice. He was too alone.

Michael had also turned back just before him. He was just too tired. He had climbed all his life and knew when it was wrong. In his own words he admits: 'It just didn't feel right. The sight of the lightning boded badly. I didn't want to carry on. My body couldn't go on. The effects of the illness were still with me. I would never have survived.' And so another brave mountaineer turned round. It takes courage to do this. Only the three of us now remained alone at the Balcony. We still waited; we had no idea they had turned back.

At 3.00 a.m., shivering uncontrollably and on the threshold of our ability to wait much longer, we saw the torches of the Sherpas below.

'Thank God, oh man, thank you,' I muttered wearily to myself. I knew that I wouldn't have been able to sit motionless much more. I felt numb with cold.

When they arrived we struggled desperately to change our tanks. This involved removing the regulators from our existing ones and putting them on the fresh canister. At Base Camp we had got this process down to a fine art. We could do it blind. Up here, in the dark and cold, it was a different game altogether.

I removed my outer mitts to be able to grip the regulator. My hand shook with the cold. I twisted it off and tried to line it up on the new tank. My shivering became frantic and in despair I screwed it on carelessly. The screw-threads jammed. It wouldn't budge. I swore at it out loud.

Neil and Allen were ready by now. Allen just got up and left, heading up the ridge. I fumbled crazily. 'Come on, damn you, come on.'

I felt the whole situation begin to slip away from me. I was losing patience and concentration as well. We had come too far to fail now. Too far. Neil shivered next to me uncontrollably. I was holding him up. He had been ready a while now.

'Come on, Bear, fucking get it working,' he stuttered through his mask. But it was jammed – there was nothing I could do. Neil had now lost any feeling in his feet. He knew what that meant. He was getting badly frostbitten with every minute I kept him waiting. He squeezed his toes tight but only felt a numbness come over them.

We both huddled above the tank, fumbling frantically, and then suddenly it came loose. I lined it up and tried again. This time it fitted snugly. My hands were freezing now and before tightening the regulator, I thrust them inside my down jacket to try and warm them up. Ten seconds later I tightened it all, squeezed the tank into my pack and heaved it onto my shoulders. We had lost precious minutes. We knew that if we were to have even a chance of the summit we had to get going soon.

One of the three Sherpas who were meant to continue then suddenly stood up, turned and headed down. This wasn't meant to happen. They should stay together as a team. What was happening? The Sherpa felt worried by the storm and the winds that were beginning to rise. They were too dangerous. He wanted to go down. There was nothing we could do.

The other two Sherpas would continue, but they wanted to rest at the Balcony for a few minutes. We couldn't argue. Neil and I turned and headed up after Allen onto the ridge that would eventually lead us to the South Summit.

Those first few minutes after we climbed over the Balcony Ledge onto the ridge, I began to warm up. I felt the blood now reach into my feet again and my legs lost the stiffness that the wait had caused. My breathing reached that level again where you just heave aggressively into your mask. My eyes stared at the snow in front of me. I noticed that it was getting lighter and that the storm had passed. As we were drawing closer it seemed as if now the mountain was beginning to open her arms to us. I felt an energy now that I had not had before. I pushed the pace on.

I moved past Neil and mumbled to him that I had to keep moving. The faster pace was keeping me warm. He nodded slowly and tiredly at me as I went past. His head was low and he looked deeply exhausted. But I knew he wouldn't stop, he was too close and he knew it. Today was 26 May, the day that his father had died some fifteen years earlier, when Neil was only nineteen. The fact that this early dawn at 28,000 feet Neil was struggling with every sinew, one last time, to achieve what had so cruelly eluded him now twice, was all the more poignant. His father somewhere up above would be cheering him on; of that I was certain. He leant over his axe, heaving into his mask. I knew, though, that he would not turn round, so carried on.

The energy that I was experiencing worried me. I thought that perhaps I was getting too much oxygen; maybe my regulator was giving me 3.5 litres per minute not 2.5. If that was the case then I would soon find my tank empty. My mind raced with the possibilities. I checked the gauge again. It firmly read 2.5. It had to be right. The memory of what happened to Mick loomed in my mind. All I could do was hope that it wouldn't fail; not now, not so close.

After an hour on the ridge we hit this deep drift snow again. I cursed. The energy that I had felt before began to trickle from my limbs with each step forward. I could see Allen just ahead, floundering in the powder. He seemed to be making no upward progress as he slid back down into the deep snow beneath him. I looked up and the Face just soared away above. It was drift snow as far as I could see.

To our right, the Face dropped sharply away. The gradient was extreme. Nothing lay between us and the plains of Tibet, 8,000 feet below. I looked back down at my feet.

I hardly even noticed the magic of the views up here, of the entire Himalaya stretched below us, bathed in the pre-dawn glow. I didn't have the energy. My mind and focus were entirely directed on what my legs were doing. Summoning up the resolve to heave one's thigh out of the deep powder and throw it a step forward was all that seemed to matter. An anger filled my head each time the snow would sink up to my waist. I knew I wouldn't be able to do this for much longer.

Somewhere beneath the South Summit we found the ropes that had been put in on the team's first attempt. I clutched at them eagerly. They posed some vague sense of comfort as I stooped and clipped in. I clipped a jumar on to the rope as well; it would stop me slipping back. Exhausted, I allowed myself to rest. The harness took my weight and I sat slumped in a ball, breathing. I closed my eyes.

As we approached the South Summit, the wind began to pick up. I noticed it at once as it swirled around my feet. It howled and whipped the surface snow up into a frenzy.

Noel Odell, one of the climbers who had attempted Everest in the pre-war years, spoke of the sight above here like this: 'the mighty summit seemed to look down with cold indifference and howl derision in windy gusts.' Nothing seemed to have changed in seventy years. I kept moving slowly, driven by the knowledge that the South Summit wasn't far.

In many ways those last few metres to the South Summit were the hardest of my life. I wasn't close enough to feel the adrenalin of being near the top. Instead, though, I just felt this deep pounding fatigue that reduced me to two steps at a time. It was all I could manage.

Neil was soon close behind me again. I had to keep moving. Just get to the South Summit, was all I thought, just get there. You're so close. Allen in front had already staggered over the snow lip and reached it. But still it never seemed to arrive.

I felt every ounce of energy now being sucked from my body. I knew that this is what it must be like to drown. My body, more than ever before, screamed at me in desperation to turn around. I moaned out loud for the first time, as if I was venting the voice that told me to turn back. I couldn't, not now.

In a drunken stupor, barely aware of anything around me, I collapsed in a small hollow on the leeward side of the South Summit, at 28,700 feet. My head leant back on the ice behind me, my eyes were tightly closed. My head then fell forward and I began to hyperventilate. My body desperately needed more oxygen; but all I had was the 2.5 litres that trickled past my nostrils every minute. It wasn't enough, but it was all I had, and the tank was getting lower by the second.

Over the top of us, arctic hurricane-force winds blew like I had never experienced before. They seemed to howl as the three of us sat huddled together. I was worried that I was low on oxygen. I couldn't reach the tank to check the gauge, it was buried in my pack; it was too cold to start fumbling around just to confirm what we should already know. I should be able to calculate it. I tried to work out the mathematics in my head. The thin air robbed me, though, of the ability to do these basic sums. I gave up, frustrated at how slow my mind was working. I would have to take the gamble. It was a chance that I had to take. I hoped it was the right decision.

Ahead I could see the final ridge and the Hillary Step that lined the route to the true summit. Only 250 feet higher above this Step was the place of dreams.

Snow was pouring from the top, as these winds raced over it. A vortex of cloud hovered below the leeward face, protected from the wind.

Staring at it, my body just felt empty, all energy had been ripped from me. The ridge was a haze in front of me. Yet somehow in the few minutes that we lay there, in the midst of all that sought to stop us, I felt a peace. Something deep inside knew that I could do it. I would somehow find the energy. The more I looked at the ridge the more I felt this energy flooding back. Hillary once said that the mountains gave him strength; until this point I don't think that I had really understood this. But lying there, at my weakest moment, I found the mountain giving me a strength I had never experienced before.

The final ridge is only about 400 feet long, but it snakes precariously along the most exposed stretch of climb on this planet. On either side, down sheer faces, lie Tibet to the east and Nepal to the west. Steep granite rock lines the Nepalese side, and snow cornices protrude over the other. Shuffling carefully along the knife-edge ridge, over the tops of intimidating snow ledges, we began to make our way towards the Hillary Step; this was all that barred our way from the top. The strength seemed to be staying with me as we moved slowly along. I was feeling it like I had never done before.

*

I knew exactly where I would see him, I had read the accounts of Rob's tragic death up here many times. They proved right. Slumped and half hidden by the passing of two years, his frozen body sat in its immortal grave. Since that final appeal from his wife over the radio, where Rob had tried with all his being to stand up and climb these ten feet over the South Summit, he had sat here. Time up here stands still. The cold ensures this. All he had to do was manage those meagre ten feet over the lip in front of him; he knew that from then on it was all downhill. The exhaustion and fatigue at this altitude had robbed him, though, of his ability to do this. He had died where he now sat, only ten feet to my left. I let my gaze return to the ridge under me. I didn't know what to think.

I knew that we would see various corpses up here, yet somehow nothing had prepared me for the sight. Everyone knows the risks involved: it's big boys' games that demand you play by big boys' rules; I knew this, yet the stark reality shook me. It is hard to describe. Rob's death had been only one of many that day, yet the proximity at which I now climbed by him cut right into me. The sight lingered in my mind as we carried on along. Concentrate now, come on, Bear, concentrate. Strangely, though, I noticed that I wasn't scared by the sight of him. Instead, I felt a quiet determination to be different – to stay alive.

*

The rope was being whipped by the wind in front of me as I shuffled along. I thrust my ice-axe into the cornice to my right to steady myself. Suddenly the snow just gave way beneath it. My ice-axe just shot through the cornice. I stumbled to regain my balance; it should have been solid. I slowly realized that we were walking literally on the lip of a ledge of frozen water – with Tibet 8,000 feet directly below. I could see the rocky plains through the hole where the snow had been. I placed my ice-axe tentatively a little lower down and tugged on my sling that secured me to the rope. It held firm.

At the end of the ridge we leant over our axes and rested. The Hillary Step now stood above us. This forty-feet ice wall was all that hid the summit from view. At sea-level this would be a relatively pleasant ice-climb that you would happily do on a sunny midwinter's day in the Lake District; but where we were now, cowering from the wind, at almost 29,000 feet above the Lake District, it was becoming our final and hardest test. A test that would result in whether we would join the ranks of those who have seen in awe what lies over the lip ahead. If so, we would become only the 31st and 32nd Britons to have ever done this. The ranks were small but exclusive. My heart burned more than ever to be one of them.

I remembered the last lip in the Icefall where I had felt my legs turn to jelly. It had worried me at the time, in case the same thing happened up here. If my legs failed me under the narcosis of high altitude, I would be powerless to fight it. I tried to dispel the thought as we rested for a few more seconds. We had to start up it soon. It was the same vertical gradient as the lip on the Icefall, only now so much higher. I struggled to stand and clipped on to the first rope. I looked weakly up above me.

As I moved laboriously and clumsily up the ice and found the first small ledge, I leant in close and tried to rest. My goggles were plastered against my face as the mask pushed into me. Ahead and to my right, I could see a cluster of ropes protruding from the ice. They were old ones from past years. They were bunched in a tangled mess. I tried to focus my mind on which was the correct rope. My brain was working so slowly.

You believe that your mind is sharp and alert until you have to actually test it. The ropes confused me. I couldn't understand why my mind couldn't discern and operate normally. I shut and opened my eyes in an attempt to focus.

Only a year previously the slumped and frozen body of a climber was found hanging by his abseiling device from these ropes. It was the body of Bruce Herrod, the British climber with the South African team who had never returned from the summit in 1996. Nobody knew what had happened. The truth was not known until a year later, when he was found here in the ropes. He had been descending down but had clipped into the wrong rope. As they began to bunch up and become entangled, he lacked the energy or mental capacity to do anything. He died as he was – swinging with the wind from his harness, trapped in a jumble of ropes. He had been cut loose as they found him. The ropes now bunched in front of me were the only reminder of him. I reached for a clear line.

As I heaved myself over the final lip, I strained to pull myself clear of the edge. I unclipped whilst still crouching, looking down at the snow around me. The line was now clear for Neil to come up. I lifted my head forward and stared.

Only 200 metres away, along a gentle, easing slope, lay the crest of the summit that I had dreamt of for so long. A wave of adrenalin flooded through my veins. I could feel this surge of strength. I had never felt so strong and yet so weak all at the same time. I got to my feet without meaning to and started staggering towards the tiny, distant cluster of prayer flags. Gently flapping in the breeze, on the crest of a snow cornice, these flags marked the true summit – the place of dreams.

I found it ironic that the last part of this immense climb should also be the flattest. Beneath here were thousands and thousands of feet of treacherous ice and snow, yet here it was a gentle slope almost beckoning us up to the top.

However many of these pathetic, desperate shuffles I made, the summit never seemed to arrive. It never appeared to get any closer. I tried to count the steps as I moved. Come on, just do four, I would feebly tell myself, yet by two I always seemed to lose track of where I was. My counting became lost in this haze of weariness. I now breathed in gulps like a wild animal, in an attempt to literally devour the oxygen that trickled from my mask. Slowly the summit loomed a little nearer.

As I drew now closer, my eyes welled up with tears. As I staggered those last few feet, I felt as if I was pulling all my emotions of the last year in a sledge behind me. Weary and broken I was slowly getting closer to the small place that had captured my imagination since I was a boy. Those last 100 metres were undoubtedly the longest of my life as they crept slowly by beneath me. Yet eventually at 7.22 a.m. on the morning of 26 May, with tears creeping down my cheeks inside my goggles, the summit of Mount Everest opened her arms and welcomed me. It was as if she now considered me somehow worthy of this place. My pulse raced; and in a vacant haze, I suddenly found myself standing on top of the world.

Allen embraced me, mumbling excitedly into his mask. We stood there, all our differences seemed to have vanished; we were here together. It was all that mattered. I turned and could see Neil staggering towards me, stumbling with exhaustion. I beckoned him on as he drew nearer and nearer.

As he approached, the wind mysteriously began to die away as the sun rose slowly over the hidden land of Tibet. The mountains below were being bathed in a crimson red. A magic was in the air.

As Neil arrived, he knelt down and crossed himself. He had never shown a faith before, but I had always seen it in him; it inexplicably just somehow showed. Here at 29,035 feet above sea-level, with our masks off to save our precious oxygen, Neil and I hugged as brothers. This early dawn was now the anniversary of his father's death and I kind of knew that this moment was meant to be.

I got to my feet and slowly began to look around. My eyes were ablaze. I swore that I could see halfway round the world.

CHAPTER SEVENTEEN

BORROWED TIME

▲

'There are certain places that are rarely ever seen; and in those
you will find a special sort of magic.'

Nineteenth-century Indian Missionary

The entire land of Tibet lay sprawled below us. I wondered if any
binoculars would be strong enough to see us from down there. I
didn't feel at all remote; instead I felt strangely at home. The
summit was only about six square feet. I stood on it and couldn't
stop smiling.

For twenty minutes we sat and just gazed. The horizon
seemed to bend at the edges. It was the curvature of our earth. I
stared in utter amazement. I wanted the moment to last for ever.
I wondered, with a small grin, what Shara or my family would be
doing at this precise moment. They would be asleep. They have
more sense than me, I thought, and smiled. How I wished they
could be here; I wanted everyone to be able to see what the
horizon had laid before us. There truly was a magic to this place.
It was sacred ground.

I had often gazed at pictures of the summit, taken by famous
Everest climbers of past years – pictures showing the greatest

mountain range in the world – the Himalaya, sprawled like a table cloth below and all around. The amazement of now standing on this precariously small summit myself and seeing the vast peaks of the world, poking like contorted limbs through the blanket cloud across the horizon, held me captive. I had always feared that I would be too tired to care – too nervous of where I was. But I was wrong. For the first time in three months I wasn't tired. Instead adrenalin and energy pounded through my veins. I hardly dared blink.

The wind gently caressed the summit under me – the roof of the world was silent. It was as if the mountain was somehow allowing us to be here.

Technology is now so advanced, so precise – yet crouching here, it amazed me to think that no amount of science could put a man on the summit of Everest. Only the dangerously slow process of actually climbing the mountain could do that. We can put a man on the moon but not up here. It made me feel a little proud.

My mask now hung beneath me – I had turned my regulator off in a bid to conserve oxygen. I lifted my head and breathed deeply. The air at 29,035 feet felt scarce and cool as it filled my lungs. I smiled.

*

The radio crackled suddenly to my left. Neil spoke into it excitedly.

'Base Camp, we need advice . . . We've run out of earth.'

The voice on the other end exploded with jubilation. It was uncontainable joy.

Neil passed the radio to me. For weeks I had planned what I would say if I reached the top, the message that I would want to give. All that just fell apart. I strained into the radio and spoke without thinking. 'I just want to get home now,' was all that came out. Not quite the speech that I had hoped for. The words wouldn't exactly change mankind, but they were all I could manage.

The two Sherpas soon arrived. Pasang and Ang-Sering appeared like spacemen on the moon. Entirely hidden by down suit, goggles and mask, they staggered together to the top of the world. They had grown up in the same village as kids and had dreamt of becoming climbing Sherpas. Today, some four years on, as they reached the summit of Sagarmatha, their lives would change for ever. They would return to their village not only now as men, but also as true Sherpas. They would join the ranks of their Sherpa heroes, the Everest summiteers, revered throughout their land. We took a picture of them arm in arm and then hugged like children astride the roof of the world. I had never seen such joy in anyone's eyes before.

*

The memory of what went on then begins to fade. Neil still assures me that for my reputation's sake it would be best not to say too much about my delirious state of being up there. I don't believe him, but I do remember having some vague conversation on the radio. Funnily enough it was with my family, some three thousand miles away – the people who had given me the inspiration to climb.

At Base Camp they had managed to set up a 'patch through' via our satellite phone. By them holding the radio next to the receiver I suddenly found that, from the pinnacle of the world, my mother's voice was booming loud. I couldn't believe it. I quickly lost the reception.

My mother still maintains that I cut her off, as she was ruining the moment; I still profess that I don't know what she is on about. 'Cut my own mother off? Please.'

Up there, the time flew by and quickly passed. Like all moments of magic – nothing can last for ever. We had to get down. It was 7.48 a.m.

Neil checked my oxygen; I knew it would be dangerously low.

'Bear, you're right down. It's on 4 out of 25. You better get going fast,' he mumbled frantically.

I had just under a fifth of a tank to get me back to the Balcony. I doubted that I could make it; I had to leave now if I was to have any chance. I heaved the pack and tank onto my shoulders, fitted my mask and turned round. I never looked back. The summit was gone. I knew that I would never see it again.

*

I had only spent twenty-five minutes there in total, a lot of which had been taken up with trying frantically to take a few pictures for my sponsors. I knew if I failed in this, then my life would be in grave danger on my return. In all, I had only spent a few of those minutes on top just looking, just being. But the views I saw and the magic I felt during those precious few minutes will remain embedded in me for ever. They had surpassed my wildest imagination. I knew that I could never forget.

Within minutes of leaving the summit, the exhaustion set in. The adrenalin of before, that had driven me to the top, was now replaced by this deep fatigue. I could never have believed how hard it could be or how much energy was required just to go down. My two steps of before that I had struggled to keep count to were now completely lost in drowsiness. I tried desperately to concentrate, but my mind seemed to drift in and out of awareness.

One of the last people I had spoken to before leaving England, now three months earlier, had offered me just one solitary piece of advice; the words now rang in my ear. Mike Town, an experienced climber with whom I had spent many a blustery New Year in Cumbria, charging round the fells with his two woolly Bernese mountain dogs, had said one thing before I left – 'Be careful, above everything on the descent, because that's the danger time.' Strangely I now remembered those words. 'That's the danger time.'

Statistically, the vast majority of accidents happen on the descent. The concentration and adrenalin of going up seem to disappear. In its place comes a weary nonchalance. Nothing matters apart from one's longing for warmth and comfort. Lost in these thoughts you become careless. The focus gone and the mind weary, it is all too easy to lose one's footing or clip carelessly into a rope. Along the route were the remnants of brave men who had been caught by these emotions. Mick was one of the few lucky ones who had lived. I had to be careful now, I had to be alert; but still the drowsiness tried to pull me away, tried to deaden my senses. It was one of the hardest times as I tried desperately to fight the fatigue. I sensed that I was losing.

I struggled to find the right rope at the top of the Hillary Step. Sifting the frozen ropes apart with my mitts on, I tried to feed it through my figure-of-eight abseil device. It wouldn't go. In frustration I just looped it twice through my karabiner in an Italian hitch (a knot that sounds very dicey, but in actual fact is a quick and effective method of descending a rope), and then just let my body-weight force the rope through my gloves. I left the summit slope irrevocably behind me. I was alone again.

I moved across the ridge and, out of fear, I scaled those ten feet that had eluded Rob Hall before, all in one go. Those vital few feet lead back up to the South Summit; it would be the turning point for me. From then on, as Rob would have known, it was all downhill.

Somewhere beneath the South Summit the two Sherpas caught me up. We had been faster than them on the ascent but now, as weariness swept over me, I found them close behind. My tiny rate of oxygen I was now using, in my effort to make it last until the Balcony, was causing my dangerously slow pace. Pasang and Ang-Sering now climbed alongside me. We had come a long way together and now for the first time I really needed their presence. It made me feel secure.

Slowly we battled against the fatigue, down through the broken snow that our floundering bodies had caused on the way up. I suddenly just felt this longing to get home, yet I knew that was still weeks away. Between us and Base camp lay three treacherous days of avalanche-prone descent. I pushed the longing from my mind.

I somehow just knew when my oxygen ran out. It was nothing sudden but, instead, was this slow realization that the meagre flow of air that I could occasionally feel against my damp cheeks was no longer running. I removed my mask; it was now of no use and would only hamper my breathing. It hung limp and redundant from my rucksack. I was too tired to stow it away.

I could see the Balcony below, it wasn't far. I just had to make it there. I knew our half-used tanks that we had cached on the ascent awaited us. I let my legs wearily drag through the deep snow. I couldn't keep going much longer. I lost sight of the Balcony as my head slumped and my goggles misted over again for the umpteenth time. I continued to collapse down the slope. Eventually too tired to even feel any relief, I slumped to the ground next to the tanks at the Balcony.

I feasted on the fresh tank, after now almost fifteen minutes without oxygen. I breathed it in gulps. Warmth flooded back into my body; we were almost down. Camp Four was somewhere below us, only 1,700 feet of descent divided us. It was the section though that had almost claimed Mick's life. No ropes would protect us on the blue ice there. The urge to hurry, as Camp Four becomes visible, would have to be resisted; the last hurdle is always the most dangerous. We were weak and vulnerable after spending nearly sixteen hours climbing in the Death Zone above the South Col. Reaching the sanctuary of Camp Four was our sole desire as we sat and stared for one last time at the Himalaya below us. We began to descend and leave the land of magic behind us.

We were all now together as a group. The Sherpas and I led the way and Allen and Neil followed behind. As the tents came into sight far below us, the excitement came again. The tents, despite looking like uninvited visitors on the exposed Col, vulnerable to everything the mountain could offer, still seemed to symbolize the finishing post of our ordeal. Oxygen, water and rest awaited us. The tents grew in size as we came slowly and carefully down the ice.

I concentrated harder than ever before as I waded down through the deep snow. We soon came out of it and onto the blue ice again. In the light of day we could see clearly where we had climbed on the ascent. I tried to contain my excitement with each step that we came down. My crampons had lasted well. They bit firmly into the blue ice beneath the deep snow gully. I knew now that I was getting near 'home'. Very near.

I wondered what had happened to Geoffrey and Michael, and prayed that they would be there safely. We hadn't heard a word. There had been nothing we could do up there. We had been struggling to survive ourselves. I knew they must have turned back and I hoped they would be in the tents. I had no idea that they were watching us long before we ever saw them.

At the Col, I moved like a drunk across the slabs of rock and granite. It felt so strange not to feel ice beneath me any longer. The teeth of the crampons scraped and groaned as they slid over the stones. I leant on my axe to steady myself. The tents were only yards away; Michael grinned out at me from within, sheltered from the wind. I am not sure whether I even managed to smile back, I was too drained.

For sixteen hours we had neither drunk nor eaten anything. As predicted our water-bottles had frozen within twenty minutes of leaving the Col. We hadn't slept for over forty hours now. Our bodies felt strangely distant from our minds. Both just ached for some relief. In the porch of Neil's and my tiny, one-skinned tent, still fully clothed and looking like a somewhat deflated Michelin man, I very unceremoniously just collapsed. Everything went black.

'Bear, come on, you've got to get in the tent. Come on. Bear, can you hear me?' Michael's voice woke me. My goggles were still on, albeit a little lop-sided. I grinned and nodded, and shuffled into the tent. My head was pounding. I was severely dehydrated. I needed to drink. I hadn't even peed for over eighteen hours. My body was in turmoil.

Neil was hovering around with Allen, shedding their crampons and harnesses. Michael and Geoffrey now squatted and talked with me. I think they found the sight of me lying like a second-century mummy somewhat amusing, or maybe it was their relief that we were down. They had waited unknowingly back here for a long time. The suspense of not knowing was now over. The evidence of what had happened was lying sprawled beside them as they made me a warm drink from the stove. I felt so happy to see them.

As the afternoon turned to evening for the second time since being above 26,000 feet, we talked. We hadn't known why Michael and Geoffrey had retreated. They told their story. The lightning, the problems with their oxygen – also the fear. Geoffrey felt some regret at turning round, but you make decisions up there that feel right and that is never a bad way to operate. After all he was alive and safe. The lesson that I had learnt in the last twenty-four hours is that staying alive is all that really matters. The corpses had shown me that.

Michael turned to me later in the evening, as we were getting ready to try to get comfortable for one last night of tossing and turning in the Death Zone. There was a twinkle in his eye. We had come through a lot together in the past few months and had shared those same frustrations at Base Camp when we were ill and all the others were preparing to leave. We had shared a tent together that last night before leaving Camp Two for our summit bid. We had started on the same journey above Camp Four that had eventually beaten him. We knew each other pretty well by now. He said quietly to me something that I have never forgotten. It was the voice of twenty years' climbing experience in the wild Rockies in Canada. He said: 'Bear, I don't think that you have any idea of the risks you guys were taking up there. In the same situation I would turn round again, you know.' I smiled at him and he hugged me.

*

At 9.00 a.m., a little later than we had hoped, we moved out from the South Col. The wind still blew and snow whipped over the rocks; nothing seemed any different from when we had arrived forty-eight hours earlier. Yet so much had happened. I clipped into the rope and began to abseil off the lip, down the Geneva Spur. The Col was hidden once more.

Neil and I climbed together. He was moving faster than me, but I no longer cared. I had nothing to keep up for any more. We had done it, I could be slow now if I wanted. The tiredness had started before we had even left the Col. My body had been unable to recover at all up at Camp Four that last night. Instead I had just lain there awake – surviving.

The fatigue of almost sixty hours without sleep showed. On the Lhotse Face as I rested and swigged from my bottle, I lost my grip and it slipped through my fingers. I didn't know how I had done this, but one moment I was drinking, and the next it was scuttling down the Face to the glacier, some 4,000 feet below. I winced; it was Ed Brandt's favourite waterbottle that I had borrowed. It had gone to the summit with me and I knew he would treasure it even more now. I just sat and watched it hurtling away like a speck below me. Sorry, Ed, I thought. He'll murder me. I grinned. At least it had gone out in glory.

Coming down the Lhotse Face seemed to take as long as going up it. Camp Two awaited us at the bottom, across the glacier, and Neil swore at me for being so slow, but he waited patiently. We were still a team. It showed. Three hours later, staggering slowly side by side, we shuffled those last few metres into the camp. Thengba was jumping on the spot with happiness. We were alive, that was all that he cared about. We embraced, and for the first time I relished his smell of diesel oil and yak meat. It was good to be with him. We had spent a lot of time together beforehand at Camp Two.

Andy and Ilgvar were also now at Camp Two. They looked tired. Andy could hardly speak from his sore throat caused by the dry air. But they had succeeded. Together they had reached the summit of Lhotse, the fourth highest mountain on our earth. The strain of the climb was written all over them. Andy smiled at me. It was as if since our climb on Ama Dablam together he had suspected that I would reach the top of Everest. I had never shared his suspicions; for me they had been only hopes. Maybe that is what makes him a friend. We shook hands like two gentlemen in a London club, then started to laugh. We had both seen that special place.

That night I slept like the dead. I drank a final litre of water, squeezed into my sleeping-bag and forgot everything. I didn't move an inch for twelve deep hours until just before dawn the next day.

My eyelids seemed sealed shut as I tried to prise them open. It was 5.30 a.m.

'Bear, let's just get going, eh? It's the last leg, come on, I can't sleep when we're this close,' Neil announced in the chilly air with condensation pouring from his mouth. I shuffled sleepily.

'Two minutes, okay? Just two minutes,' I replied.

'We'll leave at six,' he announced.

'Yeah, yeah, just belt up now, okay?' I mumbled tiredly. 'Blooming maniac.' I had been dreaming of hot chocolate back in England, and resented his interruption. I fumbled to pack my rucksack. It seemed to weigh a ton now that I was bringing everything off the mountain. It brimmed with kit. I swore quietly.

We didn't eat before leaving, in anticipation of that elusive fresh omelette at Base Camp. Instead we slowly began to get ready to leave. We were all slow putting on our crampons, and ended up leaving some five minutes late, at 6.05 a.m. 'So what? It doesn't matter, we are homeward bound,' I mumbled. Our guards were beginning to drop.

An hour along the glacier we were stopped suddenly in our tracks. The mountain around us roared violently, then the sound of an echoing crack shook the place. We crouched and waited.

To the side of us, almost exactly five minutes ahead on the exact route we were going, the side of the Nuptse Face collapsed. White thunder pounded down the slope as we stood and stared in horror. It rolled like an all-enveloping cloud across the glacier. The Cwm became obscured in this wave of snow, the spray of which rose high into the air. Slowly the sound began to fade away. We stood in disbelief, some 500 metres back. It had clean missed us. If we had left on time, five minutes earlier, it would have covered us. We stood motionless and silent. For once being late had paid off.

It brought us abruptly back to our senses. We couldn't afford to relax; not yet. Just a bit more luck, come on, we are so near, I thought. My desperation to be safe was greater than ever before. As the journey nears its end, the risks increase – there is more to lose. We had tasted the summit yet were still within the mountain's grasp. We could not afford to be careless, not now. After all, we still had one last descent through the Icefall to complete. Statistically, I knew our odds would now be at their very worst.

The familiar Army expression of 'it's not over until the fat lady sings' rang in my ears. I began to long for the sound of her voice to ring round the mountains instead.

As we crossed each crevasse, the mountain began to feel more distant behind us. We were emerging slowly from her jaws. I hadn't descended below Camp Two now for over ten days. I knew that I was leaving something extraordinary behind me. We all walked in silence, lost in our thoughts.

Twice during those few hours moving through the Cwm, I quietly wept behind my glasses. I wasn't quite sure why I was crying. I thought of my father waiting back home. Somehow I knew that he understood what I had gone through. I just longed to be home. I didn't try to stop the tears; they had been stored up for a long time. I just let them flow.

Two hours of wading through the powdery snow of the avalanche, and we sat at the lip of the Icefall. The tumbling cascade of frozen water seemed to beckon us in, one last time. We had no choice but to oblige.

Neil strangely crossed himself again at the lip and plunged in, the rope buzzing as he abseiled over the edge. He was gone from sight. I smiled; that was twice he had done that now. Something deep had happened up there with him, I could see it. I pushed the thought away, clipped in, checked the rope and followed Neil down into the glassy depths.

The route had changed beyond all recognition. There must have been a lot of movement whilst we had been up there. The new ropes snaked over the giant ice cubes and led us through treacherously angled overhangs that would crush a house in an instant if they chose that moment to come loose. I swallowed and raced through them. Geoffrey and the others followed on. The ice must have laughed at our feebleness as we hurried nervously through the dark shadows of its jaws above. With each mousetrap of ice we passed through, I felt some of the tension leave me. Each step was a step towards home.

We could see Base Camp to our left, below us. My body filled with excitement and I felt energy fill my weary limbs. I could hardly believe we were almost back. I felt like it had been an age since I had last seen Base Camp. An entire lifetime seemed to have passed up there. The tents seemed to shimmer below us, as if calling us back. I hurried through the ice.

At 12.05 p.m. we unclipped from the last rope for the final time. I let my head fall on my chest as I moved across the ice, out of the Icefall; I couldn't quite believe it, but it was true. We were home – a little ruffled, but home.

Neil and I threw our crampons to the ground and hugged like three year-olds at a birthday party. I turned excitedly and looked back up at the tumbling, broken glacier and shook my head in disbelief. I was breathing heavily. It had let us through. I thanked the mountain sincerely in my mind and looked around me.

I hardly recognized the bottom of the Icefall now that summer was coming and some of the ice was beginning to melt into stream water. Relieved, so relieved, we splashed in the puddles of freezing water. It felt cool on my sweaty face. I splashed water into the air, dunked my head in the stream and then shook it violently. Waves of worry and tension seemed to leave me as I yelped and threw my head back and forth, shaking my hair. The sun was warm and we knew we were safe at last.

We hugged again as Geoffrey, Michael, Andy and Ilgvar arrived with Pasang and Ang-Sering. It was one of the finest moments I have ever known. We shared the same emotions; the same relief swept over us all. It showed in our eyes. They were all ablaze.

The walk across the rocks to our camp, that before had been

the curse of us, suddenly became a delight. I skipped over them with renewed vigour. I could see everyone at Base Camp waiting outside the mess tent. I was dying to see Mick.

My windsuit now undone to the waist, karabiners clipped to my jacket and with water dripping off me, I dropped my pack for the last time. Neil beside me was smiling from ear to ear. He looked a different person now that the strain was lifted from him. He whacked me hard on the back and grabbed my head in his arms; we had come a long way together.

I turned to Mick and we hugged. Grinning, he shook Neil and I with excitement. We had done it together. Mick had also tasted life up high – near the top; he knew what was up there; we had climbed this mountain as a team, as brothers. Mick felt no bitterness about having got so close. He had seen and experienced too much to feel bitter. He had come within a whisker of dying, and he knew it. His family had implored him not to go back up, and a lesser man might have ignored them. He had made the only real decision and was alive now. That was all that mattered. In my mind he had reached the top. I have never thought of it as any other way. He is my bravest friend.

*

Still sweaty from the descent and soaked from the melt-water at the bottom, we drank in the morning sun. The vast jeroboam of champagne that had sat like some idol at Base Camp for two months was ceremoniously produced. It took four of us twenty minutes of hacking away with ice-axes and leatherman tools to finally get the cork off. I feared it would blow a hole in the tent at 17,450 feet in Base Camp. I squinted behind Neil as we wrestled with it.

'If it hits you, Neil, it won't make much difference to you, so let me tuck in here behind,' I argued. He chuckled as we wrestled frantically, shaking the jeroboam way beyond the recommended 'safe' limit. Neil tried to shield his head under his arm, but before he managed to get it there, the cork just erupted like some tectonic explosion. It flew round the room what seemed like four times, then lodged itself in a bucket of used tea-bags. Screams went up. The party had begun.

I groped for the cigarettes that Patrick had brought out for me over two months ago. I opened them, lit one and spluttered violently. My throat was still red and sore from my illness and the incessant coughing up high had reduced it to an inflamed mess. I spat blood-filled saliva on the floor. Much as I would have loved to have my first cigarette for ten months there and then, I just couldn't. I stubbed it out on the floor and sipped at the champagne. At least I had tried.

I felt like drinking a gallon of this Moët et Chandon that had travelled so far, yet my body just couldn't cope. Sipping slowly was all I could manage and even after a few of those I felt decidedly wobbly. People were noticing this, but I didn't care. I closed my eyes and flopped against the rock wall; a huge smile was plastered across my face.

An hour later I began to peel myself off the wall. I felt hungover, and I had only had three and a half sips. I felt sure that climbing Everest meant that I would be able to drink like a whale. Something must be wrong. I rather sheepishly got up and staggered out of the tent, squinting in the bright sun. The Sherpas were chuckling as I emerged. I smiled and waved at them to be quiet. My head hurt.

Ed Brandt announced that the sat-phone was charged. We could call home. I remembered his waterbottle that I had dropped. I winced; I would tell him some other time. I went into the communications tent, sat down and dialled home. Someone could let Colonel Anthony now know that I had really reached the top. I grinned. I am sure he would just turn and say that he knew that weeks ago.

That afternoon I lay in my tent with Mick. I peeled off my

clothes and got into fresh socks and thermals. I had reserved a set especially for this moment. It had been a good decision. Mick wore my tweed cap and plied me with questions. We sat huddled for hours and talked and talked. I had missed him.

'How come Geoffrey has lost two stone in weight, I've lost about one and a half stone, Neil looks like he's fresh out of Weight-Watchers HQ, yet you still have love handles, eh?' Mick joked.

'You know what they say, Miguel, it takes courage, faith and chocolate cake to climb Everest.' He shook his head in disbelief, and I secretly felt my sides to see if I did have those love handles. He was right.

*

Henry poked his grinning face through the tent. He had done his job well. He had orchestrated the entire expedition successfully. That in his books meant that we were all alive. To him that was what mattered. His face showed the relief.

'Well done, boy. Well done, eh?' he said to me, smiling. He had watched me on Ama Dablam, all the way through to now. He had trusted me and helped me; I owed him a lot for that trust. I had lived up to his expectations; it was all I had hoped for. I thanked him; it was his help and advice that had carved the way for me. He knew how grateful I was; I hardly needed to say it.

'I knew you had it in you,' he added.

'I've been lucky, though, Henry, you know. Very lucky,' I replied.

He reeled on me, his eyes ablaze.

'No, Bear, you haven't been lucky. No.' He spoke fast and abruptly. 'You, young man, have pushed and pushed for this. You alone got there. Do you understand? You pushed hard, didn't you?' I remembered our conversation before I had left

Base Camp. Our eyes met. I nodded. We smiled and he withdrew from the tent chuckling.

As the day dragged on, with Sherpas moving slowly around Base Camp, exhausted but exhilarated, the rest of us focused on Neil's feet. They were in the early stages of severe frostbite. The feet and toes looked blistered and puffy. He sat soaking them in warm water. They were tender and battered. He suspected that he wouldn't ever feel them again properly. We didn't know whether he would lose them or not. We didn't discuss it.

The long wait we had both had at the Balcony had left its mark on him. We had to get him evacuated as soon as possible. He would need proper medical attention on them soon, if he was to keep them. Andy helped bandage them carefully; they had to be kept warm and protected. There was no way that he would get them in a pair of boots; he needed an airlift out of here by helicopter.

The insurance company said that dawn the next day was the soonest they could get one out to us. At 17,450 feet we were on the outer limits at which helicopters can fly. Only the Nepalese military pilots have the suitable choppers and local knowledge to reach here. One would be with us, they hoped, weather permitting, at 6.30 a.m. tomorrow morning. We waited in anticipation; yet no amount of anticipation could keep sleep from me that night. I knew I would sleep like never before as my body began to wallow in the elusive rest that it had so longed for. I daydreamed for a while for some strange reason of getting a dog. Yes, I'll get a dog when I get home, I said to myself, then I fell fast asleep, smiling.

*

'One only, one only!' The Nepalese pilot bellowed over the noise of the rotors. I took no notice and hopped in.

'I am his personal doctor, I must under all circumstances be with him,' I fibbed unconvincingly. The pilot looked somewhat bemused.

'What?'

'Yes, that's right, at all costs,' I insisted, bundling Neil in. He grinned. His feet all bandaged up looked like loaves of bread. I winked at him.

The co-pilot looked bemused as well. 'Most unusual, but if you are his doctor then I'll take him down to Lobuche then come back for you. The air is too thin to take off with two passengers.' I felt a wave of guilt come over me and nodded gratefully.

'Yes, I must insist,' I continued, showing the patience of a pregnant camel in the latter stages of labour, 'I'll be waiting here.'

I pray the insurance company never gets to hear about this. I'll be stung for thousands, I thought. Oh, sod it.

The chopper struggled to lift off, then pointed its nose down and swept away across the glacier fading from sight in the glaring sun that was now rising.

Mick and Geoffrey never believed it would work.

'That's the last you'll see of them,' they joked. I sat staring into the sun, squinting to see if I could see it returning. There was no sign.

Twenty minutes later, the distant sound of rotors could be faintly heard. I could still see nothing. I dared not get too excited. I couldn't face a thirty-five-mile walk out to Lukla, in the lower foothills. I didn't have the strength. 'It has to come back.'

Slowly noise grew and on the horizon I could see the tiny speck of a helicopter winding its way through the valley. It was coming back. My heart leapt. Geoffrey and Mick shook their heads in disbelief.

'You dog, I can't believe it,' they shrieked over the noise of the chopper, now hovering above the ice. It touched down and I clambered in, grinning. I tapped the pilot on the shoulder to say okay. All I had with me was my filthy fleece and my ID documents; everything else would have to be taken down through the valleys by yak. If this was going to work then there wouldn't be room for any surplus baggage. I knew that I wouldn't see any of my equipment again for some time.

Inside the cockpit both the pilots were breathing through oxygen masks. They needed to, coming straight into this height. They pulled on the throttle and angled the blades. The chopper strained under the weight, then it slowly lifted off.

Six feet up, though, all the warning lights flashed and buzzed furiously. The chopper began to lose height then just dropped the last three feet down on to the ice. It had been an abortive take-off, the rotors didn't have enough air to bite on. We tried again and failed. The Nepalese pilot scurried round to the fuel dump and let a load out onto the ice. He scrambled back in and we tried one last time. If it didn't work then they would have to leave without me. I can't be that heavy, I thought.

The chopper struggled and just managed to lift off, then dipped its nose and swept only feet above the rocks that raced away below us. The skids missed some of them by what seemed like only a few inches. The pilot strained to get more speed and lift; the joystick shook in his hands. Their eyes darted between the dials and the rocks below, just beneath the height of the skids. They were sweating. Now would be a bad time to die, I thought, having just got off the mountain safely. I knew that only a few years ago a chopper had crashed trying to take off from here, killing everyone aboard. I swallowed, I couldn't do this as a living.

Slowly the chopper gained height and the glacier dropped away below us. The pilots sat back in their seats and looked at each other, then at me and grinned; it had been close. I think they knew that I wasn't a doctor, but they also knew when someone was desperate. That is why they had come back. I thanked them and smiled.

As we swept down through the valley, the rotors began to bite into the thicker air. On the horizon I could see a tiny figure with two big white dots on his feet. 'Neil?' I muttered, grinning to myself questioningly. We swooped down to pick him up and lifted off with ease. The pilots, still both on oxygen, looked round at us. A look of understanding came over their faces as they saw us huddled together, grinning. We were away.

Mick and Geoffrey raced ahead of the rest of the team and covered the thirty-five miles to the rocky airfield at Lukla, in some twenty-eight hours, non-stop. An amazing feat that I knew I could never have done. My body was in pieces.

As the two of them began the long journey down, Neil and I leant back in the helicopter, faces pressed against the glass, and watched our life for the past three months become a vague shimmer in the distance. The great mountain faded into a haze, hidden from sight. I leant against Neil and closed my eyes – Everest was gone.

CHAPTER EIGHTEEN

WHY

▲

'Two roads diverged in a wood –
I took the road less travelled,
And that has made all the difference.'

Robert Frost

The harsh world of the mountains – cold, white and hostile had been our life for the past ninety-three days. We were leaving that world behind us now. As the chopper swooped and wound its way back through the valleys, that hostility slowly became replaced by the rich flora of the foothills. Glaciers were exchanged for the warmth of yellow rock-beds, and snow was substituted for the buds of the late-spring flowers. I felt the richer air fill my nostrils and a warmth swept over me. We were leaving a lot behind.

The three months up there had changed every one of us. Fear, worry, pain, but also a sense of wonder had held us strongly together for all that time. But still, the long awaited dream of home held me captive. As the valleys that we knew so well flew past beneath us, I felt that dream getting ever closer.

Kathmandu was the sprawling mass of fumes and ancient

diesel buses that I remembered it to be. Nothing else seemed to have changed. I felt like a naïve stranger returning into the hustle and bustle of it all. I had been away from all this for so long, living a life of simplicity amongst the hills. The confusion of the city below frightened me as we hovered above the landing pad at the airport. A different world was now awaiting us.

*

On arriving at the Gauri Shankar hotel, I apologized to the receptionist for my smell. My clothes were black with the dirt of months of mountain living. I shifted around slightly embarrassedly. She seemed most forgiving and smiled. I returned the compliment and took the key. It had been a while since I had seen a girl.

The shower was all I had hoped it to be; it was unlikely, though, to disappoint, when my last shower had been over twelve weeks earlier.

The bathroom floor became thick with grime, as the dirt and sweat washed off me. I felt both fear and strain falling away with it. As the cold water splashed over me, I felt a deep relief. I sang quietly to myself. Neil sat on the bed, swigging a cool beer, his feet still bandaged and raised.

Leaning over the balcony of the hotel in my towel, whilst Neil showered, I saw the Russian team, who had been on the north side of Everest. They talked in low voices and moved their bags lethargically around. They looked mentally exhausted. I put on a T-shirt and, still in my towel and holding my beer, I went down to see them. As my eyes met theirs, I knew something was wrong. I knew that look. Neither of us talked for a few seconds as we just looked at each other. They had been crying; big Russian, bearded men, crying.

*

Sergei and Francys Arsentiev were recently married. They loved to climb. Everest was the culmination of a dream; a dream that had gone horribly wrong. Francys had been coming down from the summit when she collapsed. Nobody knew why. Maybe cerebral oedema, or a heart attack, or maybe just exhaustion. She didn't have the energy to carry on. She died slowly where she sat. Sergei, her husband, went off in search of help; drunkenly he staggered in a stupor of fatigue and desperation. He fell to his death and was never seen again.

The Russian I sat with asked me feebly if I had seen anyone fall whilst we had been up there, or had we seen a body, or just . . . anything. His voice was weak, he knew that it was unlikely, but he had to try. His eyes seemed dead. I felt a sickness well up inside as I thought of Sergei and his wife both dead on the mountain. 'What the hell am I doing celebrating?' Emptiness swept over me. I pushed the beer slowly aside without even looking at it.

That afternoon, lying on my bed, I struggled to understand why we had survived. Why had we even been there? I thought of Sergei and Francys Arsentiev; they hadn't been the only ones who had died in the last few weeks. Roger Buick, a New Zealand climber, had also collapsed whilst still quite low on the hill. He had died there from a heart attack. Life seemed tragically volatile, almost cheap. Mark Jennings was a British climber who had reached the top but had died on the descent. That killer symptom of collapsing to the ground from fatigue had claimed his life as well. These were all experienced, fit climbers. I wrestled to understand why we had survived when others had been robbed of precious life. What a waste, what an unnecessary waste. As I lay there I found no real answers. A year later, I still find myself bereft of any.

The Russians' faces had been buried in deep despair; they weren't interested in answers; they had lost their comrades. I closed my eyes. I remembered the words of an old corporal of mine when he had lost his best friend; they were all I could find.

Said in his broad Welsh accent he had put it down to the 'Shape of life, Bear. Shape of life.' The words didn't seem to answer anything, but they were all I had.

Human nature hungers for adventure, and true adventure has its risks. Everyone knows those risks on Everest, yet the reality of seeing it first hand makes such words seem hollow. These are real lives, with real families and it still confuses me today.

I remain loyal, though, to the belief that those brave men and women who died during those months on Everest are the true heroes. To them goes the real glory. This must be their families' only relief.

Neil had lived with death on Everest, twice now. It was twice too much. We wandered the streets of Kathmandu and tried to put it all behind us. As we walked I felt a liberation. The rickshaws honked, the street sellers scurried by clutching their wares, and the fumes lingered sordidly around the tiny, muddy backstreets. The rush of everyday life seemed to dull the memories of the mountain, and all those emotions began to lift off me.

I remembered when I had returned from Ama Dablam almost eight months earlier; the excitement, the determination – it was gone now. I had spent it all on the mountain. The photos of Everest for sale in the stalls no longer held the same magic. I looked at them out of habit more than anything.

We were due to be flying out early the next morning, to get Neil home to some proper medical attention. His feet were now really beginning to swell and blister, as the dead tissue in his toes began to decompose. He hobbled around with me like an old man. It was good to try and move them, despite the strange looks we received from passers-by. We ignored them, they didn't need to know.

Mick and Geoffrey would arrive in Kathmandu by plane from Lukla in a day or so. It would be a shame not to be together for a while in Kathmandu, but we had no idea how long they would be. We needed to get Neil back.

That last night, 'out on the tiles' in Kathmandu, Neil 'got lucky' with a beautiful Scottish girl. It hasn't taken him long, I thought, smiling. I left them kissing outside the down-market Casino. I felt strangely happy for him, almost jealous. I reassured myself by thinking that I was far too exhausted to possibly attempt that. I grinned. That would do. I went back to the hotel and fell fast asleep as if drugged by the intoxicating rich air of Kathmandu – at only 3,000 feet.

*

If a man was taken straight from sea-level to the summit of Everest, he would be unconscious in minutes, and dead soon after. The hostility of that place of dreams had allowed us through her fickle net for a few brief moments on the top. We had returned alive. But why had we done it? Or as one paper, rather too accurately, put it: 'What makes a scruffy, twenty-three-year-old want to risk it all for a view of Tibet?' Before I left, I am sure that I would have had a far more slick reply than I do now. The answer seems somehow less obvious, or maybe just less important. I don't know; I don't really think about it much. It is just good to be home.

Without any doubt, though, the draw of the mountains is their simplicity. That fierce force of nature, where the wind howls around you and you struggle for breath and life itself; it is strangely irresistible to man. The simple sound of ice beneath your crampons, crunching as the teeth bite into the frozen surface. The raw beauty of being so high and so remote, being like, as Hillary said, 'ants in a land made for giants', seeing the greatest mountain range in the world sprawled beneath you. All of it inexplicably draws us to them. I feel those emotions and see those views as I write.

I am not sure if I would return to climb other great peaks, the ones above 26,000 feet – I suspect not. I feel that I undoubtedly used up at least four of my nine lives during those months, and it is always good to keep a few in the bank for emergencies. In truth, though, it is the mountains that I love, the air, the freedom, the heather, the streams. I will always be amongst those, but maybe now in a way that I can just 'be'; free to enjoy them, with nothing any longer to prove. That, to me, is the real spirit of the mountains.

My experiences on Everest are now just memories; they may fade, but they will never leave me. It is something that maybe only those who have been there will understand.

Since our return, though, people have congratulated me on 'conquering Everest', but this feels so wrong. We never conquered any mountain. Everest allowed us to reach her summit by the skin of our teeth, and let us go with our lives where others died. We certainly never conquered her. If I have learnt a deep understanding of anything, it is this. Everest never has been nor ever will be conquered. It is what makes the mountain so special.

One of the questions I repeatedly get asked since returning is, 'Did you find God on the mountain?' The answer is no. You don't have to climb a big mountain to find a faith. I actually began my faith whilst sitting up a tree as a sixteen-year-old. It is the wonderful thing about God; He is always there, wherever you are. That's what best friends are for. If you asked me did He help me up there, then the answer would be yes. In the words of the great John Wesley when asked by some cynic whether God was his crutch, he gently replied, 'No, my God is my backbone.' He was right.

*

The return to the rich air of sea level brought with it an abundance of blessings. The wind was moist and warm, the grass grew and the air was thick with oxygen. The rush, though, from the extreme altitudes we had been to, back to virtually sea level, brought with it its dangers as well. Several of us experienced recurring nose-bleeds and Mick and Jokey had both passed out several times. These were all purely reactions, for the first time in a while, to too much oxygen. But our bodies soon adapted and within several weeks our precious acclimatization was lost.

When we were next to fly in a plane, gone would be the time when we could quietly announce to our neighbour during the safety brief that in the case of a loss in cabin pressure feel free to use our oxygen masks – we won't need them.

As for the rest of the team, well, Neil returned to his own company, Office Projects Ltd, in London. His feet healed remarkably well and now only cause him a minimum of pain. He still doesn't have much feeling in them but he managed to keep all his toes.

In 1996, whilst he was away, to his horror, his business did a record high quarterly turnover in his absence. Now, though, when he returned, his new-found confidence ensured that his business set an even higher record. He had only been back a month and he found himself winning contracts wherever he looked. He bought a huge BMW and whopping big speedboat on the proceeds.

I smile as I meet him in London and hear of all his latest 'acquisitions'. If anyone deserves them, it is him.*

Funnily enough, in the same week that he bought his speedboat, I also bought a boat. Mine, unfortunately, wasn't quite as grand as his, being only a nine-foot-long, rotting old fishing boat. Still, I felt certain that our time on the mountain had maybe created a secret yearning for the sea. Maybe it was the freedom

---

* In early 1999 Neil Laughton completed his dream of climbing the highest peak on each continent. By the summer of 1999 he had also reached the North Pole.

and peace that it offers, I don't know. I am currently writing this book on a small uninhabited island off the South Coast,* and my fishing boat has broken down. So I am cursing the day I bought it as I go hungry, awaiting the island's owner at the end of the week. Still . . .

Geoffrey left the Army, and found himself a job in the City. It had been a shame that for so much of the expedition we had been apart, but it just turned out like that. The main part of the climb, though, we had done together, and my respect for his decision to turn around above Camp Four remains immense. It showed a certain wisdom to be able to make rational decisions like that, well into the Death Zone. He remains a close friend.

Mick seemed profoundly changed by his time on Everest. He became gentler than I had ever known him to be and his gratitude for life seems to shine from him. He came all too close to losing it. He sums his thoughts up like this:

> As for 'Mick on Everest – the sequel', it seems unlikely. I feel that the money, time and exposure to danger, involved in trying to achieve those extra 300 feet, is not worth it. In my three months that I was away, I was happier than ever before, more scared than I hope ever to be again, and more stressed than any bond dealer with £10 million in the wrong place, could ever imagine. I came home alive and for that I'll always be grateful.

He has since launched a network marketing arm of Tiscali. I know he will be successful.

Henry Todd, our expedition manager, returns to the great Himalayan peaks twice a year – organizing expeditions. Almost

---

* Green Island in Poole Harbour was very kindly lent to me by the Davies family. It was magic!

half of his time is spent in these hills. They are his home. He still swears and shouts ferociously, grinning away from behind his matted beard, but the bottom line is that his expertise keeps people alive up there. We all couldn't help but like him; and the faith and trust he placed in me made all the difference.

Graham returned to his family and the good Brown Ale of Newcastle. A month later he was awarded an MBE by the Queen, for services to mountaineering and charity. It had been given to the nicest of men. Having been forced to abandon his summit attempt with us because of the illness he had, he has subsequently agreed to return to Everest in the spring of 1999 – to try again. It would be his fourth time on the mountain.*

The other climbers with us returned to their homes. As is the nature of adventure, you return home having trodden some fine lines, and nothing ever seems to have changed. Buses smell, newspaper men blurt out the headlines and people get in a panic if the milk is a day old – but it is this continuity of life that makes it so good to return to.

As for the Sherpas – they continue their extraordinary work. Pasang and Ang-Sering still climb together as best friends, under the direction of their 'sirdar' – Kami. The two Icefall doctors, Nima and Pasang, still carry out their brave task in the glacier; they remain a law unto themselves, playing poker in their tents by candlelight until the early hours and laughing out loud across Base Camp. They both still smoke incessantly. I did get the dog that I said I would buy, and called her Nima; though my dog is rather less brave than him – as she lies on her back, asleep by the fire.

Thengba, my friend with whom I spent so much time alone at Camp Two, has been given a hearing-aid by Henry. Now, for

* Graham Ratcliffe MBE reached the summit of Mount Everest from the South Side in May 1999. He is the first Briton to climb Everest from both sides.

the first time, he can hear properly. I never believed that his grin could get any wider – but Henry assures me it has. Thengba's days are now spent laughing along with his Sherpa friends' banter. I am returning to Nepal next year to see him.

Despite our different worlds, we share a common bond with these wonderful men; a bond of friendship that was forged by an extraordinary mountain.

Once, when the climber Julius Kugy was asked what sort of person a mountaineer should be, he replied: 'Truthful, distinguished and modest.'

All these men epitomize this. I made the top with them, and because of them. I owe them more than I can say.

The great Everest writer, Walt Unsworth, writes a vivid description of the characters of the men and women who pit their all on the mountain. I think it is accurate.

> But there are men for whom the unattainable has a special attraction. Usually they are not experts: their ambitions and fantasies are strong enough to brush aside the doubts which more cautious men might have. Determination and faith are their strongest weapons. At best such men are regarded as eccentric; at worst, mad ... Three things these men have in common: faith in themselves, great determination and endurance.

*

8 JUNE 1998. DORSET, ENGLAND. The day after my twenty-fourth birthday.

I looked at my watch sleepily, it was 3.20 p.m. Damn, I thought, – the pigs. I had dozed off in my bedroom, fully clothed on my bed, and time had floated by in a blissful, summery haze. The animals would be going berserk with hunger. 'I've got to stop these afternoon naps – they'll become a habit,' I mumbled to myself, as I sat upright.

Since returning, my body had slowly begun to unwind from

the exhaustion of our time on the mountain. The months had drained me more than I could have imagined. I think that it was the constant worry and strain of not knowing what lay ahead that had plagued my waking hours the most. I had found that even on rest days at Base Camp where, on the face of it there was nothing to do but wait and sleep, the gentle nagging fear never really left the recesses of my mind. The fear of what the next day would bring, that intolerable waiting for the unknown, and the fear, I guess, of possibly not seeing my family again.

The relief that I now felt was immense; for the first time the pressure had fallen away, and rest came easily. Nothing but feeding the animals at home disturbed my rest those first few weeks after getting back, and oh . . . how I now loved my duvet.

My back had held up amazingly well. During the build-up to the climb I had experienced only the mildest of twinges – on the climb itself, it had never failed me. Despite the constant strain and hard discomfort of lying on the ground, I never felt any recurring pain. It had amazed me.

Now lying at home in bed, my back mildly ached for the first time. I smiled. So much had happened. It's this flipping soft-living, I'm sure, I thought.

I slowly clambered off my bed and sat wearily looking around my room. My eyes rested on a bag in the corner. On our return, all my kit had been piled into a mass of different hold-alls and I was only now beginning to sort them out. This was one of the last ones that remained untouched, since my return four days ago.

I knelt down and began rummaging lazily through the kitbag. It was full of stinking clothes and equipment, which I had hurriedly packed that last night at Base Camp, before getting the chopper out the next morning. Socks that I had worn for months were festering in the bottom. They must have smelt like I had, when I stood proudly before the beautiful receptionist in the hotel in Kathmandu – they stank. I threw them in my pile for 'immediate' washing, and carried on sifting through the bag. Books, Walkman, tapes, medicines. They were all just as they were when I had stuffed them excitedly in at Base Camp.

As I pulled a pair of thermal long johns out, I noticed my sea-shell fall out with them. It clinked to the floor and lay on its side. I reached over and picked it up carefully. It had been my most treasured item in my tent for all that time on the mountain. I had found it with Shara on the beach in the Isle of Wight. I rolled it over in my hand and my mind wandered.

I remembered the number of times I had read the inscription on the inside of it. That lonely time, when all the others left Base Camp without me because I was ill; that fearful moment of leaving Camp Two for the final time, when I didn't know what the future held. The words in the shell were as true now as they had been then. I read them slowly. They meant the world to me.

'Be sure of this, that I am with you always, even unto the end of the earth.' Matthew 28:20.

I gripped the shell tight in the palm of my hand and remembered. It had come a long way with me.

Suddenly the voice of my mother broke the silence, as she warbled from downstairs in her high-pitched tone. I turned towards the sound.

'Bear, Beeeeaaarr. You may have climbed Everest, but whilst you are at home you jolly well pull your weight. Now hurry up and go and feed those pigs. That's your job. Beeeaarr, did you hear me?'

I smiled, got slowly to my feet, and put the shell in my pocket. I scuttled down the stairs two at a time, muttering under my breath, 'Blasted porkies.'

POSTSCRIPT

▲

In the year following Bear's ascent, Michael Matthews, a twenty-two-year-old British climber, reached the summit of Mount Everest, becoming the youngest Briton to climb the mountain at that time – an honour shared with James Allen, who also reached the summit aged twenty-two, in 1995. Tragically, Michael Matthews died of exhaustion during a storm on his descent.

Before 1995, the youngest British climber to have reached the summit was Peter Boardman. In 1975 he reached the summit aged twenty-four; sadly, he later died on Everest whilst climbing with Joe Tasker in 1982. Another British climber under the age of twenty-five to have possibly reached the summit was Andrew Irvine. Irvine died with George Mallory on their famous 1924 expedition and the mystery surrounding their ascent of Everest has still not been solved. This book is a tribute to those brave men who never came home.

You're blessed when you're at the end of your rope. With less of you there is more of God.

Matthew 5, v.2 (The Message Version)

Appendices

▲

British Everest Expedition 1998 – Official Sponsors

Davis, Langdon and Everest,
  Chartered Quantity
  Surveyors, London, UK
Gartmore Investment
  Management
SSAFA Forces Help
Eton College
Virgin and the Morelli
  Group
Karrimor
Quatar Airways
Lord Archer of
  Weston-Super-Mare
Breitling
Timex
Khyam Leisure
BT plc

John Duggan Esq
Michael Dalby Esq
The Grenadier Guards
Land Activities Sports Fund
PRI ITC Catterick
Household Division Funds
Lazards
St Hugh's College, Oxford
  University
Citibank
Smithkline Beecham
Henderson Crosthwaite
  Institutional Brokers
Sharp Panasonic
Liquid Assets!: Moët et
  Chandon
Freedom Brewery

Charity Contributors

The Expedition was raising money for Great Ormond Street Children's Hospital and SSAFA Forces Help – the national charity, helping both serving and ex-service men and women and their families in need.

Many individuals and companies generously contributed to the fund-raising efforts, for which we are very grateful. The following is a list of some of the major corporate contributors:
Theakstons Brewery. Guinness Mahon. Perpetual. Bank of Ireland
Greenflag. Alliance and Leicester. RBS Avanta. Churchill Insurance
Aberdeen Prolific. Albert E Sharp. Baring Asset Management.
  Birmingham Midshires. Britannia Building Society. Halifax
  plc
Hill Samuel Asset Management. HSBC Holdings
Harrods. Rothschild Asset Management. London and Manchester. Pearsons
Save & Prosper. Scottish Equitable. Templeton. Virgin Direct
Ludgate Communications. Bristol and West
Dresdner Kleinwort Benson Research. Henderson Investors
Kleinwort Benson. Lansons PR
Mercury Asset Management. Northern Rock
Portman Building Society. Frere Cholmeley Bichoff
Luther Pendragon. Polhill Communications
Woolwich. Nonsuch High School
MORI. Biddick Harris PR. Broadgate Marketing. Chase de Vere
Chelsea Building Society. Colonial
Coventry Building Society. Financial Dynamics
Prospero Direct. Thomas Cook
Yorkshire Building Society. Brewin Dolphin Bell Lawrie
Cazenove. Financial and Business Publications Ltd
Lansons Communications. Rathbone Bros

Skipton Building Society. Walker Cripps Waddle Beck
Brunswick PR. Norwich and Peterborough Building Society

*

A total of £52,000 has been raised for Great Ormond Street
Children's Hospital, £13,000 for SSAFA Forces Help and £30,000
for the Rainbow Trust (a charity supporting terminally ill children
and their families).

To date Bear and his expeditions have raised almost $2 mil-
lion for children around the world.

For further information on Bear Grylls see: www.beargrylls.com

FACING THE FROZEN OCEAN

ONE MAN'S DREAM TO LEAD A TEAM
ACROSS THE TREACHEROUS
NORTH ATLANTIC

To my dad, who I miss so much,

and to Shara for giving me Jesse, our little son,

whom my father would so adore.

mer'cy *n. & a.*

1. compassion towards those in distress;

2. something for which to be thankful;

3. a blessing – 'it was a mercy we got out alive'

5th November, 2003

Dear Bear,

I was mightily relieved to hear that you had returned safely from
your terrifying ordeal! I think I remember warning you that the North
Atlantic was not exactly the nicest place to be in an open boat, but you
clearly experienced some truly awful conditions and I am full of
admiration for the way that you and your team coped. I am thankful
that my message to you arrived just in time – but I cannot possibly
imagine it was at all adequate to sustain you during those freezing and
frightening conditions..!

The photographs tell your tale very well and I imagine that your
talks are sell-outs, which is, of course, excellent news for The Prince's
Trust! It really is so good of you to allow my Trust to benefit from all
these endeavours and I can assure you that the money you raise will
make an enormous difference to many lives.

This comes, as ever, with my boundless admiration for you and
your intrepid colleagues and my heartfelt thanks for all you have done
for my Trust.

Yours most sincerely

Charles

CONTENTS

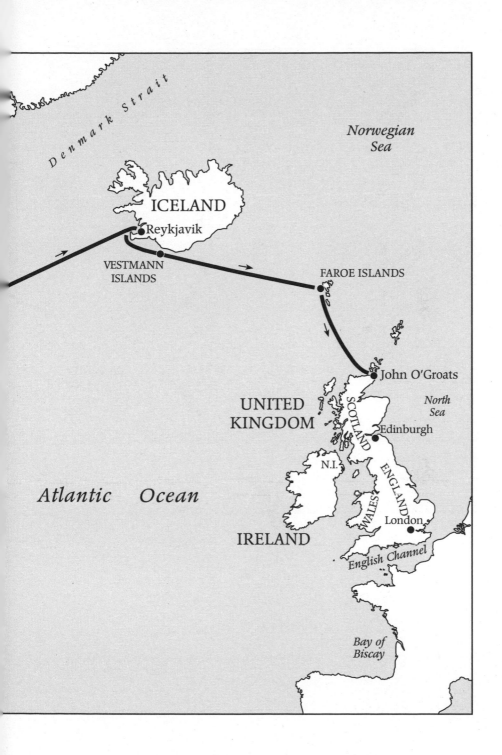

Denmark Strait

Norwegian Sea

ICELAND

Reykjavik

VESTMANN ISLANDS

FAROE ISLANDS

John O'Groats

UNITED KINGDOM

SCOTLAND

North Sea

Edinburgh

N.I.

ENGLAND

Atlantic Ocean

WALES

London

IRELAND

English Channel

Bay of Biscay

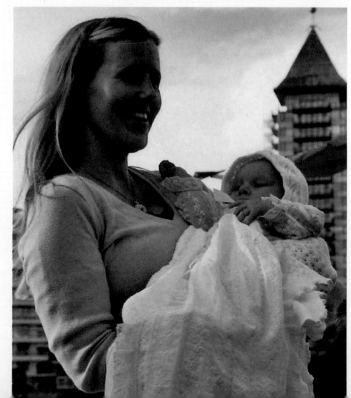

Above. My late dad
Mickey Grylls and
me aged eight

Right. My reason
for coming home:
Shara, my wife,
with Jesse on the
deck of our barge
the day of his
christening

The expedition's patron, HRH Prince of Wales with (from left to right)
Eric Loth (from The British Masters Arnold & Son, our lead sponsors),
Nigel Thompson, Mick Crosthwaite, Lt Andy Leivers, me and
Jean-Marie Florent (also from our lead sponsors)

Into the Unknown by George Lewis. The oil painting was in aid of
The Prince's Trust. *(Courtesy of Octavian Art)*

ARNOLD & SON
MASTERS OF THE LONGITUDE IN LONDON SINCE 1764
TransAtlantic Arctic Expedition 2003
Patron: HRH Prince of Wales

The *Arnold & Son Explorer*, looking a fraction of her beautiful self,
being lowered into Canadian waters for the first time

HMS *Newcastle* in heavy seas. Andy getting a perspective on what
lies ahead for us in an open boat

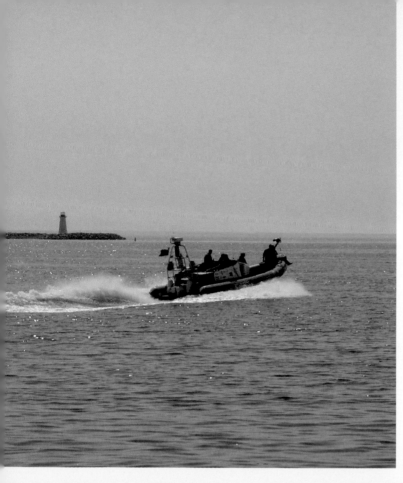

Left.
Leaving Halifax,
Nova Scotia.
The journey
begins

Below. Arriving at
night in Glace Bay,
Nova Scotia

Looking aft as we enter the sea-fog off Newfoundland, south of the
Belle Isle Strait

The remote coastline of Newfoundland, and one of the many lighthouses

Left. Bear in St Mary's harbour, Labrador

Below. The crew stare worriedly at the dark weather clouds ahead, with no idea of what we were going into

Sea-fog and swell off the Labrador coast

Charlie 'Lone Ranger' Laing, our brilliant cameraman

Trying to rest in our 'sardine tin'

The product of having soaking wet, freezing hands for days on end:
the bath effect!

1. DANGEROUS DREAMS

The man who risks nothing, gains nothing.

Neil Armstrong

We are still no closer to Base-Camp and it's getting late. I glance nervously around the Icefall. We are 19,000 vertical feet above sea level, in the mouth of Everest's killer jaws. I notice my hand is shaking as I fumble with the ropes through thick mittens. I am scared.

The sound of the metal climbing devices clinking on my harness is becoming hypnotic. I squeeze my eyes tight shut then open them. I try to breath rhythmically. I dig my crampons into the snow and wait. Mick is still ten yards away, stepping carefully across the broken blocks of ice. We have been in this crevasse-ridden, frozen death-trap for over nine hours and we are tiring. Fast.

I stand up on my feet and take a few more careful steps, testing the ice with each movement. Then I feel the ice crack under me. I hold my breath. My world stands still. It cracks again then drops and opens up beneath me. I am falling.

As I smash against the grey wall of the crevasse that was hidden beneath a thin veneer of ice, my world is spinning. The tips of my crampons catch the edge of the crevasse wall and the force throws me to the other side, crushing my shoulder and arm against the ice. I carry on falling, then suddenly I jerk to a halt as the rope somehow holds me. I can hear my screams echoing in the darkness below.

The ice that is still falling around me crashes against my skull, jerking my head backwards. I lose consciousness for a few precious seconds. I come to, and watch the ice falling away beneath me into the darkness as my body gently swings around on the end of the rope. Suddenly all is eerily silent.

Adrenalin is soaring around my body, and I find myself shaking in waves of convulsions. I scream again and the sound echoes around the walls. I look up to the ray of light above, then down to the abyss below. Panic is overwhelming me. I clutch frantically for the wall, but it is glassy smooth. I swing my ice-axe at it wildly, but it doesn't hold, and my crampons screech across the ice. In desperation I clutch the rope above me and look up.

I am 23 years of age and about to die.

The River Thames, September 2003, five years later. It is raining. I look up and hope for better weather for the day of Jesse's christening. I have it all planned.

The priest is going to stand on the old wooden deck of our barge, his robes billowing in the autumn breeze that whistles down the Thames, and, right there, with our families all around, he will christen our gorgeous son, Jesse, with snow water brought back from the summit of Mount Everest.

But first there were forms to be completed and my wife, Shara, was gradually working through the questions.

'Occupation?'

'What?'

'I have to put your occupation here.'

'OK.'

'Well,' Shara asked, 'what *is* your occupation?'

I hated this question. What would have been a simple query for most people was anything but straightforward for me.

It would be so much easier just to be an estate agent. It would be so simple to write.

Explorer? Sounds self-important.

Mountaineer? Well I have always climbed, I guess.

Motivational speaker? Partly, but that's not all.

Television presenter? When bribed.

Writer? Once in a while, but not that brilliant.

'Just put anything,' I replied unhelpfully.

In truth I feel rather as though I'm unemployable; but somehow I seem to have carved out this strange existence where I am able to do what feels natural to me, and then earn my living speaking about those experiences. And that, I guess, is my job.

'Oh, just put estate agent, my love,' I told her.

The two adjectives most often attached to the men and women who live these adventures are 'brave' and 'eccentric', but to be honest, I dislike them both. I am not especially brave: I struggle with so many things and am much too sensitive for my own good. I often feel both afraid and vulnerable in this weird world we live in, and miss my family if I leave them for twenty-four hours. As for 'eccentric', I am not eccentric: yes, I sometimes take risks, but by nature I am extremely cautious. I am only too aware of the law of averages: the more times you get lucky, the worse your odds become.

What I do know is that I have always tried to live as my dad taught me.

My father died less than three years ago. Out of the blue, unannounced. He had been recovering from a pacemaker operation and was at home and fine, sitting up in bed. A minute later he was dead – just like that. That wasn't meant to happen; he was only sixty-six. In the blink of an eye, one cold February morning, my dad had gone. All I had now was what he had taught me. I wish every day I could remember more.

Throughout my childhood in and around the Isle of Wight, he'd taught me to climb and he'd taught me to sail. I adored every day we spent together on the cliffs, every day on the sea. I adored the excitement, the thrill and the challenge, but above all I loved just being close to him.

I remember those special days all the time, often at odd moments. Maybe backstage at a big conference when I'm nervous, about to go out there and face another sea of strange faces. It can feel like the loneliest place on earth. I often think of Dad in those seconds before going onstage. I don't know why.

I remember how he once gave me an old 7-foot wooden boat with an even older 1-hp outboard engine. For Christmas he added a steering wheel, so I could potter around the harbour like a real captain.

He guided me, he moulded me and he liberated me.

'Now listen, Bear,' he would say. 'There are only two things that really matter in life. The first is to have dreams. The second is to look after your friends. The rest is detail.' That was life in a nutshell.

If my school reports were terrible, as they invariably were, he would say I should try harder, but it never seemed like the end of the world. He would pull a silly face, speak in a silly voice and hold me tight. And I learned more about life in those moments than in all my years of school.

It was soon after my eighth birthday that Dad gave me a huge framed photo of Mount Everest. This was immediately hung on the wall in my bedroom. I would stare at it for hours in the dark, trying to imagine what it would be like to climb up there. What would it really feel like, so far away, so exposed, in those storm-force conditions that inhabit high ice faces? In my little bedroom, that Everest dream was born. One day, I swore to myself, I would stand on top of the world.

After leaving school, I joined the army. During this time I served for three years as a soldier with the British Special Air Service (21 SAS) until a freak parachuting accident almost ended my life.

I was in southern Africa, it was early evening, everything was routine; then my chute failed to deploy properly. I survived the fall, the torn canopy slowing my descent, but my injuries were bad. I had broken my back in three places and was deemed by the African doctor a 'miracle man' to have survived. It had indeed been a miracle, and one I thank God for every day.

Six months in and out of military rehabilitation healed the bones but my confidence took much longer to return. The idea of climbing Everest seemed nothing but a pipe-dream now.

But from where I lay, I began to dream again. And as my movement increased I began to get restless. I soon found that my hunger to climb had returned, and that hunger became the focus of my recovery. When, two years later, the opportunity to join a team of three other climbers on Everest came around, every ounce of me knew this was my break. It was crazy, but here was my chance.

I had been earning about £45 a day as a soldier and I needed £15,000 for the expedition. I sold all I could, took out loans and got lucky with one amazing sponsor, Davis Langdon and Everest. The door had creaked open.

Together with Mick Crosthwaite, my friend since we were kids in the Isle of Wight, and an exceptional team led by Neil Laughton, an old army friend, I spent three extraordinary months on Everest. Finally, at 7.22 a.m. on 26 May 1998, exhausted as dawn broke over the high Himalayas, two of us from our team stood on the roof of the world. A strange combination of luck, friendship and heart had enabled that moment to come true for me. It was all that I had imagined it would be and more.

Two years later, I led a team that managed to circum-navigate Britain on jet-skis in aid of the RNLI. It was Shara's and my first summer of married life together, and not quite her ideal holiday, driving around behind us in a camper van laden with jerry cans. She thought it was crazy but we had a blast. We had the proper sponsorship, we were helping a charity, we were with my closest mates and we were following a dream. This became my career.

I had been drawn into the world of expeditions partly because it was what I loved but largely because I found it was one of the few things I could do all right.

Early in 2000, I read about a British team that had previously attempted to cross the North Atlantic, just below the Arctic Circle, in an open rigid inflatable boat (RIB). They had performed heroically in horrendous conditions. Close to hypothermia and fighting frostbite, they had twice had to put out a call for emergency help – once to be brought out of the pack ice near Greenland and on the other occasion to be lifted on to a fishing trawler during a storm off Iceland. But they completed their route and had all returned alive.

I was intrigued.

'Do you think it is possible to complete this North Atlantic crossing in an open RIB without needing such emergency assistance?' I began to ask various maritime friends.

Typically, they would laugh. I would look at them and wait, expecting an answer which never came.

'It must be,' I would then tell myself. 'It has to be possible to do.'

The idea lingered.

There had been a Hollywood film set in the same seas, *The Perfect Storm*, starring George Clooney, about a group of fishermen who set out and never came back. I had seen it already and been terrified. I watched it again, but this time differently. I scrutinized the scenario and the conditions – the way the waves and the storm formed. I tried to imagine how a small open boat would cope. What decisions would I take as skipper? Would I turn round or risk the vessel? Suddenly, almost without knowing it, I was hooked.

Icebergs, gale-force winds, whales, the Labrador Sea ... I started to sleep badly at night, my mind a race of imaginings. But most importantly, by day, solid research led me to believe the crossing was distinctly possible.

Three years later, we did it – just. This is the story of that journey across the freezing, ice-ridden, most northerly part of the Atlantic.

In late 2002, I was invited to write an introduction for *Debrett's People of Today*. I felt unsure about what to say. I wanted to explain the essence of exploration and why it still appeals so much to me. But that essence is extremely hard to capture. This was my best effort:

> *Exploration, I have discovered, is all about taking that one extra step. When you're nearing the pinnacle of a high-altitude mountain, breathing wildly, with your physical reserves run dry, and are reduced to crawling on your knees, it is heart that matters. It is heart that tips the balance between dragging yourself one step nearer to the summit,*

and turning back for the safety of camp. And it is in these critical moments and decisions that people distinguish themselves.

I don't think any of our team felt particularly distinguished or individually brilliant, me included; we were a group of well-trained and hungry young guys, but we had a bond, something special that held us together when it was bleak and cold and frightening. That bond is hard to define, but it's because of that bond that I explore. It is why I went in the first place, and it is because of that bond that we all came home.

And it is this 'coming home' that, in the world of exploration, is all that ever really matters.

2. BUILDING THE BEST

If you want to build a ship, before you give men tools, teach them to yearn for the vast and endless sea.

Antoine de Saint-Exupéry

The one niggle that I always had was how would I tell one of my crew's family if something went truly wrong out there? In the middle of the night, 400 miles from any landmass, in driving rain and sleet, you are so vulnerable.

Trying to move around a small, open boat with inflatable tubes that are slippery as hell and freezing is a lottery. But even in the worst conditions things needed to be done. You couldn't really avoid having to move around the boat. One slip, a careless move, and in giant waves in pitch darkness, at 25 knots, recovery of a man overboard would be near impossible, however hard we tried.

How would I tell his family? What words would justify my pursuit of this dream? No dream is worth a man's life. And I knew the buck would always stop with me. It kept me awake often.

This expedition was always going to be different. In the past, certainly on Everest, I had been happy to sit in the back row at meetings, to listen to the leader of the expedition and do as he asked. It was also my prerogative, every now and then, to have a grumble like everyone else. I was OK at being one of the crew, a follower. I quite liked it.

Now, suddenly, it was going to be me making those

difficult calls, taking the lead. It was a big deal for me and it made me very nervous. I was heading into an infamously dangerous part of the world, and men's lives would hang on my decisions. Not just any men's lives, but my friends' lives.

I did not particularly seek leadership – it just happened. Leadership is a hard thing to learn, but our past experiences have much to tell us. We've all known people who have shaped our lives – schoolteachers, instructors – but what makes some of them remembered with affection and others so feared? For me, the people who had shown me real leadership – in fact, more than that, people I would have been prepared to fight alongside and die with, especially from my military days – were the ones who made me feel special, who went out on a limb for me: my patrol sergeant who shared his last capful of water with me after four days in the desert; the man who said I was OK and stood up for me when it counted.

Neil Laughton had been an incredible leader on the Everest expedition, a friend and a man I could depend on, decisive at times when others might easily have hesitated. I thought of him and tried to think how I like to be led. I guessed that was a good place to start. It was simple: I always felt best when I was trusted, when I felt that what I did mattered, when I was responsible for an area of expertise. When the rope, or the oxygen, or the food, or whatever it was, was up to me.

So I wanted each of my team to assume responsibility in his own area and take a real stake in this expedition. I wanted him to make decisions and feel pride in what he was doing. I didn't want to be one of those leaders who tries to do everything, inevitably makes mistakes and ends up being resented by everyone. I didn't want it to be about me; I wanted it to be about us, together, doing our best.

When word went out among the maritime community about this project, CVs started to pour in – ten years of experience here, fifteen there, everyone was an expert, and everyone seemed to want a piece of the action. But for me they missed what I felt really counted in a team. I wanted people who weren't 'experts', I wanted people, yes, who were well trained and competent, but above that I wanted people to whom this expedition really mattered. People who would put their everything into it, their heart and soul, their enthusiasm, their reputation if it all went wrong; people who would be there in the bad times as well as the good.

I wanted people I knew and trusted, people who, when they hadn't slept for days and their hands were so cold and wet that they were wrinkled, blue and shaking, would still summon up from somewhere inside the ability to get on their hands and knees at 3 a.m. during a storm and rummage to find you an energy bar from the sodden food sack. That was the sort of person I wanted.

I was looking for people who were kind before they were brave, honest before they were brilliant. People who occasionally needed reassurance but who, when the chips were down, I felt would find something deep inside them that is special. It's called heart. I wasn't interested in people who were never scared – courage is not the absence of fear, but rather the understanding that fear is human and that we all have the ability to overcome it. I was looking for people who wanted the chance to find that something inside – that part that often surprises us, a part that is gut and instinct, and that is better than we often expect.

This is a something that people rarely get the chance to find.

If I was going to take an open, rigid inflatable boat into those inhospitable waters, I was going to make sure that I had people on whom I could rely. In the end, I picked friends.

The first name on the team was Mick Crosthwaite, first and foremost, if I'm honest, because he was my buddy. We had known each other for as long as either of us could remember, from childhood days, all the way through school, the army and then as climbing partners on the Everest expedition.

Over the years Mick has grown to represent a source of solid friendship, sound judgement and real support. His presence always seems so strong; somehow, with him, I never have to look over my shoulder to check, never have to cast a precautionary glance. I just know I can rely on him 100 per cent of the time. And that's very rare.

By nature Mick is incredibly single-minded. When he's at work, running the Tiscali network, the pan-European network-marketing arm of the Internet communications company, nothing else gets in his way. Likewise when he is on an expedition, he moves into a different zone and focuses totally on that.

Sure enough, on the day when he was due to fly from London to Canada for the start of our voyage, Mick arrived at Heathrow airport in his business suit, having rushed from some high-powered meeting where he had clinched, to quote him, 'a massive deal'. To the amazement of several bystanders, he then proceeded to change into his expedition gear right there in the drop-off zone at Terminal Four. His mobile was switched off and stayed off until he was back in Scotland, a 6,000-mile round trip away.

Mick's demanding work commitments meant he was unable to make as much of a contribution to the planning stages as he knew he should, and on several occasions this irritated me. At one point I told him that if he wanted to be part of this, that had to start now: 'I am not another of your employees to be curt with, Mick, get out of work mode and realize you need to start giving a little too much rather than a little too little to this expedition. Everyone is busting a gut and all they see is you leaving early or arriving late. It's not acceptable and you know it.' The phone went silent, not dead, just silent. He was thinking. 'Make a choice, Miguel.'

This was an important and difficult conversation, but it changed everything in the run-up. The others needed to know Mick would start putting his heart into what we were doing now, not just on the actual expedition itself. This was different from climbing. The logistics here were more complex than for a small team on a mountain and we needed everyone's energy in the preparation as much as when we would leave. What Mick didn't do, someone else had to – and it was too early on for people to feel resentment. It was all the more poignant because the others were now working so hard towards the expedition.

'I've got to go now, Mick.' And I replaced the receiver.

Mick arrived at the next meeting with the biggest file of meteorological data you've ever seen. As our weatherman, he was now in. He'd been the first to join me on the team but really the last to become one of us. But that didn't matter; what was important was that I had my wingman again.

I suppose our friendship was genuinely forged on Everest. We climbed together throughout, but in the final moments of those three months, when fate and weather and health proved decisive in selecting who finally stood on the roof of the world and who didn't, fate chose me. I was luckier, that was all.

Mick had climbed to within 350 feet of the summit when he ran out of oxygen. Soon he was slumped in the snow at 28,500 feet, dying. I had spoken to him on the radio from down at Camp Two. He calmly told me he reckoned he had ten minutes to live. Then he went quiet on the radio and wouldn't respond. I was over 5,000 feet below him, powerless to help as my best friend's life slowly ebbed away. And in my panic all I could think of was how I was ever going to tell his family.

During this time Neil Laughton found him, helped him to stand up, and together they stumbled down the ridge under the south summit. Exhaustion was too much for Mick though and two hours later, delirious, he slipped and fell almost 500 feet. In truth he should have died, but he survived, was rescued and eventually came back down from the mountain. He knew exactly how close he had been to death.

His response to our time on Everest, particularly after I finally reached the summit, underpins my admiration for him. I think it is a credit to him that he has never felt the need to go back to Everest and try again. He just feels lucky to be alive. To risk everything again to try to climb that extra 350 feet is not a risk worth taking. As so many climbers have learned the hard way, our team included, if you play the odds of one in eight climbers not returning alive from Everest's summit too often, you don't always win.

Some people say the summit of a mountain is everything. They're wrong. Staying alive is everything. The press had no interest in the fact that Mick climbed higher than K2. To them he 'failed' to reach the top. But to me, we reached the top together, there was no difference.

I once read that a true friend revels in your success when things are going well and is there for you in difficult times. Well, Mick has been exactly that kind of friend for me. And that's why it mattered so much that he should be with me this time.

The next challenge for both of us was to tell his parents. I thought he should do this himself.

'Mick, you're grown up, for God's sake, don't be a wet blanket,' I told him, eager that it should be he who announced the news and faced his mother's disquiet, not me. 'And don't just procrastinate and let them find out through a newspaper. You're unbelievable. You're like an ostrich, burying your head in the sand. Well, I tell you, I'm not getting the blame for this one while you walk quietly by smirking.'

Our families had been extremely close and had known each other for as long as I could remember. Mick's father was my grandfather's godson and both our mums are called Sally. However, despite all this, I was always a little bit nervous around his mum near expedition times. This had all started when, aged sixteen, Mick and I had announced that we were saving up to do a parachute jump together and we were off the next day. For some reason, this wasn't Mick's fault but mine. In the Crosthwaite household it had somehow become accepted wisdom that it was always unreliable Bear who got honest Mick into dangerous situations. They bought into it every time.

The parachute jump, unsuitable girls, the army, Everest – to this day, somehow, it is all my fault.

Nigel Thompson lives not much more than 100 yards away from our barge on the Thames in London. He knew Shara first, and shared a house with her while we were going out. But since then he has become a close of friend of mine as well. We eat far too many Danish pastries together in our local square, laugh lots and talk about Hussein and Mohammed, the local curry-house waiters, on a daily basis. He has the wickedest sense of humour of anyone I know, and a vulnerability that is gorgeous.

What is it that makes some people get along? Well, we laugh at the same things, we laugh easily. I think that's important. But there's more to it than that. We're comfortable together, and that's a good thing in a friend. Nige is also godfather to our little son, Jesse.

He has always had a passion for sailing and boats, and was a fanatical rower at both school and university. Despite my being a bit suspicious of his worryingly high level of interest in navigational gadgets, his favourite pastime was getting into trouble in little boats – and naturally, as so often happens with the sea, this made us the best of boating buddies.

I have been to more boat shows with Nige than with anyone else, and have talked more with him about RIBs than is healthy. I knew he had never tasted the extreme environments that the expedition would encounter to such a degree before but he had this latent hunger to do more with his life, to be a bit different. His knowledge, his energy, his enthusiasm to be part of this adventure would, I knew, make Nige the most lovely of people to share the dream with.

I will never forget one particular day at the London Boat Show with Nige. We had been wandering around, chatting to as many different RIB builders and designers as possible. I was beginning to flag, but not Nige. He was in full swing.

'But can the sheer bow still allow sufficient water clearance in a following sea?' he would ask. And they would be off. Talking terms I could hardly understand. I needed some air.

'Nige, let's come back here later maybe?' I suggested.

He reluctantly agreed; the boat-builder reached out to shake his hand and passed him his business card.

'If I can ever help in any way, any advice, whatever it is, just let me know. If you are really going to do this expedition, you need the best RIB ever built. Just give me a call.'

Nige thanked him. There was a pause as the designer waited for his response. Nige fumbled. Finally, he reached into his pocket, pulled out one of his property surveyor business cards and handed that over.

'Likewise,' he said, 'if I can ever offer *you* any help with . . .' He paused '. . . with buying a shopping centre. Just let me know,' he finished buoyantly. The man stood bewildered as we walked away. Shopping centre? What the hell was he on about?

Nige's sense of humour never faltered. In the cold times ahead, when he began to suffer frostbite in his feet as we emerged from the Icelandic storm, he still managed to mumble to me over the wind, 'How do you think Mohammed the curry waiter would cope with this right now, right here, balancing forty poppadoms on his trolley?'

I asked Nige right at the start if he would join the expedition, and he didn't hesitate. He was working for Lunson Mitchenall, a firm of London surveyors. But this was his chance to do something more, something extraordinary, and he knew it. Most important, he went for it, and that's not always easy to do.

For me, one of the most rewarding aspects of these adventures is that they can become a genuinely life-changing experience. I've seen it so often. It gives people pride. It may be very quiet but it's there. And it's a great thing to see.

Right from the start, Nige proved a huge support to me. We discussed the expedition endlessly, and he helped me prepare the brochures that we sent out to prospective sponsors. He would stay up late at home on weeknights to print out another batch for me. They'd always be dropped off at the barge by morning. I know that I would never have got the expedition off the ground without him.

It was with Nige that I'd spend hours gathering information, constantly weighing up the pros and cons of routes, boat designs, equipment and every aspect of the expedition. Some of what we were doing as a team was new to him, and he was one of two team members who had not had the benefit of a military training, but as time went on he responded and picked things up remarkably quickly.

My nature is to speak my mind – I always have. I dislike petty jibes or undertones, I would prefer someone to say what they mean up front. It comes from having an older sister. I think it's best to try to be honest and clear the air, even if it makes us very vulnerable. What matters is that I know everyone in the long term appreciates honesty.

One evening I felt Nige was being difficult about something and I just came out with it. 'What's up, Nige? Why did you say that?' He mumbled something and we carried on, and to be honest I forgot all about it. Until three o'clock the following morning, that is, when Nige rang to say he couldn't sleep because he'd been worrying about what he'd said. He was sorry and hadn't meant it. I told him it was fine, it was nothing – it wasn't. I was impressed though. That sort of thing is not always easy to do. But Nige is that kind of sensitive, endearing person. He makes the calls we all so often put off. I knew he would be an important man to have on board.

Charlie Laing was a year ahead of me at school. We'd always known each other and got along pretty well, but we'd never been close friends. I probably only saw him twice during the ten years that had passed since we had left, maybe across the room at a party.

Then he telephoned me out of the blue. Shara and I were living in Chamonix, in the Alps, at the time, and Charlie had gone to considerable lengths to get our telephone number. He asked if he could meet me to talk about this next expedition and said he would email over his CV. Since school he had become a freelance cameraman, and had put together an impressive portfolio: among other projects, he'd worked on *Tonight with Trevor McDonald* and *Stars in their Eyes* and had produced a twelve-part documentary on the eccentric side of American life.

When Charlie called I was frantically busy travelling around doing talks to companies and then racing back to France to be with Shara. I hardly ever had much time in London. But he insisted.

'I'll meet you at Gatwick for a coffee,' he suggested.

I was impressed, and we eventually met at Finnegan's Bar at the airport. I told him about my plan to try to cross the North Atlantic but said I had already made a commitment to another cameraman.

'I've got to be honest with you,' I said. 'This other guy is the most likely to be our cameraman. He's hugely experienced and fired-up and it looks ninety-nine per cent certain that he's going to come along. I'm sorry, buddy, but it's gone.'

Charlie said he understood. 'Just keep me in mind,' he added as we said goodbye.

He rang me every week from then on. 'Any changes?' he would ask . . . again.

I'd tell him nothing had changed, and I would hear the disappointment in his voice.

Then, in October 2002, complications arose in the arrangements with our original cameraman, Will Ingham. It became clear that the production company due to film the expedition couldn't now pay him for his time, and at that stage we were in no position to pay him a market-related fee ourselves. The expedition bank account that Nige had helped me set up still had zero in it. Not one measly penny. We couldn't make any sort of commitment to a cameraman now without the support of a production company; I mean, we didn't even have the funds for a lifejacket.

On top of this, something didn't feel quite right. I felt uneasy with the idea of paying anyone to join the expedition. People had to want to be aboard our RIB. It wasn't about the money. This couldn't be a job – I wanted it to be someone's everything.

In that sense Charlie was our man. He was the one who had chased me and chivvied me. I called him soon after Christmas and asked if he was still keen on the idea. It would be unpaid, and would cost him the best part of six months' work. I'd pay for everything for him on the expedition – kit, flights, etc. – but his time and expertise would have to be for free. It was all or nothing.

I promised myself that if he agreed to come under those conditions, I would make it up to him if I could afford it when the time came and would buy him the smartest camera available as a present. In the end, I could afford it – just – and I hope that Charlie's commitment to us paid off for him too. Certainly the money I shelled out on that camera was the best I've spent in a long time.

Just like Nige, Charlie leaped at the chance. He didn't hesitate for a moment. I liked that. He had been determined enough to hunt me down in Chamonix, resolved enough to meet me at Gatwick and gutsy enough to keep asking. It worked.

Charlie might have had little knowledge of the ocean, or much real experience with boats, but he compensated with enthusiasm and grittiness. He was like a sponge, so eager to learn and master new skills. I'd catch him reading books on rough-water boat-handling and asking Nige endless questions about navigating in the fog that we knew would be so prevalent in the Labrador Sea. Whatever it was, he wanted to know – from EPIRB frequencies and emergency call-out procedures to knots and magnetic variations. Above all, he seemed to get a real buzz out of everything.

I remember one specific moment during the sea trials when I looked across the boat and saw him just grinning to himself. He was loving every moment.

Charlie recalls:

I had just got back from Australia, and I heard about Bear's plans. I wanted more than anything to be involved and thought I would give him a call and see what happened. I had no idea what to expect because I had only ever been on a yacht off the coast of Africa, but I just had the feeling it would be amazing.

In selecting Mick, Nige and Charlie, I suppose I had essentially based my choice on character, people I knew well, people in whom I had trust, people who knew me and who I felt would bond together. Really, they were my mates.

The only exception to this rule of thumb was my choice of engineer. There was a brief and pretty desperate period when we thought Mick could be the engineer. This was mainly because he was interested in tractors. Fortunately for all concerned, this folly evaporated like mist in the morning sun when I caught him failing to jump-start his old 1940s tractor down a hill, with clouds of smoke billowing out. 'Mick, I love you,' I told him, 'but we need a professional.'

As the plans gained momentum it became blatantly obvious that for a boat that was going to be single-engined, due to the sheer distance we were going to be travelling and hence the limitations on the amount of fuel we could carry, finding a professional engineer was critical. That one engine would be our lifeline – literally – and without it working, it mattered very little how big and brave our team was.

I wasn't used to having to rely so heavily on machinery – before, it was the human factor that had been critical on high mountains. But this time, keeping that precious sole engine working was going to be the most important job on the expedition. I needed somebody who could keep it working in what would possibly be the worst conditions such an engine had ever been in.

Mick and I had both served in the armed forces, and it became clear that it made sense to try to involve the Royal Navy.

I approached a naval friend, Captain Willie Pennefather. He put me in touch with the navy's PR team, who seemed to get right behind us; and, with the promise of the main front slot at the Schroders London Boat Show assured, we had some pulling power for them as well. But it was more than that. If the expedition proved successful, the navy's involvement would demonstrate its core values of adventure, teamwork and professionalism. So we formed an agreement whereby we would take a Royal Navy engineer with us as one of the crew.

The navy would also help with the berthing of the RIB at the RN Sailing Centre at Portsmouth, under the command of Lieutenant Commander Bill Rothwell. In addition, the navy offered to supply us with 20 tonnes of fuel for the sea-trialling. It was more than I had ever hoped for.

In the end the navy's commitment to us far outweighed even this, and their proactive support was crucial, especially in linking us up with the Danish and Canadian navies, who we knew were the only people who operated the rescue ships up in the Arctic. It was slowly becoming apparent that the naval side of the expedition was fundamental to our chances of success. (That is, of course, if you can manage to restrain the navy boys from taking you out drinking, which bitter experience has taught me is always a bad idea.)

The head of Fleet Corporate Communications, Captain Alistair Halliday, placed an advertisement in the *Navy News*. 'One naval engineer volunteer needed for arduous northerly expedition. Well paid, extra leave, but cold and misery guaranteed, with no ward room to escape the wind and waves!'

We received three replies and prepared to run some form of selection process. The first candidate was Lieutenant Andy Leivers, who came to visit me on our barge in London. He seemed to enjoy the environment, telling Shara she had a lovely galley and referring to our loo as the 'heads'. He was very polite, and very naval.

It was a sunny day, so I suggested Andy and I should take the little RIB that we keep on the Thames out for a spin. I quite often take people down the river and they invariably flounder aboard rather uncomfortably and take some time to settle. Andy was different. He was obviously completely at ease on the water and I remember how precisely and professionally he tidied away the rope, tying a perfect bowline round the stanchion with one hand.

While we were preparing to climb on to the RIB, Shara had been inside the barge, on the phone to her mum. She had heard us clambering around on deck and quickly jumped to conclusions.

'I don't believe it, Mum,' she gasped. 'Bear said he would put these guys through this selection process, and I think he really means it. I can hear them on deck and he's making the Lieutenant do press-ups. Poor guy's dressed in his best trousers!'

Luckily for Andy that wasn't the case. I wasn't that harsh (although I subsequently found out he would have loved to have done some press-ups) and in any case I was quickly becoming convinced that Andy Leivers was exactly the kind of person we needed. He had joined the Royal Navy as a marine apprentice at the age of seventeen, risen through the ranks to become an officer, then read engineering at South-ampton University. He was now serving as Deputy Marine Engineer on HMS *Newcastle*. He was eminently qualified, and he seemed fun, diligent and cautious.

I didn't even see the other two candidates.

Andy recalls:

I have my mother to thank first of all, because as an avid *Daily Telegraph* reader, she had read an article by Bear about his forthcoming record attempt across the North Atlantic. The article was titled: 'Is this the frozen limit?' She sent it to me saying it looked up my street and maybe I should apply.

I soon found myself up in London ready for an interview. I got an interview of sorts, but an interview the Bear Grylls way: on an RIB going up the Thames at forty knots! We had a blast and the more I heard about it all, the more I began to get seriously excited about the prospect of joining the team.

I knew Andy was the right guy. So we worked out a deal with Captain Halliday, whereby Andy would essentially be seconded to us from the Royal Navy.

I sought two assurances from the navy: the first was that they would allow Andy to be 100 per cent committed to our expedition and would not call him away for other duties or operations. I felt it was essential for Andy to understand that if the men he had been in charge of were sent to Iraq, or elsewhere, his commitment was still to be to this expedition. I understood how hard this might be for him if war broke out. They were his men, whom he'd looked after. But he knew what I was after and agreed. As it transpired, his men were used in coping with the fire service strikes at home, and not in the Gulf, so Andy really only missed an alternative way of getting soaked.

The second assurance I needed from the navy was that they would support me as leader of this expedition and I would have the authority of the navy behind me if I needed it. I felt it was important to lay this down early and for Andy to know he was on secondment and that I was in charge.

Both these conditions were agreed.

I was immensely relieved to have pulled this off. It was a huge deal for us. I felt tremendously privileged to have secured the services of a first-rate engineer from the finest navy in the world.

Through the weeks that followed, I became increasingly impressed by Andy's professionalism. He took total responsibility for the engine and fuel systems, and regularly brought me charts indicating how we could maximize the boat's performance. Cautious by nature and conservative in his analysis, he seemed to provide the ideal counterbalance to me. But on top of this, I reckoned that he was the kind of person who would help me make the right decisions under pressure in the middle of the ocean.

Mick had really pushed me to involve the Royal Navy somehow. He felt that it provided important security. He said that if the navy were just 'sponsors' and it all went wrong, they might be less inclined to send out the search-and-rescue than if we had one of their personnel on board. I agreed; but it was more than that. We now had an engineer who had been trained to the highest level, a man who also had a real understanding of the sea, weather and fuel management. And I knew that the more knowledge we had on this little boat, the better.

Finally, Andy came across as a kind man. I didn't want somebody who was just super-strong and super-confident in whatever they did. It was as important to me that I found someone who would work through a tough night and then be kind enough to offer you the roll-mat at the end. And Andy was exactly that sort of person.

So this was the crew: Mick, Nige, Charlie and Andy. I was convinced of their individual qualities, and hopeful we would bond together well. But there is always an element of the unknown and probably the most intense few months of our lives lay ahead.

But that bonding did come. And I remember when it happened.

It was one evening, not long before we left for Canada, when the whole team were together, meticulously going through each stage of the route point by point. At the start, this type of meeting had been dominated by me, talking them through all the plans, but this time it was different. They were all talking, buried in maps, fuel-ratio diagrams, wave-chart data, Danish naval emergency procedures, call signs, you name it. They talked about stuff I didn't even under-stand. It was fantastic. I just sat quietly and watched. I could sense in their voices the anticipation of what lay ahead. This was their expedition as much as it was mine. We were all in this together now.

This was what I had always wanted. I smiled to myself and opened a bottle of wine.

'To the times ahead,' I said, raising a glass.

'To the times ahead,' they replied, hardly even looking up as they continued poring over the charts.

This was my team. I knew I'd got lucky.

3. COUNTDOWN

Fall down seven times. Get up eight.

Japanese proverb

One glance at the long list of sponsors provided at the end of this book might create the impression that this was one of the most effortlessly funded expeditions in the history of exploration.

It wasn't.

In truth, the expedition was originally scheduled for the summer of 2002 but had to be postponed because we hadn't raised enough money. In fact, after two years we had still raised no money. Nothing at all.

I think people often assume that the world of expeditions is glamorous and romantic, but the reality is very different. Most of the actual expeditions themselves involve being continually cold, wet and frightened. And any notions of 'romance' tend to dissipate pretty quickly when the temperature drops below freezing and stays there. Whereas in the movies it is all OK again two hours later, the bottom line for us is that two hours later you are still there – no change, still cold, still wet and still frightened.

The other reality of an expedition is that 90 per cent of your time is spent in the preparation. And for us that preparation time was two years of uncertainty and self-doubt. As rejection letters poured in as quickly as the proposals were dispatched, I questioned myself constantly: 'Why is this not working?'

I struggled every day to find an answer.

When you put all your being into something afresh each morning, and it continually gets thrown back in your face, it's hard. But life is rarely easy. And the bottom line is that we eventually reached our target only because we were bloody-minded enough to keep going.

So many times people advised me to accept reality and try something else, and there were definitely moments when I thought they might be right. Day after day, the arrival of an envelope with a company logo would provoke a surge of excitement, but this was invariably followed by deep frustration when I read the politely worded but negative response. Month after month, it was the same. But somehow I found it even harder to give up; instead, I just became difficult to live with.

Nige and I dispatched literally hundreds of proposals in the course of two years, all neatly printed and bound. We raised absolutely nothing, although there were a few moments when we glimpsed success.

Our initial strategy was to seek one overall title sponsor who would take all the commercial benefits on offer in return for the sum of £250,000. This, we hoped, would be the knockout punch: the one big deal that would fund the expedition and end our worries.

For many months, these hugely optimistic right hooks kept missing the target. Then, just as hope was fading, British

Telecom appeared to be moving within range. They seemed genuinely interested and we were invited to make a presentation at their offices in Ipswich. Mick and Nige took an afternoon off work and we drove up there together. We soon found ourselves standing in BT's huge boardroom and we gave it our all. But it soon became clear they couldn't write that size of cheque. It was just too much. So the bargaining began.

After some time they asked: 'Do you think you could do it for £90,000?'

'Well, yes . . . just,' I replied.

After so many rejections, I would have accepted anything. All I wanted was to do the expedition, and there in the BT boardroom we started to calculate how we could do it for £90,000, how much we could save if we bought a second-hand boat, cut back on this piece of kit and scrimped on communications. Deep down I knew it was madness.

Thankfully, in the end, BT said no, and our bank balance remained at zero. If they had, and we had gone ahead with a cut-price expedition, we would have seriously compromised our safety. It would have been sacrificing a safety margin that we already didn't have.

The explorer Sir Ranulph Fiennes once said, 'Staying the course is what counts – them that stick it out is them that win.' I had read this in a magazine, saved the cutting and tucked it just inside the frame of the mirror in our bedroom. I read it all the time. But, mentally, we were in the trenches. Sponsorship is always a process of attrition but I felt I was losing. It was clear that we needed a fresh approach.

Robert Swan is another man I really admire. He has led expeditions to both the North and South Poles, and had become a friend. We had bought our barge from him in London, and his old boat was now our home. Rob is a good man and one I respect. He just quietly gets on with things, and does them well. I like that. Around this time, I bumped into him at a lecture at the Royal Geographical Society one balmy summer evening. We cut away from the crowds who were milling around drinking afterwards, and sat on the steps in the garden. I needed his advice and some help. I soon knew that what he was telling me was like gold dust.

He said that rather than seek one overall sponsor, we should just create smaller, simpler packages and look for a larger number of sponsors. It seemed too obvious. 'Make it manageable,' he continued. 'You have a whole host of companies whose conferences you've spoken at, who like what you do. They'll buy into this dream if it's less money and justifiable.' I listened carefully. 'Offer them a free talk and a day out on the boat afterwards and for £15,000, rather than £250,000, they have the branding and a simple way for their staff to feel part of the adventure.'

He was absolutely right.

For a company to write a cheque for £250,000, not only do they need the approval of the board, but the timing has to be perfect and the proposal must match all their corporate values, etc. That's not always easy. It is much simpler for them to write out a cheque for £15,000 if it gives them a way of keeping involved with what you are doing and benefits the staff internally as much as the exposure does externally. 'All you have to do,' Rob concluded, 'is find twelve companies who will take this kind of package.'

So I did as he advised, to the letter. We created these new £15,000 packages and sent them to everyone again. But somehow the rejections still poured in.

I couldn't understand why.

I sent out more.

Then one day in September 2002, we suffered particularly heavy losses. Four rejections arrived in the same post, all from key companies I had targeted. 'I can't believe they've said "no",' I muttered to myself out of frustration. 'Those were my best hopes.' I was confused. I held my head in my hands. Nima, our dog, came over and sat on my feet as she often did. Then I heard a voice from outside the door. 'Bear, are you OK?'

It was one of our neighbours on the quay, Heidi-Jane Smith.

Our barge is one of ten house-boats moored at the same pier on the Thames, and I live there for one reason. In this big, faceless city we have something special: a community. People care and tend to look out for one another. It makes coming home so good.

I told Heidi things were not going well, and she listened.

'Well,' she said after a while, 'why don't you give me one of your proposals? I can't promise anything, but I will give it to the people at work, at Vitol, and we'll see what happens.'

The following day I saw Heidi again. She was smiling as she banged on the door.

'They'll do it,' she said as I opened the hatch.

'What?'

'We'll take one of the £15,000 packages. Vitol have said they will be a sponsor.'

I could hardly believe it. I literally picked Heidi up and squeezed her. After so many months of people saying no, someone was actually saying yes. Vitol, an oil-marketing company, had become our first sponsor. That night, I started working out if we could do the expedition on only £15,000.

We were off the mark.

Not long afterwards, Lunson Mitchenall, the company of property surveyors that Nige works for, also agreed to take one of the packages. That news sent me scampering off again to calculate whether we could make it now with just £30,000. It was beginning to happen. Yes by yes, our hopes and expectations started to gain ground. Then Shell agreed, then Lafarge Aggregates. Even BT came back. It was affordable now.

We had found a formula and it was working: the more talks I found myself doing, the more I would follow them up with a proposal. And people just got it; it was simple and justifiable and it made sense. My belief in it grew, and companies sensed that. There was a momentum behind us now.

In the end we filled all the lead sponsor slots within two months. In total a dozen companies, from General Motors in Canada to the *Daily Telegraph* over here in the UK, took the £15,000 package, and we still had the title sponsorship to sell.

We were prepared to name the entire project after one

company, in all the press coverage and branding. It would include the boat's name, the title logos, talks and corporate days afterwards, and this bundle was going to cost someone £50,000.

Early in 2003, just before the Boat Show, I learned that a Swiss–British company, British Masters, a specialist watch-making group, was trying to contact me through a speakers' agency. They had read an article on 'risk' I had done in the *Daily Telegraph* and they had liked it. But more importantly, they saw an opportunity. The company was headed up by a couple of Swiss guys from Lausanne, Eric Loth and Jean-Marie Florent, and when I contacted them, they explained they were eager to revive a connection with British exploration which the company had developed in the days of Shackleton and Scott. They had a brand they wanted to relaunch world-wide – it was called Arnold and Son.

'Well,' I replied, 'the title sponsorship is still available, and . . .' I paused, then I just went for it . . . 'if you can make your mind up within the next forty-eight hours, we will have time to get the boat covered in Arnold and Son logos by the time it appears at the London Boat Show in three weeks' time. It could be amazing.'

Some time before, I had agreed with the organizers of the Boat Show at Earl's Court to display our boat on a podium at the front of the exhibition. It was the same place where Sir Francis Chichester's *Gypsy Moth* had stood during the Boat Show in 1967. I felt honoured and also a little daunted, but I knew it was the chance of a lifetime. We just ran with it.

Arnold and Son instantly recognized the opportunity. They wanted to call us the 'Arnold and Son Trans Atlantic Arctic Expedition'. It was a bit of a mouthful and took me seven attempts to say fluently on our answer-machine, but it was really happening now. They called back the following day to say they would like to take the title sponsorship slot at £50,000. We had never met in person and we agreed all this on our word alone. That was it, and it was a great way to cement a deal.

Their corporate logos went to print, and the first time we met was on a freezing January morning outside the Boat Show. There was snow on the ground, and the partially completed boat stood proudly at an angle, floodlit for all to see. When Eric and Jean-Marie saw it, they smiled to themselves. She was perfect. We knew we had been given our final break, and we had sufficient funding to set up the expedition just as we wanted. We were truly up and running.

Both the boat-builders and I had bust a gut to get everything ready in time for the show, and together we had done it. It had gone to the wire and a whole team of people were helping late into the night before the show opened.

The logos were sealed round the base of the stand, the maps waterproofed and sealed to the sides, and a Musto mannequin, dressed in full survival suit, was perched on the half-finished tubes of the hull, high above the ground. It gave the whole boat life. Each night before I left for home, I patted her hull. She was to be our home and our only lifeline out there in the ice-strewn seas. Sitting there silhouetted at night, with the hull covered in the signatures of so many well-wishers, she was already looking beautiful.

I was exhausted though, and so was Shara. She had seen her carefully maintained home slowly become buried under a mountain of equipment, logos and survival gear. Even Christmas had been a washout of phone calls and late nights. I tried desperately to keep home as home, but it never quite happened. By New Year Shara was four months pregnant and was still trying to help me. But I could tell she was drained.

She had been pregnant earlier in the year but it hadn't worked out for us. Shara had been distraught. As I held her in my arms, sobbing in the hospital, I knew we had just lost everything we had ever hoped for together. But what broke my heart even more was seeing her pain. Her miscarriage left us both feeling empty.

Life had thrown us some bitter deals. Within two years of marriage, we had both lost our fathers, Shara's dad, Brian, having passed away only ten weeks before mine. We had cried in bed together for so many nights since. Her getting pregnant was a way forward. But then we lost it. Life was sick. And we were struggling. I just felt this ache inside. But Shara was incredibly strong and, like so many women before her, she quietly and slowly picked herself up and carried on. She was truly an inspiration.

Six months later, she was pregnant again. But this time she was terrified. As I held her each morning, with her hand in mine, and felt her caress her tummy nervously, I promised her everything would be OK. She'd close her eyes and say she believed me.

Deep down, I knew that this next year was going to change everything. I prayed to God I wouldn't let her down.

4. FIRST BLOOD

The world often steps aside for people who know where they're going.

Miriam Viola Larsen

So the money was finally raised, and a myth developed in exploration circles that I had, somehow, discovered the secret of securing sponsorship to fund an expedition. Many people have contacted me since to ask for advice, perhaps thinking I have an address book full of contacts just waiting to write cheques. I wish that was true. In fact the secret was nothing more glamorous than that Ranulph Fiennes quote which so simply said, 'them that stick it out is them that win'.

As time went by, I became increasingly grateful that the Royal Navy was on board, and I recognized that its level of involvement and enthusiasm owed much to the contacts and help of Captain Willie Pennefather.

I had first met Willie a year earlier. We had started talking about the sea and I told him about my hopes for this North Atlantic crossing. He was hugely enthusiastic about it all, and in no time I began to recognize his expertise. Ever since that evening, and particularly since my father died, he has been somebody whom I can trust and turn to; someone whom I can be sure has my best interests at heart. That means a lot to me.

He used his access to the highest echelons of the Royal Navy and eloquently explained why he thought it should get involved in our project. The First Sea Lord agreed, and doors began to swing open.

Beyond this, we had Willie as a constant and reliable source of support and advice. With his experience and contacts, he was the ideal man to stand quietly in the background, ready and willing to make the vital decisions at crucial moments, and in this decisive role he would in time prove absolutely invaluable.

I asked Willie to speak at the naming ceremony of the boat, on 29 April 2003 down in Portsmouth, and he used the opportunity to explain why he felt so strongly about this expedition.

You will all know what the challenge is – it is to cross the Atlantic by the Arctic route in an open, rigid inflatable boat some ten metres long, through some of the most testing conditions and waters that the Almighty has made available to people like Bear Grylls and his team . . .

Quite mad, I hear you say, but is it? Yes, it's all about endurance and achievement, but, more importantly, it's about the team. The bonds you create in those extremes. The sea offers an abundance of opportunity for challenge, but also for belonging, and so often I have seen it transform nervous, under-confident people into fulfilled team players. Men with a much greater and enduring purpose in life.

Such adventurers as these are an inspiration to us all. It takes guts and imagination, and often a short memory, to delve into the unknown. Often, management accounts and targets tend to dominate today, but these count for nothing if we lose our spirit. It is this spirit that these adventurers stir in us all. They bring joy and smiles to people's faces and they fire up something that often lurks too far beneath the surface in the rest of us.

The adventurers are the ones who show opportunity to others, through their visible determination to risk everything, to have a go, and through their determination to succeed.

Bear, I can't tell you what a tremendous honour it was for me when you asked me to speak at the naming of your boat, your pride and joy, and the First Sea Lord has asked me to say that the navy much admires your values and is thrilled to have been able to help and take part in the expedition under your leadership.

Good luck, God bless, and above all come home safe and sound.

The combined effect of finally having money in the bank and the navy on our side gave enormous impetus to our preparations, but the single most significant consequence of these developments was that we could afford to build exactly the kind of boat that we wanted to take into these precarious, icy waters.

I first came across Ocean Dynamics when I was casually browsing through a trade boating magazine and noticed their small advertisement in the classified section. They sold themselves as specialists in building tough, resilient boats, and when we saw they made lifeboats for the RNLI (Royal National Lifeboat Institute), worked with clients in Scandinavia and didn't do too many drinks trays, we sensed we had found the right people to build our boat.

They were based at Pembroke docks, far away in west Wales, so Mick, Nige and I drove five hours from London and found ourselves sitting in a Portakabin describing the boat we needed.

Shaun White and his team listened patiently. We said we wanted a boat with a range of 1,000 miles, and we needed extreme durability; we wanted an aluminium hull that wouldn't crack if it hit small, submerged icebergs at night, and we needed a jet engine instead of a propeller that, again, wouldn't get damaged by hitting any floating debris or random containers. None of us wanted to spend the amount of time and energy preparing as we had and then find ourselves 500 miles offshore without a prop, having clipped something in the night. It was a risk we could minimize and it made sense to give ourselves the best advantage at this early stage.

Other boat-builders had considered our requirements but said we were asking for the impossible. It was too difficult, too risky. So we looked again. These men didn't say that, but they quickly and bluntly identified our main challenge as finding a way to carry the required amount of fuel in an efficient manner.

'I think it's possible . . .' Shaun White said, smiling.

That was what we wanted to hear.

Through all the deliberations and discussions that followed, as we pored over power ratios, different types of engine and various configurations of storing the fuel, we accepted professional advice when it was given and constantly focused our efforts on minimizing the expedition's technical risks.

Shaun became a friend and a confidant and I ended up

calling him, 'Uncle'. The name has stuck. When we finally came to leave, Shaun was determined to be there with us in Nova Scotia. He flew out with us and looked so proud as hundreds of well-wishers looked round the boat on the quayside in Halifax. It had been his baby too, and he had put his heart and soul into its construction. Part of me wished 'Uncle Shaun' was coming with us as well.

Difficult decisions were unavoidable in the design phase, because we were going into new territory with the specification. For example, the ideal would have been to fit two engines, but with the range we needed there simply was not room for double the fuel load. Our need for fuel economy meant we could have only one engine. I know Andy was taken aback when he saw this arrangement because it left us with no fallback option – the navy follows the belt-and-braces principle where you make sure you always have a Plan B – but RIBs are generally designed to have a range of around 100, not 1,000, miles. It was a risk we had no choice in taking.

Even to achieve this kind of extended range, we needed to carry 4,000 litres of fuel and the reality was that we could go further by using one engine rather than two. That was the bottom line.

The question of how to store the fuel occupied the team's minds for a long time. We knew the performance of the boat would be poor at the start of each leg because we would be so heavy with fuel, but we had to try to ensure the weight was spread as economically as possible across the boat. It would be a deciding factor in really heavy seas. Move two tonnes of weight and it makes a huge difference to the trim and pitch of the boat. I was forced to sit back and let the experts work out these different ratios – my job was to probe, to question and then to trust their decisions.

Andy was coming into his own now. He was brilliant in this area, and as soon as he joined the team full-time I took real confidence from his presence in all these vital early discussions. He was diligent and exact, and he was cautious and conservative by nature: vital ingredients in a craft where we were dependent on only one engine.

As soon as the boat was ready, we began to plan the sea trials. These were always going to be critical. We had been designing a boat that was in many ways unique. No one really knew how she would perform fully laden in a swell. Only our trials would tell us that. We needed to test and trial at different payloads in different conditions, and then retest. A thousand miles was already at our outermost limit of range. If we got these small calculations wrong, it could be critical.

We also needed to trial the human factor; how we, the team, would cope. Living in what was described by one journalist as 'an area the size of an open-top car' for over 3,000 miles of wild seas, with no shelter, strapped in day after day, would take its toll on us physically. We needed to begin to get used to her and learn how to feel at home on board.

My plan was that these trials should be short and focused, intensive weekends when the team would be on the boat, seeing what worked, what didn't, getting used to the way she handled and finding out how we would cope when it cut rough.

There was a balance to be found: we had to get a reasonable number of miles on the engine and get the early services out of the way before we set out on the ocean but, on the other hand, I didn't want any of us to be sick and tired of the boat by the time we reached Canada. It still needed to be fresh and exciting.

So, for the first sea trial weekend, we planned to take the boat from Portsmouth to the Scilly Isles and back. The weather was not great and within an hour or so of the start most of us were feeling sick. I had forgotten quite how debilitating seasickness can be. You fix your eyes on the horizon, but that doesn't stop the world inside you starting to spin. We would need an endless supply of anti-seasickness pills.

We learned lessons, and took notes.

We would have to wear our helmets when the sea was rough, to protect our heads if we fell or slipped as we shifted around the boat. Pot Noodles made us vomit. Talcum powder needed to be at hand to ease the gradual biting of the neck and wrist seals of the dry-suits into our skin. Vaseline protected our nostrils from the salt and spray and prevented them becoming raw.

The idea of having an inflatable mattress in the 'sardine tin', the area at the back of the boat where two, maybe three of us, could lie down and rest, seemed inspired. It wasn't. The mattress made us feel sick and was easily punctured. OK, so we needed to get some absorbent foam instead.

We hadn't planned where we would put our feet when we were helming, so they dangled uncomfortably in mid-air. Right, we would need to weld some kind of footrest into position.

The boat, in the final stages of building, became a test bed for many maritime companies. Many people approached us with new ideas. Some were bonkers; some were amazing.

By the end we were trialling seats for the new naval fast-response crafts, testing a small exterior water heater that would take the pounding of all poundings and only worked periodically. We were also experimenting with a marine tracking device that would send back a signal every half-hour with our speed and latitude and longitude, as given by the GPS (Global Positioning System). This data was sent via satellite to the Internet and became a lifeline to those waiting for news back in the UK. But it had its dangers too, and when all our systems went down in a storm, including this device, people understandably jumped to conclusions. They would see our speed gradually falling away and the weather patterns worsening. When we went blank and offline, we were in trouble, but it wasn't fatal. We were still upright, but they weren't to know.

Yet when it worked, it gave people hope; hope that slowly we were coming home, wave by wave.

By the end of that first night of our sea trial, we were all starting to feel really cold, which was not promising. This was a midsummer's night off the south coast of England, not the frozen North Atlantic. We weren't even that wet, but it became obvious we were going to need much more kit if we weren't to freeze. But already we were looking like Michelin men in all our gear.

More notes were made.

The wind always whistled behind us wherever we sat and we lost a lot of heat like this; roll-mats to sit on would shield our backsides.

We needed better lifelines: the clips were far too small – in a storm at night, in mittens, we'd never get clipped on. They needed to run the whole length of the boat, and be big and strong.

These were all small details but, in my experience, on any expedition it is the small things that make the biggest difference. Something that seems insignificant and minor on shore can make a life-altering difference at sea, so I was determined that every little glitch and problem should be identified and resolved at this stage. When we finally left, it would be too late for this sort of refinement. This was the time to iron things out, when it was calm and when it was good, before it got nasty.

The truth is that our first night aboard the boat had not been much fun and, weighed down by fuel and hindered by rough weather, we had not made very good progress towards the Scilly Isles. We were all tired and wet, so at four in the morning it seemed sensible to tie up on a buoy at Salcombe harbour in Devon. Our performance might not have been outstanding, but it was our first time out and there was no point in going completely mad. We waited until dawn, then headed off to find some breakfast on shore.

I had spoken to Neil Laughton, the leader of our Everest expedition, during the previous week and knew he was planning to be in the Salcombe area over the weekend. We bumped into him in the village and he casually asked if we could take him and a couple of friends out for a spin on the water.

'No problem,' I replied; it would be fun, just like the old days. We were laughing and joking. The mood was good. Neil was excited to see the boat.

Somewhere in the dark recesses of my mind, however, a bell was ringing. I remembered that Salcombe was known for a raised strip of sand and rock just beneath the water's surface, somewhere near the front of the harbour. 'Salcombe Bar', as it is called, was reputed to be one of the most treacherous hazards on the British coastline.

The conditions were wind over tide now. Later – too late – I read the view of a round-the-world yachtsman who said he had seen awkward conditions all around the globe but nothing quite so bad as the Salcombe Bar.

But this was only a muffled bell at the back of my mind as we headed out into the harbour. Neil was standing right at the bow of the boat, with two of his friends, and all seemed well. I did notice the waves were beginning to build just a bit, but everybody was relaxed and smiling, shooting the breeze.

Then I looked straight ahead and saw what can only be described as a monster wave approaching. It was probably around 200 yards away, but it was very obviously heading in our direction.

Standing at the helm, my first instinct was to turn the boat and run away from this thing. Then I decided there was not enough time. We would have to face the wave head-on and try to ride it. Seconds passed like minutes. Nobody was laughing any more. This rogue wave rolled irrepressibly towards us. People grabbed at handholds. We were doing only 10 knots.

It connected head-on, and our boat literally took off, nose up, out of the water. Then we dropped straight down 15 feet as the wave fell with a crash on to the stern of the boat. She pitched forward wildly. It felt as though we had all been standing in an elevator and the cable had broken, and we had fallen down two storeys and smashed into the bottom.

Andy gashed his knee. I was shaking like a leaf. Neil was still just clinging on.

'You guys are insane,' he said, smiling, after we had turned the boat round and run back to shore with the subsequent waves. 'You wouldn't catch me 500 miles offshore in this thing, in a big sea. Bloody hell! It'll be nuts.'

To be honest, my legs were still shaking a couple of hours later, but in time we would learn to deal with waves like that. It was a matter of confidence and trust. We were learning how to handle her in these conditions, slowly but surely, day by day.

On our second sea trial, we encountered some similar

conditions around Portland Bill, Dorset, when the sea was breaking up and coming at us wildly from every direction. The area was infamous for its rough waters. Although it was only a small taste of what we would find out in the big ocean, we began to feel the boat responding really well to the challenge. It was what she was designed for and she loved it.

Andy was handling the throttle, I was helming and the boat was alive. We were being thrown around, but we were making progress, finding our way, starting to enjoy the challenge. The adrenalin was up.

The following day, with everyone back at work, each of the guys – Mick, Nige, Charlie and Andy – called me individually to say they could hardly move because of the physical battering they had taken on the water. I felt it too. We were stiff and sore, and that was after only fifteen hours in no more than tricky conditions.

Our early trials left us in no doubt about the scale and nature of what lay ahead. Legs of almost 900 miles over several days would leave us battered and bruised, and that worried me. I was wiped out after only a day and a night – in summertime.

It became increasingly obvious that the real challenge for us was the fact that we were in a completely open boat, with nowhere to hide. I had underestimated this. In a round-the-world yacht you have a cabin where you can shelter from the worst of the weather, a place to get out of the rain and spray, a place to rest and get dry in. We had no such luxury, no respite from the elements. Whatever the weather and sea conditions, whether it was rain, sleet, waves, hail or spray, this was where we would live, eat and sleep. It was to become our most exhausting factor: the relentless wet, cold and exposure. And we all learned to dread it.

For our final sea trial, we travelled the 90 or so miles from Portsmouth to Jersey and back. We took the time to run through all our safety procedures: deploying the life raft, putting out the parachute sea anchor, rehearsing our 'man-overboard' drills. It wasn't the same as the real thing, but these were necessary disciplines to have learnt by heart. Being able to deploy the sea anchor in under two minutes as waves pounded over the foredeck at night had to be instinctive; and that takes time to learn.

I threw endless fenders overboard for the guys to retrieve, all of us learning how to handle the boat delicately in a pitching sea. I did it again at dusk. They were getting it.

By 3 a.m., Mick was on watch. Everyone was tired. It was time for a live test of the 'man-overboard' drill; I had decided to be the dummy, and I wasn't looking forward to it. I was lying in the sardine tin with Nige, unable to sleep. I looked anxiously at my watch. We were exactly mid-Channel now. It was the worst time on the worst shift. I sat up, gave Nige a nudge just to make sure he was awake, stood on the tubes and jumped into the black.

As per the drills, everyone leaped into action and Mick brought the boat round into the sea. The spotlight flickered on and they soon had me in the lee of the RIB, Mick carefully balancing the jet controls holding me off by 5 yards.

'What's it worth, skipper?' he shouted into the night. I was cold now and my heart was still pounding. I laughed, but only a little.

'England is sixty miles that-a-way,' he chuckled. 'See you for breakfast.' He drove off.

A short dogleg, and he was back alongside me.

'Mick, you've got ten seconds to bring me in or I *will* kill you.' Strong hands dragged me in, floundering. Andy threw me one of his diesel rags to dry myself, laughing. But it had been a good drill to do.

The night was perfect, the sea was still and the stars and sky were bright. It was as easy as pie. We all sat quietly afterwards and could only imagine what it would be like in a wind-whipped gale with icebergs all around. It would be a different game altogether. The truth is that getting back to a man overboard would be near impossible, and we all knew it. We turned and headed for home.

In many ways, the expedition was beginning to assume its own momentum. The funds were in the bank; the boat-building process was finally complete. We were talking to shipping agents, managing relationships with sponsors, discussing finer details of the route and working out possible dates of departure bearing in mind the state of the ice-packs in the Arctic and the weather patterns coming in. We were busier than ever.

There had been times, especially in the early days, when it had sometimes felt as though the entire expedition was resting on my shoulders. It was my dream and I was struggling to make it happen. Those days had gone now, and most of the time I was able to stand back and oversee all the activity. I loved that.

Everything was happening all around me.

We had arranged two major crew meetings before the expedition, one six months before our scheduled departure and one just a week before. Every aspect of the expedition was discussed and checked. Nige had all his maps laid out and carefully went over the routes and the contingency plans once again; Andy talked about the engine and the refuelling requirements; Mick went over the emergency coastguard procedures and weather plans, and Chloë distributed her logistics folders.

Chloë Boyes was working for Goldman Sachs in London when we met. I told her one evening, as we chatted after a talk I had given, about the administrative challenges – to put it mildly – that existed in my life. Shara was pregnant, everything was hectic and I was struggling to stay afloat.

She saw the problem as clearly as I did. I needed some help. More than this, she proposed a solution; she wanted some excitement and I wanted an efficient number two. I should employ her as a PA to handle all the admin. I felt a burden lift off me.

It was always going to be hard for me to trust somebody enough to allow them to liaise with the people who provided my living: the CEOs of the companies who use me as a speaker, or the sponsors and contacts surrounding the expedition. But it didn't take long for me to feel comfortable with Chloë in this role.

She was easygoing and efficient and her impact was immediate. It meant the world to me to be able to have the occasional relaxed evening at home with Shara, rather than working late into the night catching up on an inbox full of emails.

Chloë's role within the expedition soon became a vital one. She was going to operate our base from London and the expedition HQ was moved to the offices of Liaison Media, our PR guys, only 100 yards away from our barge. It worked perfectly and was always a hub of banter and fun, the rooms piled high with radios, maps and logos.

I wanted to keep the barge clear for Shara. The London base was going to be our first point of contact with the outside world. Day or night, when we needed help out there, Chloë and that office were to be our lifeline. It was a big responsibility for her.

Most of the crew didn't know much about her to start with, but as soon as she handed out her neatly prepared folders, packed with logistics and contact numbers, at our meeting, they started to recognize the importance of her role.

Perhaps the best measure of her enormous contribution was the fact that as soon as we finally reached Scotland, Mick, Nige, Charlie and Andy all told me they wanted to get her something special to say thank you; thank you for those times she was there for us, coordinating and crisis-managing situations in real time. They all chipped in to buy her a glass and silver bowl, engraved with the words 'for always being there'.

Chloë had teamed up with our PR company, Liaison Media, which was headed up by a real live-wire of a guy called Alex Rayner. When Alex had first heard about our expedition he had suggested he become involved, and had been immensely excited from day one. And it showed. 'Ha,' he would announce, having arranged another interview for one of us, 'I just love this.' And off he would go.

The final member of our base team was Andy Billing. He had agreed to build a website for the expedition, at minimal cost, and to keep it constantly updated, streaming information as we went along. In the early days we were getting four hits a day, and that was probably me checking to see if anyone was visiting the site. However, during the expedition, as the dramas unfolded, we were registering more than 30,000 hits every day. Andy was in his element. He was so enthusiastic, always obliging and above all professional. And everyone loved it whenever he appeared with his customary greeting: 'Good morning, fine sirs!'

Shara had decided she didn't want to be alone in London while I was away. I agreed with her. She and Jesse would be much happier with her mother out of London. It would be quieter. Andy agreed to live on our barge for the entire duration of the expedition: manning the phones by night.

Just knowing he was always there to help Chloë and answer the telephone gave me the reassurance we all felt we needed. This was the final piece of the jigsaw.

In 2001 I was invited to become an ambassador for the Prince's Trust. It was a huge honour and in return I promised that our next expedition would be in aid of the charity. Ever since then, through various events I have been involved with, I have seen at first hand how effectively and genuinely the Trust provides thousands of young people in Britain with both the incentive and the opportunity to build their dreams. It gives them a chance to get out there and do the very best they can, to start businesses, to find work. It offers a break to people who would never normally get the chance. It is a brilliant idea and it changes lives.

I wrote to HRH The Prince of Wales, the founder of the charity, to explain that we would like his Trust to become our official beneficiary; I also asked if he might ever consider becoming the patron of our expedition. He not only agreed to take on this role but also expressed the desire to meet the entire team before our departure. I couldn't believe it.

On the appointed day, at the appointed time, smartly dressed in our expedition fleeces, we gathered at the barge and hailed a couple of taxis to take us to St James's Palace. I had also invited the two top execs from Arnold and Son, our title sponsors, Eric and Jean-Marie, as a small additional gesture of thanks to them for their support. They looked immaculate, dressed in their suits.

The Prince had obviously been well briefed, and as he entered the room he walked towards me and started to mime the act of spraying deodorant under his arms. He was taking the mickey out of me already, as I had recently featured in the Sure for Men deodorant TV commercials.

'How is the deodorant?' he asked playfully.

'It's fine, thank you, sir,' I replied awkwardly.

Then, after a moment of silence, I added, 'Well . . .' I paused, 'at least I wasn't asked to do an advert for Anusol.'

My impromptu reference to a remedy for haemorrhoids prompted a rapid shuffling of feet behind me from the guys, but the Prince laughed and the ice was broken. He then told us how during his naval career he had served on a frigate in the North Atlantic. He had encountered a storm so ferocious and powerful that the force of the waves had literally bent a reinforced steel ladder. He looked at me intently.

'And you're going up there in a small rubber-tubed boat. What will you do in that kind of sea?' he asked.

I paused awkwardly.

'We'll call you for some advice when that happens, sir, rest assured,' I replied. There was more shuffling behind me.

He asked Nige how his astral navigation was coming along, and Nige admitted it was something of a grey area. The Prince laughed out loud. The atmosphere was light and fun, and we had some photographs of us all taken outside afterwards.

'Well, I think you're all insane,' the Prince concluded as he turned to leave, 'but I'll be thinking of you.'

As the final day of departure drew nearer, inevitably there were several last-minute crises that needed to be solved in a hurry. At one point Andy Leivers called to say he needed a particular seal for the jet housing. If we couldn't get this specific part quickly, plus a spare, the boat would not be able to leave for Canada, and we would suffer the consequences of that delay. The ice was fragmenting now in the Arctic. The timing was perfect; we had no room for such a delay.

I was making a speech for Fujitsu on that particular morning, and I recall being backstage, all dressed up in my Everest climbing kit, waiting to go on. But I had to make the call to make sure we got this seal, and I had to make it now. I was literally phoning the jet manufacturers when the master of ceremonies stood up to introduce me.

'Can you get the part to the naval yard for tomorrow?' I asked in hushed tones.

'Yes, we can, if I get it sent this morning,' said the voice of Martin Jackson, their marketing director, on the line.

'Thanks, Martin. You're a star. I've got to go. I'm onstage in five seconds. Bye.'

I took a deep breath and walked out onstage to another sea of faces. I was sweating already.

My two lives had almost overlapped, but luckily not quite collided.

The long-running debate over how we would store the fuel reached a critical stage only two weeks before the boat was due to leave. It slowly dawned on us over the final trials that if we were to get the necessary mileage and range, we would need to install an extra fuel bladder under the front deck of the boat. The area was meant to be our storage for food and supplies, but would have to be sacrificed.

The problem was that this particular piece of specialist equipment had a list price of £15,000, and we didn't have that sort of money left in the budget. It was a huge problem to be faced with so late, and it threatened to hold up the entire effort.

I called one company, explained the situation, gave them the sales patter, and they responded by offering us a £500 discount on the fifteen grand. That was kind – of course, they were not obliged to offer us anything at all – but I needed a better deal. In desperation I called the best company in the UK at designing such bladders, specialist suppliers to the armed forces and much, much more expensive than £15,000. I phoned one of the directors at FPT Industries.

This time I simply told them what we were trying to do, what had happened and how desperate we were for help.

'OK, we'll be happy to help,' said Mark Butler, the CEO.

He immediately dispatched a couple of his specialists to see the boat at the naval base in Portsmouth, and, over the next few days, in constant contact with Andy, FPT Industries completed an intensely intricate and professional job.

The fuel bladder they fitted was custom-made from Kevlar, the bullet-proof and flame-resistant material they use to make fuel bladders for fighter planes. Nobody could say they weren't thorough! It was carefully moulded under the bow by a team of experts, plus Andy, and all for no charge at all. I was so grateful. At the final hurdle they had bust a gut, put other orders on hold and cleared the way for us. They made me promise one thing: that we would 'come home safe'.

Such generosity, such professional services so freely given, amazed me time and time again. I was deeply touched by the many companies, and indeed individuals, telling us that if we needed any help at all, we only had to ask.

Perhaps this spirit originates from the maritime culture that if anyone is ever in trouble on the sea, ships in the vicinity will always offer assistance. It is a great culture and is one of the great strengths of the climbing world as well: when lives are on the line, people drop everything to help.

As Captain Pennefather told us afterwards, the whole expedition grew to be much more than an attempt to complete a crossing or break a record. It involved hundreds of people in hundreds of ways, all doing their bit and all as important as the next man. In many ways, we were just the front men for an extraordinary group of people behind the scenes who got us to the start line. In return, I hoped our endeavour would continue to bring out that spirit in people and I wanted to do everything to make sure the magic got spread around.

The final morning before the boat was to leave for Canada was special. I had planned to be alone on board. It was very early on a grey, drizzly Monday morning when I drove down to Portsmouth and went to fetch the boat from the naval base. The sea was glassy calm, disturbed only by the steady rain. I glanced at my watch and saw I had some time to spare before I was due to arrive at Southampton docks, so I decided to make a slight detour, to the south and my childhood, and pointed the boat towards the Isle of Wight.

Everything was still and quiet when I arrived at Bembridge harbour, not a sound; but it had never been like this when I was a child. In the morning mist, all I could see was memories of jostling boats and dinghies, me and my friends messing around, our fathers frantically shouting from the beach, of fun and happiness, of bumps and bruises and laughter, above all of laughter. Right there I felt Dad standing quietly beside me.

The engine was scarcely idling as I chugged quietly around the harbour. And, as if from somewhere deep inside, I found tears were now running freely down my cheeks for the first time in ages.

I passed slowly by the pontoon at the Sailing Club. The members of this club had so much wanted to support this expedition; they were awash with friendship but not with funds. None the less, they organized a whip-round in the bar for the Prince's Trust, and I placed their sticker on the boat. That was the only logo placed on the boat for free. It was different. It was part of me.

As I left Bembridge harbour, I found myself waving nostalgically, not at anyone or anything in particular, just waving goodbye.

When I eventually reached Southampton, I tied up near

an enormous container ship alongside massive grey fenders that dwarfed our tiny boat. Everything suddenly felt very small. A huge crane swung over and plucked the boat out and on to a trailer. The tubes were deflated, and everything was neatly packed away before our precious cargo was steered through the vast gates in the bow, right into the guts of the ship.

Between us, we had designed and built what must have been one of the most advanced RIBs in the world. But beside this cavernous container ship it looked like a Dinky toy. As she disappeared from view, I felt that sense of sadness you experience when you reach the end of a long road.

There had been many days when the expedition seemed unlikely to get off the ground, but now we were here on the docks. The next time I would see her would be in a very different harbour, thousands of miles away and further north, on the remote Nova Scotia coastline. I was meant to be doing a BBC TV interview on the quayside but found it hard to make much sense. The container ship's gates closed. I glanced over my shoulder and our RIB was gone.

There wasn't much more we could now do. For the first time in months, the kit was ready and packed, the boat had gone, the logistics were in place as far as they could be, and the team's mood was high. The final countdown had started, and this stage can be frightening. Everything goes quiet and, maybe for the first time in ages, you have the opportunity to think about what really lies ahead.

I was beginning to understand a bit more now about what

we were undertaking. It was no longer happening 'next year'. It was almost upon us; and suddenly it felt so soon.

Shara had given birth to our son Jesse only four weeks earlier. It had been the most intense and intimate day of my life. He was perfect, and Shara, in those moments, had looked so alive. But in those first few weeks afterwards, I began to feel real doubts about everything ahead. I wasn't even sure why I was leaving at all, and when I sat and thought about it, I felt utterly torn.

It had been different with the Everest expedition. Then I was younger and maybe more rash, but Everest had changed me. When friends die in the mountains, you reconsider what those odds really mean. They are not just statistics any longer. They are real, and if you play them often enough you don't always come out on top.

Now my life was different. I was a husband and a father. I had much more to lose. I was no longer prepared to die up a mountain. Shara and Jesse had given me life after Dad passed on. I had everything to live for, and I wanted to stay alive. The idea of taking that level of risk again terrified me.

I didn't even know what the risks were here. No one did. So few people had tried to cross the North Atlantic in an open RIB that there were no stark statistics like the one in eight fatalities on Everest. There was nothing: no quantifiable ratio, no survival odds, just the unknown.

I tried to look for the positives. I tried to tell myself that my new family would make me more cautious, more determined to get home safely. But I wasn't sure that I believed it.

Only a matter of days before we were due to leave, I woke up in the middle of the night and knew I should a write a letter to Shara, just in case. I'd hand this letter to my best buddy, Charlie Mackesy, and ask him to give it to her only in one event – if I didn't come home. It was the hardest letter I have ever written. As I wrote, my palms clammy with sweat, the night seemed to stand still. I was confronting the worst option and trying to deal with the consequences. All the time I was praying – praying my wife would never have to read these words.

The last two years had been hard for Shara. And I owe her so much. It's obviously not ideal for any new mother that her husband should have to be away when their child is so small; and it's definitely not ideal that 'away' should mean setting off across a dangerous ocean in a small, open boat. Yet as the days neared we somehow never spoke of saying goodbye. It was our unwritten rule.

Charlie, Shaun White, the boat-builder, and I were due to fly from Heathrow to Nova Scotia on the Monday evening. Andy had already been there for three days, preparing the boat, while Mick and Nige were going to fly a day later. On the Friday evening, Shara gave me a little photograph album she had made, full of pictures of her and Jesse. It was beautiful.

Early the following morning I woke early and spoke for

the first time into the Dictaphone that would be my companion for so much of the time ahead.

It's 5 a.m., and I can't sleep. Shara is lying beside me, and Jesse is asleep on my pillow. I am trying to get packed up quietly, but I am so scared now. I am used to leaving for expeditions, but this is different – I feel strangely alone. Just looking at Shara and Jesse asleep is so hard. It breaks my heart.

I am so excited to be seeing those cold waters, but I am under no illusions that it's going to be anything but many weeks of being wet and frightened. But I still firmly believe it is possible. I just have to remind myself of that, and always remember that each wave is a wave closer back to my home.

As a team we had agreed to take $10,000 in cash, just in case we found ourselves in situations where perhaps a fisherman or a helicopter pilot, or anyone, needed some persuading. I wandered down to the bank and collected the money. It was a beautiful summer's day, and I was wearing just an old pair of shorts. I collected the money, and also bought a crate of Bell's whisky from the off-licence next door. With dollars and whisky, we now had international currency.

I played a last game of squash with Danny, the second-hand car dealer who plays a wily game with me several times a week. Afterwards he said, very gently, 'You know, Bear, I really don't want you to go.'

I just smiled back.

'Can't I just puncture the boat or something?' he asked.

In the afternoon we gathered everything Shara and Jesse needed to take to her mother's house and packed it into our car. We laughed. They were going down to the country with all seventeen suitcases. I was going across the North Atlantic, and I had two small bags.

Sunday drifted by. The sun shone, Charlie Mackesy came down, and we all lay on the grass and drank tea. I went for a walk with Shara and held her hand as I love to do. And then it was time to leave for the airport.

British Airways had generously provided our one-way tickets to Canada and they had kindly offered to show us around the weather centre at their headquarters at Heathrow before we left. As we approached their corporate head-quarters, I saw a welcoming party of BA staff, dressed in hats and uniforms. It was a lovely gesture on their part, but my mind was elsewhere. They were all watching.

I gave Jesse a little kiss, then turned to face Shara. She was crying already.

'Trust me, my love, all will be fine.'

I held her tight to try to stop the tears.

'We'll be safe and back together in no time. I promise.'

It was a promise I knew wasn't mine to make.

As we toured round BA's Compass House, I was in a daze. I couldn't take anything in. All I could think about was them both driving home, and Shara being so afraid. But I didn't know what else I could do. It was time to be a leader now, time to make sure we did this job properly, time to make sure I was right when I promised her we'd be OK. It was time to look ahead.

When we eventually reached the check-in area, I received

a text message from my sister Lara saying she hoped every-thing would go 'swimmingly'. It was quite funny.

My great-uncle Edward, aged ninety-three, called soon afterwards to wish me well. 'God bless you,' he said very slowly, and then he added in the softest and most tender of voices, 'We do so love you.'

What a gorgeous man he is.

I was feeling pretty drained, physically and emotionally, by the time Charlie and I settled into our seats. BA had put us in business class and we were soon being spoiled with champagne and food. Charlie was really buzzing, chatting to the crew about the expedition and generally enjoying every minute. He was in heaven. He eventually fell asleep snoring.

I just sat quietly, alone with my thoughts, staring out of the window. Now and then I could see the ocean, briefly visible between the clouds, and watch the white horses far below. I eventually closed my eyes as well, warm and snug, knowing that the way home would be a very different story.

5. NORTH FROM NOVA SCOTIA

A real friend is one who walks in when the rest of the world walks out.

Ronald Reagan

Even if all five of us had been born and bred in Halifax, Nova Scotia, it is hard to imagine how the people of this open-hearted Canadian city could have been more hospitable and supportive. The fact was that we were five British men who happened to have chosen their city as the starting point of our transatlantic expedition, and we had certainly not expected, nor did we deserve, the warm generosity shown to us by so many people.

Our boat, the *Arnold and Son Explorer*, was moored at the central quay in the middle of a waterfront development, and as soon as one of us stepped past the spectators to go aboard, we were asked for autographs and quizzed about the boat.

We were given free use of two nearby apartments for as long as we needed, and local officers of the Canadian navy gave us 3,000 litres of fuel, for which they refused to let us pay. Ordinary citizens of Halifax seemed drawn to the boat, coming to wish us well, offering us some piece of advice about the waters ahead. We were showered with kindness and all felt looked after and special.

Andy had already spent three days out here before us and seemed to have become something of a local celebrity through his press and television interviews. It was great to see. He was clearly enjoying himself and, just as I had hoped, he had really started to take ownership of his part of the expedition.

Amid the high spirits, though, there was plenty of work to be done to get the boat ready, and it soon became clear Andy had done a superb job in this respect as well. He had fitted a new alternator the day before we arrived, and it seemed to have solved a last-minute issue we had had with a faulty power supply. The boat was neatly stowed with most of the kit, apart from our personal stuff, and she looked fantastic. I felt so proud and very protective.

She had started out as a rough idea in our minds, advanced to the drawing board, been to the Boat Show, on to the sea trials, across the Atlantic in the huge container ship, and now here she stood in pride of place on the Halifax waterfront.

The food packages had been carefully sorted out into days, and Andy had been meticulous in making sure that everything was neat and tidy on board. That was important to me. Even before the building process was complete, I had gone out and bought more than 100 bungee elastic cords, and roll after roll of Gaffa sticky tape. Andy had laughed incessantly about this.

'I hope that crane is strong enough when she is lifted over the docks,' I said, as our pride and joy first went into the water in Portsmouth.

'Well, we could always bungee or Gaffa tape her together if it isn't,' Andy instantly replied.

Whatever we were doing on the boat, there was always a bungee near at hand. It became a running joke. In my experience, the army would grind to a halt if it wasn't for bungees and Gaffa tape. They are the meat and drink of any unit.

'We'll use 'em all,' I would always reply.

And I was right. By the end of the expedition, when we were finally packing up in Scotland, I took immense satisfaction from seeing Andy rummaging around in the hold of the boat, looking for a bungee to keep his holdall together, and then hearing him say, 'I don't believe it. We're out of bungees.'

Come Halifax, the stores were all lashed neatly down in place. Nothing could budge. The bungees were all working.

We knew we were going to be thrown around violently on the ocean, so everything needed to be really well secured. The flares, the food, the spares, everything – even down to the box of ear defenders that were never used. (This was because they made us sick, as they took away our instinctive balance.) The sea anchor was neatly folded and stowed ready for deployment and, all in all, our little yellow boat looked ready for anything. It was a fantastic sight.

I had brought with me around forty laminated stickers, featuring little motivational slogans, which I placed in strategic positions around the boat. All of the guys teased me incessantly about these. They told me they were quite unBritish, but I thought these sayings would help us get through when times were tough.

They served their purpose well, although I did concede that the sticker reading, 'Make sure you watch the sunset once a year it will give you a whole new perspective on life' was starting to wear a little thin by the end. As Charlie wryly pointed out at the end of the 3,000 miles: 'Well, that's my sunsets done for the next twenty years.'

Our entire experience in Halifax was facilitated by the enthusiastic support of one of our lead sponsors, General Motors (Canada). I had made a speech at a GM conference in Italy some time before, and they had agreed to take one of the £15,000 sponsorship packages. They also effectively adopted this stage of the expedition, helping to generate publicity, raising money for a local charity – the Nova Scotia Sailing School, which teaches local kids how to build a boat and take trips into the wilderness (not round the Arctic if they've got any sense!) – and also hosting a farewell banquet for 500 people the night before we were to leave.

It was an emotional occasion. I had been asked to speak and accepted, even though I knew I would be speaking at about 3 a.m. British time, which I was still on, having arrived the day before.

The worst thing about speaking after dinner, though, is that it ruins your appetite. 'So much for taking this last chance to bulk up,' I thought, as I nervously played with my steak.

In fact I was too nervous to eat at all. It's weird how, after all the speeches I make – almost a hundred a year – I still get terrified. I dread those moments before you stand up, that silence as all eyes are on you, that intensity, but I guess to do it well you have to *use* that intensity. It's any speaker's best tool.

The first speaker was Michael Grimaldi, the president of General Motors (Canada), and he spoke concisely and directly about his company's pioneering spirit and how it constantly aimed to push back the boundaries in the automotive industry.

Then I stood up. All I really wanted to say was this: how so often people look at us and think that we are the pioneers and the guys breaking new boundaries, but it's not really true. In truth we are just normal guys who have been given a chance, a chance to follow a dream made possible by the likes of them. 'I'm not feeling very oratory-like right now,' I went on. 'I am nervous and we leave in only a few hours. But what I really want to say is thank you. It's because of your pioneering spirit that we are here. And when it comes down to those crunch times, somewhere out there in the waves and ice, the times when it really matters, I hope we can show that same spirit; and that we come home safe and can say, "We did you proud as well." Thank you.'

I sat down relieved, my job done. It was our last night, and I needed a bar and a strong drink.

As we left we said our thanks and farewells to the president of General Motors, and on the spur of the moment I offered him a quick spin on the boat the following day before we left.

'Unfortunately I am flying back to Toronto for a meeting tomorrow morning,' he said.

I paused, then asked again. 'How about doing it early?'

'That would be wonderful,' he smiled.

So at 6 a.m. the following day, in a crisp early-morning chill, under a clear Halifax sky, three of us took GM's president around the harbour. We were flying along over still, glassy seas at 25 knots. We watched the first of those sunrises, and it was a magical time.

Just before nine o'clock on that morning of Thursday, 31 July 2003, with barely an hour left before our scheduled departure, we were all sitting quietly around the boat, waiting. This was a rare period of calm and, in crisp sunshine, I decided it was the ideal time to convey a message. Standing on the bow, I asked Andy, Nige, Mick and Charlie for their attention. They turned to face me.

'Chloë has just faxed me a letter that was delivered to our base in London earlier this morning,' I said. 'I want to read it to you.' The letter was from the Prince of Wales.

Dear Bear,

I did just want to wish you and your team 'God Speed' for your intrepid adventure. I am delighted that the spirit of the Great British Eccentric Adventurer is alive and well and I much look forward to seeing you on your return.

Never has a Prince's Trust Ambassador gone to such lengths to support my Trust, and I am hugely grateful to you!

This comes with every possible thought and countless best wishes.

Yours most sincerely,

Charles

We were far from home, standing nervously on the brink of a life-changing challenge, and everybody was apprehensive. As messages of encouragement go, this handwritten letter from the Prince of Wales was hard to beat, and I could see it on the others' faces.

At last we were ready, and a flotilla of boats had gathered just off the quayside to escort us away from Halifax. There were 3,050 miles ahead of us. It was all systems go.

Almost.

It was 10 a.m., our time of departure, but there was no sign of Carol, the American journalist.

I had told her very firmly the previous evening that if she was late, we would leave without her.

She was late. So we were leaving.

'No, we can't go,' said Mick. 'You have to give her another ten minutes.'

'Five,' I replied.

The fleet of tugs, yachts and icebreakers was now moving out of the harbour, and people were glancing at their watches, wondering what was going on, what was causing the delay.

Quarter past ten, twenty past ten, half past ten. All our patience was being stretched. I could sense it. This wasn't what the guys needed. We were ready to go.

Carol McFadden was a beautiful, extremely glamorous and very game journalist from New York. The whole idea of taking her along for the first ten hours of the first leg of the expedition had started when she came to London and said she wanted to write an article about the world of expeditions for *Cosmopolitan*.

She was engaging, bright and entertaining, and, even though we were meeting at a time when the corporate rejection letters were arriving on a regular basis, I really enjoyed our conversation on the top deck of our barge.

'Well,' I said, 'if you want to get a real taste of the expedition, you should come with us for a bit of the first leg, from Halifax up the Nova Scotia coast.'

Carol's eyes literally flared into life, and she asked, 'Could I?'

'It would be a one-off and it would have a price,' I continued. 'Usually, press time is press time, expedition time is expedition time; we never mix it. But this would be an exception.'

'Well, that sounds a great idea,' she said.

'OK, this is the deal,' I said, thinking on my feet, intensely aware of what was then our very real need to raise funds. 'You can either write a normal article on the basis of our interview today or you could come along for part of the first leg, have the adventure of a lifetime and write a story about what it's *really* like to be on an expedition with five men on a small boat.'

I said it would have a price tag of £25,000.

Carol thought about it. It was a one-off opportunity. 'Inside an expedition' was a hundred times more saleable than just 'an expedition'. She agreed right there on the deck.

I knew we were offering a unique experience, and we were asking a premium price, but it was her call. On balance, I hoped it was a reasonable proposal.

Carol was a mother of four, leading a comfortable home life, but, there and then, she showed she was also gutsy, spontaneous and, above all, willing to grab life and have a go.

When I told Mick about the arrangement I had made with her, he congratulated me on what seemed a novel way of raising funds, but said we must make sure she signed some kind of indemnity.

'If anything happens to her, those Manhattan lawyers will sue you at the drop of a hat,' he warned.

'Well, will you write this indemnity form for me?' I asked him. 'Thanks, Miguel.'

Mick eventually produced a brief, very blunt document which, remarkably, managed to include the word 'death' eleven times in the space of only five lines.

'Mick, I can't send that to Carol,' I replied. 'She'll run a mile.' He told me just to send it. So I did. I think the wording surprised her but, again to her great credit, she signed on the dotted line the very same day.

She later told me, 'I sure wasn't going to let my husband see that. You Brits, you're nuts. You're meant to be looking after me, not sending through suicide notes to sign!'

Well, she'd passed Mick's litmus test.

We kept in regular touch during the preparations. At one stage, I arranged to take Carol over to Cowes for an afternoon on the boat. The aim was to give her all her kit and introduce her to what it was like on board. It was actually quite a blustery, overcast day, and I told her the sea could get pretty rough.

She didn't seem too concerned, but I glanced apprehensively at her equipment, which seemed to include, instead of a Musto offshore jacket, an Apple Mac i-pod, a silver-plated Theo Fennell pot of lip-balm and a Dolce and Gabbana headdress.

'Seriously, I would store some of that away,' I said.

'Baa,' she said, laughing.

It was one hell of an afternoon.

And sure enough, for the next month, we kept finding lip-gloss and Armani scrunchies wedged in between fuel filters or bilge alarms. Several times Andy appeared from the engine compartment staring at some beauty accessory in disbelief. It became a running joke.

Carol evidently lived in style and, true to form, she arrived in Halifax with her husband, the high-profile New York financier George McFadden, and their children. From the word go, they all joined in the spirit of the expedition. I remember one night in Halifax when Charlie leaned over to George, nudged him and told him to hurry up and drink his beer. He wanted to move on. No one usually talked to George like that and he loved it. It was a pleasure to have the McFaddens around.

The original plan was that Carol would remain on the

boat for the entire first leg but, when it emerged that there was no decent landing strip for her to be able to fly back from Port aux Basques, we modified the itinerary. Instead, we agreed we should take her up the coast for some ten hours, until late on the first night, then drop her off at a small inlet called Glace Bay, on the northernmost tip of Nova Scotia. There was a small airport there.

As arranged, she came down to the quay the day before we were due to leave, and I presented her with all her remaining equipment. With the kids standing by and clearly loving every minute, I gave their mum a big survival knife and harness, protective waterproof clothing, flares, torches, EPIRBs and the rest.

'OK, Carol,' I said finally. 'That's you set. You've got all your gear. Now, please make sure you are here at ten o'clock in the morning. We will leave at ten prompt.'

Those were the famous last words. It was now 10.35 and there was still no sign of Carol.

Finally, in a frenzied flurry of bags and taxis, she arrived at 10.40, forty minutes late.

'I'm so sorry,' she said as she kissed her family goodbye and clambered aboard.

'Come on, Carol,' I said. 'We'll talk about this later.'

I subsequently learned Carol was late because she was on the telephone to poor Chloë in London checking on all our insurance policies for her. I had taken personal cover for all the crew while we were in Canadian waters and included her on the policy.

'Well, if you hadn't got me so worried with that death warrant you sent me . . .' she explained, and as she spoke I saw Mick fumbling with the rope he was stowing.

I smiled and kind of understood. She was aboard, and she was fine, and we were finally on our way.

So, with the nose of our boat pointing north, we edged away from Halifax, escorted by this wonderful flotilla of local boats. We waved at them, and they waved at us, and I found my heart was pounding. So many people in this town had done so much for so little reward. We'd miss them, but we had a job to do now.

As we left the city behind us, I felt a peace, a quietness. It was such a relief after so long to just be us. Alone. No mass of people, no more interviews, no more anything apart from what we could bring to this ourselves. We were as well equipped and trained as we could be and we all felt proud to be here. The sea was mirror calm, the sky clear, and I sat on my own with my feet over the prow. I closed my eyes and breathed in the cold Nova Scotia air. The hull, with all those signatures from the Boat Show now painted over, glided though the water with ease, and I found myself thinking of Shara all those miles away, safe at home.

Carol settled as we picked up speed, and I quietly sat back and thanked God that we had a calm day and a flat sea. She was not short on courage, but I am not sure whether she would have coped very well if conditions had been really rough.

Several days later, when the boat was being thrown around and we were all being repeatedly drenched by sprays of icy water, Charlie suddenly piped up from deep within his survival suit pulled over his head: 'I think Carol would be looking for an exit strategy by now, don't you reckon?'

I think that was a fair response. But to her credit she had agreed to come whatever the weather, more or less.

Mick obviously gave the whole subject some thought and, some weeks later, over a beer in Iceland, he turned quite serious and said, 'Do you know, if we had been caught in a storm when Carol was on board, I think we would have had no option.'

'To do what?'

Carefully measuring his words, he replied, 'In those sort of horrendous conditions, not just with Carol but with any-one who was unprepared for that kind of onslaught, I think you would have had no choice but to tie their arms and legs together and strap them down in the sardine tin until we were out of trouble.

'She wouldn't have liked it,' he added between sips, 'but at least she would have survived.'

We all looked at Mick, a little concerned.

Mercifully, the conditions did not arise where Mick had the opportunity to test his theory on Carol. A gentle breeze ensured her day unfolded with no greater alarm than our first sighting of a minke whale.

Into the afternoon, we gave her a chance to helm. I told her it was her watch, and she should take the wheel. She seemed uncertain whether I was serious but, in exactly the manner we had grown to expect, and actually respect, she just got up and took over.

I gave her the bearings and showed her the direction we needed to take. She stared intently ahead, but we were soon doing figures of eight in the ocean. Anybody watching our path from above would have assumed we were trying to signal SOS in the water, but Mick stepped forward as Carol's personal tutor.

'OK, now this is going to be easy,' he began. 'Just imagine . . . you are driving this boat down Fifth Avenue in Manhattan. Prada is over on your right, Dolce and Gabbana is on your left. Go straight ahead up Fifth, aiming straight towards Gucci on the horizon.'

Her course became as straight as an arrow.

She was laughing, and was always a good sport. Despite all the endless jokes, each of us was highly impressed by the fact that someone like her had risen to the challenge, done everything expected and walked the walk. For all she knew, it could have been blowing a Force Eight gale out there. And as for the banter, well, that just meant everyone had accepted her.

We arrived at Glace Bay just before midnight, still in calm seas. The sun had long since disappeared in a distant glow of orange across the sky and we had all sat mesmerized, lost in our own thoughts. I felt so calm and content.

Nige had navigated us carefully through the myriad of tiny islets around the bay itself, and it was strange to pass by so many moss-covered rocks, sometimes just 30 yards away. Nige was concentrating intently on the GPS screen.

'Left five degrees, and hold the course for 300 metres,' he would say quietly. He was in his element, using the precision accuracy of the Simrad navigational equipment to chart a safe course and ensure we avoided those lethal outcrops.

Finally, we entered the tiny harbour itself, and noticed more than a hundred little fishing boats moored together in a small bay. The fishermen were working in silence by halogen light, processing their catch, and the whole place was dominated by an overpowering stench of fish innards. As we glided silently up the narrowing creek, the locals seemed to hardly notice us.

We moored and found that the only place open around the dock was the small ambulance station, with its doors open, so we went in there. The crew on the nightshift seemed surprised to see five massively overdressed men shuffle into their hangar, and they were intrigued to hear what we were doing. They could not have been more friendly, and they generously plied us with sandwiches and cups of hot tea.

It was soon time for us to say our goodbyes to Carol, and we found her a taxi that would take her on to the hotel she was staying at, near the airport, from where she would fly home.

'Thank you all so much,' she said. 'It's been amazing. It's been a real privilege to have shared these early moments with you. I will think of you all every moment until you are home safe. Look after each other, eh?'

'We will,' we promised.

Soon after 1 a.m., we were heading on out again towards Port aux Basques, a small town on the southern tip of Newfoundland, the huge island that sits to the north of Nova Scotia. Once again we wove a careful path through the small islands and rocks, each still beautifully silhouetted in the moonlight, until finally we were in open water.

It was 100 miles straight across this stretch of water to Port aux Basques, where we planned to refuel before heading up to our final Canadian port on the tip end of the Labrador coast, far to the north.

At about 3 a.m. Charlie was on watch and his attention was drawn by a green glow in the sky to the north.

'What's that?'

'It must be the lights of Newfoundland,' Nige suggested.

But Newfoundland is a huge, magnificent wilderness, not a city electrified and lit for 10 million inhabitants.

'Or maybe it's an oil rig,' I wondered.

'No way,' Andy replied. 'That's the northern lights.'

And it was. This was nature's famous lightshow, staged every night at the northern end of the planet. We sat in wonder. The effect was stunning, as if the sky was being illuminated by the stage-lights of some sort of heavenly concert. We sat entranced, in the world's biggest and most spectacular arena.

Our expectation after that first night was that we would be treated to this natural extravaganza most nights across the freezing ocean ahead. However, we never saw them again.

The weather made sure of that. More often than not, dense cloud cover obscured the northern lights and gave us long, dark nights.

But that was all in the future. For now, on this first night of the expedition, the five of us settled back, enjoyed the view and picked contentedly at our boil-in-the-bag sachets of baked beans. That night, it was impossible not to feel richly blessed.

The northern lights lasted until around 4 a.m., and Mick and I helmed through that last night-time shift before dawn, while the others snatched a couple of hours' rest in the sardine tin. In a tranquil, misty dawn we pulled into Port aux Basques at just after 6.30 a.m.

We could hardly have been luckier with the way things were going so far. Everyone was slipping into their role and feeling confident. Each of us was playing our part with one clear goal in mind: to stay alive and complete the crossing. If it was going to be like this every day and night, then it would be easy. Privately, we knew that wouldn't happen. It was only ever a matter of time before the skies and seas would change.

As we approached the quay at Port aux Basques, I spotted the harbourmaster standing by to welcome us. He had been telephoned and forewarned by Chloë. The tracker system had kept her informed of our every move, and her attention to small details like this had an enormous impact on the expedition. It was the difference between being warmly greeted on arrival at a far-flung outpost and arriving and trying to find someone to talk to and having to explain who we were.

'Welcome to Port aux Basques,' declared the harbour-master with a broad smile.

I had expected this place to be a major hub for shipping in the area. It was, after all, one of the last 'big' ports before the northern waters of the Arctic ahead and a staging post for shipping between Newfoundland and mainland Canada. Instead, there were just a few old concrete and wooden piers stretching out to sea, where the big icebreakers and ferries could refuel and disembark.

The rapidly rising sun was warming the cold air of dawn, and, happy to have arrived, we all began to peel off the layers of dry suits, thermals, Gortex and waterproofs.

A group of local fishermen were sitting on the wooden walkway at the head of our pier. Leaning over the railings, side by side, smoking silently, they were dressed in lumber-jack shirts and chest-high rough waterproofs and were watch-ing us cautiously as we bustled about the boat.

I was now down to my undies, and felt deeply relieved to have got rid of all the heavy, stinking kit, which now lay in a pile on the foredeck. Right then, I realized we needed some more rope and, on the foreshore, I happened to spot an old corrugated building with a sign marked 'supplies'.

They would have what we needed, but I really didn't fancy getting dressed in all my kit again. I glanced over at the fishermen and thought, well, I am sure they have seen a man in his underwear before. So I pulled on my Musto ocean boots, took a deep breath and, dressed in nothing apart from underpants and boots, walked gingerly past the fishermen to the shop.

They looked at me, looked at each other, then stared out to sea, puffing on their cigarettes, without saying a word. Charlie, chortling, caught the whole scene on camera.

The sun was shining on a clear morning, and I was wandering around a chandlery in my pants. I was in heaven.

6. SURFING THE WAVES

Man cannot discover new oceans unless he first loses sight of the shore.

Christopher Columbus

British people traditionally seem fascinated by trying to forecast the weather. It's a national obsession: we watch the news and then we watch the weather. It never serves much purpose, save the vague satisfaction, upon hearing the rain on the roof, of noting whether or not the forecasters were correct. This is a strange pastime, and one at which my mother-in-law is a maestro.

'Hmm,' Vinnie often muses from her sofa when it starts to pour outside, 'they were right.'

She assumes this is, of course, highly irregular.

Out on the North Atlantic, though, the stakes were a bit higher than whether or not it would drizzle during the summer fête.

For us, the weather forecast was everything. If our expedition was going to go smoothly, it would probably be because we got the weather forecast right. Similarly, if the expedition ended in disaster, it was more than likely going to be because our weather forecast was wrong. This worried me. So much seemed to hang on these forecasts ... our lives in particular; and so many of those forecasts, ultimately, appeared to be down to luck.

We were not looking for rough seas and storms – there

was too much at stake. We didn't want to be heroes – all we wanted was to be safe. We would stay safe by getting the forecast right.

It was as simple as that.

Everything I wanted most in the world – to get back safely to Shara and Jesse, to be the best husband and the best dad I could be – depended on accurate weather forecasting and staying away from the bad stuff.

Plenty of other factors could go wrong, but the implications of bad weather were by far the greatest danger. In such an exposed, small boat, we were highly vulnerable.

Andy, with his experience of the sea, was well aware of our precarious circumstances. In March, some months before we set off, he was on board HMS *Newcastle* in heavy seas off the coast of Cornwall. HMS *Newcastle* is a type-42 Destroyer, 462 feet in length, and, from his position on the bridge, with hundreds of tonnes of wild water pouring over her bows, the ship pitching wildly as she battled through the blackness, Andy began to understand how vulnerable we would be in an open RIB, only 33 feet long. He knew as well as we all did that the forecasting really mattered.

As soon as we arrived in Port aux Basques, I took time with Mick to check the weather forecast. This would become a ritual: whenever we arrived in port, Mick and I would use our first spare moments to research the weather and call Mike Town in the UK.

Mike is one of the top meteorologists in Britain and was

one of the few experts to predict the hurricane in 1987. We were extremely lucky to have him on hand.

We got through to him on the satellite (SAT) phone first time.

It was our first call back from the boat. Our system of hunting good weather had begun. It was midday back in England, and this was just about the only occasion when Mike Town would be called at a sensible time of day. Unfortunately, we ended up calling him at all times of the nights ahead, but he was kind enough to expect and accept these calls whenever they came. He understood only too well how much we relied on him.

'We're in Port aux Basques. How does the weather look from here?'

'It's looking OK,' he replied. 'You shouldn't have any problems for the next twenty-four hours.'

'So it's clear?' Mick asked.

'Pretty much. There are a few localized small fronts but nothing really menacing. There's a big storm passing to your south, but that should miss you. The temperature will drop from here onwards, but you shouldn't find more than Force Five northerlies, and they're going your way. It should be fine.'

When I first met Mike I called him 'sir'. He was my geography teacher at school, but he soon became a friend as well. He was a climber and a martial artist and a real character, loved by many of his students. He used to arrange climbing trips to the Lake District, which Mick and I, aged fifteen, adored and took very seriously. For both of us, he became genuinely inspirational, and we have stayed in touch with him ever since leaving school.

Soon after meeting Shara, I planned to take her away for a weekend's climbing. Shara was under the impression it was purely a romantic getaway weekend, which it was of sorts, but it did also involve two ascents of Skiddaw, the hard way. It was Mike who lent me the keys to his cottage in Cumbria.

In the years when I was training with the army, Mike used to pack stones in my rucksack and run off ahead up the mountains, dragged by two abnormally large Bernese mountain dogs, telling me to hurry up because he had the sandwiches.

Time and again, Mike has been a source of support and friendship, a man I have learned to trust absolutely. And I loved the fact that he had been one of the few to predict the hurricane!

Some people might think it is a bit unusual, maybe a bit amateurish, to set out across the North Atlantic with your old geography teacher as one of your main sources of meteorological advice. But I liked that. I suppose I was just lucky that my old geography teacher happened to be such an expert in this field.

The Fleet Weather Centre, operated by the navy, also provided us with invaluable information at various stages of the expedition, and when Internet access was available in port we logged on to various weather websites, including one maintained by, and designed for, the US military.

Our third source of guidance was the local population. The people living in these isolated and far-flung places were not slow to offer their opinions on the weather. Down the years, through the generations, they had learned to interpret and recognize patterns; to look at the sky, feel the wind and trust their instincts.

The bottom line was that we were trying to avoid the storms, and these people were fishermen by trade. Avoiding the storms was what they had to do every day of every year of their lives.

In Port aux Basques, the local people seemed relaxed about the weather. Wizened old men appeared near the dock later in the morning and told us how they had only just emerged from nineteen days of dense fog, but now things seemed to be clearing.

'You should still be careful,' said one old man, dressed in a thick woollen jersey and faded jeans. 'Things can change very quickly out there.'

Routinely, we were used to predicting the weather for a journey of, say, 60 miles offshore. That is still a long way out to sea. But we needed now to estimate the conditions for a crossing as long as almost 1,000 miles. That was a whole different beast.

You might be told that wind speed was only 5 to 10 knots, and think that is all right, but a wind just 20 per cent over that can still produce enormous swells. This in turn reduces the speed of the boat, and suddenly your carefully planned two-day forecast would have to become a three- or four-day guestimate . . . and it was that extra time that was so unknown and dangerous.

We had always known that accurate forecasting would be difficult, not least because we would be passing through waters that were, to a large extent, uncharted. Where little shipping traffic passes, the authorities understandably don't place too many weather buoys, so information was sketchy and forecasts often unreliable.

Most of the time, we simply had to be satisfied with an accurate twenty-four-hour forecast, and thereafter we would make a reasonable assessment and hope. Above all, we simply tried to be cautious and sensible.

It was just before ten o'clock on another brisk and clear morning when the *Arnold and Son Explorer* pulled away from Port aux Basques. We had refuelled, paying for the diesel with a heavy fistful of our US$50 bills, taken from a watertight container in the depths of the hold where we stored our cash, passports, wallets and photographs of home. We said goodbye to the locals and once again pointed our nose north.

Within fifteen minutes, though, we were in dense sea fog, and we found ourselves edging through what felt like thick, soggy soup. The fog was so intense that at times it was impossible to see the bow of the boat. We were driving blind.

We had been warned of magnetic variables in this region, and the compass started to behave erratically. This was worrying. We were now relying entirely on the accuracy of our electrical instruments to make any progress at all.

Every now and then, through the mist, we caught a

glimpse of Newfoundland away to our right, a craggy stretch of coast or a distant lighthouse; then everything would go grey and damp again, enveloping us in mist. Everything gets wet in seconds as this type of fog hits you. Inexorably and quietly, it covers you in moisture.

The sea though stayed calm and flat, and we moved steadily on through this strange, silent seascape. Minute by minute, we were beginning to settle into a routine.

As the afternoon drew on, the temperature began to drop and the waves started to build steadily into a swell. The change was slow and gradual, but we were clearly approaching much bigger seas. We knew we were heading up towards the Belle Isle Strait, a natural funnel of water where the wind and currents drive the ice down between Newfoundland and Labrador. It was an infamous stretch of water, and not much used. It was dangerous and unpredictable and was now less than 300 miles to the north. We were readying ourselves.

Perceptibly, the feel of everything was changing. We were alone and heading north. It was only going to get colder and more isolated from now on and ice was ahead, somewhere. We had no idea how long it would be until we saw it, but it was out there, waiting, floating massively to our north. We knew that Port aux Basques was to be our last port of accessible civilization for a long time.

We were starting to quieten into our own worlds, checking and rechecking, lashing ourselves to the boat when we moved around, taking nothing for granted, keeping our own personal grab bags clipped to our waists. These small waterproof holdalls contained essential items such as a torch, a knife, a hand-held VHF radio and mini-flares.

Each of us was well stocked with anti sickness pills, and these were working well. I took my pills on the dot every eight hours. I had to keep alert and avoid that debilitating sense of feeling wretched and disoriented.

The seasickness, we soon discovered, was often worst in the sardine tin, and if it hit you, it was utterly incapacitating. You lie there, desperately needing some decent rest, overwhelmed by the invasive smell of diesel and the deafening roar of the engine, and you are wet and cold. You can taste the salt water in your mouth and your nostrils are sore and raw, and your stomach churns, and nothing can stop it. You want nothing more than to curl up and die.

They say seasickness has two stages: one is when you don't care if you die; the second is when you start praying to die.

Whenever anybody was sick over the side, it was vital to try to rehydrate afterwards. You'd have to pump water from the large jerry cans strapped to the side of the console and start drinking again. It was the last thing you felt like doing, but it was absolutely necessary to recover your strength.

'Drink water. Replace the liquids. Keep drinking.' This became one of our mantras. Experience had told us that dehydration could be a big issue in an open boat, especially when it is rough. The sheer amount of waves and spray that was eventually to come over us meant that we swallowed a lot of salt water – it was impossible to avoid. This means your salt intake becomes very high and you need twice the amount of fresh water to compensate. But on the sea you never feel like drinking, which is why it has to be a discipline.

As we progressed, the rota seemed to be settling down and working well. We had decided to sustain a five-hour rota. Each crew member would helm for an hour, navigate for an hour, spend the next hour sitting in the 'deckchair', a piece of rubber material on one side, slung between two metal struts and angled down, and lastly rest in the sardine tin for two hours. Every hour on the hour, almost without exception, the five of us rotated religiously through this circuit of tasks and responsibilities.

Our concept was logical and straightforward: make the big challenges manageable by breaking them into smaller tasks. We reckoned that on a 1,000-mile leg you had to have something short-term to focus on. The days and hours passed very slowly sometimes, especially if you were sick. It was much easier to focus on getting through a single hour and then addressing a new situation than it was to have nothing to think about apart from watching the GPS plotter and seeing how slowly we were moving.

We humans are creatures of habit and we need something to focus on. This routine was something tangible that would hold us together when it struck rough, and I was determined that whatever happened, we would stick to it. Even when you were resting in the sardine tin, after one hour you would roll over to the other side as the guy to your right got up, and another body crawled in to your left.

There were times in those early days when we would be coasting along in calm seas under clear skies and one of us would suggest we stayed as we were because everyone was OK, but I was adamant we stuck to the rota.

This was our discipline. In extreme environments people depend on routines, and the more familiar you are with the routine, the less frightening the unfamiliar becomes. On the ocean, life gets much easier when you have something you can hold on to, something you know is predictable and reliable and constant. Whatever else might change, I wanted the rota to remain on track.

The only drawback of the system was that you had to get on well with whoever was next to you. The rota meant you really only had regular contact with the people either side of you. When the seas were rough, you would be wearing your helmet and full survival suit, and, even though you were sharing a living space of a few square yards, you would scarcely be aware of the other two members of the crew one seat away from you. It sounds strange, but at various stages of the expedition twenty-four hours would pass during which I would not see Andy even though we were never more than a yard apart.

Mick just loved this. He would say that this was his ideal holiday: no chit-chat, no small-talk, just the roar of the engine. He announced that if the rota format could be duplicated in England, life would definitely be better. This is a sure sign that a man is working too hard and getting too many phone calls.

Growing used to our equipment, and settling into the

hourly routine, we continued to make good progress, at times reaching speeds of 25 knots as the following seas propelled the boat forward.

I remembered how Andy had told me one evening that one of the reasons why he was so keen to do this expedition was his desire to experience some unusual sea conditions and, towards evening on this first day out of Port aux Basques, it was beginning to happen. We were being treated to the spectacular sensation of 'surfing' on big ocean breakers.

We had been aware of the sea building in size and strength throughout the day. Increasingly powerful waves would roll up from behind and raise the boat high above the ocean; then the crest of the wave would break, and we would surge forward. It was amazing. We would look back to see the wave frothing away in white water and, within moments, another surge of marine power would lift us high once again.

Roller followed roller, surge followed surge.

By dusk, the dense fog was returning, but we were still surfing forward at good speeds, more than ever trusting in our instruments to keep us on course. I started to wonder what would happen if while racing down one of these rollers we were propelled into a collision with an iceberg. At these speeds, and in the dark, we would have no time to react with the energy of the waves behind us. It was not a good thought, but I consoled myself by remembering being told that at this time of year we would not hit ice until much further north. We had to trust that and keep the speed on through the fog.

It had been a strange kind of day.

First the fog, then the falling temperatures, then the slowly swelling waves, then the darkness, finally all of this together. Piece by piece, element by element, the ocean seemed to be assembling its forces against us. Individually, none of these factors would have been a concern but, as they all massed together that first night, each of us had the distinct feeling that we were entering a new phase of the expedition. We were beginning the work in earnest. The playtime was over and we were entering the arena where mistakes would become extremely costly.

Each mile travelled to the north felt like a mile travelled to a different level. It was exciting, it was what we had put so much time and energy into preparing for, but I would be lying if I did not admit that my heart was beginning to pound.

The distant flash of a lighthouse through the mist and darkness reminded us how close we were to the coast, as the Belle Isle Strait narrowed towards its most northerly gap. The boat really needed to be driven now. Concentrate. Control her. Compensate for the power of the waves pulling you off course. Feel her.

The RIB was built for these conditions and she was thriving in the surf and this was what we had trained for. This was why we were here. There was nobody else around: just the waves, the fog, the boat and the five of us. This was living; these were the moments when I felt most alive.

As we approached the Strait, now only 50 miles to the north, I found myself privately trying to work out how the rota would unfold; who would be helming at the critical hour, guiding us through the currents and funnel of sea and racing tidal water. It would be me or Mick; I knew Mick would be thinking the same.

It was going to be difficult. There were no stars out, and in the fog it would be easy to lose all sense of direction and perspective.

At around midnight, when Charlie was at the helm, we found ourselves travelling in completely the wrong direction before he made a 180-degree turn and set us back on course. He cursed himself out loud, but it was so easy to do. The horizon and sea become a confused blend of rolling black-ness. The chart-plotter screen is an eye-aching blur of green and reds. Tiredness pounds at your eyelids. The waves yank you violently off course and every small over-correction is replicated by the jet drive at the stern. The boat is so sensitive to helm.

Just before 1 a.m., I came off watch and Mick took over. It would be he who would helm us through the Belle Isle Strait ahead. He needed his concentration now and we all knew it. None of us slept and we all sat up and watched him guide us through, struggling to keep us on course in the roar of the surf behind.

It felt as if we were riding some kind of wild beast, all the time knowing that we could never be completely in control of something so powerful and untameable. As we surged forward, I found myself praying again that there would be no ice.

Again and again the boat rose and fell, as huge waves

lifted her hull before throwing us down the face of the wave in front.

Both time and sea were now racing.

An hour later, I was crouching down in the pitch black beside the console with my torch, trying to check one of the fuel gauges, when the boat was hit violently by a wave side-on. My head smashed against the metal console and I slumped back into the seat holding my forehead in my hands.

I shouted out loud, my eyes closed tight. I was feeling dazed and soon I had a splitting headache.

Charlie asked, 'Are you OK?'

'Yes, I'm fine,' I replied, wincing. 'Can you hold the torch while I just recheck this fuel gauge.'

This was always a tricky task; the fuel was stored in four areas and, for reasons relating to the distribution of weight and maximizing the boat's performance, we needed to drain the fuel from the centre tank first, then from the tanks on the side and lastly from the bladder at the front.

The whole system operated on a complex series of fuel drain levers and manifolds. Andy had marked them all for us to be able to read and understand, even at night.

I was on my knees trying to check the dial of the centre tank we were using, just to make sure it wasn't time to change over. This check involved pumping air into the tank and giving the dial time to settle before taking the reading.

'It looks fine,' I shouted to Charlie who was right next to me. 'The reading looks OK.'

The engine typically ticks over at 2,600 revs per minute,

producing a roar that would seem invasive for a short period but which, for us on the ocean, became almost hypnotically comforting after a while. That roar represented raw power and movement in the right direction, homewards. We grew to love it.

Fifteen minutes later, for no apparent reason, the noise began to die. The revs plummeted. Then it stopped. All of a sudden, our loud mechanical world plunged into a terrifying silence. From 450 hp to nothing, the boat was now running on momentum. The engine was dead.

Our hearts stopped.

It was approaching 2.30 a.m., and we were still in the last port of the Strait. Everyone was immediately awake and alert, fired with adrenalin, desperately trying to work out what needed to be done. Andy had been in the sardine tin, but he was out on his feet in a second, checking the levers, the filters, the engine monitoring systems, all lightning-fast, instinctively moving into reaction mode.

'Get the engine lid up now,' he said calmly and firmly.

The rest of us reached for the latches and lifted the lid, as our naval engineer set about his work.

'She's out of fuel,' he said, his face contorting with strain as he grappled with the engine primer. 'We need to act fast. The turbo is not going to like this at all.'

He started frantically pumping the engine primer; pumping then priming. I stood over him, acutely aware that we were drifting powerlessly in one of the world's most treacherous stretches of water, vulnerable to any rogue wave.

Without the roar of the engine, for the first time we could hear the wind licking violently off the waves. It was much stronger, much more threatening than I had realized.

The sea was churning white and black, and suddenly we were just a little boat at the mercy of the sea. With no propulsion from the engine, we would have no ability to respond if one of these rollers hit us side-on. In the darkness, in what was the first major crisis of the expedition, I just hoped and prayed that Andy could get her working again.

Time seemed to be suspended.

We waited and waited.

Two and a half minutes passed like hours.

Then Andy looked at me, then back at the engine, and said loudly, 'Try her now.'

I took a breath and turned the key in the ignition.

There was a bubbling noise, a spluttering.

Then nothing.

'Again, Bear,' he said. 'And hold it.'

I did.

A deeper noise, and then a different noise, and then finally that comforting roar as the engine sprang into life and the boat came alive again.

Several hours later, Mick told me how his legs had turned to jelly when he heard that silence descend. Mine had too, and they stayed that way for several hours afterwards.

'Well done, buddy,' I said to Andy. 'Good work.'

'The central tank was empty. But I don't know how. Who last checked it?'

Central tank? Empty?

I knew what they meant.

'It was me,' I told everyone over the roar of the engine. 'I'm so sorry. I must have misread it. It won't happen again, I promise.'

We carried on in silence.

I knew I had caused the crisis. I had checked that tank just a few moments before and I must have misread the dial. Hitting my head was no excuse. I was angry with myself. It could have been disastrous. How could I have been so stupid, so careless?

With hindsight, it might have been a good thing that it was me who made the first mistake of the expedition. It was inevitable that there were going to be mistakes – it was only natural – but nobody wanted to be the first.

Maybe the fact that it was me, as leader, who had made the first cock-up took the pressure off the others, but I felt I had let them down a little. I remember my late father saying that if you want a good team, then pick people who are better than you. Most people do the opposite. It makes them feel better. But I had picked people who were better than me.

It was always our great strength.

It was with huge relief that we eventually turned and watched the Belle Isle Strait fade into the darkness behind.

The rest of the night wore on and just before dawn the mist lifted to reveal the black outline of the Labrador coast away to our left. The wind was biting and dramatically colder now, but we knew we had survived our first test.

'Wow, look at that!' Mick shouted suddenly.

I turned around to see an iceberg, which must have been the size of Buckingham Palace, half a mile away on the port side. It was incredible: huge, cold and grey. The waves rolled past it furiously.

We stared in disbelief. If we had collided with that during the night, there would only have been one survivor, and it would not have been us. Thank God, the fog was clearing.

'This is too early to be seeing ice,' I thought to myself. We had been told we wouldn't see ice until we were off the coast of Greenland. Seeing icebergs this far south was not a good sign. But I knew what I was seeing here off the port side. What worried me most though was what else we had been told that was wrong.

We had read that what you see of an iceberg represents no more than 6 per cent of its total mass; based on that fact, this berg was enormous. It seemed to belong here. In our small, yellow-tubed boat, I felt we didn't. We were trespassing, and we were alone. I felt as though the iceberg was looking at us, angry to be disturbed in its territory.

Some experts had warned us that icebergs might not show up on our radar screens, but this wasn't generally the case. In fact, the Canadian coastguards place radar reflectors on the large ones, and this gave us some reassurance – though not much.

The following seas continued to drive us on towards our destination, and we reckoned we would reach St Mary's harbour, on the Labrador coast, at around 6.30 a.m., approximately three hours ahead of schedule.

Andy was due to helm at five o'clock but he had just got off to sleep and, as a small gesture of apology for getting him up in the middle of the night when the engine stopped, I suggested I would do some of his shift. We were all tired.

By dawn, and only three miles from shore, we suddenly felt a rush of warm air on our faces. It was a welcome change from the cold winds that had been blowing all night, and with this wind came a rich aroma of heather. Labrador looked and smelled like the wilds of Scotland and, as we carefully wound our way from Battle Harbour down the mouth of the remote estuary to the port of St Mary's, all five of us were buzzing.

The land on either side of this narrow inlet was barren and untamed, but eventually we turned a corner and found a small harbour full of fishing boats, surrounded by a cluster of corrugated-iron buildings. It was early morning, but people were already at work on the one concrete quay, preparing thousands of freshly caught crabs.

Our early arrival had caught the local reception party by surprise, and we pulled alongside an old wooden pier to wait. We began to unwind and enjoy the quiet of the moment as we waited for the local contact to arrive and guide us to where we were to moor. We were so pleased to be here, safe and with some time to prepare for the first of our real tests ahead: the Labrador Sea.

We dug out the bottle of Mumm champagne we had brought to mark our first sighting of an iceberg and removed it from its bubble wrap. The cork flew off and the five of us drank contentedly.

However, within minutes, we were being bitten to shreds by giant mosquitoes and blood was pouring down Charlie's neck.

'Get the cigarettes out, quick,' he shouted, slapping his forehead frantically. 'That'll keep them away.'

It didn't.

Before long, each of us was covered in huge bites that oozed blood. They itched like hell. None of us had seen mosquitoes this big, and Nige said they obviously had to be this huge to survive so far north – they would need to be well insulated. Well, after such a feast of English blood, they would certainly be that all right.

As we scurried around, each clutching four cigarettes in both hands in a vain attempt to dispel the insects, we heard a voice behind us.

'Welcome! We weren't expecting you until half past nine.' The booming voice belonged to Alton Rumbolt, mayor of St Mary's.

'How do you do?' I replied, putting out my hand. 'Yes, we had following seas, and we've made good time.'

'OK, well, as soon as you are all sorted out, I will show you to where you are staying.'

Alton led us along a dirt track up the hill towards the harbour buildings, and almost everybody stopped to greet us as we walked by. They all seemed to know what we were doing, and they all seemed eager to help.

'Enjoy your stay in St Mary's,' said one of the fishermen.

'Thanks,' Nige replied.

We walked on.

Alton Rumbolt noted, 'That was Robert Rumbolt.'

'I see,' Nige said innocently. 'Is he your brother?'

'No ... just a relative.'

It soon became clear that the majority of the population of St Mary's, which did not exceed 250 in total, was also named Rumbolt. And when it came to naming shops or businesses, it seemed they didn't like to venture too far from the path of convention: 'Rumbolt General Stores'; 'Rumbolt Fishing'; 'Rumbolt Supplies'.

Nige persevered: 'Is that your shop over there, Alton?'

'Nope,' Alton replied, 'that's my cousin's.'

'What about Rumbolt Repairs?'

By this stage, Nige was finding everything quite amusing. He had, after all, been at sea for a while.

'Not mine,' Alton replied. 'That's my second cousin's.'

We reached our rooms and crashed. Everyone was drained. Nobody had got much sleep in the sardine tin during the past two nights. It's not easy to fall asleep beside a roaring engine, bracing yourself every time a wave hits the boat. Sleep only tends to come when you are so exhausted that you physically can't stay awake. As Andy would tell people when asked how we slept, 'You can sleep anywhere if you're tired enough.'

In due course, Mick and I headed back down to the boat. We clambered inside the cubby, where Andy's spares and our supplies were stowed during passage, and dialled home on the SAT phone. We needed to speak first to Chloë, to update her on our progress, and then to Mike Town for an updated forecast.

More than ever, we were determined to get this next judgement exactly right. The next leg, across the infamous Labrador Sea to Greenland, would be one of the toughest of the entire expedition, and we didn't want to take any unnecessary risks. The passage through the Belle Isle Strait had been rougher than we'd expected and that had taught us a vital lesson. The forecast might say the outlook is fine, but the reality for a small boat in unpredictable seas can be very different. We weren't a big cruise liner or a frigate. We were effectively a rugged, inshore speedboat, and as far as forecasts were concerned, this was worth remembering.

Mike Town was not overly optimistic about the prospects.

'There's a north-westerly wind of around Force Four to Five,' he said, 'and you'll be heading north-east, so that will probably give you a beam sea for the crossing.'

'That's not ideal but it's manageable,' I said.

We checked a couple of websites, and they confirmed the likely direction of the wind. The data all forecast north-westerlies, and, for us, that meant beam seas.

Our kind of boat was most vulnerable in a beam sea. With the waves rolling across us, we have little lateral stability compared with either a head-on or following sea. I didn't like this.

Mike added cautiously, 'It looks as if the winds are going to get stronger, not weaker, after about forty-eight hours. But if you do decide to wait, you could be in St Mary's for a while.'

It made the decision much more difficult. Did we sit and wait, or risk it, getting most of the 700-mile crossing completed before the bad weather really kicked in?

I discussed this with Mick. He agreed we didn't want to get stuck, but we also had to be safe.

In the end, we decided we would prepare the boat to leave the following day, but we would not make a final decision until we had checked the weather forecast again in the morning. That kept our options open. It also meant we would be ready if we did decide to try to beat the bad weather that was coming straight down from the Arctic through the Labrador Sea.

Throughout the afternoon as Andy, now rested, pottered around the boat, doing various maintenance tasks, I mulled over the issues. Mick and I were almost certain we should get a good night's sleep and leave at first light in the morning. The forecast was not that bad, and my instinct was to keep moving.

It would be great to stay in St Mary's a bit longer and spend time with the people there, but we all knew we needed to be well across the worst of the Labrador Sea before the strong winds reached our latitude. Conditions of Force Four to Five over the next two days were a reasonable option.

I felt confident we would be OK. My only concern was that this was such a crucial leg to get right, and I knew there would be no room for error once we were 400 miles offshore. It would be too late. I had never been anything like that far from land before. The furthest I had been was about 50 miles and even that had felt very exposed. I reached for the Dicta-phone, and spoke . . .

I'm still feeling tired, and I'm apprehensive. I'm not sure about the forecast. It's awkward whether to go before the bad stuff or to wait. It's the toughest call yet.

I remember Annabel, my sister-in-law, telling me before we left that I would have to make some hard decisions out here as leader – and this is one of them.

I miss Shara and little Jesse; I really miss us just being together, especially at times like this.

I feel edgy and vulnerable when there are these difficult choices to be made, especially as the person leading the team. I just want to keep everyone together and happy, and to make the right decisions. I hope I can.

Later on I spoke to Chloë again on the SAT phone. She had received a phone call from Mary, Mick's girlfriend. It was bad news. Mary's father had suddenly passed away. It had happened the hour we had left Halifax. I found Mick prepping his kit and told him to telephone Mary. I warned him it wasn't good news. Mick was devastated, but also torn. Torn between the team and wishing he could be there for Mary at this awful time.

Mary broke down and cried. Her father had just fallen

from the cliff of life, and Mick, her boyfriend, was now treading precariously near the edge. It all became too much for her later that day when she found an envelope. It was Mick's will, which he had written the day before he left. This was the final straw.

Mick and I spoke for a while, partly about Mary, partly about what to do now. We were trying to rationalize everything, but soon we were interrupted by a familiar voice.

'So we're all looking forward to seeing you tonight.'

It was Mayor Rumbolt again, extending the warm hand of hospitality, inviting us to an occasion at the town hall where, it seemed, we were to be the guests of honour.

'We would like to initiate you all as honorary Labradoreans,' he grinned. That sounded worrying. I had done initiations in the army, and they were rarely good news. Ever.

'Um ... yep, that would be a pleasure,' I said.

The words tumbled out. We had all planned on an early night but it would have been ungracious to turn him down.

'We'll go along for a short time, show our faces and present the mayor with a decent bottle of whisky as a thanks for all he has done, and then bed,' I told the others.

As it was, they were all much keener to go than me. 'It'll be fun,' Charlie added.

So we went.

Everybody was in high spirits as we approached the house where we had been asked to meet before going on to what Alton cheerfully referred to as the 'town hall'. The guys were now in the frame of mind to celebrate our progress so far.

'They've got pretty good roads for such a small place,' Nige noted as we walked along.

'I know,' Charlie added, 'especially when you think they only go round the town and that's it. They don't actually lead anywhere. There is no road from here to Toronto, or any-where for that matter. The only way out of here is by plane or sea.'

We arrived at the house, full of festive fishermen, and found the beer flowing fast. The local people could not have been more friendly, and they made us feel quite proud when they said they could hardly believe we had travelled up from Nova Scotia in our small, yellow 32-foot rigid inflatable boat.

'You must go easy from now on, mind,' said another Rumbolt. 'You are heading into difficult waters from here on.'

Another asked, 'When are you leaving?'

I replied that we would probably leave the following day, and this remark provoked a chorus of amazement.

'You can't do that. It's northerly winds,' the fishermen said. 'We never go out in northerlies.'

'Really?' Andy asked.

'No, never.'

The locals were absolutely adamant, and I sensed eyes glancing in my direction.

'Why not?' I asked.

'The northerlies are the vicious ones,' they said. 'They blow onshore and come straight from the Arctic. They're cold and dangerous. It's a rule in our fleet. When the wind is a northerly, we wait for the winds to change.'

It made sense, but I tried to rationalize the situation.

First, I told myself, the fishermen were dealing with conditions maybe 50 miles, maximum 100 miles, offshore. We had to think bigger. We were trying to get it right for over 700 miles straight across this ocean. That made the decision a different call altogether. We had to see the whole picture.

Second, the thought did cross my mind that it wasn't every day they have visitors, and that, even with Charlie and Nige's terrible jokes, they might not want us to leave quite so soon. At the very least, our arrival had broken their routine.

It was soon eleven o'clock, the time when I had promised myself we would all be back asleep in our beds, but the evening was only just starting. Mayor Rumbolt announced it was time to move on and join the rest of the folks at the town hall. We arrived, and quickly realized not only that almost the entire town was present but also that the night's entertainment seemed to be ... us.

There was no escape from this local kindness, so I decided I might as well enter into the spirit of the occasion. We got drinks and I even had a dance with Mrs Rumbolt ... although I wasn't sure exactly which Mrs Rumbolt I was dancing with.

We were soon led to a kind of wooden stage where, in preparation for our initiation as honorary Labradoreans, we were told to get dressed in chest-high boots, aprons, hair-nets and long rubber gloves, and to carry a crab net round our midriffs.

This was looking bad.

Amid hoots of laughter from the assembled crowd, who

were all having the time of their lives, we were asked to drink down pints of home-brewed beer and eat hunks of bread dipped in some very suspect looking local paste. On top of all this, and at the same time, we had to sing a song.

And this was just the warm-up.

We were each then handed a clearly rotting sardine and told to eat it, head and all. Things were getting out of hand. We all hesitated, but Mick decided he had definitely had enough.

'Listen, Bear, I'm all for being a good sport, but this is getting ridiculous,' he said, suddenly looking very serious. 'If we eat this sort of thing, we could all get sick for days. I hate to say it, but our mission is to complete this expedition, not to be initiated as a Labradorean, nice as it is. We have to be sensible here.'

He was right. Andy, Charlie and Mick were able tactfully to toss the sardines to one side, but Nige and I were the last in line, and people were watching us very closely. There was no escape, so I looked at Nige, took a deep breath, and together we bit the heads off the revolting sardines and chewed.

We eventually managed to leave at 1.30 a.m. 'Give me the sea over the sardines any day,' I told Mick as we finally reached our hotel room.

Our plan remained to leave at 6 a.m., so long as the final weather forecast was all right. Whatever our doubts about the wind and a beam sea, whatever the local fishermen said, the bottom line was that worse weather was on the way. If we waited we would get caught in it for certain.

We had forty-eight hours' clear weather ahead of us, and I believed we could handle the Force Five winds if they did happen to come early.

I tossed around my bed sleeplessly. Wondering. Questioning. Then finally, thankfully, out of exhaustion, I fell asleep.

7. UNSEEN CREW

Man must live by faith – faith in himself,
and faith in others.

Anon.

Everyone was awake by 4.30 in the morning after our initiation at St Mary's, ready to set out on the second-longest leg of the entire voyage, just over 700 miles straight across the Labrador Sea. We checked the weather forecast. It was still no change, and by 6 a.m. we were on our way.

Once again, Canadian hospitality had been so warm. It was sad to be finally leaving these shores and lovely to see a small group of the locals gathered on the jetty, even so early in the morning, to wave goodbye.

As we left, I had passed Alton a sack of surplus chocolates for his fishing trips, and we were all shouting thanks to him across the water. It was a lovely moment, but I did feel rather bad when I realized later that by mistake I had also included in Alton's goodie bag a leftover medical kit of Carol's.

It was not just any old medical kit. It was a personal enema kit that Carol, for some bizarre reason, had deemed indispensable. Alton was going to get the shock of his life when he rummaged through the bag on a cold fishing trip looking for a Mars bar.

None the less, everything was going smoothly, and all of us felt a surge of confidence and excitement. We were moving through a beautiful part of the world, down the narrow inlet from St Mary's to Battle Harbour, past rolling mountains on either side, through the now familiar strong scent of heather and fir trees. The water was mirror calm, and I recall thinking to myself that there was nowhere in the world where I would rather be at this moment than right here with these four guys. It was magical and free.

Andy was checking the engine; Mick had been on the SAT phone, getting a final up-to-date forecast from Mike Town; Nige had been punching in the new waypoints on the plotter; and Charlie was checking the waterproofing on his camera. Everyone was getting on with their specific tasks, and everyone was feeling strong.

We had no idea how much we would need our strength.

Privately, I felt as though I had been tested back in St Mary's, and had managed to pull through with a tough decision. I felt certain it was right to go. Even as we cruised down the inlet, I was running over the logic again: the fishermen said the northerly winds were bad, but they had also talked about the sea being full of ice; we had to take the weather windows when they became available, and the immediate forecast was not bad.

I spoke into the Dictaphone:

I just want to get the first twenty-four hours of this leg out of the way. That could be the tough time because we are heavy with fuel and so slow and vulnerable to big seas. We need a day and night's grace before we hit the big stuff; that's when we will need all our power and manoeuvrability. There is an element of risk and unpredictability in all this. I know that, but I just hope and pray we have made the right decision.

454

With that, I flicked the stop button on the recorder and took a piece of paper, wrapped in plastic, out of my grab bag. On this I had written out one particular verse from the Bible.

Nicky Gumbel is another squash friend of mine in London; he also happens to be a priest. Everyone at the gym simply calls him 'the Pope'. It makes us laugh. Nicky had phoned me as I was checking in my luggage at Heathrow, and given me a little verse that he and his wife Pippa had felt strongly that morning applied to me. It had lifted my spirits then as it did now when I read it leaving Labrador.

When you walk through the waters, they shall not pass over you. I have saved you. I have called you by name. You are precious in my eyes.

(Isaiah 43:2)

That was good to know. I read it again, took a deep breath and tucked it away in my bag. I remember a famous round-the-world sailor once saying, 'There's no such thing as an atheist in the Arctic Ocean.' I had always liked that. It had soul.

We duly passed Battle Harbour and headed out northeast into the Labrador Sea, the stretch of water I had read so much about. As we advanced we felt noticeably colder air on our faces. The next land we would see would be Greenland.

I had done my fair share of reading in advance of the expedition, and this research included a science journal which had described these particular waters as follows:

The Labrador Current originates in western Greenland. The outflow from Hudson Strait combines with the Baffin Island Current to become the Labrador Current. This Labrador Current travels 1–2 knots an hour, and carries with it pack ice, cold water and icebergs.

It was one of these icebergs that sank the *Titanic* off the Grand Banks in 1912. Upwards of 10,000 bergs are released each year, as many as 1,300 bergs from Greenland's Jacobshavener Glacier alone. The bergs slowly disintegrate as they are carried south from Baffin Bay, and a grand spectacle of about 2,500 giant ice chunks parade past the Labrador coast each year. More than half of these icebergs pass the Belle Isle Strait, and this whole area poses a substantial hazard to shipping, particularly when the area is thick with the Labrador's prevalent sea fog.

Nobody could say we hadn't been warned but we were only half a mile out from the coastline, when I noticed something strange.

'Hold on.'

'What?'

'This wind is not quite a northerly. It's coming from more north-east. It's going to give us a head sea. Look at the waves already beginning.'

In layman's terms, the waves were not rolling across us, they were building and rolling directly towards us. Already laden down with full tanks of fuel for the long crossing, we now faced the harsh reality of heading straight into the waves and weather.

My instant reaction was that we should turn back, retreat to St Mary's and revise our plans. These were not the conditions that we had expected, the conditions upon which we had based all our calculations. A different wind and a different kind of sea meant we would be playing a completely different game.

Then I looked at the waves. They were pretty small, just gentle rollers. They didn't look that bad, and the wind was steady. We were expecting it to strengthen significantly over the next twenty-four hours or so, but not unmanageably.

We all had a quick word together, to discuss the situation. It was not ideal but, we agreed, no reason to retreat. We were on our way and all of us were hungry to get this leg done.

Our spirits were raised soon afterwards by the sighting of our first big whale, spouting magnificently on the port side, and within the hour we had passed another massive, majestic iceberg. If we had been passengers aboard a big cruise ship, we would have been able to sit back and savour the Arctic wonders. That would have been great, gin and tonic in hand. Instead, we were perched on our open RIB, anxiously studying the state of the wind and waves, trying to predict the future.

We didn't like what we saw. Hour by hour, unmistakably, the conditions were deteriorating.

The swell was building slowly and the temperature was dropping fast. By mid-afternoon we were in full gear: waterproofs, two balaclavas, gloves and helmets. Each of us was working hard to stay warm. We had given up trying to stay dry.

The boat was hitting the waves head-on now. Every wave was steep and sharp. They were pitching us up about ten feet as they connected, then crashing down on top of us – over and over again. Each time we were lifted up we braced ourselves, tensing every muscle; and each time we slammed back down every bone in our bodies shuddered with the impact. We winced on contact.

By late afternoon the light was fading and the temperature was still dropping. I was shivering uncontrollably. This was not good. It wasn't even night yet. I looked around at the others. Some were lying in the sardine tin, eyes closed. Charlie was awake but he was shivering too. We had to do something before it got dark, otherwise we would freeze to death.

'Stop the boat, Andy,' I said, tapping his shoulder. 'People are getting really cold, me included. We need our final layers.'

The boat lolled about in the swell. We could no longer see land and the sea was a dark and menacing grey.

The two guys who had all the kit on, every last fleece, seemed to be managing. They weren't as cold as us three. I had wanted to wait until it got dark and much colder before putting on my last fleece layer, but that time had come sooner than expected. My hands were shaking.

'Mick, can you help me get this zip undone on my drysuit?' I asked him urgently. 'It's jammed.'

It had also started to rain steadily.

He undid the zip, fed the fleece over my head and pulled the arms down sharply.

'Thanks, buddy,' I muttered as he helped rezip the drysuit over me. Then we both checked Charlie. He was looking warmer.

Cold is so dangerous and this was a different sort of cold to that found on high mountains. This was a constant damp, wet cold that penetrated everything. Everest might have been technically colder, but it was not so all-consuming. The temperature there might drop to −40 degrees, but it was powder-dry. Nothing ever got the chance to melt. This was different: it was not so far below zero but it was wet, and, with the constant wind chill of 20 knots forward speed plus the head wind, it got bitingly cold. And the wind and wet got in everywhere.

Now we were wearing everything we possessed. If any of us got cold now, there was nothing else to rely on.

We were soon under way again, sticking to our rota, but nothing seemed straightforward any more. Helming became much more difficult because it was now imperative to keep the boat straight into the oncoming waves. But our course was just off that angle. That meant we had to weave our way forward, bringing the nose back into the sea when the waves were breaking ahead of us.

Navigating was awkward because it was difficult to follow the course when the instruments were being continually covered in spray. When it was your turn to rest in the sardine tin, all you could do was huddle under the tarpaulin and curl up in a ball to try to keep warm.

I heard a murmur next to me. Nige rolled towards me and spoke through his helmet.

'Just think, we could be in the old speedboat I had in

Poole. Remember? The one that almost sank when a yacht went by, where you would get swamped by a ripple. Just imagine how that little boat would have coped out here.'

Nige chuckled at the thought, then was forced back again as he braced against another wave. This was Nige through and through. His approach helped keep us all smiling at many hard moments, in spite of genuinely miserable conditions.

Each of us was feeling tired as darkness fell. We had been hoping for a break from the relentless head seas but through the night they gradually built up even more. Hour by hour, shifting through the rota, we just focused on the next wave, concentrating, surviving, advancing out to sea.

The violence with which the boat crashed off the waves as they disappeared under us was exhausting, but one factor debilitated us more than anything: the incessant wet, the feeling of being continually drenched, over and over again. Each time a wave broke across the boat, we were covered in gallons and gallons of icy water, and absolutely everything was getting soaked. Every few seconds we'd hit another wave, and wherever we were in the boat, the spray would wash over us. We'd close our eyes as the salt water trickled down the inside of our visors, down our cheeks, into our mouths and around our neck seals.

Every bag and tarpaulin was drenched. I opened the watertight zip of my grab bag to take another anti-seasickness pill, and a wave flooded the bag. The pills became soaked and crumbly. The zips were going brown from rust after just a few days.

The sound of water was everywhere, an incessant drip-ping. It was like living in an open-top car in a car wash, in a washing machine, in a deep-freeze.

Icy water seeped down our arms into our gloves. These were properly sealed diving gloves, but still, after twenty-four hours of such conditions, they were sodden and cold like everything else.

As we ploughed on through the night, some of us were starting to feel sick. Even Andy was struggling. The familiar cure of fixing your gaze on the horizon didn't apply here because there was no horizon, just blackness. Alton Rum-bolt's wife had kindly given us a round of crab sandwiches in St Mary's, but the stench of them, soaked in diesel and salt water, made us all want to retch. I threw them overboard, apologizing.

By morning, after twenty-four hours at sea, we were exhausted. We had set out from St Mary's aware that we were trying to cross the Labrador in a tight window of decent weather. I still believed we had made the correct decision, but the predicted wind direction had turned out to be wrong and that small window had been dramatically tightened.

I looked around the boat, at Mick and Andy, Charlie and Nige. Everybody was focused. We had one common aim: to reach Greenland and safety. But Greenland was still over 400 miles off and, on the chart, Labrador still looked only a blip away. This was going to be a real struggle and every glance down at the chart-plotter while on watch told us the same story. We were making perilously slow progress.

At times, you would come off watch and the estimated 'time to destination' dial would say 'two days, eighteen hours and forty-one minutes'. By the next time you were navigating, four hours later, you hoped that the time remaining would be significantly less. But often it was more. If our speed dropped only slightly due to the conditions, the 'time to destination' dial would rise dramatically. It would now say 'three days, eleven hours and ten minutes'. This was so demoralizing. We should have covered the dial.

In those dark hours curled up in a ball in the pouring rain, shivering, I often thought of home and our unseen crew, which for me was my dad. It wasn't advice I was after, or even guidance, it was just comfort, a familiar, warm hand to hold.

Mickey Grylls was born on 21 February 1934, and he died on 7 February 2001, only a couple of weeks before his sixty-seventh birthday. He was a true gentleman: a family man, a man of faith and a kind soul.

To me, he was always just Dad, and that was enough. And on this wild, grey, windy North Atlantic morning, 300 miles from anywhere, I peered from the sardine tin out across the endless sea and remembered him.

Silly things, like the dewdrop that used to hang from the end of his nose when he was walking in the cold; the coarse stubble when he hadn't shaved; the warm kiss; the smiling pride in his eyes when I achieved something … anything. And his laughter.

There was that poem that my father loved so much, written by a soldier just before a battle during the English Civil War. 'Oh Lord, you know how busy I must be this day,' he wrote. 'If I forget you, I pray do not forget me.' I could see the poem where it always sat, wedged in the frame of his mirror.

The second verse of Dad's favourite hymn, 'I vow to thee, my country,' said it all. It was him in a nutshell, although he never knew it.

And there's another country, I've heard of long ago,
Most dear to them that love her, most great to them that
    know;
We may not count her armies, we may not see her King;
Her fortress is a faithful heart, her pride is suffering;
And soul by soul and silently her shining bounds increase,
And her ways are ways of gentleness,
And all her paths are peace.

I missed him so much. In these difficult moments particularly, I so wished he could be here with me.

It was early morning at our barge on the Thames. We were just getting up. There was a knock on the door. It was a policeman. That was strange. Shara sat beside me as he told me my father had died. My mother was many hours away and so the police were asked to tell me. The officer did so, and with great gentleness. I even thanked him for his time. I was completely numb.

Then going with Shara to the funeral directors, to give

them my dad's favourite boxer shorts to be buried in. I held them in my hand feeling ridiculous. But I couldn't even do it. I was unable to go into the funeral parlour. I tried three times but instead broke down with Shara in the alleyway outside.

Then, at 2 a.m. at my parents' home, sitting beside his coffin the night before the funeral, alone. Laying his old Royal Marine beret on the coffin. Afraid. Afraid of how I would cope in this world without him.

Then finally, carrying his coffin down the aisle of the church, flanked by five of my closest friends in the world – Ed Amies, Mick Crosthwaite, Trucker Goodwin-Hudson, Charlie Mackesy and Hugo Mackenzie-Smith – our arms linked, being literally held by their strength. How I needed them. All I could hear was the strange, hollow click of our shoes down the aisle. Dad felt so heavy.

He had written a reading for me to do at Shara's father's funeral. I read it again at my dad's funeral only a few months later. The words were so tender, and had turned out to be so prophetic.

This was what he wrote:

I have passed on.
Remember my time with you.
Treasure all those moments together,
Those moments of fun and laughter;
As you remember, know that I am with you.
It is not the number of years we live that counts,
It's how we live that matters.
As you live your lives, remember I am with you.

Build on the beliefs we created together.
Hold on to that which is right.
Discard all that is wrong.
When you are happy, know that I am with you.
When you are sad or in pain, know that I am with you.
True love does not need a physical presence;
What is called death is no more than the removal of the
      physical being.
Now that I have passed on I understand it all.
I am hand in hand with our Lord, yet I am with you.

The words were so simple: 'When you are in pain, I am with you.' But was it true? Even out here? When I was afraid?

The words 'I am hand in hand with our Lord, yet I am with you.' But would you hold my hand now? Could I really believe in this 'Lord' of yours? Would you give me faith when it counted?

Andy was having the same kinds of feeling midway across the Labrador Sea. He had lost his father as well, but at a much younger age. That is harder. But I understood. Days later, he told me that he had asked his dad for help. He hadn't done that in years.

'Maybe that seagull is my dad,' Andy had mused, looking at one of the birds following us.

He smiled at the thought, hoping he was right.

None of the crew was particularly religious. It was never really something that we discussed. Faith is very intimate, if it is to be real. For me, here on the Labrador Sea, alone and in terrifying conditions, my Christian faith was all I really had; not some sort of blind, all-conquering faith, but an intimate, at times faltering faith. The sort that says I'm not quite sure about everything, especially the very 'religious' bits, but I love the sound of this Jesus. The one my dad knew.

Faith is always a risk, just like love. It has taken me a long time to admit this, but I am no longer frightened to say I need it. I need that comfort. I often feel lost, but my faith says I'm never lost to Him. That means the world to me, and faith is a risk I want always to take. At the end of the day, it's all I have.

C. S. Lewis once wrote about this Jesus: 'Safe? Who said anything about safe? 'Course he isn't safe. But he's good.'

Dad would have agreed with that.

To me, faith is not about us. It's about Him. It is about being loved and about being held, unconditionally, regardless of how well or badly we may be doing.

This Jesus always seems so much bigger than me, so much stronger than all my self-doubt and fears. He has this habit of stealing in when I least expect Him, and always when I least deserve it. When I am right at my wits' end, when I feel I am losing the precious hope we all need so dearly. These are the moments when I sense Him near me, and I can never quite believe it. He never condemns, He just sustains. He doesn't judge, He understands. He gives me my hope again, and says be brave. He helps me when I most need it.

Why does this love mean so much to me? Maybe because I don't expect it. Because I don't deserve it. It just comes, regardless. It is like the sea and the waves and the tides.

You can't keep God out. He's all around us, if we're just still enough to listen.

'Do not be terrified; do not be discouraged, for the Lord your God will be with you wherever you go.' A man called Joshua in the Bible heard God say that, and he went on to lead a nation.

Faith does this. It hopes. It holds us. It feels like home and I'm lost without it.

Dad wrote that he was 'with me'. I hope every night that this is true. Whether I am kneeling beside Jesse's cot or out on the ocean or on some mountain, I pray for this always. For Dad and my Jesus to be right beside me.

And right here, right now, in the waves and wind, I knew that, somehow, the unseen crew were at our side.

8. RUNNING ON VAPOUR

There can only be true courage when first there is genuine fear.

Dr David Livingstone

Andy was sitting bolt upright in the sardine tin.

I didn't know why.

More than thirty hours into this bone-shuddering, relentless storm, the winds were still at fever pitch, and the 20-foot waves were now coming at us head-on. Each wave was taking us further and deeper into the heart of the storm. We had no choice but to hang on, clinging to the routine by which we would stay afloat and continue this painfully slow progress across the Labrador Sea.

But Andy sitting bolt upright in the sardine tin was not part of this routine.

In these harrowing conditions, we had adapted the rota so that while two of us would stay at the console, one helming and the other navigating, the other three would squeeze into the sardine tin. We would spoon, body to body, trying awkwardly to get some rest and shelter beneath the tarpaulin sheet. Three of us in the sardine tin together meant we kept warmer.

But Andy was sitting bolt upright, staring out to sea. Water was still crashing over his head, but he hardly moved.

Something was wrong. I knew it.

A minute later I looked again.

Andy was up now, checking the fuel gauges, pressing the dial, taking a reading, looking up, checking the gauges again. I couldn't see the expression on his face through his helmet, but his slow, deliberate body language suggested he was agitated and concerned.

When Andy was happy, I knew it; he would be wearing his Peruvian woollen hat, eating with his green plastic spoon, cosy in his own cocoon, at peace with the world. That was a very different Andy to now.

Still the wind licked across the boat, and the incessant waves were crashing over the bows and console every thirty seconds or so. The sea just didn't seem to care. It had no regard for our struggles. The waves just roared towards us with a deafening mass of white water; then our world would drop away under us. One wave was gone and the next would be upon us.

Looking behind me, I was stunned by the speed at which the waves were racing away from us, and the sheer energy and force by which they travelled, unhindered, unbridled. They were like wild horses galloping.

Even the most basic kinds of communication and move-ment had become almost impossible. I wanted to turn to Andy and ask him if there was a problem. But this was not easily done. I could only watch him through my visor.

Andy recalls:

My responsibility was to make sure the fuel and engine systems worked efficiently, but it wasn't easy because the weather had such an impact on how fast we burnt through the fuel.

In planning each leg of the expedition, I tried to take account of this uncertainty by loading at least 20 per cent more fuel than was necessary. But the legs were so long and the boat so relatively small that there wasn't physically room for much greater margin.

During the storm in the Labrador Sea, when we were still about 300 miles off Greenland, I started to get concerned. The head sea meant we were on 2,600 engine revs, moving forward at only 12 knots. It was dangerously inefficient and our fuel reserves were running low. I did a calculation – back-of-a-fag-packet stuff – and worked out that at this rate we would run dry between 100 and 150 miles short of Greenland. I couldn't see how we could narrow this and still make any progress.

I checked and rechecked the levels; I was worried. Our lives were not imminently in danger if we could get a Mayday off; the Danish icebreakers could get to us in a day possibly, but it would have been so gutting if we ran out of fuel and had to abandon the expedition. This was my area of responsibility and I would have felt as if I had let everyone down.

So much preparation: two years' worth of Bear's and the others' work, and it would have been my fault. And what a bloody stupid way to fail – running out of juice.

I waited a further minute and then finally Andy beckoned me over. We stood side by side, braced against the constant pitching of the boat, shouting to each other to make ourselves heard above the wind and waves.

'Bear, we're running short on fuel,' Andy yelled.

'How bad is it?'

'Pretty bad. We're struggling.'

'Well, what can we do to reduce our burn rate?'

'We need to reduce our speed. That's the only way of making the fuel last longer.'

'Reduce it to what?'

'Eight knots.'

'Eight knots?'

'Yeah, I know it's crazy, but it's our only choice.'

It didn't take me long to work out the consequences of slowing to 8 knots. It would mean that from this point it would take us another thirty-six hours to reach Greenland instead of the twenty hours we were expecting. We would be off the planing speed and the boat would be very vulnerable, completely at the mercy of the sea. We would hardly have the speed to push through these big head seas. Everyone was freezing cold and soaking wet, and I knew this would now take our struggle up to a new level. I wasn't sure we could cope with a further thirty-six hours like this.

But we had no option.

'If we do this, will we make Greenland?' I asked.

'Touch and go . . . but if the seas die down a bit, well, then we should make it . . . just,' he replied.

'OK, do it.'

I turned and gazed across the restless grey ocean, trying to keep calm. We had been confronted by a major problem, and we had taken prompt, decisive action, but I was still deeply worried.

The prospect of aborting the expedition because we ran out of fuel haunted me. It would not go down as a very glamorous failure. It would be a stark, brutal waste of two years' planning; gone – just like that.

The bottom line was this: we needed a break in the weather. Given some decent conditions, we would almost certainly get to Greenland. However, if the winds and the head seas remained as strong as they were, there would probably be nothing we could do to avoid calling the rescue services.

We needed help.

Not for the first time, I tried to pray. Truly pray.

Anyone looking out of the window of a jumbo jet flying overhead would never even see us down here. We were so small and insignificant in this unforgiving sea. We were effectively invisible. Tiny. Lost in a sea of white horses.

'Please, God,' I prayed, eyes closed, 'I know it is asking for quite a big one, but please make these seas go calm.'

I was waiting, eyes squeezed shut. A few moments passed – as long as I dared – before I slowly opened my eyes, looking for the miracle; but there was none.

I wondered how many times through the centuries God must have heard this same prayer from men fighting for their lives at sea. Thousands. I knew this. But I prayed again.

Massive amounts of water were still pouring over the boat. We were being drenched by the spray, and the RIB was really labouring against the giant waves. The engine would peak, and then seem to stall as the boat was suspended in mid-air as it dropped off the back of a steep wave. We would all cling on, motionless, until we landed, often on our side, with a crash. Then, instantly, the engine would pick up revs again. Its computer system would be carefully monitoring the impact and revs. I had no idea how the hell it was still working but it was, and slowly we were edging towards Greenland.

Most of us had not eaten anything for twenty-four hours, partly because we were feeling so sick but also because it was impossible to eat when the boat was being thrown around so violently. Andy said it was like trying to eat while sitting on a fairground rollercoaster ride. Just the thought of cold, salt water-soaked Lancashire hotpot and baked beans made me retch. We just accepted the reality that in a storm, eating anything more than the odd flapjack was almost impossible.

Drinking was just as hard, but more important. No matter how bad we were feeling, we had to drink. Charlie was sick again over the side of the boat. Then he laboured over to the jerry can to refill his water bottle to drink. It was a horrible task.

I squeezed into the sardine tin, so tight against Mick that I could feel the zip on his dry-suit back pressing against me. I put the Dictaphone's watertight pouch to my mouth . . .

We seem to have been going for ever; then I look at the chart and see we've still got hundreds of miles to Greenland. I'm not sure if we can keep going like this. Everything is so wet. My head is freezing, as my balaclava has been continually drenched for almost two days and nights.

Our dry-suits are being amazing and I have no idea how the hell they are keeping this amount of water out. But still inevi-

476

Above. Our first iceberg. To give some perspective, this one is over eight miles away

Right. Arnold & Son Explorer in the Greenland fjords

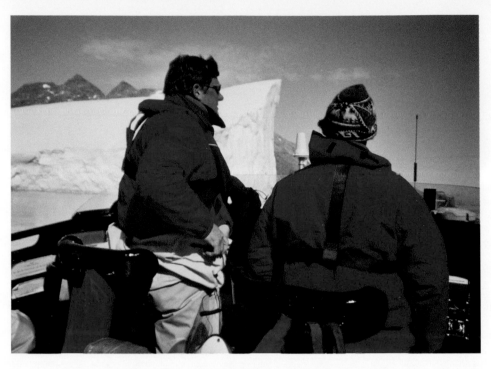

Leaving Nanortalik, following the ice towards the mouth of
the Prince Christiansen Sound

Nige taking time out to write his diary midway through
the Prince Christiansen Sound

Above. Repacking and stowing kit in the Prince Christiansen Sound

Right. Trying to catch up with some precious sleep as we leave the coast of Greenland. We are sleeping in the bows to try and bring the weight forward to increase our speed

The sun sets over the ice plateaux of Greenland behind us

Entering the big head seas. We knuckle down as the conditions
dramatically deteriorate. The barometer plummets some 400 miles from Iceland.
In the worst conditions, taking photos became impossible

Dawn finally arrives after a night of terrifying storms off Iceland

Andy stares out longingly towards Iceland, only fifteen miles away but
still hidden, at the end of our frightening ordeal

One of the rare clear sunsets captured as we leave the Vestmann Islands

Against the backdrop of the remote, northern coast of Scotland,
the *Arnold & Son Explorer* completes its journey. *(Kinloch)*

Above. We finally hit land! The homecoming on the beach of a small cove at Kinloch, north Scotland

Right. Nige's face says it all. Scotland at last! *(Kinloch)*

Below. Lt Andy Leivers and Bear Grylls, holding the Royal Navy's White Ensign aloft as they arrive in John O'Groats. *(David Cheskin / PA Photos)*

The moment we had all been longing for: celebrating the 'Mumm' way in Scotland! *(David Cheskin / PA Photos)*

Holding my little son Jesse the day I returned. His look says: 'Dad, take a bath'

tably water gets in, all down your legs. This happens when your zip is undone to try to pee, or when you stretch out at the wrong time and break the seal on your wrists or neck. This sea is just so cold and so penetrating.

Nige's lifejacket has just gone off. These lifejackets are very high-spec commercial ones and they are supposed to inflate only when you are in the water. Nige's has just gone off in the sardine tin. That's how sodding wet it is in here.

These seas are ferocious. We are into deeper ocean now, so that means the waves should become longer and it should be more comfortable. But there's no sign of that yet. It is just black all around us. I am cold and damp, and I am just dreaming of Greenland with each bit of salt water I taste.

We were approaching the end of our second day on the Labrador Sea, and the North Atlantic was doing what the North Atlantic does best. Creating chaos. Andy understood the seriousness of the situation. 'I'm not a very religious person,' he would recall later, 'but I lay in the sardine tin that night and prayed. I prayed that my late dad would help us with the weather. I might not be a huge believer in God, but I believed in my dad, and I knew we needed help from somewhere.'

As dusk approached, we checked all the gauges again and ran through the calculations. We were burning only 70 litres of fuel per hour, compared to 90 litres per hour earlier, and we had only lost one knot of speed. That was encouraging, but reaching Greenland was still going to be touch and go.

Everyone knew the plain facts. If the sea died down a

bit we stood a real chance of making it. But in our heart of hearts we all knew that if the weather conditions did not improve, we would almost certainly have no chance of getting there. Now, forty hours into the storm, and still with no sign of reprieve, everyone sensed that rescue was beginning to look like the most likely outcome. We were powerless to do anything more.

We simply weren't getting any breaks in these conditions. The seas were still running wild and huge.

The physical battering was taking its toll. Every twenty minutes or so we all made a point of looking around the boat, checking how the person next to us was coping. I had started to suspect that all of us, including me, were suffering from the early stages of hypothermia. Our reactions were more sluggish than usual, and it felt impossible to concentrate on anything. We were drained and we were cold. Even the most straightforward tasks – whether it was checking the fuel gauges, tying a knot or just having a pee – now took on the dimensions of a major undertaking.

But I needed to pee. I tried to stave it off. To perform even this simple task was a nightmare. I tried to block it in my mind. Ten minutes later, I knew I had to go. I clambered out of the sardine tin and tried to steady myself against the console.

The drill normally was to go to the stern of the RIB, harness on so that you felt confident enough to use both hands to undo the dry-suit zip, and then pee. But in these conditions, to move even that far around the boat was dangerous and unnecessary. I wedged myself between the console side and the sardine tin and started to fumble with my dry-suit zip.

A wave crashed over the back of me and I frantically grabbed the edge of the console. I steadied myself again and tried to hold on with one hand and undo my fly with the other. It was impossible. In desperation, I realized there was only one way to pee in these conditions: kneeling down.

I crouched down on the floor and using my elbows as a brace, I found I could hold myself steady against the violent motion of the waves. I undid the zip and peed on the floor. Another wave poured over and washed it away in seconds. I spat the salt water from my mouth and clambered back alongside Nige.

To do 'number twos' in this sort of condition just wouldn't happen. It would be lethal. Most of us managed to crap in calm seas, hanging inelegantly off the back of the jet platform, but in this sort of sea it was unthinkable. Somehow our mindset and the adrenalin ensured we never needed to go when it was rough. I guess we weren't eating much, which helped. But looking back, it is strange how we managed to last out for days at a time.

Andy was helming now, but he was drowsy and veering wildly off his course. His head was drooping and he was struggling, although he was only twenty-five minutes into his shift. His concentration had gone and the waves that were smashing into the side of the RIB were hardly even drawing his attention. He was going down with exhaustion. To his credit, he recognized this. He turned to Charlie and asked him to take over. He couldn't focus his eyes. The chart plotter had become a blur to him. He needed Charlie to help him this time.

This kind of gesture takes real courage, but it was what I had wanted from the team all along: an honesty, a humanity, a willingness to be vulnerable and draw on our strengths together. That was what made us stronger. Collectively, we were always going to be better than when we were on our own.

I had no doubt that Charlie himself would need Andy's help sooner or later, but for now it was Andy's turn to need that help. They swapped helm and the boat carried on into the waves.

But all our bodies were slowing down, and I for one was shivering. I had seen hypothermia among climbers high on Everest, and I knew that there was not much we could do. We just needed that break in the weather.

But that wasn't happening, and with every minute that passed, we seemed to be drawing nearer and nearer to the moment I had been dreading, the moment when we called for help. It would be my decision, and a terrible one to make.

'We shouldn't leave it too late,' Mick told me sensibly at one stage. 'I mean, if this is the situation, well, there's no point waiting until we have run out of fuel before we put out a Mayday. We don't want to be floating around for a day with no power. We can at least put them on standby and let them know our position.'

He was right. It was logical.

It was just that I didn't want to face it.

'OK,' I said, relenting in the face of common sense. 'I'm going to call Chloë and just let her know what's happening.'

Mick nodded. 'She does need to be informed,' he affirmed. 'It gives us a backup if we do run out of fuel.'

I agreed. 'Slow the boat right down, will you, Nige?' I asked.

Whenever we wanted to use the SAT phone, we had to reduce our speed to a knot or two. Then one of us was able to crawl on hands and knees into the tiny cramped console, under the helm position, in order to dial. This space was jammed with spares, food and supplies; it was dark and stank of leaking diesel. It was a miserable place on land, in a big sea it was hell. Idling along at just 1 knot keeping the boat head to sea made her loll about awkwardly. Most of us would start feeling sick. These calls needed to be made as quickly as possible.

I crawled inside on all-fours, banging my head on the metal hatch. I cursed. Nige swung his feet out of the way to let me crawl past. I took off my diving gloves. My hands were shaking as I pulled out the SAT phone and began to unwrap it from its plastic bag. I fumbled to attach the charger, then the antenna wire. Time was ticking on. I could hear my own breathing – it was nervous and rapid. I could also hear Charlie being sick again. More than any of us, he hated having to stop the boat.

I carefully dialled Chloë's number in London, holding

the phone a few inches from my soaking head in an effort to keep it dry. This phone was our lifeline, and needed to be kept out of the water at all costs. I waited.

Nothing. No dial tone.

Lying half in and half out of this tiny hatch, desperately trying to stop my head banging on the metal rails on the console roof inches above me, I dialled again. Still nothing.

'Bloody work,' I cursed at the phone.

Finally, on the fourth try, I heard a telephone ringing far away in London, in a different world, a warm and comfortable place where all was safe and dry and OK, a world away from here.

'Hello, Chloë?'

'Hi, Bear, how are you?' she replied, bright and breezy.

'Get a pen and paper,' I told her. 'We're in trouble.'

It was around eight in the evening in London, and Chloë seemed to be in a restaurant somewhere. I could hear noises behind her. She was back in seconds. 'Go for it,' she said.

'Mick, I need our lat and longs,' I screamed to him. He would be able to read these off the plotter.

'Four-ah, two-ah, seven-ah.' Mick was shouting them in his loudest, most clipped voice. It made me smile. This sure had his concentration; Mick didn't want any errors here. I relayed the numbers on, shouting them out above the clamour of the wind. Chloë repeated them correctly. Then I told her we were running critically low on fuel.

'We've got about 1,200 litres of fuel left,' I shouted down the phone. 'We reckon that should last us for eighteen hours, and get us maybe 140 miles closer. Right now, we are 195 miles from Greenland in terrible conditions.'

'OK, I've got that,' Chloë said. Her tone of voice had changed. She knew it was serious.

'One more thing,' I added. 'Please call Captain Pennefather and tell him what's happening. We're OK, and will call again when we reckon we have two hours' running time left.'

I replaced the SAT phone and wriggled back out of the hatch, trying to yank my gloves back on. Andy revved the engine, and we started to move again. We struggled on, the RIB crawling up and over the waves at a pathetic 9 knots.

Chloë was aware that Willie Pennefather was in Scotland, where, among other things, he was sorting out various aspects of our scheduled return to John O'Groats. She eventually tracked him down to Edinburgh.

Willie recalls:

I had left for Scotland on 2 August with a slight feeling of detachment from the expedition, although I had followed the crew's progress every day on the Internet. I had been invited to be part of the official party attending the Edinburgh Military Tattoo. It was a very formal occasion involving drinks and a black-tie dinner, before we were to travel in official cars with police outriders to Edinburgh Castle, arriving in time to allow us to be seated in the Royal Box at exactly the start of the display.

At dinner, the sergeant came to tell me that Chloë Boyes was on the telephone for me.

I told him to ask if I could ring her after dinner. I assumed it was to discuss the plans for the crew's return. The sergeant reported that after dinner would be OK, but said Chloë had sounded a bit alarmed.

I thought of leaving the table unseen, but my host General Nick Parker and his guests, General Sir Mike Jackson and Menzies Campbell among others, were not the type of people who would not have noticed. Thoughts of Sir Francis Drake and his game of bowls crossed my mind, but I eased out and called her back some fifteen minutes later.

She then dropped the bombshell.

'They are 200 miles west of Greenland in a gale,' she told me calmly, 'and Bear says they are critically close to running out of fuel. I don't know what to do.'

The next hour was frantic as I somehow tried to combine the jovialities and formalities of the Tattoo parade with also trying to instigate some rescue contingency plans. I found myself conducting analysis discussions with the London team at the desk of the GOC Scotland, then in the back of a car on the ADC's mobile phone, with flashing blue lights all around, then at the back of the Royal Box at Edinburgh Castle with pipes swirling in the background. It was strangely surreal to know that at this precise moment of such pomp and ceremony here in Edinburgh, these guys were struggling for their lives in a lonely, terrifying sea.

I must say I could easily watch the Edinburgh Tattoo again, having had my mind so firmly elsewhere! On this occasion, I could only think of the boys and what they were going through out there.

Our task was to do everything possible to prepare for whatever fate would decide was to happen.

We knew we could do no more than alert the rescue services,

keep them informed, and ensure Bear told us at least an hour before they ran out of fuel, so that they could be rescued from a boat which still had steerage – this could be critical if the weather was still atrocious. We also decided to keep the team's families in the dark for the time being, and to contact the Duty Fleet Controller at Northwood, who gave us vital access to the Naval Weather Centre.

All this done, I returned to the party, even if my thoughts were elsewhere.

Meanwhile, nothing was giving at all. We were still battling against the brutal ocean. Waves as large as houses kept thundering towards us, picking us up, dumping us down and soaking us in icy water. Perhaps it was the cold and fatigue, but I started to personify the waves. To me, as they flew past, they seemed to turn and look at us strangely, as if they were asking, 'What the hell are you doing out here in such a boat?'

I didn't have an answer. Then the wave was gone.

We were all becoming frightened and I knew it; we were so completely exposed and vulnerable, dangerously out of place.

I prayed again.

'Please, God, please calm these seas,' I said under my breath, lying in the sardine tin, hugging Mick in front of me not just to keep warm, but because I was scared. 'You've helped me so many times before, but I really need you now. I really need you to hear me. I really need you to help us.'

None of us had managed more than a brief doze over the past two days, and a couple of hours later I was helming again. For this particular shift, from 11 p.m. till midnight, Charlie and I sat shoulder to shoulder at the console, fighting to keep the boat on course and under control.

As I helmed, I noticed a small piece of coloured plastic flapping around on the anchor, attached to the foredeck. I knew it was some sort of Chinese lucky charm that a stranger had placed on the side of the boat while a bunch of well-wishers were crowding around us on the quay in Halifax, Canada. Most of them had draped flowers and things on the boat, but this particular woman had presented this small, peculiar token.

I saw her, and didn't really like the idea of the charm, but it would have been rude not to accept the gesture and I let it pass. I hadn't given it another thought until now – in trouble, so far out in the ocean. I began to wonder whether this could be the reason why God was not answering my prayers. Maybe this charm was keeping His goodness out. It sounds crazy and superstitious now, but right there, in the darkness, I was clutch-ing at anything and praying like never before. I was desperate.

As the minutes passed, I felt compelled somehow to get rid of the charm. Everything might be OK then, I thought. The sea might die down. 'Just forget it and concentrate, Bear,' I told myself.

But the more I dismissed this idea as ridiculous, the more I believed it to be the case. And a minute later, it was all I could think about again. I couldn't take my eyes off this ruddy little plastic thing, swinging hypnotically with the motion of the bow.

The problem was, however, that it was wrapped around the anchor arm at the very front of the boat, and I knew that getting to that area would be extremely risky, especially while the boat was being thrown around in the storm. One slip on those slippery tubes, one awkward pitch of the boat, and I could easily be washed overboard. My lifeline should hold me, but at 10 knots, in the black of night, in these waves, I would be dragged until I drowned.

'Forget it,' I told myself. 'God might not like the charm, but He doesn't want to me drown either.'

I did forget about it.

For about thirty seconds.

Damn it, I had to get rid of that thing. Charlie hadn't noticed this and I didn't want to tell him what was on my mind. He would have said to stay put and that I was being irrational, which may have been true. So I made up a story about the sea anchor looking as if it was coming loose from its housing. That would do.

'Don't bother, Bear,' Charlie said. 'It's fine.'

'No,' I persisted. 'I'm going. Take the helm.'

So I slid from my seat and began to fumble for my harness. I swung myself over the edge of the console and began to edge, step by step, along the tubes, round to the front of the boat.

Once on the foredeck, I grabbed for the handholds and steadied myself as she pitched on top of another wave. Water flooded over the tubes and all around my feet. I snatched at the charm. It wouldn't come away because it had become tangled around the anchor warp. I yanked again, but still it wouldn't break. I was becoming annoyed. So, summoning every bit of strength left after two nights without sleep, I grabbed it and pulled.

It finally came free, and I hurled it into the waves.

On reaching Charlie again, I felt a surge of relief. I again took the helm and waited ... waited for the miracle of calm seas. But the sea never even looked like subsiding. It stayed just as rough through both our shifts, and I was tiring.

This vast ocean just didn't care about us, didn't care if we reached Greenland or not, if we capsized and drowned. It was so immense, and we were so very small. This can be the sea's greatest quality – the way it reminds us of our own mortality. But that reminder is also very humbling. Being big or brave doesn't seem to count for much. In fact, even just trying your best and slogging your guts out means very little. It is irrelevant, and only the sea decides who wins the battle.

All we could do was endure. Waiting, like ants on a motorway.

Once again, as shadows of exasperation closed in, I reached for the Dictaphone's pouch and pressed record ...

I am getting exhausted. The other guys are as well. They are doing so well, trying to knuckle through this thing, but it has been exhausting. I just want to get to Greenland. I am going to sleep, and I'm not going to move for six months. I don't care. I'm not going on another adventure like this. It's too intense, too exhausting. It's so different from climbing Everest: there we had that stillness, and you could always climb into a tent and get away. But this is so relentless – the pounding and the wet. There is no escape. I just long for it to be calm.

This is an endurance exercise, and it gets much more frightening at night, because you just can't see the waves. All you see is the white water.

We're still going at 8 knots, not much faster than running pace. But the guys have been incredible. I feel so genuinely proud of them right now. I thought the people without military backgrounds would be struggling, but Nige and Charlie have been an inspiration.

Charlie happened to be helming when I climbed along to the foredeck. My whole life was in his hands, and he held everything together. Not long ago, he was asking for advice, but now he has mastered the helm, he's in control, and I trust him completely. That's very special.

Nige is coping amazingly, considering. He's wet through and should be bloody miserable, but he just turned to me to say he could murder a Danish pastry and a cappuccino. He smiled faintly. But Nige's great quality is that he just gets on with things. It's these small things that make such a huge difference.

So much can go wrong on this boat: if the engine stops, we're in big trouble; if the forecast is wrong, we're in big trouble; if the navigation is not done properly, we're lost. But each of these guys has taken responsibility for his job, and everyone trusts that person to do it. Not just with words but with their life.

Things are really bad right now, but there's something pretty unique about this situation: five men in a small boat, all trusting one another, looking after one another. Caring.

I had told everyone so often that there would be times when we would be at our wits' ends, but also that it is in those times that I need them to give that little bit extra. To laugh, to watch out for someone as they pee, to dig out a chocolate bar for the guy on watch, when you're exhausted. This is what really matters, and they have all done this over and over again.

These four guys are just bloody brilliant British people. They show so much quiet, cheerful strength, and yet I know how cold and wet they are because I can feel them shivering alongside me. I will buy the biggest round ever if we reach Greenland, I promise.

When I finished recording these thoughts, it took me some time to push the stop button on the Dictaphone. It should have been the simplest task, but my fingers were numb, and I fumbled around angrily for several minutes.

By midnight, three o'clock in the morning back home, I decided to call Chloë again, to keep her informed of our progress and to check that the Danish navy had been alerted to our situation.

I got through second go this time and told her our status.

'And one other thing,' I added.

'Yes?' she said.

'Can you call Charlie Mackesy and ask him to pray for us? He'll understand, even if it is three in the morning. I really need his help.'

Charlie was my best man at our wedding and one of my closest friends. An artist in London, he is also Jesse's godfather, and in this desperate situation I needed to feel that he was praying for us, praying that everything would somehow be all right.

Charlie recalls:

I was staying with my sister in Yorkshire, fast asleep when the mobile rang under my pillow. I woke up, looked at the display, saw it was Chloë and immediately knew Bear was either in real trouble or was dead. It would have to be something terrible for her to call me at three o'clock in the morning.

She told me Bear wanted me to pray for him because he was stuck in this storm. It was getting worse, there were icebergs about and he didn't think he was going to get out of it.

To be honest, I wasn't feeling very full of any sort of faith at the time, but I went downstairs, sat quietly in a chair and said a prayer. I simply asked God to calm the storm. I slowly became aware of a strange, but very clear image, where it was pitch black, ice was everywhere and people were screaming. I prayed for it to go quiet, and then fell asleep in the chair. I woke up in the early hours of the morning with a sense of calm, and went back upstairs to bed with no idea what had happened.

Meanwhile, three of us were soon back in the sardine tin, once again trying to ignore the stinging, salty spray and the relentless battering of being lifted up and then thumped down. I was done in. I lay there, wedged against Nige and Mick, and out of sheer exhaustion I somehow fell asleep. It was a magic relief from the grim reality of our slow-burning failure.

I woke with a start. It was just after 5.30 a.m., and immediately I became aware that something was different. The boat was planing. We were surging forward smoothly and the sea was millpond-calm. I blinked hard, suspended in that demi-world between sleep and being awake. I blinked again.

This was for real.

Andy and Charlie were helming, and chatting. Then Andy turned towards me and smiled.

'Things are starting to look up, Bear,' he said. 'We're doing twenty-two knots.'

I sat up and looked around. I couldn't believe my eyes. The sea had just died away. The apparently endless storm had ended. The sky was clear blue. It was a beautiful day. I sat and stared.

'We've got about 400 litres in the centre line tank,' Andy continued. 'I think we might just do it.'

He grinned at me.

Elated, I began to get up from the sardine tin. For the first time, we had a real chance of making it.

I knew we should call the base team in London, just to let them know our situation had improved, and I duly phoned Chloë. She in turn contacted Shara to say everything was all right; Shara then phoned Charlie Mackesy in Yorkshire, just to let him know all was well and that his prayers had been answered. Charlie suddenly adopted this guru-like status. It was very funny. But God had shone on us very clearly and I was in no doubt of that at all.

We were not quite out of trouble but we were all beginning to believe we could make it to Greenland. Everybody was wide awake, enjoying the sunshine and our newfound speed. Andy was carefully monitoring the fuel situation, with Charlie helping him read the dials. Mick's lifejacket had also gone off sometime during the last twenty-four hours, and he and Nige were laughing at themselves, looking like drowned rats dressed in bright yellow blow-up jackets. It was our finest time on the entire expedition so far. We forgot the wet, the cold and the hunger and enjoyed being able to talk for the first time in days. The wind had disappeared and the boat was flying.

At last, at 9 a.m., Greenland appeared on the horizon.

We were still 65 nautical miles offshore, but even from that distance we could identify the gigantic mountains and broken glaciers of this, the largest and most remote island on the planet.

'How are we doing on fuel, Andy?'

He looked up from the console. 'I'm trying to drain all the different tanks into one. It's hard to tell exactly but we're still going, eh?'

The sea was like glass, and there was a crisp chill in the air. I had never before seen sea like glass at that distance offshore. It was incredible, and I felt the mercy of God that morning. We were exhausted, but we were so relieved.

Seagulls were swooping above us, playful puffins fluttered frantically in front of our bow, and stunning-shaped icebergs were dotted along the coastline as far as we could see. The miles were dropping off behind us fast. It was a dream.

We eventually eased carefully past a cluster of giant growler icebergs that surrounded the small harbour of Nanor-talik. They floated freely, sculpted like vast statues, and you could see their huge mass of cobalt blue ice under the surface of the calm water. We had finally reached Greenland.

We were met at the small harbour pier by the mayor and a group of locals. They held out strong hands to help us ashore. I had never felt so pleased to arrive anywhere.

Andy took a look at the last tank.

'How much fuel is left?'

'About fifty litres, I reckon,' Andy replied.

Fifty litres? That was perhaps enough to have kept us going for another half-hour on the ocean. We had started the leg with 4,000 litres. Fifty? It was the tightest of margins. It was nothing. Bluntly put, if that storm had raged for thirty minutes longer, we would not have made it. It had been that close.

We had been lucky, very lucky. I knew that, and I was with four men who were deeply grateful to reach dry land.

We all were desperate to lie down and sleep, but first there were a couple of SAT phone calls to be made.

I called Chloë to tell her the good news that we had finally arrived in Nanortalik; then I called Captain Penne-father direct.

'What was your fuel state when you arrived?' he asked.

'Vapour,' I replied, smiling.

9. GOOD NEWS, BAD NEWS

Indecision is the thief of opportunity.

Napoleon Bonaparte

Sleeping for a couple of hours, taking a hot shower, getting something decent to eat: these are the kinds of thing most of us take for granted every day of our lives. After 700 miles of living in an open boat on the Labrador Sea, exhausted and salt-burnt, these simple acts took on a meaning that is hard to describe.

The Inuit mayor showed us to our 'hotel', which was a relatively large corrugated building surrounded by several rows of smaller corrugated houses. But at that moment, a five-star West End hotel could not have been more enticing.

We hung our soaking kit up to dry in the dusty boiler room, and Nige, Mick and I were asleep, fully clothed, before we had even closed the door of our small bedroom. The shower could wait a few minutes longer.

We woke an hour or so later; it was mid-afternoon. Andy and Charlie were beginning to let their hair down and have a few beers with some of the locals. They had certainly earned a night off.

There was an Internet terminal in the hotel reception and I stayed behind with Mick to check the weather forecast on the increasingly familiar series of websites.

Our next leg was going to be the longest of the expedition, and probably the most challenging: just over 800 miles round

Greenland, across the Denmark Strait and on to Reykjavik in Iceland. The web pages took a while to download, and I watched them slowly unfold on the screen.

My heart sank as I read what appeared.

'There will be a Force Three weather pattern for the next forty-eight hours ... and severe storms are expected to arrive in the Denmark Strait by Friday afternoon.'

It was already Tuesday evening.

There was no problem with a Force Three weather pattern. That would be ideal. That was about as good as the weather was ever going to get in this part of the world. The real problem was that, for the second time on the expedition, just like in St Mary's, I was being presented with a dangerous dilemma, a fifty–fifty decision, a roll of the dice.

The choice was straightforward: either we seized the latter part of the forty-eight-hour weather window, banking on reaching Iceland before the main storms hit this far north, or we played safe and waited in Nanortalik until conditions improved.

Was forty-eight hours long enough to reach Iceland? Maybe it was just, if we left now, but that was impossible. We couldn't even refuel until 10 a.m. the following day. That reduced the forty-eight-hour window to thirty-six hours. But what was the alternative? A wait that might not break until the ice-packs returned in earnest?

Yet again, I felt as though I was being challenged to gamble with our lives. And I hate gambling. It just takes one bad call to make it your last. Mick looked at me. Only a matter of hours ago we had been pleading for land, dreaming of respite from the fury of the sea, and here we were debating whether we should put ourselves back into that furnace. It didn't sit easy at all.

I leaned back in the chair and wished I could be in a situation where the forecast meant the decision was obvious, either way.

Mick wrote all the data down, to spell it out clearly.

The advantages of staying were that we would all get the few days of rest that we so desperately needed after our ordeal in the Labrador Sea. The drawback was that the bad weather could remain in place for three to four weeks by the look of the weather patterns moving up from the south. That would mean we could be stuck in Greenland until September when winter would begin to draw in again. The temperatures then drop even further, the ice starts to compact, and it would become impossible to complete the expedition.

'Who dares wins,' rolls off the tongue so easily. It is much harder to say when your life is in that dare.

No doubt the benefit of leaving Greenland as soon as possible, most probably the following morning, was that we would sustain the momentum of the expedition and, with a bit of luck, reach Iceland before the predicted lows and rough weather really took hold. The danger was if these lows came early; no one wanted to find themselves in another, bigger storm.

An additional factor was that this time we would be racing towards the bad weather, trying to beat it to Iceland. On the

Labrador we had been travelling through the storm, eventually away from trouble. Now the front would be blowing into us, so if we hit it, there would be no respite until port. The longer we took, the worse it would get. We knew that.

The others were now well into the drinking. I could hear them next door in the bar. The tension of the Labrador was getting drowned away in time-honoured fashion.

The little voice at the back of my head was urging me not to be impatient, to be responsible and cautious. I didn't mind waiting, I had always wanted to have some time in this remote, beautiful part of the world, but we had a goal in mind, and instinct told me we had to seize this window of opportunity.

Once again, five lives seemed to rest in my hands. Why couldn't this decision be simple? Mick presented me with the facts in black and white, on paper, in his scrawl that I knew so well. Mike Town concurred. It was my call. But I couldn't make it.

This was a massive decision, and I didn't feel able to make it alone. In search of calm, wise advice, I called Captain Pennefather. He listened quietly as I explained the situation, sketching out the pros and cons.

Willie didn't say much because he didn't need to. He just let me talk through the situation and, as I talked, I gradually began to realize there was really no choice at all. Yes, it was exhausting, it was too soon in an ideal world, and it was maybe a shade risky, but if we were going to complete the expedition, we basically had little choice.

Willie simply, cleverly, gave me the space to reach my own conclusion.

We rang Mike Town once more. Again he confirmed that two big fronts were on their way from the south and that if we didn't leave soon, we would probably have to remain in Greenland for several weeks. Mick looked once more at the charts, estimating wave heights and our chances of reaching Iceland in the time that this weather window seemed to allow us.

I asked Mick for his honest view on what we should do, no holds barred. I knew it was important to be decisive with the other guys, but Mick was different; he was my closest mate. I could share everything with him, without shame, my real fears and doubts, the sheer uncertainty of it all. I looked at him. His eyes looked tired. Tired of the salt water and now tired of the computer screen.

'So?'

He frowned, paused, then said quietly, 'Bear, I guess we've got to leave in the morning.' He continued, 'Every minute will count. How early do you think we will be able to get away?'

'Well, if we refuel on time, we should be able to leave at around eleven thirty, at a push.'

This didn't even give us time to dry our clothes.

'Instinct is the nose of the mind ... trust it.' This was one of the quotes that we had laminated and stuck on the boat. 'Bloody quotes,' I swore. But it was our answer.

Now I had to break the news to the others.

As I stood outside the bar, grey clouds of doubt scudded in all over again. Was I putting my ambition to complete this expedition ahead of our lives? Was I being impulsive and foolish?

I knew that 80 per cent of the time people die on high mountains because they push on when common sense says they should turn back. Was I doing just that? We had been let off the hook on the Labrador Sea. How smart was it to go straight back out, into possibly even worse weather? But how would we know if we never even tried?

I called them together in a room alongside the bar. They were enjoying a few beers and were not really in the mood for a meeting. I would have felt exactly the same in their position. I felt a strange pang of envy. I didn't want this burden.

'Well, there is good news and bad news,' I began, realizing that none of them was expecting what they were about to hear. 'The good news is that we have a window of good weather, and the bad news is that, to take this opportunity, we must leave as soon as possible in the morning.'

They stood motionless. Nobody said a word.

'It will mean we need to get up at five,' I continued, filling the void, 'and start prepping the boat. It's not great, but it seems our only choice if we are ever to reach Iceland.'

I paused.

'And I'm really sorry we can't delay the weather.'

Mick, at least, had been prepared. Andy, Nige and Charlie just looked understandably fed up. The long-awaited period of rest and recovery after the Labrador crossing was being cancelled. This, I am certain, was the single most difficult moment of the entire expedition.

Mick outlined the reasons for the decision, explaining the weather forecast and how forty-eight, possibly seventy-two, hours of clear weather would be followed by weeks of storms, but Andy was clearly hesitant and uncomfortable.

'Bear, the one thing we all said when we arrived here was that, above all, we didn't want to get caught in bad weather again,' he reminded us. 'We were bloody lucky out there this time. Now you're telling us to go back into it with a shit forecast, with little chance of beating that weather to Iceland. What happens if the fronts come sooner rather than later?'

'I know that's the risk. I don't have an answer for that,' I replied. 'I only have the facts. Study the charts Mick's done and see what you reckon. If we don't all agree, we don't go.'

This took Andy a few minutes to digest. And part of me, if I am honest, longed for someone to say no. The idea of another storm terrified me. Anyone who thinks these expeditions are romantic should have felt the tension in that room. It was palpable. These decisions were critical. My hands were sweating.

'Let's try and get a few hours' sleep now,' I said.

The guys had arrived in high spirits; they returned to their rooms in silence. I was knackered, in mind and body, and as I fell into bed and gazed at the white patterned ceiling, I just hoped we had made the correct decision.

Charlie recalls:

Bear's announcement was a shock, and we did question it, but not in a negative way. In the end, we understood and accepted his logic, and the team ethic came through. Such team spirit was new for me.

By nature, I have tended to be a loner, working as a freelance cameraman and often travelling on my own. I live my own life, and I have always been happy with that. However, on this small boat, being part of the team was everything, relying on other people and knowing that they relied on me. It felt good.

So, when Bear said he wanted to leave in the morning, we didn't just accept it without question. This wasn't the army. We studied the data and discussed the issues, but, in the end, we agreed and moved forward together. That was it. Whatever happened after that, there would be no recriminations.

Nige recalls:

It wasn't a great moment when Mick and Bear said we would have to leave, and it wasn't too great when, the next morning, I discovered that my boots were still sodden wet. It was not ideal that I had to start the leg by putting soaking wet boots on; but I guess the weather didn't give us much choice.

There are not many situations that don't look better after a decent night's sleep, and when we all woke at 5.30, everyone appeared more cheerful and purposeful. Everyone now accepted the logic. We had agreed on the decision together, and the team was moving forward as one. Nobody was on the touchlines. We were all players and had made our own calls.

Mick and Andy started preparing the boat, which still looked a mess after the Labrador crossing; Charlie and Nige were doing their best to dry and repack all the equipment, and I settled the hotel bill, arranged the refuelling and sorted out the customs forms. With luck, I reckoned, we would be able to get away before noon.

We all knew the blue sky above us would not last for ever and the forty-eight-hour clock was ticking.

The mayor had invited us to lunch, but I dropped by his home to say this was no longer possible. I explained that every minute counted in our race to cross the Denmark Strait and reach Iceland before the storms arrived. He understood completely.

It was almost half past eleven when I reached the quay-side. The guys had done a fantastic job, and we were almost ready to leave.

Alex Rayner, our PR man in London, had been asking us repeatedly to do a select few radio interviews. I knew that I should do these, but I felt uncomfortable. This just wasn't the right time. I reneged on my promise to Alex, turned off the SAT phone, and quietly hoped he would understand.

However, a minute later, a radio station got through on Nige's mobile phone. It was BBC Radio Five Live.

'Bear, we'll call you back in twenty minutes for a live slot,' said the producer in London. 'Is that OK?'

The guys were waiting in the boat. We were refuelled and ready to go. They had met our deadline exactly. It was 11.30 a.m. precisely. They all looked at me.

I put the phone to my ear again. 'I'm really sorry, but we just don't have the time.'

'Just twenty minutes?'

'Not this time; we have to leave now. I'm really sorry.'

They were clearly a bit put out, but away in their London studio they were not to know that for us to wait another twenty minutes could turn out to be the difference between reaching Iceland safely and getting trapped in the oncoming gales.

We didn't have that sort of time to waste. I jumped aboard the boat and Andy turned the key once more. If all went to plan, this engine would run continuously until we reached Iceland. And that was a long way from here. Iceland, in my little son Jesse's *Children's Atlas of the World*, was still one whole page away.

The first ten hours of this leg unfolded as one of those experiences that will remain with me for ever. It was a privilege to behold.

Our route took us down the south-west coast of Greenland and then through the Prince Christiansen Sound, effectively cutting off the southern cape of Greenland and bringing us out on the eastern side. The natural features of Prince Christiansen Sound are some of the most remote and unsung beauties of the world. Maybe this is what makes them so magical. They are so rarely seen.

I can only think of one word to describe our reaction as we began to weave our way through the sheer fjords in front of us: stunned.

Sheer, vertical walls of rock, at least 2,000 feet high, rose straight out of the water into giant, snow-capped, jagged peaks. The depth of this fjord was such that it went off the scale of our instruments. Several times, we took the boat up to the rock face, stared upwards, and marvelled at these natural skyscrapers.

This was a living, changing landscape. Glaciers tumbled down thousands of feet into the still, icy water. I had seen icefalls on Everest, where the frozen ice ruptures and breaks its way dramatically down cliff faces. But here, the glacier crashed directly into the fjord.

Thousands of pieces of ice, ranging from small lumps to enormous bergs, were floating in the water, and it was exhilarating to see and feel the ice knocking against the aluminium hull, as we wove our way through the bergs. The *Arnold and Son Explorer* had been designed for these conditions, and it eased its way elegantly through the Sound.

Twice, the black mass of a whale appeared, suddenly rising out of the water within 50 yards of the boat and then disappearing with a casual swish of its 6-foot tail. It was unbelievable to sit and watch.

We passed through this wonderland in awe. The sun was bright in the midday sky, without a cloud in sight, and we were dressed in light clothes and fleeces. For the only time on the entire expedition we let the rota slip, each of us simply took turns in helming, while the rest sprawled out on the foredeck, writing diaries, listening to their Walkmans or just basking in the wonder of this place. It was a special time and for once we could recoup a bit of energy. We would need it.

Not another person for miles around; just us, in this frozen paradise.

Charlie recalls:

The icebergs were colossal, coming in all sorts of weird shapes and sizes. Some had these strange kinds of spires and they genuinely resembled cathedrals. They were certainly that big. They had a translucent tinge, and many had these incredible cracks of bright blue running through them. They were astonishing.

We saw a variety of whales – Humpback, Minke – but none came much closer than 50 metres, probably because our jet drive was making such a racket, and that meant that, unfortunately, despite all the sightings, I never got my 'Attenborough' shot on camera!

We all felt a sense of peace, a quiet contentment. It was the moment I had hungered for so much. It was just nature and my friends. Pure magic.

These beautiful, isolated places, where just one hidden rockface, high above a glistening glacier, stands out so proud and majestic, feed a man's soul. They are untouched by human contact, like a tiny flower in a dense jungle that serves no purpose for mankind – a flower that will remain unseen for ever. To me, such places are simply God's extravagance.

We had come to this place, far from civilization and completely uninhabited, and we found glaciers, mountains and icebergs that were truly exquisite. But we knew it couldn't last for ever, and all of us dreaded the next bend in the fjord being the last.

Eventually we turned the final corner of the Sound and were confronted by 20 miles of fjord leading straight to the ocean. This spectacular stretch of water was bordered on either side by even larger mountains, which would part every once in a while to afford a glimpse of the snow-capped plateaux of Greenland behind.

But our gaze was fixed on what lay ahead of us in the open seas, and for the first time that day we could feel the cold Arctic wind on our faces. This wind was being funnelled down the fjord but it was nothing violent, just a stiff, steady breeze, almost like a warning. It was announcing the ocean ahead. And it was beckoning us forward.

Each of us put on extra fleeces and began to clamber into our survival suits. We made certain everything was correctly stowed and the boat properly organized. We had learnt a lot from the Labrador: about rough-water stowing of food and supplies, about waterproofing kit effectively, about wearing the right amount of layers. In some ways, we had been caught out by that storm, and we didn't want to make the same mistakes again. Everyone could feel the stakes were rising.

Before long we were dressed in our full gear – balaclavas, helmets, inner and outer gloves, two pairs of thermal socks, five layers of clothing under the dry-suits, the lot – and a quietness, a tension descended on the boat. It was 7.20 p.m. We could hardly move now, we were so bulked up. But experience had taught us to be ready. We sat in silence. The mouth of the fjord was still flat calm, with only the ripples of the funnelled wind bristling on the water.

'OK, Nige, how far to Iceland?' I asked.

'In a straight line, 630 nautical miles,' he replied.

'All right then, with a bit of luck we should reach Reykjavik by 15.30 hrs the day after tomorrow.'

As we reached the edge of the fjord, where the Sound runs into the wide open ocean and the Denmark Strait, we stopped one last time. The boat idled lazily, dwarfed by the glaciers and cliffs on either side of us. We had one last SAT phone call to make.

Mike Town was waiting for us to call. He checked the weather forecast again. It was still clear for the next thirty-six hours, with Force Fives or Sixes coming up towards Iceland after that. If we could be within reach of Iceland by that time, we could manage these winds for the last stage into port. That was good enough for us. Now we just had one last box to tick before we set out to sea.

Tucked into the edge of the cliffs, at the mouth of the Sound, is one of the remotest weather stations in this part of the world. The scientists there are more familiar than anyone with these waters, and they understand how unpredictable they can be. Their advice would be invaluable.

We saw their aerials and a cluster of huts from a few miles down the Sound, and we managed to get them on the radio.

'Hi. Where are you heading?' they asked.

'To Iceland,' I replied.

There was a pause.

'What's the weather looking like?' I continued. I didn't want to put words in their mouths.

'Well, it looks good for twenty-four hours, then it *should* be OK for another twelve hours after that; then it's deteriorating towards Iceland. It depends on how fast that low pressure sweeps north. But I reckon you should be OK. Wouldn't you like a cup of tea and something to eat before you leave?'

'Thanks,' I said, 'but we're all dressed up like astronauts and ready to go. We really ought to keep moving.'

We thanked them and signed off.

The forecasts sounded consistent with what we had had from the UK, but I also knew we were moving into some of the most uncharted waters on the planet. The US military had only recently put weather buoys in place to measure the wave heights. They had no need for such data previously.

We had taken good advice, we knew the facts and we were going for it. I packed the SAT phone away in its watertight pouch in the console and crawled back out.

We were still drifting around slowly, weaving among a small cluster of icebergs in the last little inlet before the ocean. It was as if these small bergs were wary of moving into the open seas. To be honest, I felt a little bit the same.

We eased the throttle open, turned the boat's nose from land and headed out into the Denmark Strait between Greenland and Iceland, and almost 700 miles of open sea.

In all my research, I hadn't found much about this part of the route. What I did discover in one geographical document was pretty blunt: 'The Denmark Strait is one of the most difficult of large ocean straits in which to carry out any sort of research. Inhospitable weather and the frequent presence of ice make ship operation severely difficult. Try somewhere warmer.'

This wasn't quite what I was looking for.

As we headed away from the ice plateaux of the Greenland coastline, the sea was glassy-calm before us. Not even a ripple of wind now anywhere.

'It's like the *Marie Céleste*,' Nige said.

He was right.

We had reached the ocean to find, not the severe conditions that we had feared, but an eerie stillness. Dusk was falling, the sea was like a mirror, and a dense fog was descending. Before long it had completely obscured Greenland from sight.

I knew what Nige meant. It did feel as though we had been transported to the *Marie Céleste*, the fabled ship that was found drifting on the ocean, untouched and unmanned.

A flock of puffins were floundering around in the water, and as we headed towards them they flapped awkwardly as they tried to take off. How the hell did such small, clumsy birds survive the storms these waters must see? I had no idea. They looked so fragile and out of place. But they did, and it was spectacular and humbling to watch these wonders of nature fussing all around us.

We were managing a speed of only 13 knots because the boat was still so heavy with fuel at the start of such a long leg, but the rocking motion of the gently rolling waves was ideal for sleep. As we maintained the rota, each of us managed to get some rest during our hours in the sardine tin.

It was a glorious night and I remember waking apprehensively, opening my eyes and half expecting to find the sea churning and throwing the boat around, but it wasn't. It was still calm.

However, I still felt very nervous. I wasn't sure why.

I knew that every hour that passed was an hour nearer Iceland, but I longed to go faster, to get more miles under our belt while the weather was so good.

'How are we doing?' I asked Mick.

'Yeah, it looks OK,' he replied. 'We've done 205 miles since we left.'

I looked around the boat. Everything was neat and ready, and everyone was resting.

The dawn felt a little cooler, but that was to be expected; we were heading in a north-easterly direction all the time, towards a latitude of 64 degrees north. It was still calm as we ploughed on through the gentle rollers.

A few hours later, Charlie and I were sitting together at the console when, out of nowhere, we were confronted by a cruise ship ahead on the horizon. It had been a real surprise to me that we had seen so little other shipping on the expedition so far. I had expected to see much more. The truth was that this was the first ship we had seen in almost 2,000 miles. We were so excited. I tried to raise the captain on the radio, to get some further info on the weather conditions ahead (even though there wasn't much we would have been able to do about it out here).

We couldn't see the name of the vessel. So we tried this instead:

'Hello, big ship, this is little yellow boat.'

A Danish voice replied, 'Hello, how are you?'

'Fine,' I responded. 'Just fine.'

He said he had heard about our expedition, and he wished us luck. I detected an element of foreboding in his voice when he said that the 'fair weather had lasted well in the Denmark Strait'. He asked if there was much ice around the southern edges of Greenland, where he was heading, and we told him it was broken up and passable.

As he spoke, a cluster of people appeared on the deck of the cruise ship. They were all peering down on the small yellow boat passing in the shadow of their ship. We just sat there, feeling a bit ridiculous and very small, imagining what they were thinking.

'Oh well,' said Mick, waving from the sardine tin, 'at least the captain won't be getting too many complaints from his passengers about the state of their cabins. I think we have given them a new perspective on the words "living quarters".'

It was nearly midday on Thursday, our second day at sea after leaving Greenland, conditions were still good and we were making reasonable progress. If our weather forecasts were right, there was almost another twenty-four hours in our window of decent weather, and that should be enough time to get us within reach of Iceland. All seemed well and we had no reason to imagine that anything would change.

We noticed the wind freshen into the afternoon. It was not dramatic, but it was marked. Where we had been expecting Force Four, we were moving into Force Five winds.

But that was OK, I told myself. The bad weather was still 1,000 miles to our south.

Or it was supposed to be.

By evening, the sea was building and the spray had returned, every thirty seconds or so, cold and uncomfortable, and I started to notice the movement of the boat becoming more pronounced. She was taking these head-on waves well, digging the deep-V hull into the water as it rose to meet her bows.

It wasn't too bad.

'It's OK, isn't it?' I said to Nige that second evening.

'Yep, this is nothing like the Labrador,' he replied.

'No,' I said. 'No dramas.'

Three hours later, I happened to glance over at Nige. It was our habit to keep a vague look out for each other. I looked again. He was staring intently at his watch. I knew what he was staring at. His barometer.

A barometer simply measures the air pressure, but it is still, in this modern age of electronics, the most accurate and reliable indicator of any bad weather ahead. It had read 1,026 millibars when we left Greenland and had remained pretty much unchanged ever since.

But something had obviously changed now. Nige looked blank and frightened.

I was watching him.

'What's it say?' I asked.

'It dropped to 996 millibars,' he replied. 'That's impossible I have never seen anything like this before.'

The barometer had dropped 30 millibars. Much later, Mike Town would say this was almost a meteorological impossibility – it was too steep. But it happened. We all saw it.

Our weather window had slammed shut. The night was just beginning and we didn't know what the hell we were going into.

Three hundred miles out to sea, almost exactly midway between Greenland and Iceland, there was no longer any-where to hide.

Our ordeal would soon begin.

10. TERROR

When you are going through hell, keep walking.

Sir Winston Churchill

Our hopes plunged with the barometer.

All of us knew we had been racing against the weather. But now we were racing *into* that weather. There would be no respite until we reached Iceland, and we knew we were in difficulty.

We had been told the weather window would last forty-eight hours, but the low pressure had moved north at an alarming speed. That precious window had lasted only thirty hours.

The rota meant it was my turn to rest in the sardine tin, and I desperately went over the situation in my head. Clear, logical thought was hard. 'How did this happen? Was this my fault? Should we, after all, have stayed longer in Greenland?'

In confusion, I reached for the Dictaphone.

We're back in the really big seas now. Waves are crashing over the boat again, and we're all getting soaked. Our kit that we had laid out so carefully on the tubes to dry whilst in the Sound is now getting drenched once more.

Our bodies are being slammed around the boat, and it's just relentless. When you're not on watch, sitting at the console, you have to brace yourself in your seat, tensing your stomach muscles, over and over again. The boat seems to get picked up every thirty seconds or so. If it lands on the keel, it's OK. If it lands on its side, it sounds as if the boat is breaking apart under us.

I am dehydrated, but I can't get across the boat to get a drink. Moving around is so hard. I've got a really bad headache from the slamming, and each wave makes me wince. It's impossible to have a pee: I tried clinging to the console, but you need both hands to undo your fly-zip. In the end, I just gave up. There's no chance of getting a drink, eating or having a pee so long as these conditions continue. We just cling on for all we're worth.

We're 325 miles off Iceland. That's still a hell of a long way, when we can hardly make nine knots; and this storm is getting worse; that is what frightens me the most.

Twenty-five-foot waves were rolling, breaking and crashing all around us. And from the level of a small, open RIB, they felt immense and terrifying.

The water pouring over us, hour after hour, was icy. We were now just south of the Arctic Circle, in seas that were freezing enough to sustain tens of thousands of icebergs. This wet cold was terrible. Our underclothes inevitably, over time, got damp because the seams began to let in small amounts of water, and slowly all this then seeped down our arms and chests. Every part of our bodies felt drenched, but it was the wind that really made us cold.

This wind whipped over the console and chilled every exposed part of us; every gust carried with it more of the freezing sea spray. Heading *into* this wind made it twice as strong. It was both the storm and our forward speed combined. Wherever we sat or curled up, there was nowhere to hide from it. All we could do was hug one another in the sardine tin, pull the tarpaulin up to our waists and try to get through the next hour.

In these conditions, our salvation was the kit we wore. From the very first night on the Labrador Sea, when it had got so cold that we had had to stop the boat and put on extra layers, we had learned the hard way how to try to keep as warm as possible. Our survival depended on it.

From the inside out, the full kit was an unbelievable amount: next to the skin, we wore a thick, fleecy long-sleeved top and thick thermal long-john trousers; then a heavy-duty fleece, then Gortex salopettes and a Gortex fleece jacket; on top of all this went an all-in-one survival dry-suit, and another windproof and waterproof ocean jacket on top of that.

On our hands we had inner fleece gloves inside big waterproof mittens. We also had sealed fleece diving gloves, but both sets inevitably ended up sodden. You just interchanged in a futile attempt to warm your fingers.

On our heads we had fleece balaclavas and a Gortex balaclava over that; on top of these we wore RNLI Gecko helmets. But even these couldn't keep the water out. It got in everywhere: our hair was soaked and our faces and necks had water constantly dripping down them.

Most of this kit was provided by Musto, and I will never forget standing in Musto's headquarters, in Basildon, a year earlier. It was a swelteringly hot summer's day, and Keith Musto, the founder of the clothing company, was helping me try all this on. Within minutes, I was sweating. Keith found it very amusing, me standing in the stock room like a giant Mr Blobby, dreading it as he approached me to add yet another layer.

'You will need it all,' he added, as he tugged me into another fleece. 'This kit will keep you alive. It's the best in the world. But have no doubt about it, if it gets really bad out there, whatever you are wearing, you will still be cold.'

I truly could never have then imagined any conditions being cold enough to make me shiver with all this amount of fleece and Gortex kit on. I could hardly move. But then I had never been in this sort of wet wind chill, this far north, so exposed, for so long before. Here in this tiny corner of the vast, 41-million-square-mile ocean, curled in a ball on the floor of this small, open boat, I found myself shivering uncontrollably.

The key to coping with cold is not to allow yourself to get to the stage of being really cold. That might sound obvious, but I have learned from climbing that if you allow yourself to get that cold, it's almost too late to do anything about it. It's much harder to get warm again. But here there was nothing we could do: we had no shelter in which to hide from the wind and rain and spray, and we had nothing more we could wear. All we had was what we stood in.

We relied entirely on one another to keep an eye out for signs of hypothermia, to be constantly aware of the telltale signs of extreme cold – shaking hands, slow reactions and sluggish responses – and to help anyone who seemed in trouble. Hypothermia hits silently and often very quickly. The team needed to look after themselves, and everyone needed to be aware of the indicators. If somebody is feeling cold and is crunched up in a ball, trying to protect their core warmth, that's a good sign that they are aware and rational; on the other hand, if they are lying on their back, with their arms at their side, head and body exposed, not caring, then that is not good.

It's good if someone sits up, offers you a Mars bar and shouts, 'Hey, catch'; and it's not good if they don't even have the energy to sit up and get the Mars bars, let alone try to eat one.

We tried to drink something, maybe a cupful of water poured over our face and mouth, every few hours to stay hydrated. I ended up trying to do this once every full rota, i.e. every five hours. It gave me a focus, and I stuck to it. If one of us wasn't drinking, someone needed to notice.

Every little ritual became recognizable and important to us: the way in which each of us sat, or ate, or helmed, or slept. We recognized what was normal for each of us. Any change in the ritual, like any other change in the routine, was often an early sign of something starting to go wrong.

This expedition wasn't about trying to be brave or strong in front of one another, or thinking it was somehow stoic never to admit that you were struggling or something was wrong. It was about being brave enough to say just how you felt, weak or strong; it was about being honest enough to admit occasionally we needed some comfort or a helping hand, being able to say we were frightened. It was about being together, about staying close. All said and done, it was simply about staying alive.

But we were suffering now. We were being lashed by the rain, and our eyes were stinging from the spray. We were getting tired from continually bracing ourselves against the violence of the waves, and our heads were aching from the deafening roar of the engine.

Darkness made things even worse. It became impossible to see the waves, to know where to guide the boat to minimize the slamming. We would stare ahead transfixed, trying desperately to determine the oncoming sea. All we could see of the horizon was a vague line between the pitch black sea and the dark grey, menacing sky. Suddenly, this horizon would disappear and be replaced by a wall of black water, then a final burst of white as the crest of the wave came into view, and then there would be the roar as it crashed over the boat. Those final moments of frothing white water were always the most terrifying, as you braced yourself once more.

You'd cling on to something, anything, and pray.

Often, it seemed the best place to be was sitting in the so-called 'deckchair' on the side of the boat. We had worked out how we could pull a thin plastic storm sheet over us and hide away. If we trapped the bottom of this sheet under our feet and sat on the rest of it, we could just about escape the spray and the wind, and convince ourselves, for a few precious moments, that we were safe. This thin veneer of orange plastic was our comfort blanket, an opportunity to float away into our dreams. For me, they were always dreams of being at home.

It was Charlie's turn in the deckchair now. I was back in the sardine tin, trying to ignore the discomfort. I heard Mick shouting at me, even though his head was only inches from mine.

'This bloody weather – it's not supposed to be here!' he screamed over the noise.

Mick recalls:

I felt this heavy guilt. The weather window had closed much earlier than we expected, and getting the forecast right was my area of responsibility. I started to feel as if the guys were looking at me across the boat and wondering: 'Mick, what's happening?' I felt it was my fault.

Of course it wasn't Mick's fault. It wasn't anybody's fault. The only fair way to judge our decision to leave Greenland is to assess the decision in the circumstances that prevailed at the time. The reality was that in Nanortalik we received advice from three separate sources of information and they all gave us a forty-eight- to seventy-two-hour window. We had had to go. But nobody was to know that this front would arrive sooner than forecast, or that it would be much deeper and more sinister than anticipated.

There were no recriminations. We had to look forward, not back.

As time moved on past eleven o'clock on this second night in the Denmark Strait, six hours into the heavy seas and howling gale, Nige and I found ourselves in the dark, squatting on the floor, trying to hold on while opening the food sack to grab something to eat – anything. Nige pulled out a crushed and split flapjack. The wrapper was broken and it was wet. He steadied himself, broke it in two and handed one half to me. I ate it in one.

'Ooh, I'd love to be in the curry house now,' Nige gushed, 'with Hussein and Mohammed and the trolley, laden with murgs and poppadoms! Absolutely lovely!'

He was smiling at me with relish, and for a moment, a brief moment, we were a million miles away.

It had become almost customary that every Sunday we would all go to the Indian restaurant in our local square. Hussein and Mohammed, the waiters, knew our orders by heart.

'Oh, and don't forget a bit of extra zing in the korma,' I would remind them jokingly, while whistling and twiddling my fingers in imitation of adding a bit of extra chilli. Hussein would laugh, and Shara would roll her eyes; it was always the same old jokes between us. It all felt a long, long way from our small, open boat in this tiny part of the North Atlantic Ocean. But the memory provided us with a fleeting moment of comfort in the nightmare.

Nige looked back at me. He was tired, I could tell. But he still managed a smile.

Charlie was doing OK, but he was also starting to get really cold. One of the first things the army instils in you is the ability to look after yourself when it gets miserable. It is simple self-discipline. Charlie was always a really tough and gritty character, but he didn't have a military background, and his clothing and equipment always seemed to be a bit more chaotic and disorganized than ours. My stuff is always a mess back home, but somehow, when I am away, I become much more careful and neat. I need to know where everything is. It's just habit.

However, as a result, Charlie had to put up with much worse conditions than the rest of us. His spare gloves, for example, were soaking long before ours. He hadn't had them wrapped up well enough in their waterproofing. But he never seemed to grumble. He just got on with it.

For so much of the expedition, Charlie had an almost impossible task. Filming under these conditions was nigh on impossible. Yet despite this, I would often see him fumbling with a radio microphone with cold, shaky fingers, trying to stuff it into its waterproof housing. But no sooner had he taped it to the console or elsewhere, then a wave would tear it loose. Sea-water is a killer to sensitive electronic equipment, and it is a tribute to Charlie that in the early stages of the storm he was filming at all. Despite his best efforts, the bottom line was that, whenever conditions reached gale-force, we were fighting for our lives and neither photography nor filming was possible. The world around us was black and soaking, accompanied by a 120-decibel soundtrack. Not quite ideal lighting or sound conditions.

Still so far from land, our condition was getting serious. We were moving into survival mode. We were nervously fumbling for our harnesses in the dark, feeling them beneath us, concentrating on what we were doing. There was no room for error: fuel readings had to be correct, helming needed to be perfect. One bad reaction could breach the boat in these seas. It was the blackest of nights, and the conditions were still deteriorating.

Things had suddenly got very dangerous very quickly, and it soon became clear that for the second time on the expedition, I would have to call our UK base and alert them to the situation. If conditions continued to plummet at this rate, we would lose all control. Our lives would then rest in the hands of the rescue services, although this far from land, none of us had any idea what sort of rescue could be mounted.

I urged everyone to keep focused as we slowed the boat to a crawl so I could make the call to London.

Once again, in the new, unfamiliar quiet, without the roar of the engine, I knelt down and crawled into the cubbyhole. My hand was shaking now, not just because I was cold but because I was frightened. I patiently waited to get through. It was eight minutes to midnight, their time.

Chloë had just turned out the lights in the hallway of her flat, on her way to bed. She looked at her phone ringing, and her heart sank when she recognized the +88 number identification on the LCD screen and realized this late-night call was coming from the boat. She knew, having been following our tracker, that at this time we were still a long way from Iceland. She realized almost immediately that something was wrong.

'Chloë?'

'Yes, I'm here. What's happening?'

'Get a pen quickly. I need to give you our position.'

I turned to Mick and shouted at him: 'OK, Mick, give me the lat and longs. Loud and clear!'

He yelled at me: 'Six-ah, two-ah, two-ah, seven-ah.'

'Six two, two seven,' I screamed down the receiver, trying to make myself heard above the engine and the storm. 'Did you get that?'

'Yes,' she replied, writing down the numbers on the only piece of paper she could find – a copy of *Time Out*, the London listings magazine.

'Read the numbers back to me, Chloë,' I shouted.

I was cold, wet and exhausted, and I was painfully wedged in this small, dark hole. I needed Chloë to be certain of our precise position so that she could relay this to the rescue services. One number mispronounced or misheard could prove disastrous, even fatal.

'Four-ah, one-ah, three-ah,' Mick shouted in my ear.

'Four one three,' I yelled into the phone. 'So that's six ... two ... two ... seven ... four ... one ... three ... North, OK?'

She had the coordinates, and she soon had the latitude reading as well: 31.18.912 West.

'Chloë,' I concluded, 'we're OK, but we're struggling. These seas are much, much bigger than they were on the Labrador. Contact the Icelandic coastguard and give them our position, and keep them posted.'

I turned to Andy, still screaming: 'What's the fuel situation?'

Andy paused, then shouted that the fuel was looking OK; we were still around 250 miles from Reykjavik. I relayed this to Chloë.

I remembered how she had left her safe job at Goldman Sachs for a bit of adventure. Well, now she had it – in spades.

'And please phone Willie as well.'

'OK.'

'We'll phone again in an hour.'

Chloë passed on the message to the rescue services in Reykjavik, as requested, then called Andy Billing, who was awake on our barge in London. She also woke Willie. She would need all the help she could muster.

Chloë recalls:

The call from Bear was brief and troubled; it had come out of the blue. But I had come to expect this. We had agreed before the start of the expedition, when they left England, that Bear would call me at 3 p.m. every day. This never really happened because from the start, even in Halifax, the team were busy at different times with boat preparations, last-minute weather checks and press. It is unfortunately the nature of the beast, and any form of routine was damn near impossible from so far away.

There always seemed so much to do, so many things to sort out, and in the midst of bad weather it seemed impossible to keep track of time. I had promised Chloë I would call again in an hour, so she was sitting up, coffee in hand, waiting for my call. London was in the midst of an uncomfortable heatwave, but it was her concern for us on the ocean, rather than the humidity, that was keeping her wide awake in the early hours of the morning.

In the end, we didn't call until 2.30 a.m., more than an hour and a half late, and Mick spoke to her. I couldn't face the cubbyhole again, I was feeling so seasick. Mick had volunteered instead. He told Chloë the conditions were not improving, but that we were stable and hanging on. We would call again at 8.30 in the morning. Chloë duly passed the news on to Willie. Our base team was all working well, but right now there was nothing they could do to help us. We were going to have to get through this alone.

This night was the time I needed to lead. This was no longer the time to stand back. It was the moment for me to step forward.

Throughout my life, from my army days to the Everest expedition and since, I have never regarded myself as a natural athlete. There have always been people, in all these different fields, who were stronger and fitter than me. But when it comes down to the crunch times, I have always somehow managed to find a little bit extra when it matters most. I've never understood where it comes from.

On Everest, for many weeks early on, I really struggled on the lower sections of the mountain, and there were times when I felt weak and slow, as a climber. But as the months passed and just two of us were finally approaching the summit, I somehow felt my strength return. It shouldn't have been returning then: we hadn't eaten for days, or even peed for over thirty-six hours, our bodies were not functioning and our reserves were gone – we were in the Death Zone and our bodies were physiologically dying, above 26,000 feet. But something was keeping me moving. This strength is not athleticism, it's not fitness; I think it is heart.

And as I clung on in the boat, I felt this was another of those critical moments. It was 1 a.m. and the sea was winning. We were in a crisis, and this was my time to find that heart again.

I didn't want to be impulsive and I didn't want to be cavalier. I was aware that I had to be calm and responsible, and concentrate; I also knew that right now I had to lead. I had been helming for an hour, getting a feel of the conditions, coping, every cell in my body focused, and I knew I shouldn't let go.

'We're stopping the rota,' I shouted. 'I'm going to keep the wheel with Mick for the rest of this night.' The RIB was then hit side-on by a wave that had appeared from nowhere. We all braced against the impact, and then I continued: 'I want you three to get in the sardine tin together and get some rest. I'm going to need your strength for the morning.'

That was my decision. This time, there was no discussion.

I had been as terrified as anyone else as the storm had built up. It was now in full force. We were being pummelled by waves that came at us out of the dark, drenching us, battering us and hitting from all angles. But now, in the heart of this Force Eight gale, hundreds of miles from any land, I felt this strange determination return.

So I kept the helm. I felt emotional and raw, but I was also clear about what Mick and I were doing. Together, the two of us would bring the boat through the storm and through the night. We would keep the boat upright; we would bring it into port. I would need the others to rest and be ready to take over when it was light, but I needed Mick, my oldest friend, to be with me now, beside me.

I didn't want any loose helming during the night as our margin for error had been reduced from maybe 10 per cent to 2 per cent. One mistake, one slip, and the boat could be taken and rolled. You make the right call a thousand times, but just one error of judgement can so often prove fatal. The mountains had shown me that. There was no longer the margin for someone to misjudge a wave or react nervously to a breaking wall of water in front of the bows. The only way I was going to make certain we survived the darkness and the night was by doing the helming myself.

I had pushed everyone to leave Greenland. I had got us all into this hellhole. I would get us through it as well. These were my best friends' lives, and I wouldn't tire now.

Every time we had reached the safety of port before, we had felt as though we had been pardoned. When you walk down a street, it's solid and it doesn't move. There are no surprises. But the ocean is different. It rolls and heaves. It is unpredictable. When you put out to sea – far out to sea, in a small boat – it's like being put out for sacrifice, and ultimately it is the monster of the sea that decides your fate.

That's how I felt. We were being put out for sacrifice, like the heroes in the children's books my mum used to read me when I was young. Waiting to be consumed, devoured, forgotten, never even missed. But I wanted, with every bone in my body, to be home, to hold my wife and son again, and to be safe.

Mick and I would do this together, this one last time.

Mick recalls:

It was the right decision. We were really struggling in the twenty-five-foot waves, and they seemed to be increasing in height and ferocity as the night closed in. Bear and I were just finishing our watch, but Bear had learned how to handle these conditions; he had got the feel of the boat and the sea, and it was just more sensible for the two of us to soldier on through the night than for each guy to come in and start all over again from scratch.

Throughout the previous hour, out of desperation, I had been experimenting with the jet bucket at the stern of the boat. This is a large hood that lowers hydraulically over the jet to give you, effectively, a reverse gear. But we knew that if we lowered it partially over the jet, it would begin to dig the nose of the boat down into the sea slightly. Lowered even further though, it made all the difference, providing stability and grip in the waves. Instead of taking off wildly and slamming off the wave crests, the boat could edge her way over the face of the waves; when the bucket was dipped as she punched through the crest, it pulled the bows sharply down the other side of the wave. Our speed would drop dramatically but it held us more tightly on to the waves' surface.

This all took control though: to feel the different pitch of the bucket and to know at which point to apply it. We were ploughing through the swell at around 10 knots, and by trial and error we learned how the bucket could have a positive effect.

As a wave approached, I would bring the bucket right down, forcing the bow into the sea as the wave tried to pick us up. It was working – the slamming was being reduced.

Up until now we had been nearing a point where we knew something would give way soon. The boat would not be able to take this sort of punishment for ever. Something would go. The engine was labouring under the pounding the hull was taking from these waves. And each whine we heard made us hold our breath until it regained its momentum. But the bucket helped: we were regaining some control over the ferocity of the sea.

This strengthened my resolve to keep helming until dawn. I seemed to have caught the rhythm and the feel of the waves. The boat was still upright and I wasn't going to let her go now.

My decision to helm was not about wanting to be a hero. I just didn't want to die.

I had only one goal in my head, and that was to pull the boat through the night and eventually into port. It wasn't even about being the best helmsman. I wasn't – Andy and Nige were probably better. But right there and then I had this thing under some semblance of control and my instinct said hold on.

So I did.

By 3 a.m., Mick and I were still firing on adrenalin in our determination to keep the RIB level. Every sinew in our exhausted bodies was reacting to the sea beneath us.

Suddenly, though, the boat was struck by two waves simultaneously. Two converging walls of water collided over us. The *Arnold and Son Explorer* lurched violently to starboard and began to corkscrew. I clearly remember thinking she was going over. But she rose up again. The three bodies in the sardine tin were lifted at least 4 inches off the soaking wet thin foam covering, then landed in a heap as the boat crashed back into the water.

Mick was literally washed off his seat, and the force of the water threw him on top of me. We both clutched at anything solid around us. In the dark, and in blind panic, I grabbed hold of the wheel again and frantically tried to guess where the next freak wave was coming from. We were like blind men in a boxing ring, alone and afraid, taking punches from every direction.

Over and over again we were picked up like a feather on the swell and then dropped back to the water surface, with an impact equivalent to 7 tonnes of aluminium and fuel being dropped from the second storey of a house.

We had no idea how long our electrical equipment could withstand the combined effects of the relentless physical battering and the regular drenching by water pouring over the boat.

I was more frightened than I have ever been in my life, yet I have never wanted so desperately to live.

Our forward speed was almost zero, and we still had such a long way to go. The weather was getting worse, not better, and I wondered how much longer we could stay upright.

And what if we capsized?

I recalled how in diver training we had been told we would be able to survive for about fifteen minutes in the waters of the North Sea. We would have much less time up here in these icy seas just south of the Arctic Circle. We knew the drill: to try to clamber to the stern of the boat, which would then be upside down. Then keep together. But if you were separated in the capsize, the bottom line was that you would be lost to the waves. You would die.

I remember looking back at Charlie and seeing a look of terror on his face. He was ashen-white. His eyes looked a million miles away. They stared at me blankly. Empty. He didn't even bother to spit the water away from his mouth as the spray hit him in the face. He just lay there, beyond caring.

Nige was in the deckchair. He was holding his knife in one hand and his flares in the other. He looked deadly serious and truly scared. I looked back to the helm. I had seen all I needed to in those three brief seconds.

Time was moving so slowly, but everything was hurtling through my head at treble speed. I suddenly saw familiar faces in the sea and the waves. I reached out to touch Mick. I just needed to know he was there.

I was tiring. I had to be stronger.

The only light on the boat was a dull green glow from the

screen but it was enough to see what I had spotted. Glued to the edge of the console was a small, laminated photograph of Shara, holding our little Jesse; and she was smiling at me.

I had never felt in such danger of not seeing them again. I felt sick. I stared at Jesse, my little son. It broke my heart. 'How have I got into this situation?' I murmured. 'I promise you I will come home. I will see you again.'

I started muttering even louder to myself, almost talking out loud. I was speaking to Shara. My love.

'I will get this boat back safely. I will get back to you. Watch me, baby, this one last time.'

Shara has always believed in me. She thinks I am stronger than I am. She thinks I am nicer than I am. She defends me and always takes my side. If I am annoyed with someone, so is she. If I am exhausted, she soothes me. She makes me calm when I am nervous. And I have always loved her. She's my buddy. I would not break the promise I had made her at Heathrow.

Together, we had the world to live for. We had a son.

My mind raced back to that afternoon when little Jesse was born. I remember so vividly how people had warned me against watching my wife give birth: 'It's so animalistic,' they said.

It was a strange word. Yet every ounce of me wanted to be alongside her. It was our time, the biggest moment of our lives, and I knew we should be together.

It felt as though the world was standing still. I sat there

and held her as she writhed in pain. In her weakness, she somehow looked so strong, so feminine, so pretty. Not animalistic. I was witnessing so much more than the birth of a child; I was also watching the birth of a woman. Shara.

This was my family, all I had ever dreamed of, and the two of them both looked so frail as they lay there wiped out, exhausted. We had always wanted to call him Jesse. Shara said it was after King David's father in the Bible. King David had been quite a player. He even killed a giant called Goliath when he was only a kid. I liked the name though because it reminded me of Uncle Jesse in *The Dukes of Hazzard* – in dungarees, with a big white dirty beard.

But Jesse also means 'God's gift'. That felt so right to us.

As I watched them both sleep in the hospital, I was overwhelmed by a feeling of protectiveness. I would do anything for them; I would even die for them. I had never felt that before.

And right here, in the pitch black of the storm, utterly drained, sodden and frightened, I felt as though I was being asked, 'Could I now live for them?'

'**Come on, Bear,** we'll get through this,' Mick shouted in my ear, thumping me on the back. 'We've been through worse than this and come out alive. We'll do it again. We'll just get through this ... then we'll never go anywhere again!' And he slapped me once more.

Then Mick rummaged through the sodden food sack and pulled out another can of Red Bull. He swigged at it, then lifted my visor. I opened my mouth and tilted my head back so he could pour the liquid caffeine down my throat. It went everywhere.

'Come on, Bear, you're doing great, keep going! We can do this, buddy. Just keep going.'

Adrenalin was still surging through our bodies as on and on, through the night, we kept shouting at each other, punching each other, encouraging each other. And somehow we kept going.

Ever since Mick and I were eight years old, playing around in the Isle of Wight, there has been a bond between us. That bond was built through school, strengthened on the cold south-east ridge of Everest when he so nearly died; and now it was being reforged in the icy, choppy waters of the frozen North Atlantic.

While we were fighting our own battles at the console, there were three other men on that boat, huddled in the sardine tin, desperately trying to cope with their own worlds of terror inside their heads.

Charlie recalls:

For ten hours or so, I was absolutely convinced I was going to die. It was not just a question of being afraid; rather, an utter conviction that I was near the end.

It was not a question of 'if'; it was rather a matter of 'when', because I really believed the boat was going to flip.

Strangely, I had thought about this kind of near-death experience in advance. Before the expedition, I would get fit by running in the streets around my home in Manchester and, whenever I needed to motivate myself to push harder, I just imagined I had been thrown into the freezing water and I was swimming to get back to the boat. That image was very clear in my mind, and now it seemed to be about to happen, for real.

In some ways, the thought of drowning had always sounded quite relaxing. That's a bit morbid, I know, but the idea of being in the water, floating away, being numb to everything, thinking how nice it was not to have to worry about the bank manager – I must admit that I found that whole concept to be quite relaxing.

However, when it came to the crunch, the human instinct for preservation did kick in. I remember deciding I really did want to do quite a lot of things before I die. I didn't want to die here and now. I was not going to give up lightly. I was quite surprised by this. I thought of my immediate family: that kicked in, and very strongly. It was practical, not emotional. It was my decision: I didn't want to die. I wanted to get through this.

For me, time passed quite quickly. If you tell someone to sit in the corner, the first ten minutes go slowly, but then the hours pass quickly; and I wasn't really aware of Bear and Mick although I could see them hitting each other and shouting at each other. When things had started getting serious, they had gone all military; they were both practical and impressive, but I was still terrified.

Huddled beside Charlie, almost indistinguishable in a cold, wet heap, Nige shook with the cold and with his thoughts.

He recalls:

I understood Bear's decision to helm through the night. He felt that was what he had to do in the circumstances, and, from my point of view, well, it meant I didn't have to move – it was a bit of a result.

My main concern, though, was that the boat would flip, and I was trying to plan how I would get out of the boat from where I was lying. I imagined it would happen very quickly, and my strategy was to get myself around the back of the boat, pull the life raft out from where it was stowed and then help any of the guys who might be caught inside. We would set off our EPIRB distress signals, and call for help on the VHF radio.

This was my plan, but, lying there in the sardine tin, I knew it would be futile. If that boat flipped, there was no doubt at all that there would have been five dead bodies in the ocean. That is for certain. We were more than 200 miles from land, and there was no sign of any other shipping in our vicinity.

I didn't know exactly what it would take to make the boat go over, but it felt as if it was going to go over at every wave. It was going upright, and slamming down; then we would get hit from the side. I have never wanted to be somewhere else so much. I'm not religious, but I did find myself asking for someone to help us.

I prayed. We all prayed. We were praying for our lives.

And, somehow, we kept the boat upright.

Dawn seemed never to arrive. It was the blackest night I had ever seen. Mick and I would imagine the dawn ahead of us, to the east. We would then be convinced we could see it. But it was always an illusion; or worse, another wall of white water.

We knew that dawn would bring the light with it, and that would mean we would be able to read the seas once more.

Finally, though, the night sky began to brighten in the east. Together, shoulder to shoulder, Mick and I watched as dawn crept slowly over the distant horizon. The wind was just as strong, and the waves were just as menacing; we were still in danger, but we knew that our greatest enemy, the darkness, was disappearing before us.

My eyes settled on one of the laminated sayings stuck around the boat. It had been placed on the console just beside the photograph of Shara and Jesse and read, 'Each day ends so that a new beginning can be made.'

As the early morning of Friday, 8 August 2003 dawned over the Denmark Strait, it was indeed a new beginning.

I asked Mick to get all the guys up and huddle round. I wanted to encourage them. We could get through this now. There was hope. We had been through hell together, but I felt we were emerging out the other side.

So we cramped together, all of us freezing cold, the others squatting behind us on the edge of the sardine tin. I felt the cold chill of dawn on my face as I turned to them. It was 5.15 a.m. We were all exhausted and bedraggled, wearing full gear and helmets, squashed on this small boat in the midst of a still-heaving ocean.

'OK, guys,' I began, shouting again to make myself heard. 'First of all, I am sorry that I broke the rota. I found a way of handling the boat, using the bucket to control her, so I wanted to keep going rather than stop in the middle of the night and have to explain how we could each do this.

'I know it's been a tough and bloody cold night for

everyone, but we're going to get through this. It's daylight now. The sea has just lost its greatest ally – the darkness. There is no reason why we shouldn't make it out of this. We're going to reach Iceland.

'Only two things will stop us.

'The first is that we run out of fuel. But there is no need for this to happen. Andy has control of this, and we have enough to reach Iceland. But, Charlie, help him. Look out for him. Get him something to eat. Help him manage the fuel systems. Andy, we need all your skill and attention for these last few hundred miles.'

Andy nodded.

'The second is that we flip the boat. But I am telling you, we will not flip her if we concentrate and helm her correctly. We *will* flip if anyone loses concentration. Whoever is helming needs to be 120 per cent alert. There was margin for helming error before; that does not exist in this sea state.

'From now on, we go back to the rota. Everybody will helm for only half an hour at a time now, and we must help each other. We must all dig deeper than ever before. If we do this, we *will* reach Iceland before nightfall.'

Then I took a couple of minutes with everyone in turn, to show them how we could minimize the slamming by adjusting the position of the bucket over the jet. They all saw our defiant, plucky RIB respond, hugging the breaking waves as she punched through them.

Charlie later described my whole speech as 'almost Churchillian'. I'm not sure that's quite true, but I was just trying to keep everyone hanging on in there, just a little bit longer.

Mick and I were exhausted by now, and we collapsed into the sardine tin. Nige and Andy began to share the helming. Charlie had told me he didn't want to take the responsibility at this stage. I respected him for saying that. It was time for Andy and Nige to become the most important men on the boat, with our lives in their hands. And Charlie, as ever, kept their spirits up by feeding them chocolate and water.

Together, we had survived our longest night.

Back home in England, our friends and families were starting what would very soon become their longest day.

11. LOST AND FOUND

**Do not be terrified; do not be discouraged,
for the Lord your God will be with you,
wherever you go.**

Joshua 1:9

We had said we would call the base team at 8.30 a.m.

This was impossible.

As we had feared, the physical battering had taken its toll on our equipment, knocking out the compass, the radio and the SAT phone. The five of us had somehow survived the night of Force Eight gales, but, one by one, our carefully installed electronic systems had packed up and died.

By dawn, only the Simrad plotter and the Caterpillar engine were still in working order. And without the power to charge the SAT phone, we had no way of making these vital calls back to the UK. Our families, friends and our UK base would hear nothing, and there was little we could do.

The waves were still dangerous and wild, and the wind was still holding at gale strength; even in the daylight, when we could see the waves, we were fighting to survive.

Without precious electrical power, we had no way of telling if our tracking device was working.

It wasn't. We had dropped off the screen completely. Just like that.

It subsequently became clear we had lost power at 3.16 a.m.; that was the time when the tracker unit had stopped transmitting the signals, indicating our precise position and speed.

We knew that many people, up to 30,000 a day, and most importantly our friends and families, had been following our progress, live, through the website. They had grown accustomed to logging on and checking our latest position, as broadcast by the tracking unit every thirty minutes. At 3.16 that morning, the blips stopped and we effectively disappeared.

Back home, people were waking up and could see clearly that there was some kind of problem.

Shara recalls:

I had become obsessed with tracking Bear's position on the Internet. I was staying with my mother in the country, and she had become obsessed by it as well. So we got up at about quarter to eight on the Friday morning, and logged on as usual. But something was wrong. Their position had not been updated since 3 a.m. I thought that was a bit weird, but then there had been the odd little gap before, so I didn't panic.

I called Chloë, and she said not to worry. She told me Mick had called at two thirty in the morning, and had promised they would phone her again at eight thirty. She didn't say what Mick had told her about the storm. So I assumed all was OK. Chloë promised she would give me a call as soon as she heard from them.

I was busy getting Jesse ready because we were driving up to London for his eight-week check-up, but I noticed half past eight come and go with no call from Chloë. I didn't want to be a nuisance, but I was just beginning to get a bit concerned, so I called her at nine thirty. She told me they had still not called.

Chloë found herself in the midst of a nightmare. She was speaking to the families, assuring them everything was OK, explaining that we had been warned that the tracker unit might not function so far north; maybe that was all that was wrong. She was also trying to supply Captain Pennefather with the information he needed to work out what had happened to us. She was in at the deep end and was desperately worried.

Andy Billing was at his post on our barge, and he threw himself into sourcing relevant information, narrowing down the possibilities. He spoke to the team at MarineTrack, the manufacturers of our tracking system, and they posted a reassuring message on their website, explaining the system might be disrupted this far north. Chloë contacted Shaun White at Ocean Dynamics, seeking information about the electrical systems on the boat. He gave her the telephone number of the electrician at Mustang Marine who had actually fitted the systems, but he was away on holiday.

Meanwhile, we were continuing to make slow, steady progress in heavy seas, oblivious to the fact that back home, so many individuals were getting very nervous in an effort to track us down.

As soon as Captain Pennefather logged on to the Internet at 6 a.m. and saw our tracker had gone down he swung into action. This was his moment. He had always said that if we were in trouble he would drop everything and take over. He understood the sea and the procedures better than Chloë or Andy. And I always knew he would be there in the background – ready.

Willie recalls:

The analysis started at six in the morning, and it was crucial that we made the right calls. The Icelanders were only going to dispatch a rescuc team if we asked them, and if we agreed to pay for it. Right from the start of this long and demanding day, the ball was in our court.

My first thought was that the crew had not put out an EPIRB emergency call, so the chances were they were OK. I was not overly concerned, even when Bear didn't call at eight thirty, as he had promised. Although I did remember mentioning to the crew before they left that I reckoned if the boat was turned over in a storm, it would be pretty bloody hard to swim and set that EPIRB off, but all the same, I tried not to go down that road yet.

We discovered the voltage on their tracker had been slowing over a period of hours and that if they had lost their electrics, this would explain not only why the tracker unit was dead, but also why they were unable to make any calls on the SAT phone. By mid-morning, the people at Iridium told us the crew had tried to make a call at ten thirty, but no connection had been made.

Of course, we were dealing with probabilities. Anything could have happened out there, and the base team, specifically Chloë and Andy, did a tremendous job holding things together this end.

I had indeed tried to call, albeit a bit later than scheduled, but conditions were not very conducive to phone calls in that storm. We had gone through the procedure of slowing the boat, and then I had crawled into the cubbyhole again and unwrapped the receiver with wet, shaking hands. I had tried and tried, but the connection never happened. I felt desperate. I tried again, to no avail.

I never found out why it failed. But I had no choice but to give up. All we could do was keep going and pray.

Friday, 8 August was unfolding as the hottest day of the year in London, with temperatures touching over 100°F. Out in the Denmark Strait, it was freezing. The high was sitting comfortably over the UK and it wasn't shifting. This was resulting in very deep depressions and low pressures up where we were, 1,000 miles north. We were shivering and wet. The sea was still a confused mess of white horses, hitting us from every angle, but Andy and Nige were doing an amazing job at the helm, keeping the boat in the right direction, withstanding the towers of freezing water that collapsed over the boat every now and then.

Everyone was emotionally and physically exhausted, but we were ploughing on, occasionally now boosting our speed to 14 or 15 knots, but then dropping again to 8 or 9.

We didn't speak much, but I felt that the night's terror had eased. We knew deep down that if we kept our heads, we would be able to reach Iceland in safety.

Unfortunately, back in the UK, there was still no evidence to help Shara and everyone else reach that same conclusion. She fought her way through the traffic coming up to London, but with Jesse hot, uncomfortable and frequently crying in the back of the car, she was starting to feel the strain of uncertainty. She couldn't even begin to contemplate the worst.

Shara recalls:

I arrived at the barge just before eleven, and found Andy Billing there. The telephone rang, and I just took the call because I was standing nearest the phone. It was a man called Howard, from MarineTrack. He asked for Chloë; I said it was Bear's wife speaking. He explained that the battery had probably failed. He couldn't tell me why, but it was pretty obvious, even to me. Batteries go wrong when they get wet. But I knew that their batteries were designed specially for the boat. So what had happened? I didn't even want to think about a capsize in those seas.

I just carried on, but was getting in more and more of a state. It was such a hot day, and I hadn't really eaten. I took Jesse to the doctor and the check-up didn't go particularly well – they told me there was something dodgy with his hip. It was the final straw. I burst into tears. I sat in my car like this, crying in the rush-hour traffic all the way back to my mum's.

There was still no news when I got to my mother's house. I sat outside in tears. I called Chloë and said something must have gone wrong because Bear had said he would call, and if Bear says he will call, then he always calls. My legs were shaking under me.

Then my mum started crying, and I asked her, 'Why are you crying?' Then I cried even more.

Willie called to ask if I had phoned Sally, Bear's mother. I said I hadn't because they were all having their holiday on the Isle of Wight and I didn't want to ruin it; at least not until we had firm news, either way. I was just petrified – petrified that something really bad had happened.

As that long day wore on, the base team worked hard to keep our families as calm and reassured as possible under the circumstances. They worked out what they would say, making sure they got their facts right and synchronized.

Chloë, Andy and Willie agreed on the following: 1) Say the EPIRB had not gone off, suggesting there had not been any disaster; 2) Say the electronics had probably failed; 3) Point out that, although the tracker had failed at 0300, we had tried to make a satellite phone call at 1030, so at least at that time we were upright. 4) Stress that these conditions were manageable for any rescue services that might be employed.

One thing worried Willie. He had quietly done some research of his own with the Naval Weather Centre. The conditions at the time the systems went down, they told him, were gale force. That was all he needed, and he thanked them. He didn't even want to imagine what we were dealing with out there. He had been a Royal Naval officer for thirty-four years. He knew what the sea could do.

Meanwhile, we were ploughing on. Progress was slow, but progress was progress. However, I was starting to worry about Nige. He was looking sluggish and exhausted.

Nige had exceeded all my expectations of him since the start of the expedition. He had never experienced anything remotely like this before, but had never once grumbled or made a fuss. He had quietly got on with it and had been incredibly strong. Nige, to me, is the typically understated, uncomplaining, brave British hero. The kind that would have been on Arctic patrols during the war, dressed in a duffel coat on the bridge of some small naval vessel, for months on end, seeking no recognition, just doing his job . . . a genuine, quiet, funny, tough Brit.

At the end of the leg from St Mary's to Greenland, Nige had been absolutely exhausted and, just like the rest of us, he really needed that rest, which the appearance of the weather window then proceeded to deny him.

As a result, when we started out from Greenland, his boots were still damp and his body ached. He didn't moan, because that is not his nature; he suffered the discomfort in silence.

'Nige, how you doing, buddy?' I said, prodding his shoulders.

He stirred and murmured he was fine.

I lay with him for a while, sometimes holding him, just being close. We were struggling in these relentlessly massive, heaving seas, and the wind was still freezing. But by going from minute to minute, hour after hour, through what amounted to the most terrifying period of any of our lives, we had survived together. We were not safe yet, but we were no more than 120 miles from Iceland.

Nige recalls:

Feeling cold was one thing but I was beginning to hallucinate as well. I was dozing in and out of sleep, and having really powerful, vivid dreams. At one point, my parents were beside me. At another time, in the height of the storm during the night, I had seen the most bizarre image: I could very clearly see an old man sitting on the side of the boat. He was in his seventies, wearing a yellow jersey and beige trousers, and he looked curiously like

Bob Hope! He seemed to have come down a rope ladder and, even though it was raining, he was completely dry.

'Do you want to come with me?' the old man asked.

'No. I don't think so,' I replied.

Then he smiled and disappeared. I wasn't sure whether it was an angel or whether it really was Bob Hope! It was odd, but it was OK. I wasn't concerned after this.

I just wanted to be warm and dry.

Looking back, I am certain that at critical times, when we needed it most, a presence, a guardian angel, was looking over us. I think we all felt it that night, and it was comforting. Maybe there is much more going on out there, around us, than we realize. I hope so.

Huddled close to Nige, I reached out for the Dictaphone. My hands were still shaking, and my skin had turned completely white, as if it had been submerged in a bath for three days – which I guess we all had.

Nothing was easy, even turning the Dictaphone on with shaky fingers. Time seemed to be passing so slowly. All I wanted was for this leg to be over, to reach Iceland, phone home and tell Shara all was OK. I had not spoken to her since Tuesday night, and this was almost Friday night. I knew she would be getting desperate, with no contact for so long.

Every word was an effort, as I spoke slowly and deliberately:

My God, this has been intense. We have been through so much together. Everyone is tired, and nothing works. The SAT phone and radio are dead. We have been through hell, and are coming out the other side. I think it was Churchill who said: 'When you go through hell . . . keep walking.'

That's what these guys have done. I'm so proud of them. They're just normal guys, but they have been put in these terrible conditions, and they have come through with real courage. They are not professional explorers or adventurers. They have normal jobs, and will go back to them and no one will have any idea of what they have been through. 'Good summer, Nige?' they'll probably ask him back at work! But these guys have been bloody brilliant. Quiet, brave, terrified, yet even cheerful . . . in short, just bloody brilliant.

I turned back to Nige. He had opened his eyes and was looking a bit better.

'Nige, you're not getting too cold, are you?' I shouted from behind my visor, above the roar of the engine. 'Can you move your fingers and toes all right?'

'Not really,' he replied. 'My toes have been numb since the Labrador.'

This wasn't good. The sardine tin was not the best place to hold a detailed medical conversation, but it transpired that Nige had experienced no feeling in his fingers or toes since the first storm, on our way over to Greenland. He had had no time to recover in Nanortalik, and his condition was deteriorating.

'Bear, what do you think is wrong?' he got around to asking me a few days later.

'It sounds like you've got frostnip,' I replied. 'It's not as bad as frostbite, but it's still pretty horrible.'

'Oh,' said Nige, 'and how long does it usually take to get better?'

'Well,' I replied, pausing because I knew this was going to be a bad one, 'usually for ever. It rarely gets much better.'

'Ah, thanks, buddy,' Nige replied, smiling. 'Great bloody bedside manner you've got.'

Typically, Nige now reflects and says he doesn't mind too much if he regains all the feeling in his toes or not. He is not in pain and, as he points out wryly, at least he will always have something to remember the Labrador Sea by.

I always remember someone once telling me that high mountains and big oceans often leave us with something to remember them by. Maybe this was the Labrador's legacy.

Back in the UK, Captain Pennefather knew that darkness was barely three hours away for us. He was drawing nearer and nearer to the moment when he would have to decide whether or not to dispatch the rescue services to hunt for our RIB.

There was still no news from us; the day seemed to be drawing on for ever, and all our families were now extremely concerned. Except the Grylls, because nobody wanted to ruin their holiday in the Isle of Wight! Until there was news, everyone would keep quiet.

In fact, the first that my mother heard about something being wrong was via a news placard outside the local news-agent. It was written in badly spelt English, and the headline simply read: 'Artic [sic] heroes in terror storm.' Whoever wrote it must have seen it on the newswire from one of the agencies keeping track of us, live.

My poor mum, who ever since Dad passed away always came back to the Isle of Wight for her summers, to relax, was back in the deep end. She couldn't believe that once again her son was in such trouble. Her sky had just turned black, and she rushed back to the house to find Lara, my sister, for some support.

Mick's parents also happened to be in the Isle of Wight at the same time, and news now began filtering through to everyone very fast. They were frantic, and all getting desperate for more news. The bright summer day was becoming less rosy by the minute.

However, the judgement call still rested firmly in the lap of Captain Pennefather, now on his mobile, on his boat in the hot Solent.

Willie recalls:

Chloë and Andy had been in contact with the Icelandic coastguard, requesting information on any search-and-rescue vessels available in the area, both sea and air. By mid-afternoon, the coastguard said they would send out a rescue team, but hinted where the financial costs would fall. It would be on us. Decision time, they suggested, was by 1900 hrs. This would give them time to reach the boat's last known position and return by nightfall.

I felt they were being too hasty though. The seven o'clock deadline was based on sending the team in a helicopter, but I felt it would be equally effective, and cheaper, to send a fixed-wing aircraft. On top of this, they would be able to cover a much greater search area in less time.

We were continually assessing the balance of probabilities throughout the day, and were greatly helped by the staff at the Fleet Weather Centre, who supplied up-to-date forecasts of the wind speed and direction, the wave heights and the currents, all of which enabled us to make a full analysis.

In the end, taking everything into account, we agreed to hold off until just before seven thirty in the evening. If there was still no news, we would send out a fixed-wing aircraft.

For this we would have to bear the financial costs.

When this news reached Mick's parents on their mobile, they were shopping in Tesco's. They were told the cost, and Mick's mother, Sally, replied plainly: 'Whatever it takes; we'll remortgage the house. This is our son's life.'

Chloë and Andy Billing remained together at the barge, supporting each other throughout the day.

Chloë recalls:

It was a really surreal time for us. We were sitting in the home of this crazy adventurer surrounded by his family photographs, all these images of smiling happy times, and all I could imagine was Bear and the crew in real trouble on those Arctic seas. We had to do everything possible to bring them home safely. But, in reality, we could do so little.

Shara recalls:

By half past six in the evening, I was in a terrible state. A friend rang and asked how everything was going, and I replied: 'It's not looking that great, actually.' I was panicking. I had these images of Bear's body floating around in the ocean, bobbing away, face down, and I began wondering how Jesse and I were going to cope without him. My imagination was racing out of control.

Then I spoke to my sister and almost convinced myself that Bear would never be coming back. I was in shock really.

I had to do something, so I phoned Willie and said he had to send out the rescue plane immediately. I said I knew that he and Chloë had Bear's best interests at heart, but they were not attached to him like I was. I was being a bit bossy, but we needed to know what had happened. I just felt that a delay could be fatal.

Out on the ocean it was early evening, and Andy and I were staring hard at the plotter. It clearly said we were just thirty-six nautical miles from Iceland. Together, we raised our eyes and stared straight ahead into a grey gloom of indistinguishable sea, spray and cloud, and we saw nothing.

'This is strange,' Andy said. 'We were able to see Greenland from sixty miles away. Where is this place?'

Andy rechecked the screen, then looked ahead once more.

'Is there any way the instruments could be wrong?' I asked.

'I don't think so,' he replied.

'This is so odd.'

Maybe the reading was wrong. Maybe something had gone wrong when we lost power. Maybe we had to recalibrate the GPS plotter after a power loss. My head was racing. I was exhausted and emotional, and I just wanted this struggle to have been worthwhile. I didn't want to have gone through all this and then, at the end, find we were in the wrong part of this vast ocean, because of an electronics error. I wasn't sure we could cope with another crisis.

Where was Iceland?

It was a grey, overcast evening, and it was drizzling persistently, but it wasn't foggy and the visibility wasn't too bad. It was just murky. We really should be able to see something as big as Iceland. We all stared at the plotter, and held our breath as the miles ticked away. It was strangely surreal.

We carried on through the rain, the *Arnold and Son Explorer* bounding forward now through the decreasing swell. We were all up, gazing ahead, straining our eyes, searching for the first sight of land.

Charlie asked, 'What does the plotter say now?'

'Twelve miles,' Andy replied.

We still saw nothing. We were all beginning to believe we had missed Iceland.

Nige was back in the sardine tin and he wasn't looking good. I glanced round at him. He just looked cold and wet and gaunt.

'We're pretty bloody close now, Nige,' I leaned over and told him. He smiled and pulled the sodden tarpaulin up to his waist, as if it was a duvet, not a soaking wet bit of thin material. He curled in tight, not really dozing, just existing. I moved across and pulled the tarpaulin higher – not that it made much difference.

But where was Iceland?

Slowly something appeared, dark and defined on the horizon. Nobody said anything. We weren't sure. A minute or so passed. This something looked vast and bleak. It was land. It was Iceland, and the lee of the Reykjavik Peninsula.

I suddenly felt an incredible surge of elation. We had all been through so much, and we had survived.

Together.

I grabbed Andy's shoulders and hugged him. Through these last few day, when all of us had really started to feel the effects of no sleep, he had emerged as a quiet, brave, true professional. I knew it had been worth keeping Andy's strength for the last quarter of this ordeal. We had needed him.

Andy recalls:

It had been a very long, hard crossing. To be honest, my real worry was the effect that the constant slamming of the waves would have on the material state of the boat. Any mechanical failure in these conditions would have been very serious, if not fatal.

We were very small against the vastness of the ocean all around us. It is very humbling; but the strong sense of teamwork gave me strength when I needed it. We were looking out for each other and focused on exactly the same goal – saving our arses!

It's hard to describe the feeling of relief when Iceland came into view but it meant that for the first time in days, I could stop listening to the tone of the engine and transmission with a critical ear. Constantly listening and desperately trying to detect any sign of problems had been both draining and at times very worrying.

It was my job to keep the engine going and, with a bit of luck, the bottom line was that Iceland was now just ahead.

Time was moving on back in the UK, and Captain Penne-father was on tenterhooks.

Willie recalls:

Soon after seven o'clock, I decided to call the coastguard in Iceland myself. I wanted to ask him if he was able to see a small yellow boat at all from their observation point. I thought he would be able to see fifteen miles out to sea.

He replied he couldn't see much. He said there was low cloud and steady drizzle, and visibility was poor. I had not had that information before, and that was enough for me.

I cracked. I decided that, if the pilots of a fixed-wing aircraft were going to have a chance of finding them in those conditions, they would need every minute of daylight they could get.

The boys had been tired, emotional, and frightened, and that had been when Chloë last spoke to them on the telephone sixteen hours before. I could only imagine what they were like now. I decided we had to send out the search plane. At the very least, the boys needed to know we were there, monitoring their position; on top of this, the families were desperate to know their husbands, sons and brothers were safe.

This longest day was reaching a dramatic conclusion.

19.26: At an airfield in Reykjavik, a fixed-wing aircraft is wheeled out of its hangar and prepares to fly out towards a precise position in the Denmark Strait, the position broadcast by our tracker unit at 0316 hrs that Friday morning, the very last positional broadcast before power failed. The pilots have been told to search for five British men, who are hopefully still aboard a small, open, yellow rigid inflatable boat.

19.28: Bear is sitting up in the bow of the boat, they are now only three miles from the west coast of Iceland. The SAT phone still has no power. Nige has been looking at his mobile phone, waiting to come within range of an Icelandic network, to get a signal. It eventually happens. He shouts to Bear and hands him the phone, still in its watertight pouch.

Bear scrolls down to the name 'Chloë Boyes' in the menu, and clicks the call button.

19.29: Chloë and Andy Billing are sitting at the kitchen table on the barge, relieved that at last a decision has been made. The rescue aircraft will be on its way anytime now. They wait and hope that this stomach-churning uncertainty will soon be resolved.

Suddenly, Chloë's mobile starts to ring. She looks down and sees the name 'Nigel Thompson' flashing on the screen, and all of a sudden she feels as though her heart has thudded against the inside of her ribcage.

'Hi, Chloë, it's Bear. I've got reception on Nige's mobile.'

'Where are you?'

'About fifteen minutes from the coast of Iceland.'

19.30: Andy phones the Icelandic coastguard and tells them to call off the fixed-wing aircraft. The message is relayed to the pilots, and they taxi back to the hangar, maybe relieved, probably irritated by the false alarm. They were on the tarmac, waiting for clearance to take off. Their flight was aborted with seconds to spare.

19.31: At her mother's house in the country, Shara is talking to her sister on the mobile. Desperate. The house phone rings, and her mother takes the call.

'They're fine, Shara,' she screams down the corridor. 'They're safe.'

Mother and daughter embrace, still in tears, but no longer tears of fear. Tears of relief.

It was almost 7.50 p.m. when we eventually pulled into the main harbour of Reykjavik. There wasn't even a ripple on the water now, just the pitter-patter of lightly falling rain. It was gloomy and the light was fading.

A lone fisherman emerged on the deck of a big icebreaker moored in the harbour. He waved nonchalantly. He hadn't any idea where we had just come from, or what we had been through. He carried on with his work, casually smoking. We idled on past. We couldn't quite believe we were finally here, alive.

I knew the Sir Ranulph Fiennes quote would still be wedged on the mirror in our bedroom back home. 'Them that stick it out, is them that win.' It was true. The only difference was that we had had no bloody choice but to stick it out. On this boat, there had been nowhere for us to hide.

I thought of home. I missed our cosy bedroom.

As we pulled alongside the wooden jetty in the marina part of the harbour, we began to set about the routine of tying up. Everyone was exhausted. Nobody was there to meet us because nobody had known where we were.

As Nige began to unpack some of the kit, he turned to me, smiling, and said, 'So guess which of our friends would have had the biggest fit if they had been out in the boat with us for five minutes last night?' Once again, he was chuckling to himself.

I thought for about one second only and then, in unison, we both looked at each other and said, 'Caroline and Shara.'

Shara's best friend, Caroline, loved sailing, but only with a gin and tonic in hand and a rather fit man in tight white trousers close by. The pair of them would have had the fireball of all fireballs in this boat all right. We laughed at the thought.

Moored alongside that quay in Reykjavik, our relief was written all over us. The spectacle of five men – dressed like yellow Michelin men, all of us pale, wrinkly and drained, clambering up on to the dock and crouching to kiss a jetty that stank of diesel and dead fish – was magical. We had done it.

But we had taken it to the wire.

Willie recalls:

I was mightily relieved they were safe, and also that the fixed-wing aircraft had been recalled before it took off to search for them. And I could now stop fingering Mick's American Express card, which was to be used as a guarantee for the flight!

Mick had proved himself almost unstoppable, but that bill, I suspect, would have wiped the smile off his stubbly face. He grabbed me warmly on the quay at Reykjavik. We had no idea of the drama that had unfolded at home, but we were on land at last. That was all that mattered.

The ice and the unpredictable Arctic seas were behind us. From here we would be heading down into northern European waters; we were no longer a million miles from home.

12. NO MORE HEROICS

Chance favours only those who know how to court her.

Hannibal

Sleep came easily in Iceland. We were all exhausted, in mind, body and spirit. Ever since we had arrived, the driving rain and wind had not relented, and we were just so relieved to be off the sea.

We went out that first night around midnight and found the finest steak-house in the city, where we drank cocktails without a thought of the expense. No one cared. We were safe, we were warm and we were together.

I had phoned Shara after we checked into the hotel and I was missing her like crazy now. As we ate and drank, I remember longing for her to be with us: celebrating, without a care in the world. I can't even remember what time we eventually got back to the hotel.

I would have given anything to have had Shara there that night, to put my arms around and sleep beside her – no offence to Nige, with whom I was sharing a room, but by now I had spent too many nights with him, curled up spooning in what had started to feel like a metal coffin on the ocean.

'The coastguards were pretty trigger-happy, don't you reckon?' Mick said, sitting around at breakfast the next morning. 'If we'd arrived ten minutes later, their plane would have been in the air and we would have had a bill for thousands.'

He was talking to himself as much as anyone. 'Then again, if you want anyone to be trigger-happy, it is them, I suppose.' That was true. He carried on eating his cereal.

The realities of what had been going on back home the previous long day, when we were out of contact for so long, were just starting to sink in. I felt terrible, and a bit guilty. But we had been lucky all round: lucky to have survived that storm and lucky that the rescue had been called off in time.

We had been let off the hook twice, once in the Labrador Sea and once off Iceland, and now we had to make certain we were safe. I was determined that we would not take any more risks on the two legs that remained, the first from Iceland to the Faroe Islands, and then from the Faroe Islands to the northern tip of Scotland.

Nobody wanted any more heroics.

We had slipped through the net twice, and we had been mightily humbled.

That day, as the white, flaky skin on my fingers was slowly beginning to regain a more familiar colour and texture, I slipped away to my hotel room, and spoke into my Dictaphone . . .

The others are still talking downstairs, and we have been in Iceland for nearly twenty-four hours now. We're slowly becoming human again. We're starting to hear other things apart from the diesel engine, and we all had these very vivid dreams last night. It's almost as if each of us is processing everything in our minds: the shock of what we experienced out there and the fact that we all felt a very real and genuine fear of dying.

I really want this to be over now. There is a kind of urge inside of me – to complete this properly, safely. I just want to get home. I don't want to put my crew through that kind of terror ever again. I don't want to look at Charlie, sitting in the deck-chair, his face literally white with fear, as if the spirit had been sucked out of him. I don't want to see the expression that spread across Nigc's face when he saw the barometer plunge so dramatically. I don't want to have to find the reserves I somehow found when Mick and I helmed through the night.

It has been too intense and too exhausting.

We need a rest now and, when our minds are clear, we can plan these last two legs. One thing is certain: I'm not going out in bad weather or a head sea. I'm not gambling again. I want good weather and a following sea and, if we have to wait to get it, then so be it.

Everyone feels the same. Unless it is 100 per cent clear, wild horses would not get us back on that boat.

Once again, we were touched by the hospitality and generosity of the local people. Even people we met in the bars seemed to have been following our progress on the Icelandic TV news bulletins. Charlie was eager for conversation and, as he pointed out eleven times in one hour, 'My God, these Icelandic women are beautiful.' These words were invariably followed by: 'Excuse me? Hello … yes, I was the cameraman on board that boat, you know.' He was in heaven.

This paradise was slightly clouded though by the fact that our days in Iceland coincided with the Gay Pride Festival in town. The sight of us five, fresh off the boat, laughing, hugging and joking our way through the beers did rather limit the guys' chances with the ladies. As far as they were concerned we were quite plainly just five more Icelandic queens.

During our stay in Iceland, one man was more hospitable and generous than anyone before: a local boating enthusiast called Bogi Baldursson. He had not only read the news pieces but had even contacted our base in the UK and offered to help – with anything. Bogi took three days off work and virtually adopted us during our stay in Reykjavik.

'Bogi, we need help with this alternator.'

'No worries. A mate of my brother owns a big garage. I'll take you there.'

And he did.

Bogi also told us that we all looked terrible, white and exhausted. Thanks, Bogi, I thought. So he insisted that we should take a trip out to a natural springs spa, where Icelanders strip down to their undies and relax in the pure waters. Charlie remembered the calibre of the girls he had seen the night before and didn't need much encouragement to come along. But things looked less promising in that department when we were joined by a friend of Bogi's called Omar, who was physically vast and evidently well built in all areas. And it was with him that we would be sharing the spring. Ah.

On the drive back to Reykjavik, we were all talking.

'Bogi, some of our kit is still wet. The hotel staff are going nuts with it all everywhere. Do you know somewhere where we can get it dry?' I asked.

'Sure,' he replied. 'Omar can do it. He has a very big facility.'

I prodded Nige in the ribs, and neither of us could breathe for the next half hour.

Back at the hotel, we got serious again and started to address the real issue of getting the weather forecast right for the next leg: another 500 nautical miles through to the Faroe Islands. Our task was made easier by the fact that we would now be passing through comprehensively charted waters, where the availability of data meant the forecast was more accurate than the 'guestimates' we had been relying on in the Denmark Strait.

The guys at the Fleet Weather Centre were correct when they said Force Seven winds were running in this area at the moment. We could sit and watch the rain and wind beating at the windows. They also said it was because the high-pressure system was still settled over Britain, pushing more of these lows up to the north. They suggested conditions should improve later in the week and that, all going well, we would be able to get on our way by then.

Mick and I visited the Icelandic weather centre just outside of the city, and came back with the same picture of bad conditions at the moment, improving on Wednesday or Thursday.

Our third source of information to confirm this forecast was Mike Town; almost down to the last detail, he produced the same predictions as the two fully equipped, professional weather centres. If only the data from the previous two legs had been as consistent as now, but it had been almost impossible to predict the conditions on remote, distant oceans with 100 per cent accuracy. We had always known this was one of the major risks involved in the expedition, but Mike had done a professional and dedicated job for us. He had always given his assessment of the weather patterns diligently and cautiously. We had been very lucky to have him there for us, day and night.

'Right, guys,' I told the crew, relieved that for once I was not having to tell them we would be leaving at 5 a.m. the following day, 'it looks as if we have until Wednesday to get the boat right.' Each of them looked as though I had just placed a golden nugget in their hands.

The *Arnold and Son Explorer* was a mess: the electrics were down, there was water and diesel all over the place, and she looked as if squatters had been camping in her for a month.

Charlie and Nige set about the minor repairs, and Andy spent almost an entire day trying to resolve the electrical problem. His assessment was that when we had crashed down off a huge wave, the batteries had been thrown upwards and shorted on the aluminium. In due course, the boat-builders would hardly believe this – they had never known the actual stern of the boat to be lifted and thrown so violently by a wave as to catapult the batteries loose from their housing, but then not many of them had seen what happens to an RIB in a storm in the Denmark Strait. The fact that the batteries had been so dramatically dislodged offered a fair indication of just what the seas had thrown at us out there.

The result of this 'short' was that we had lost our entire 12V system, bringing down all communications. It could so easily have affected the engine management system as well, but in this respect, yet again, we had been lucky; it was as simple as that.

The more we examined the boat, the more we realized just how fortunate we had been. It was the strange sixth element of luck that no one can ever quite put a finger on – but we all knew it had played a huge part in what had happened so far.

With the help of Bogi and his mates, who were kind enough to open their garage out of hours and make sure all our batteries were fully charged, we got the electrical system up and running again. By dusk, the guys were still sorting out the kit and finishing some final minor repairs around the lockers and console but the RIB was slowly starting to look herself again.

While we were down on the quay, we met a round-the-world sailor, a Frenchman called Frédéric, who had just pulled into port from Scandinavia. He was preparing to cross to Greenland and was awaiting a break in the weather.

'What's it like out there?' he asked nervously.

'Oh, it can be a little bumpy at times,' Mick replied nonchalantly. Charlie shook his head, smiling.

We also met some of the crew of a large ice-going maritime research ship, the *Oreanos*, which had just made the same crossing from Greenland as we had, but about twenty-four hours later. They also said conditions had been horrendous, and told how the waves had been coming over their bridge. I looked up at their bridge: it was 35 feet up from the water.

I glanced across at Mick, and he glanced back at me. We had been let through by the skin of our teeth this time, but the sea doesn't always let you win.

We were looking forward now, though: we were going home. The unsettled weather had moved on, and after double-checking the forecast we agreed we would leave early on Wednesday morning.

Our last evening in Reykjavik was spent in the company of Ulruga Olassi, a mountaineer who had become the first Icelander to reach the summit of Everest three years before. He had read about our expedition and asked if he could come and have a look around the boat. In his late thirties, he was smart and kind-faced, and he obviously understood what we had been through. Both Everest and the big oceans make similar demands: they require heart, humility and a bit of luck to survive.

'Tell me,' he asked, 'why did you decide to make the crossing from Canada to Scotland? Isn't this against the current? It would have been easier the other way round.'

I explained that to be heading home, with each wave and each mouthful of seawater, was what really counted. I had always wanted us to be homeward bound.

He smiled, and understood.

To err on the side of caution, we had decided to include a refuelling stopover at the Vestmann Islands en route to the Faroes. These isolated patches of land out in the sea, some 80 miles from Reykjavik, would give us another opportunity to check the latest weather forecast, make sure we were clear to go, and ensure we completed this final stretch without any drama.

I didn't want any mistakes at this late stage. The highest mountains in the world are strewn with bodies of climbers who reach the summit but die on the descent, and so many war memorials list the names of soldiers who survived the main war only to die in the last few skirmishes.

We had to see this through. Properly.

Just before we left Reykjavik that final morning, I was tracked down on my mobile by Alex Rayner, our PR man, and minutes later, outside the hotel lobby, I was on the phone doing a live radio piece back to the BBC. In the interview, I was saying we hoped the weather would at last be kind to us.

'Yes ... we can hear the Arctic winds howling behind you,' the presenter said dramatically. He seemed a little surprised when I explained that the noise he heard was actually Reykjavik rush-hour traffic on the main road behind me. It wasn't quite the blast of icy winds he had hoped for!

Our last act in Iceland was to take Bogi and his young son, also, by good coincidence, named Bear, out on the boat for a quick spin around the harbour. This was to say thank you, and they both loved it. We would soon meet Bogi again, when he made a surprise visit to London to attend our homecoming party at St Katharine Docks. All the team's faces lit up when they saw him again. He had become a friend, and Nige couldn't resist asking how 'Omar's big facility' was doing. Bogi laughed.

Throughout the expedition, every day of departure had brought its own sense of tension, and the time for leaving Iceland was no different. The guys were quieter, and there were fewer jokes as we all focused our minds on getting everything ready. Now and then, someone would look up at the sky, just a little nervously, as if checking the weather one last time.

Part foreboding at what lay ahead, part excitement, part relief that we would soon be moving ever nearer home – these times were always special. There was a special atmosphere and, to be honest, they were almost the moments I loved the most. Just the team, all together, at work.

It was a few minutes after seven o'clock on a calm morning when we slipped our mooring in the Icelandic capital's harbour.

Light on fuel, because the Vestmann Islands were so nearby, we began to power through the gentle seas at 21 knots, which was a welcome change from the 12 knots we usually managed when we were heavy with diesel at the start of a new leg.

I reached for the Dictaphone, and spoke . . .

Everything is rock 'n' roll now. The boat is working well, and everything seems more waterproof in the lockers. Little things, like the problem of the drinking water that used to fizz out of the jerry cans inside the cubbyhole with all the slamming, have been solved. We are learning and getting better all the time.

I'm just praying this weather holds. I have such a strong memory of leaving Prince Christiansen Sound, and how beautiful and calm the sea was for twelve hours, and how it all turned so dramatically different after that. And it happened so fast. I'm a bit tentative about the 'good forecast' now and I sense the same hesitation in everyone else.

We're passing huge cliffs around southern Iceland, and we have a steady following sea. This is so good. I hope it stays like this. We're getting there. Come on!

Arriving in the Vestmann Islands, we found a stunning natural harbour surrounded by deep, lush, green grass that looked as if it had been glued to the dramatic, sheer cliffs. There was the usual stench of fish and there was an array of large fishing boats along the jetty. These boats were all tough and hardy, and proud, and they looked as though they were used to working in these ruthless and demanding northerly seas.

We refuelled as planned, while Mick put a call through to the Fleet Weather Centre. He reported back to say they had given us the all clear and were predicting westerly winds; that meant that the wind would be blowing from almost directly behind us right the way through to the Faroes. It was ideal. We would push straight on.

As we skirted round the last few remaining islands, the ice-capped plateau of southern Iceland appeared on the port side: huge, majestic and cold. We were soon surging through the gentle swell, trying to relax and settle into the familiar rota once more. As Iceland slipped away behind us, we just lapped up the natural beauty all around.

A school of dolphins appeared in our wake, cheerfully playing in the waves, and all kinds of birds seemed to fly overhead, as if to satisfy their curiosity about what such a small yellow boat was doing out here in these seas. This was what we had waited 2,500 miles for, and each of us savoured every precious moment.

But we still felt cautious. We had been here before, and if we had learned anything from this ocean, it was that the sea must always be respected, never taken for granted, always feared.

The sea knows no rules. It is a law unto itself, and it moves at will. It's this incredible force that is always heaving beneath you. Sometimes it can be magnificent; sometimes it can be brutal. But either way, it doesn't care. It just is. And when you begin to think you understand it, and have it taped, that's the time when it rises up in defiance. Even when it is calm, as it was when we were surging on towards the Faroe Islands, you can still sense the huge, silent force beneath you, and you fear what that force can do.

As I sat there and stared across the vast grey ocean, I sensed a strange kind of paradox. As individuals, we spend a short time on this planet. We exist, and try to follow our dreams and live with meaning, but the sea is different. It is so much greater than us, timeless, unending, relentless, and it just churns on, always evolving. In many ways, this makes it the supreme arena. And yet, even as we experienced this huge ocean, with its capacity for rage and ruthlessness, even as we felt so vulnerable to its whims, I somehow felt a part of it as well.

Why is it that storms are so often followed by periods of intense calm and quiet? Is this just coincidence, or is this the living ocean speaking to us, feeding us a small part of its vibrant life force? Surely it is touching our souls and desires, ever drawing us in, testing us.

Our frail dreams and survival instincts are also part of this natural world. We are human, after all, born from nature. We may not always feel welcome, but we are a part of the ocean as well. We have a small place here. Maybe that's what God intended: that in these quiet moments we should understand we are not utterly insignificant, but are in fact special. We belong, and we each have a home in this vast corner called 'nature'.

Perched on the prow of the boat, alone with these thoughts, heading south-east, I had time to reflect and to feel. I realized then that maybe I have two homes: one back in England, with Shara and Jesse, where we are together, holding one another, warm and safe; and the other out here in this wilderness, feeling tiny among the elements, but living, and free. Maybe it is these two parts, these two homes, that make up the person I am.

All of a sudden I was brought back to the here and now by the sound of laughter from the console area. I could see Andy trying to teach Charlie magnetic variations in northern hemispherical navigation. Charlie was looking confused.

Andy had always been very correct in using maritime terms: 'for'ard' and 'aft', 'windward' and 'leeward', 'sheet' and 'knot'. But throughout the expedition, Charlie never got this.

'What's wrong with "forward", "back", "left" and "right" and "rope" and "mph"?' he would insist, and now he finally cracked.

'Let me teach you about boats, the Manchester way,' Charlie continued with a wry smile, and he started stomping around the boat, using Andy's fuel-marker pencil to scrawl 'front', 'back', 'left' and 'right' all over the appropriate tubes.

Andy was cringing with despair. It was very funny.

Conditions remained calm as night fell and, for the first time any of us could remember, we were able to sit back and enjoy the most stunning of sunsets, as inch by inch the bright orange glow was consumed by the distant crimson and cobalt blue horizon. We sat and watched, lost in our thoughts and also in our memories.

Even on the night watches we sat transfixed, mesmerized by the simple beauty of the night under clear northern skies.

We had always expected the nights to be much lighter than usual during the expedition, but we seemed to have been followed by heavy clouds and most nights had been pitch dark. Now it was clear and we gazed up at the shooting stars and the full moon and marvelled at the phosphorus under the RIB's bow. Charlie and I were on watch together from 1 a.m. to 2 a.m. and for the first time, this 'graveyard' shift was an hour of sheer pleasure.

As dawn broke, we emerged into a few gentle squalls of rain, which softly pebbled the surface of the flat sea. Mick and I lay in the sardine tin in the rain, chatting about army days and holidays, and what we were going to do when we got home. It was the best of times. Even the soft rain was a joy.

We were less than a mile from the Faroes when they finally materialized through the cloud. Rough landscapes of hills and craggy rocks were interspersed with lush green pastures all around and we soon passed a huge, natural cave, worn in the cliff face by the relentless battering of the sea. It was remarkable, large enough to enclose a decent-sized house. We moved inside and sat quietly, all alone, silenced by nature's creation.

By the time we pulled into the small port of Thorshavn, it was raining heavily. The harbour was surrounded by rows of small houses, most of which were grass-roofed. Some of them were perched precariously on the cliffs.

A lady from the local sailing club came bounding down to greet us.

'Welcome to the Faroes,' she declared. 'Chloë has just called from London.'

Right to the end, our base team were on the ball.

'We have arranged for you to use the sailing club as a base to rest. Please treat it as your home. I hope that it is going to be all right for you.'

It was perfect. We could hang out our kit, drink cups of tea, and doze on the floor.

We ate well in the local bar, made the necessary phone calls to the base team and the weather centre and, before long, the five of us were settling down for a few hours' sleep in the sailing club's small upstairs room.

Within moments of the light going out, Charlie was snoring.

'I'm not sure which is worse,' Nige muttered in the darkness, lying awake on the floor, 'Charlie's nostrils or the roar of a 450-horsepower Caterpillar engine.'

He had a point.

13. SAFE IN SCOTLAND

We are the Pilgrims, Master; we shall go
Always a little bit further; it may be
Beyond that last blue mountain barred with snow,
Across that angry or that glimmering sea.

Special Air Service regimental verse

It was strange. I had spent most of the past few weeks doing everything possible within my grasp to reach the final destination of this expedition safely, and yet, now that we were only 275 miles from the north coast of Scotland, I found myself feeling almost sad that the end was so near.

We woke just before 3 a.m. and I became aware that we were probably pulling on all our kit and dry-suits for the last time. I looked around. The crew were quiet.

'OK, guys, I need your concentration for twelve more hours,' I told everyone as we stood in the cold night air, preparing to slip our mooring on the quayside for the last time. 'Twelve more hours, that's all. Let's just keep this boat pointing due south, steer a good course and make sure we don't make any stupid mistakes. If we just stay focused and do what we do so well together, then we will reach Scotland.'

We all knew what needed to be done.

'One last effort,' said Mick quietly.

There was a relief in us all, waiting just on the other side of the door. We were so close to achieving our target. But there was also a sense of loss that the spirit that had carried us through so many dangerous situations could not last for ever.

Of course, the five of us would stay in touch and see one

another whenever we could, and we would regularly look back and laugh, and feel proud of what we had done; yet the reality was that as soon as we touched British soil, the precious magic we all felt so intensely would begin to disappear.

That is just how it is.

'I'd love to helm this first bit, if that's all right?' Charlie asked. The night was glorious, and he took the wheel.

There was scarcely a breath of wind on the water, and the moon was reflected on the still harbour water around us. We untied the ropes and quietly left the Faroes.

We had decided to leave at 3 a.m. because the early departure meant we would reach Scotland in daylight, and therefore would actually be able to see the end of our expedition. Which would be nice!

In fact, we had originally planned to leave even earlier but Force Six and Seven winds had been blowing through the area to our south and our meteorologist, Mike Town, suggested we should wait until they had passed. We hoped they now had. Still determined to minimize any risks, we waited until the hour he suggested.

The few flickering lights of Thorshavn, the small town in the Faroes, were soon receding into the distance. We were yet again leaving behind people who had been incredibly kind and generous. What was it about these maritime communities that always made their reception of us so warm? It had become such a feature of this expedition: arriving in isolated communities as total strangers, and leaving as friends.

While we had been refuelling the previous evening, people had approached the boat freely, chatting, many of them just wanting to touch the tubes and wish us well; and in Thorshavn, as in so many other remote places we had been, they had wished us 'calm seas and God's speed'.

But above everything, they all seemed to have time ... time for us, time for themselves, time just to be.

That is what I hunger for: space, the time just to sit and be. The freedom from the rush, the little moments, the ones that we so often overlook and miss, even forget exist.

In supposedly more developed parts of the world, we have so little patience. We want it all, and we want it now. We rush from one thing to the next. We have no time for what really matters, and our lives become a blur. How often do I struggle to remember what I did yesterday, let alone last week? That's terrible, really.

'So are you busy at the moment?' We hear it the whole time, as if to be busy is something we should strive for. A friendly everyday question, but it speaks volumes. I think we are all so busy that we lose touch with who we really are.

'The heart of a man is like deep water,' I once read. No wonder so many of us struggle with our identity. We are too busy to find it, too busy to listen to those deep waters.

Those men and women in Labrador who told us to stay in port had tried to warn us and protect us from the northerly winds we eventually ran into. But we had rushed ahead.

Perhaps I should have listened more.

On two occasions on the expedition, in St Mary's and then again in Nanortalik, we had rushed, and so nearly fallen.

We were powering ahead by the time dawn burst over the eastern horizon, reaching 22 knots in a following sea. It was just before 5 a.m. We were homeward bound and gradually starting to believe we would make it. I took the Dictaphone and carefully made my way to the foredeck...

It's all looking fine. The forecasters predicted a following sea and good conditions, and that's what we have got. High winds have passed through this area now and all that remains are the cresting, driving waves behind us – the remnants of that bad weather. And the boat feels alive. She has been amazing. She feels somehow stronger now, as if forged by the wild seas to our north, so far behind us. I don't want to leave her. She did everything we ever asked of her, and I can't stop remembering that night at the start of the Boat Show back in January, where on my own I stroked her hull and prayed we would come through this together.

And she has never faltered.

I'm sitting at the bow of the boat, on my own, and the sun is shining more strongly than at any other stage of the expedition. The sea is rolling with us, and the boat is eating it up.

The guys have been brilliant as well. I think it's very rare to ask four mates to risk their lives alongside you for no reward except the bonds you create together in the hard times. To see those same men come up with the sort of courage and quiet fortitude I saw in them during those two terrifying storms is special. They have truly impressed me. They have risked everything over the past few weeks, and they have all over-delivered, and proved themselves stronger than I reckon they ever knew. That's a good thing to discover.

I received a message last night saying that I have been asked to appear on David Frost's Sunday-morning programme this week, but, as I sit here now, that kind of thing seems a million miles away. To be honest, I would prefer to be here with these guys, away from the bright lights of that weird world.

Deep down, all of us are dying to see Scotland. It's all we ever talk about.

My hour at the helm followed soon afterwards, and for most of the time my eyes seemed to dart from the seas ahead to the dial that indicated the number of nautical miles remaining on the leg, and I was lucky enough to be watching the dial when it ticked down from 100 to 99 miles. Charlie took the helm after me, and he seemed to be making good progress when Nige leaned forward and stared intently at the small screen on the console. The small arrow indicated the direction in which we were moving, and it was pointing 180 degrees the wrong way.

'Charlie, where are you going?' Nige asked.

No reply.

'Scotland is that way,' Nige said, pointing at the stern behind him, laughing out loud.

Charlie quickly realized his error and swung the helm around. He had been away in his own world for a few minutes and had lost concentration.

'Did you leave something behind?' Nige teased.

'Yeah, those Icelandic girls,' Charlie replied, chuckling. 'I can't get them out of my head.'

We were so close to home that even travelling in the wrong direction only made us laugh. 'How far to go?' I asked.

'Sixty-one miles,' Nige replied. 'Sorry, sixty two now.' Charlie hit him.

An hour later, Mick was helming. Andy was asleep and Scotland was getting ever closer, but still remained out of sight. We should see it soon, I thought to myself.

Everyone else was quiet.

Then suddenly, as if from nowhere, I heard that terrible, fateful sound. I knew what was happening. The engine was dying, the revs were plummeting, the throttle was no longer responding to Mick's acceleration.

Within seconds, we were silent.

No, God, not this close, please no, I said to myself. Please.

Then I thought, no, it's all right. We'll be OK. It will be the fuel again. We can sort this. All we need to do is switch to another tank and get the engine going again. It should be easy. Shouldn't it?

Andy leaped into the engine bay and set to work.

Five minutes passed.

I glanced at Mick. He was beginning to look anxious. The process shouldn't take this long.

Eight minutes. Andy had switched the tanks over and had tried to reprime, but the engine wasn't responding.

We were still bobbing helplessly.

Ten minutes.

My mind was racing: How could we survive the Labrador Sea and cross the Denmark Strait in a storm, and then fail in this gentle following sea, just short of home? It must work. Come on.

Andy was working frantically. I said nothing.

Another turn of the key, still no splutter of life.

Twelve minutes.

Then, once more, a final turn of the key, a spark, a splutter, another splutter ... a roar, a fantastic surge of power. We had movement again.

'Just keeping you all on your toes.' Andy smiled.

We all were grinning, so relieved.

The miles started to fly by. Adrenalin was pulsing through us as we all gathered in the bows, with Nige helming, our eyes glued on the horizon. We couldn't quite comprehend that we were about to see the mountains of north Scotland. This moment had been so long in coming.

It was 2.20 p.m. when we finally spotted the distant purple outline of the mountains, dead ahead. We were still 33 miles from land, but the end was literally within sight.

This was the moment to phone Shara.

She had initially planned to travel north and meet us in Scotland, but moving Jesse when he was still so young and just getting settled seemed crazy. I had told her to stay at her mum's. It meant we would only have to wait a day longer to see each other again. In any case, I knew we would be so busy in Scotland, doing the press stuff and sorting out the boat. I was happy to wait another twenty-four hours and see them both in earnest at Gatwick airport. I had waited so long and travelled so far. I wanted our reunion to be perfect.

She answered on the second ring.

'We can see Scotland, my love,' I told her, struggling to hold my emotions, 'dead ahead, getting clearer as we speak. I can see Ben Loyal. You know, the mountain I dragged you up when we first met, and everyone else got vertigo. Remember? It's on our nose, straight ahead. I cannot wait to see you, my angel. I told you we would be OK, didn't I?'

I could hear the relief in her voice when she said gently, 'My God, this has been a bad one.'

I looked up at Ben Loyal ahead. It seemed to be watching us, willing us on. There was magic in the air.

The plan had always been to arrive in Scotland in this small estuary, near to the lodge belonging to an old friend of Shara's and mine.

Sam Sykes and his family lived in a small, remote part of Sutherland, on the north coast, at a place called Kinloch. Shara and I had met there, many years ago, at New Year. It was one of the best days I can remember. I had been staying up there with Sam, training and climbing. It was two months before the Everest expedition in 1998, and I had everything apart from girls on my mind.

I was climbing every day, pushing myself, preparing myself mentally and physically for the months ahead in the Himalayas. I was very solitary and focused, and probably a bit of a nightmare. Then this girl called Shara walked in, dressed in a tatty red coat, and life has never been the same.

Together, we made up silly dances, kissed in the woods and fell asleep on the sofa in our boots, with my big duffel coat over us. Kinloch would always be special to us both.

I had planned with Sam to have just a small band of family, friends and sponsors meet us 'unofficially' a few miles off Kinloch in his boat. We would then come in and spend a night at his lodge before heading back out the following morning and cruising along the coast to John O'Groats for the official homecoming.

To me, however, there was only ever going to be one real homecoming and that was our arrival here in Kinloch, with the five of us in the bows, staring ahead, gaze fixed, straining to see the outlying shadow of Rabbit Island at the mouth of the Kinloch estuary.

However, the plan wasn't quite going so smoothly at Sam's end. The two guys from Arnold and Son, Eric and Jean-Marie, were delayed in transit from Zurich to Inverness. Despite a mad dash in a small hired car that apparently resembled a scene from the film *Trains, Planes and Automobiles*, with these two smart Swiss businessmen racing like rally drivers along the narrow Scottish lanes, they couldn't reach this remote corner of Scotland in time to get aboard Sam's boat and meet us at sea.

So it was Chloë, Charlie's father, James Laing, Alex Rayner, Jamie Curtis, a cameraman, and Lorraine, Andy's girlfriend, who clambered aboard Sam's boat and ventured out, earnestly searching for us through the haze of rolling Scottish waves.

Linking up wasn't straightforward. For some time they couldn't see us, and we couldn't see them. Radio contact was intermittent and poor.

Eventually, Chloë spotted some spray on the horizon, and as we drew nearer, they saw what they hoped would be our small yellow boat on the horizon. Then radio contact became clearer and we heard Sam's voice over the intercom.

'I think we can see you,' he shouted excitedly.

The boat was dipping between the troughs of the waves, rolling in towards them. They waved frantically. We still couldn't see them. And then we could. A small blue dot to starboard. We came back on the radio and they heard our voice for the first time:

'This is the *Arnold and Son Explorer* to Sam – we have you in sight, we're coming home.'

We circled their boat, waving madly. Sam was going berserk, Chloë was shouting and Lorraine was crying. We had done it. We were almost there. Sam escorted us in towards a beautiful, sandy cove, and we drove the RIB up on to the beach. We killed the engine one last time, leaped ashore and hugged everyone, jumping up and down in the surf.

In the time it had taken for them to escort us in, Eric and Jean-Marie had finally arrived. Just in time. As they pulled up with a skid on the track above the beach, they saw the boat that their vision had made possible pull into the cove.

When I saw Eric, I ran across the beach to where he was standing. I just wanted to thank him for everything he had done to make this dream happen. However, as I went to hug him, and he squeezed me, my dry-suit released a stench of stale, unwashed body odour from my neck seal. It was horrendous, he told me later, laughing.

Through almost 3,000 miles on the ocean, it had been impossible to maintain any kind of personal hygiene in the RIB, even though, to his credit, Andy was meticulous in brushing his teeth every morning, wherever we were. For the most part, we just lived and slept and did everything in what we wore.

I hugged Eric again for good measure.

We then knotted several lengths of rope together so we could secure the RIB safely to the harbour wall, and began swigging from bottles of Mumm champagne. Eric toasted us, Alex toasted us, Andy kissed Lorraine (poor girl!), and the moment was perfect.

So, on this quiet Scottish beach, with just a handful of the most important people around us, we celebrated the safe return of our expedition. We had faced the frozen ocean, and we had survived. We were home and alive.

After a while, we drove up to Sam's house and threw our kit down in a heap. Then I wandered down to the small brook below his house, where Shara and I had so often swum together. The water was bubbling over the rocks into the pool. I stripped off, stood on the overhanging rock above the pool, and dived in. As I came up for air, I felt the emotion, the strain and the fear of the last two years wash off me. Literally. I couldn't help smiling. I had been so worried I would not deliver on my promise to Shara and return safely. But we had. I shook the water from my hair, took a deep breath, and went under once more.

While we had still been in the Faroes, during a telephone conversation Chloë had asked me if there was anything special we would like for dinner on our first night in Kinloch. There could only ever be one thing: roast beef with all the trimmings. And it was duly delivered.

We ate like kings – in fact, to be more specific, we probably ate like King Henry VIII, gnawing the finest beef off huge bones, laughing at the same old jokes and drinking far too much red wine. It was the best of meals – cosy, intimate and wild.

As we sat round that table in Scotland, I felt overwhelmed by pride at what we had achieved and enormous gratitude to be surrounded by such truly good people.

Everyone had their own private feelings on the expedition, drawing their own conclusions from what we had all experienced.

Charlie reflects:

Almost the first thing I said to my father when I saw him on the beach in Scotland was that I could hardly believe how five men could have travelled 3,000 miles in this tiny living space, and endured so much pressure and strain, and yet there had not been a single cross word between any of us.

The expedition was amazing for the bond that developed between us, but I think I most enjoyed the sense of being so alone with the elements. We were travelling in an open, rigid inflatable boat, and, in explaining what we went through, the most significant of those adjectives is certainly 'open'.

I only now appreciate what this really meant. There was absolutely no protection from the wind, the waves and the noise on that boat. Everything was in your face, all the time, soaking you, deafening you, numbing you, burning you.

Of course, it wasn't always fun. There were times when it was 100 per cent horrible. However, all in all, it has been the most mind-blowing experience. To be made to feel so vulnerable, but to survive – it's not a bad thing to go through.

People still ask me what it was like on the ocean, and the best I can do is say that it was like parking an open-topped people-carrier in a car wash, and living in it for two weeks with four other men, during an earthquake, in sub-zero temperatures.

Sometime later, my dad asked me if I thought I had changed as a person because of the expedition, and I gave him an honest answer: 'Not really.' I have just got on with my life. Maybe I have learned to appreciate things a bit more than before, but it's marginal. I just feel very lucky to have had this extraordinary opportunity.

Andy reflects:

In some ways, it all ended too quickly. I felt a bit like a chef who had spent so long preparing a meal, which was then eaten in twenty minutes. For me, sixteen days passed like twenty minutes.

It was a great experience. There were good times and hard times, but never bad times, although I did have a sense of foreboding when we set out for Iceland with bad weather ahead.

Looking back, I am certain the sea could have thrown even worse at us. I think we all realize we got away with it this time and, with one twist of the dice, it could have been so different. It might very easily not have been such a happy ending to such an exciting expedition.

None the less, we got home safely and, in the days ahead on HMS *Newcastle*, I have no doubt that I will miss the feeling of being part of a team and having done something out of the ordinary.

This sums Andy up, modest as ever. But as Trucker, an old army friend, pointed out, 'Andy is the type of person that wins Britain its wars': self-effacing, diligent, reliable and resilient. He had done the Royal Navy proud as part of our team and I am so pleased to have made a friend for life.

Some weeks after our return, out of the blue, Andy phoned me. He was on a run ashore in Scotland. He had been on board HMS *Newcastle*, the 425-foot destroyer he is stationed with, off the Scottish coast, and it had been blowing a gale. He had gone up to the bridge and stood transfixed.

'It was almost identical conditions to that storm we were in off Iceland,' he told me. 'Force Eights, howling winds and wild white horses everywhere.'

All he could see from the bridge was the foaming sea pouring over the decks of the ship, tonnes upon tonnes of white water. As he stared, he said, it was only then that he started to realize just what we had lived through.

'Maybe at the time your mind shuts out those feelings,' he said 'But there, on the bridge, all I could think was, to be out on that sea in a small RIB, you'd have to be suicidal.'

Nige reflects:

I suppose, more than anything, an experience like this expedition gives you a real sense of perspective. For me, I had never before felt my life was in danger, and certainly not for such a long period of time. I remember thinking, well, after dealing with that, how can a problem at work ever feel really serious, how can I ever be really worried by a deadline or an angry client?

Then that feeling wears off, and you soon get sucked back into a normal way of life again.

With hindsight, if I had known what it was going to be like, I'm not sure I would have joined the expedition, and I really don't want to put myself in such dangerous situations again.

All that said, it was a fantastic experience. I discovered how resilient I could be and, even if I never get any feeling back in my toes, because of the frostnip, I will always be grateful for that self-belief I have gained: that I can achieve something extraordinary.

Mick reflects:

When I returned home from Everest in 1998, I told people I had experienced a wider range of human emotions in three months on the mountain than in the twenty-three years of my life before that. My first response to this expedition is that I have similar feelings about those weeks on the ocean. It was unbelievably intense.

Whether I was feeling fear or friendship, it was a privilege to be involved and to be part of the team. We were a small, tight-knit group of men fighting through adversity to achieve a goal. When you are together like that, more than 300 miles from land, battling fierce seas and you're terrified for your life, that is when you start to understand the real value of life. You begin to know what it feels like to be truly alive.

I would do it all again tomorrow, but don't tell Mary or my

mother that. I think when you experience something like this, you learn to value life. It wakes you up a bit, and it reminds you that life can be amazing.

Each of us has a choice: you can either get out there and do something, or you can just sit on your arse and moan about work. I suppose we got out there, and it was brilliant. I wouldn't have missed it for the world.

Towards the end of the dinner at Kinloch, Mick stood up and said he wanted to tell me something. The room fell quiet, and I suddenly began to feel a bit embarrassed in front of everyone.

Mick looked at me, much more seriously now, and paused. He continued: 'I guess being a leader is all about coming through at the really key moments, and that moment in the middle of the night, in the middle of that storm, was when we really needed you, and you came through for us. On behalf of all your crew, I just want to say thank you for bringing us home safely.'

He reached over and shook my hand.

It was probably the nicest thing anyone has ever said to me.

14. HOME THOUGHTS

Good character is not given – we have to build it by thought, choice, courage and determination.

Mahatma Gandhi

The following morning, we waded out to the *Arnold and Son Explorer* and cruised along the coast to John O'Groats. Alex Rayner had all the press in place, and we approached the harbour waving the white ensign that the navy had lent us for this very moment. We all raised our arms – it was from relief more than triumph.

After an hour or so of interviews, we unpacked the RIB for the last time and took a few photos for ourselves. We then watched our pride and joy being dragged unceremoniously from the water by an old tractor, ready to be lifted on to the lorry that would carry her south. None of us knew what to think, and I, for one, suddenly felt a bit lost.

The atmosphere was lightened by an old lady who came up to Charlie as we were finishing the last few interviews, and looked him up and down very carefully.

'You're mad for sure, but how lucky you have been to have had such perfect weather for your crossing.' She smiled sweetly. Britain had been basking in a heatwave; she wasn't to know that for us, it had been the coldest time of our lives.

Charlie smiled back, shook her hand and signed her John O'Groats certificate graciously. We returned to Sam's house by road and prepared to catch the flight the following morning, from Inverness to Gatwick airport, where my wife and son would be waiting.

As I came through the arrivals lounge at Gatwick, I spotted them at once, Jesse held high on Shara's hip. His eyes were wide open, obsessed with seeing everything going on around him. Airports are serious fun, I saw him thinking. Shara's kiss told me I was truly home.

One morning, a few weeks later, I woke early and turned to look at Jesse asleep on the pillow beside me. He had woken early too and Shara had brought him through for a cuddle.

As I looked at his angelic, sleeping face, I realized it had been this little person, so innocent and powerless, who had sustained me through those stormy nights when I faced the very real prospect of never seeing him again, of not getting back to be his dad.

I thought how strange it was that during those crises he had wielded such power over me, yet he had no idea of what we went through, what had happened, no idea of the strength he helped me find.

Then I looked over at Shara, asleep as well. Together, side by side: my son and my wife. And right then I understood just how much they mean to me. They mean the world.

Sometimes I look back on all this and reckon I had to go a long way just to understand what I have at home.

Within five minutes of having stepped foot on dry land at John O'Groats, I got asked the inevitable question for the first time. I wasn't ready for it, and part of me couldn't believe someone had just asked it.

'So . . . what's next, Bear?' the journalist inquired.

I was still in my dry-suit. I stared at him. I could hardly answer him. I hadn't even seen my family yet.

'Well, be sure to let us know,' he continued.

But the truth is, I'm not sure I want to put myself in that sort of danger again, not in that terrifying position where I stand no better than an even chance of coming home. I'm not sure I'm brave enough any longer.

If I really look inside me, I still find this fire burning, but it burns for my family. I want to be with them, to protect them and to mess about with them. I want to be a good husband, and I want to be as good a father for Jesse as my dad was for me. I want to teach him to sail and to climb. I want to be there. I don't want to disappear on some great expedition and not come home. A dead hero is worth nothing to a young boy.

And yet, isn't that what I do? Live on the edge? Try to be bold?

Maybe. But I also want to stay alive.

That's all.

The reality of the first few days, in fact weeks, after our return, was that so many people needed my time as well – from press to sponsors, to the navy, to the boat-builders. It seemed unending. I just craved peace and time – already.

Inevitably, a frenetic schedule developed. I had more

speaking engagements than ever before and within a week of our return we had done *Blue Peter*, *Good Morning*, BBC News, the Southampton Boat Show, CBBC and *London Tonight*. It was surreal.

We received so many kind letters from different people. They were all relieved to hear we had survived the crossing intact. One of the most lovely letters was from my great-uncle Edward, who, I think, captured the feelings of many of those who had followed our progress.

'Many congratulations on your achievement, to all five of you,' he wrote.

> Don't think that it has not caused your families and friends unbearable anxiety, particularly when your communication systems failed . . . The sea can be so menacing, please don't repeat anything so terrible again, if only to save your family from having sympathetic heart attacks. Which aged as old as I am is never a good thing.

> Funny still, at ninety-three: fantastic.

Vice-Admiral Mark Stanhope, Deputy Commander-in-Chief Fleet, also took the trouble to write on behalf of the navy:

> With the successful conclusion of your epic voyage, I would like to offer you, on behalf of both myself and the First Sea Lord, my heartiest congratulations on your achievement. Crossing the Atlantic at any time can be a hairy experience and to have achieved it in a little RIB across the Arctic is a huge feat indeed. I for one was

closely monitoring your progress day by day, and we were all fully aware that you had some pretty appalling weather on some of the legs. But you did it. Well done you all, on getting home.

During one of our first free moments back in London, I grabbed time for a quick game of squash with my friend Ted Heywood. It was so good to be back and see Danny and Nicky and all my mates at the gym again. Ted began telling me with great relish how, completely by coincidence, his mother had been on a cruise ship, the *Pearl*, sailing around Iceland at the same time as us, in the same storm.

'Anyway,' Ted went on, 'she said they were caught in this huge squall. Well, at one point a wave hit the liner side-on, broaching the boat and dumping tonnes of icy water across the decks. Ornaments and cutlery slid across the tables and the captain made the decision to turn back. He decided conditions were so bad they could not continue.'

Danny shook his head at me, smiling. 'You daft bugger,' he said.

'And Bear,' Ted continued, 'those sorts of cruise ships don't just turn around in bad weather, especially when they have several hundred paying passengers on board.' The story put into stark perspective the conditions we had survived that night. I proceeded to lose the game of squash.

Other little things began to come out that confirmed just how lucky we had been to complete the expedition. After a series of public appearances, the boat was sent for an overhaul at MIT, the company that had supplied the jet drive and gear-box. The engineers there reported back that a belt in the engine had been incorrectly aligned and had become so worn that, in their estimation, it would not have lasted another twenty minutes at sea. They had never seen a belt that was so worn and yet, somehow, was still doing its job.

'That's OK,' I replied. 'We had two spares in the engine bay.'

'Yeah, we saw those too,' the engineer said. 'You had been supplied with spares that were the wrong size.'

Someone had been watching over us.

But there was more.

Subsequently, the RIB was based in the Solent, and one late afternoon, at the end of a sponsors' day out on the boat, we got a bit of rope caught in the jet intake. We had to be towed unceremoniously back into harbour, where we freed the rope and left the boat for the night, ready, we thought, for our next corporate day on her.

The phone rang at dawn next day. It was the boatman at Bembridge Sailing Club where she was moored. He was in a state. Water was pouring into the RIB. The jet housing was leaking. The aft tubes were under water, the engine had been flooded and the gear-box and electrics were being ruined. There was panic. We managed to recover her, but it took a month to repair her and a bill on our loyal Navigators and General Insurance tab of nearly £25,000.

If we had caught that bit of rope in the jet intake while arriving among one of the many small fishing communities that we visited – and it would have been the easiest thing in the world to do, especially since we so often arrived in the dark – the expedition would have been over.

We had been very fortunate; it seemed that God's Grace had followed us all the way home.

We had planned a party at St Katharine Docks in the City of London a week after our arrival back in the UK. This was partly to celebrate our safe return but mainly to thank our sponsors and formally to present a cheque to the Prince's Trust.

It was the most lovely of days. The sun shone, the five of us were wearing our expedition fleeces, and we were surrounded by all the people who had made the expedition possible: from our closest friends and families to Captain Pennefather; from our base team to all the lead sponsors – including Mattel Toys and the Computer Sciences Corporation.

As we neared the end of the day, Eric and Jean-Marie from Arnold and Son caught us by surprise when they presented us with an original letter, written by a famous old French explorer on Royal Geographical Society-headed paper. The letter was from one of the earliest polar challenges around the start of the last century. It was a lovely touch.

Will Young had agreed to accept the cheque on behalf of the Prince's Trust. As a fellow ambassador of the Trust, he had offered to come and support us. He was fantastic with everyone, including all the kids, and even tolerated two of my elderly relatives running up the walkway with their dicky legs and hips in an effort to get his autograph. I must admit

I was cringing a little at that point. But above all, he was just fun to have around.

'You must be so relieved,' Will said to me. He was right, but it seemed as if people had been saying exactly those words right from the start, and it had never been true before.

'You must be so relieved to have a sponsor' . . . 'You must be so relieved that the boat has arrived in Nova Scotia' . . . 'You must be so relieved that you had enough fuel to reach Greenland.'

And over and over again, I would smile and say, 'Well, sort of.'

The truth was, I never really felt relieved until after that final party at St Katharine Docks. Somehow I could never let it all go before then. There always seemed to be something else. But there wasn't now. At last.

That day in London, the sun had shone on us all afternoon but, just as the last guests left, it started to drizzle. Shara told me I was the 'jammiest man around'.

It was the perfect ending.

The five of us soon said our goodbyes and went our separate ways, back to our normal lives.

Now, as I reflect, my enduring image of the entire expedition is of five men who came together and made one fantastic team. Working as one, we had beaten the odds and survived.

Our strength was that we made decisions on instinct, pursued them with heart and soul and looked after one another when this was needed. We were a peculiar mix: a naval officer, a surveyor, an Internet businessman, a cameraman. They were just ordinary guys, but when it mattered, they came up with an extraordinary bravery and spirit.

Above everything, we were good friends.

Yes, I am proud of what we achieved, but I am much more proud of how we did it. The little things, like hearing Charlie tell his dad he couldn't believe there had not been any kind of cross word between us; listening to Mick thank me over dinner at Kinloch; the feeling of being hugged by Andy and Nige on the headland at John O'Groats. Those are the moments that really last.

Andy went straight back to work with the navy after stealing two days away with Lorraine and switching off his mobile phone. As far as everyone at work was concerned, he was 'defrosting'. He has been on board HMS *Newcastle* almost continually ever since.

Nige returned to Lunson Mitchenall, only to discover that on his first day back at work he was asked to attend a corporate boating day on the Solent – as if he had not had enough of the water for a while.

True to form, Mick changed from his expedition gear into his business suit and leaped straight back into the zone of building the Tiscali empire. But the Atlantic had taken its toll. Three weeks later, he phoned to say he was still feeling drained and exhausted. I was relieved to hear that someone else was also wiped out.

Charlie went back to Manchester and resumed his life as

a television cameraman. Part of this work meant we were still together, and he was the cameraman on an adventure series in the Brecon Beacons we were doing for Channel 4. Lying in a soaking ditch with me one night, up a mountain in Wales in sub-zero winter conditions, Charlie muttered that life had definitely got colder since we met. I apologized, laughing.

As for the sixth member of our team, our faithful boat, we finished the corporate days on her and said our farewells. We are currently in the process of trying to find a sponsor for her that will enable us to donate the boat to the sea-based charity the Meridian Trust. This trust offers disadvantaged kids the chance to experience the magic of the sea. I hope we manage to pull this off and allow these young people to benefit from this extraordinary craft. She was our life in those storms and never failed once. I hope others will grow to love her as we did.

For me, the experience of leadership had been much more demanding than I had ever imagined.

The bad part of me had hoped it would mean I would get more sleep, not less. I always assumed there would have to be some privileges for the leader of the expedition.

In practice, though, to lead properly, you end up being the last one to go to bed at night, and the first one to wake in the morning. There were times when Andy had to wake at 5 a.m. to change the oil filters, so I would aim to get up with him to have a cup of tea together first. Then, in the afternoon, while Andy might be grabbing an hour of sleep, I would be with Mick checking the weather forecasts on the Internet.

As somebody who in previous expeditions had always taken great pleasure in oversleeping, the responsibility of leadership was something that required me to give my all. That is a good thing: the result was worth it. Every time.

But what *would* be next? This time the question wasn't coming from some journalist; it was coming from within me.

Sometimes I sense that people live their own dreams through explorers. It is a form of escape from life, something safe upon which to quench their thirst for danger. But I am not sure I want to be the sacrifice for these people's urges any longer.

When asked 'What next?', the easy answer is to say K2, or the South Pole. It all rolls off the tongue so easily. But in many ways it is a coward's answer.

Explorers, climbers and sailors are meant to be brave. But so often we aren't brave enough to be honest.

Honest enough to say, 'I am feeling a bit frightened of those things at the moment.'

Honest enough to say, 'You've caught me at a very vulnerable time, and I am not sure I have an answer right now.'

I hope I am brave enough to say all this.

But I know for certain that life is so much more than always having to top something or better the last achievement.

That's not the way I want to lead my life.

We all so often live in the shadow of people's expectations. But as soon as we do that, we lose our power. The magic dies. I don't want that. I hope to keep living as I have always lived – by heart.

I hope always to be among the elements, to be in beautiful, isolated places, far from the big cities, places where life is simple and pure, places where I can feel God's quiet presence around me.

I want to keep connecting with people, whether in a small boat or on a mountain, in an audience or on the TV; even in a book. It is all about giving humanity. It's about being brutally straight with yourself, even to your own detriment. That is sometimes so hard to do.

I want people to know I am normal, with just as many doubts and weaknesses and struggles as anyone else, but if we can just hang on, we can come through – and maybe even find ourselves a little stronger.

For us, though, the truth is we got lucky on Everest, and we got lucky on the frozen North Atlantic; and you don't have to be a mathematician to realize that you can't keep playing those sorts of odds and always win.

I only have to think of my late friend, Ginette Harrison, whom I first met while climbing in Nepal. We were together on the so-called unclimbable mountain, Ama Dablam, in the Himalayas. It was the year before our attempt on Everest. Ginette was a kind, strong, beautiful woman, and probably the best female climber of her age. She was intelligent and cautious and, in my eyes, as a climber, she was nothing less than invincible.

However, two years later, back in the Himalayas she was attempting to climb another great peak. Just one more. She was struck by an avalanche and killed. Just like that. Only a month earlier we had been having lunch together in London.

The avalanche wasn't her fault. She had done nothing wrong. Humans are strong, but nature is stronger. And if you play the odds long enough, it is true: you cannot always win.

But I am no longer prepared to die on some distant mountain or senseless sea. And if I have learned anything from these wild forces of nature, it is a quiet determination to stay alive.

Several months later, the Royal Geographical Society hosted the crew of the Arnold and Son Transatlantic Arctic Expedition to give a presentation on our experiences. The five of us gathered at the awe-inspiring, historic venue, on the south side of London's Hyde Park, and we told our story.

At the end of the evening, I stood up to conclude. I noticed the side door open, and some light fill the room. It was Shara re-emerging into the hall, carrying Jesse in her arms. He was meant to be in bed – it was 8.30 p.m., but she had arranged for him to be here.

On impulse, I stepped down from the stage and took him in my arms. We all then stood onstage together: the team and myself, with Jesse wrapped up in a little blanket. As he peeked out from under his little hat at the sea of faces, I had never felt so proud.

Not long afterwards, Jesse was christened on our barge, just as I had always hoped he would be.

Nicky, the priest, stood on the upper deck, and his robes billowed in the autumn breeze that whistles down the Thames.

He reached for the little bottle of snow water that I had brought back from the summit of Everest some five years ago and had kept for this very occasion. He dabbed it on Jesse's tiny forehead. And right there, he christened our lovely son.

Right from the start, this had been the plan.

And the plan had worked. By Grace.

I hope Jesse's grandfather, my late dad, felt proud.

If I go up to the Heavens, you are there;
if I go down to the place of the dead, you are there also.
If I ride the morning wind to the ends of the ocean,
even there your hand will guide,
your strength will support me . . .
I can never be lost to your Spirit.

Psalm 139:5–10

**Don't be afraid to go on the odd wild goose chase,
that's what wild geese are for!**

Anon.

GLOSSARY

EPIRB frequencies – Emergency Position Indicating Radio
    Beacon. A globally detectable, emergency broadcast signal
    sent via satellite and transmitted on the 406MHz frequency

GPS – Global Positioning System. Signals from 24 satellites
    provide precise geodetic positioning and navigation

prop – propeller

payloads – weight

helming – steering

lifelines – ropes running the length of a boat on to which a
    sailor clips his safety harness

stern – back of a boat

bow – front end of a boat

prow – front of a boat

foredeck – front deck of a boat

hull – the body or bottom of a boat

jet housing – the casing for the internal propeller

lee – sheltered side

fenders – buffers slung over the sides of the boat to protect it
    from damage

parachute sea anchor – an anchor for use in deep water.
    The 'parachute', which is made of fabric, fills with water
    and holds the boat in place

Gortex – air-permeable waterproof material

GLOSSARY

chandlery – a store selling boating supplies

jet drive – a form of propulsion for a boat

beam seas – where the waves arrive side-on to the boat

head sea – where the waves arrive head-on to the boat

ACKNOWLEDGEMENTS

Sponsors of www.arctic2003.com

Title Sponsor

Arnold and Son Watches, British Masters,
Switzerland and London

Lead Sponsors

Royal Navy   Daily Telegraph   Shell
BT Exact and NVP Brightstar   Lafarge Aggregates   CSC
Lunson Mitchenall   London Speaker Bureau
MIT Group – Twin Disc   Davis Langdon UK   Vitol
Simrad   Finnings CAT   Sage   Mattel – Hot Wheels
General Motors (Canada)

With special thanks to

HRH The Prince of Wales   British Airways plc
The Royal Geographical Society, London
The Canadian Navy   The Danish Navy
London and Southampton Boat Shows   Schroders
E Squadron, 21st Special Air Service   Musto Clothing
White Stuff Clothing   Navigators and General Insurance

ACKNOWLEDGEMENTS

Gecko Headgear   Professor Robert Swan
Ocean Dynamics RIBs   Mustang Marine
Gunwharf Quay, Portsmouth   Food Ferry – supplies
Deliverance – supplies   Bembridge Sailing Club
Echomax – radar reflectors   C-Map – charts   MarineTrack
Sartech – survival equipment   Barnstead Int. Electro-thermal
Soltron – fuel additive   Dampire – kit-drying systems
Nova Scotia Sailing School   Rightons Aluminium
Seastart – recovery   Pan Macmillan
Peter Fraser and Dunlop Literary Agents
George and Carol McFadden   Bruce Cameron
Morris and Jill Marshment   Cranham Builders
The Crosthwaite family   The Laing family
The Thompson family   The Liever family
The Proctor family   The Vyner-Brooks family
Ed Griffiths and family   The McGregor family   Hy Money
Ludgrove School   Canons Gym   Dronsfield Technologies
www.octavianart.com   Stargate3 Satellite Communications
Iridium satellite technology   Carabina Logistics
FPT Industries – fuel systems   Sigma Displays
Wallenius Wilhelmsen Lines UK – boat transport
Premier Promotions   Mumm Champagne
Cunningham Management   Liaison Media – PR
Whitbread Foundation   Cosalt – life rafts
Ocean Safety supplies   Col Henry Hughe-Smith
NSA Int. Juice Plus +   Alpine Club
Royal Navy Sailing Centre
SAS Regimental Association

The Charity

The Prince's Trust strives to help fourteen- to thirty-year-olds develop confidence, learn new skills, get into work and start businesses. Their message, 'Yes You Can', encourages young people to believe in themselves whatever obstacles they face.

Bear Grylls has been an ambassador for the Prince's Trust since 2003 and is also now Chief Scout and figurehead to 28 million Scouts worldwide, a post that encourages young people to learn adventure skills and enjoy the outdoors with good friends.

For further information on the Prince's Trust, see:
www.princes-trust.org.uk.

For further information on Bear Grylls, see:
www.beargrylls.com.